⊷⧉⧈⧉⊷

INTRODUCTION TO
PHILOSOPHICAL
INQUIRIES

⊷⧉⧈⧉⊷

Tibor R. Machan
State University of New York
College at Fredonia

ALLYN AND BACON, INC.
Boston · London · Sydney · Toronto

Library of Congress Cataloging in Publication Data

Machan, Tibor R
    Introduction to philosophical inquiries.

    Bibliography: p.
    Includes index.
1. Philosophy—Introductions.   2. Philosophy—
Dictionaries.   I. Title.
BD21.M18   100   76-22174
ISBN 0-205-05536-2

❧Contents

৵Preface

Note to the Instructor

This work exists because other introductory philosophy texts are not introductions to philosophy. Instead, most simply jump right in and assume from the start an intense interest on the part of the student. With very few exceptions, most "introductory" textbooks assume undivided interest; however, many students require persuasion about the value of even getting involved in philosophy.

Hundreds of thousands of students enter philosophy classes with only a bit of curiosity, in the spirit of window shopping. This work is for them. It is not intended for those high school graduates who can be identified as graduate school material. This book will guide students through the various stages required in an introduction to philosophy. The focus is on students who have had no previous contact with the field. This book will provide an idea of philosophy's value as well as indications of the nature of its content.

The general plan is to discuss traditional broad issues in philosophy, not the more specialized topics emphasized in contemporary philosophy. The scope incorporates problems that are part and parcel to any philosopher's concern.

There is, to start with, a discussion of philosophy as a kind of purposive human activity, a field aiming at certain kinds of understanding. (All along the controversial character of some of the

book's theses is kept in focus.)   Then we move on to a discussion of
how philosophy fits into the rest of the familiar human activities and
endeavors—science, art, and religion.   There is special concern with
the standards of clarity and meaningfulness to be expected within
philosophy, as distinct from what many students are accustomed to
in the sciences.   The emphasis is on showing that philosophy is a
rational, systematic endeavor without using exactly the same standards of precision and meaningfulness expected in the sciences.

The introductory discussion of the general character and distinctiveness of philosophy is followed by an exposition of philosophy's various branches and topics.   Six chapters follow: one each on
metaphysics, epistemology, logic, ethics, political philosophy, and, in
conclusion, on the possibility of philosophical truth.   Although con-
troversies abound on the issue of how to organize and interrelate
philosophy's numerous topics and concerns, the present book's traditional format is familiar and easily altered to suit special purposes.
The last chapter deals with a question raised frequently by students—
the issue of the results of so much philosophical controversy.   What,
in short, is one to believe in the light of so much controversy?   Despite the risk taken here, this chapter should prove something of a
testing ground, a focus of debate, for the initiated reader.

While the book was written for those not familiar with philosophy, it is not a casual, "hip" introductory text.   Philosophy
texts should not be tailored to fit short-lived fads, however intensely
felt these can be, however much real personal significance they may
hold.   Many books aimed at such fads become dated by the time
they are published.   This is not to demean the quality of such books
out of hand.   However, they usually lack the lasting, unifying significance of philosophy and, thus, perpetrate an unnecessary mis-
conception.   Philosophy can be shown to have its point, a very
important one, without making it appear to be something it is not.

Many positions and ideas discussed in this work are given
cursory treatment in comparison with standards used in fuller, more
advanced expositions.   Names are often invoked when the ideas of
their bearers cannot be given their due.   It remains for the reader
and critic to tell whether the balance intended for purposes of
introduction is advisable and useful.   This book is intended to
be a successful philosophical mind-teaser, not an encyclopedia of
philosophy.

The bibliographies, which are arranged by chapter at the end of the book, indicate my own inclinations, although the text does not always do so. But the goal was to provide a broad selection, with a variety appropriate in the context of contemporary philosophical trends, and with special attention to the level of sophistication required to appreciate the content.

The glossary, like those in other introductory texts, will provide students with basic indicators, or pointers, when the need arises (e.g., in reviewing positions and arguments treated in the ·book). Important terms will appear in boldface when they are introduced in the text, alerting the reader to the fact that these key terms are defined briefly in the glossary. It is important that exclusive use of the glossary be discouraged. Students will be helped only by consulting the glossary as a supplement to the main text.

Note to the Student

The purpose of this book is to indicate and explain how philosophy emerges from and fits within our lives. As the title points out, this is a work that is preliminary to more detailed philosophical explorations. It will also be useful to realize at the outset that this is both an introduction to philosophy and to one person's views about philosophy. Thus, this work is in part a record of my thoughts about philosophy and it reveals much of my own philosophical orientation.

A work such as this should prove helpful because many people have only vague notions about the nature of philosophy. Few know what occupies the attention of philosophers, and why. Reading and studying this book will encourage further and more advanced study of philosophy. It should serve as an introduction to the contributions made by great philosophers to the subject matter, for, as with all fields of study, the work concerns not only the subject matter itself but what others have thought about it.

A clue to the character of this book is that we will treat philosophy as one of many fields which study something systematically. Philosophers philosophize in order to gain an understanding of their subject matter.

In this book we will explore the unique features of philosophy, so that the reader will have a clear idea of what philosophy is and what it is not. The reader will also discover various modes of philosophizing and many of the conclusions that have emerged from employing these methods in certain philosophical inquiries.

The reader should consider carefully the ideas encountered in all philosophical literature. One should be mentally active from the start and check for problems, confusions, and errors, as best one can. In reading a rendition of another philosopher's views, it helps to guard against subtle, perhaps quite unintended, distortion by the author. With introductory sketches, especially, there is always the risk of misstatement. Here and there the reader will do well to either suspend judgment about the issues covered or take special care by consulting outside sources.

Finally, it will help if everyone taking courses in philosophy feels at ease about asking questions. Unfortunately, this is not often the case. Many students think that not asking the most brilliant, cogent question is a severe liability and that it is better to hide than to take the risk of being exposed. What should be kept in mind, however, is that students have the right to be ignorant, even confused, when they begin inquiry into a field. The way to improve on one's ability to be inquisitive is to take some risky plunges. Instructors will not be critical of imprecise, "foolish" questions; they will fully appreciate the interest shown and help to eliminate both fear and confusion about the subject matter.

ACKNOWLEDGMENTS

Several individuals have helped me in the development and preparation of this work. First of all I owe many philosophical debts to teachers and to others who gained my attention during my own education. Thus, there is little in this work that is completely original.

The friends who helped on this book can and should be named. J. Roger Lee's patient and extensive assistance could not be over-estimated. James Chesher, Doug Den Uyl, Eric Mack, and Morton Schagrin gave very valuable advice on several topics discussed in the book. My students Mike Parker, John Beiter, Barbara Turkewitz, and Steve Barone provided me with hints and comments that had an influence. Several young people without college preparation read the work, and their suggestions left marks. Mr. Robert J. Patterson and Sheryl Avruch at Allyn and Bacon worked hard with me on the final manuscript. The suggestions of the numerous reviewers were very valuable. My wife, Marty Zupan, stands out, as usual, with her trust and generosity in the support she gave during my work on this ambitious project.

I should mention that I am fully responsible for the final product, for better or worse. In the end I had to decide what advice to take, what to set aside. I am sure those who gave it will be all too aware of my judgments in this matter.

The Institute for Humane Studies' help in providing me with copying facilities and other secretarial assistance as I worked on the last stages of this book is gratefully acknowledged.

Tibor R. Machan

Philosophy and Its Purpose

⁓§ 1 §⁓

HUMAN LIFE AND PHILOSOPHY

In what sense does *everyone's* life relate to philosophy or to certain philosophical views? Although most people have probably not considered how philosophy can or does touch their life, some simple examples may show this connection. When, in anger perhaps, someone *blames the world* for his misfortunes, he states a *basic belief*—even if he later might wish to modify or abandon it. When someone declares his love of life, in some joyous moment, he, too, is expressing a view of the world in general. Such explicit statements as "Everything is relative," "Words mean whatever one wishes them to mean," "None of us can help what we are," "Human existence is without meaning or purpose," and "Whatever the majority chooses is what should be done" all indicate very broad beliefs—ideas not just about one or two instances of a person's life or of what he witnesses. These ideas cover all cases of a certain sort. All of the statements cited above are about some class of things, events, or relationships; some actually refer to everything that exists, others to everything in human life, and yet others to everything in the area of morality or politics.

Some may never have given expression to ideas such as those cited, but that is doubtful. In all of human history, in ancient

1

civilizations as well as in modern cultures, these types of statements occur. Often they are part of poetry, music, or drama; at other times they are offered sincerely and seriously in conversation and are believed to be true. They are not just expressions, clichés, or idioms, although they often become no more than that for some people.

On and off these and similar ideas are even defended and supported with arguments, evidence, or personal experiences. Philosophers have made it their profession, however, to provide such ideas, when they consider them sound, with the best defense and support they know possible. It is to this task that they attend. Philosophy is the field in which these types of statements are treated with great seriousness, where they are tested, examined, and subjected to very intense debate. Although they are frequently broken down or "translated" into more elaborate and thus less familiar versions, in philosophy the subject matter of the field is what these and related statements are about—namely, the very general facts of existence and our relationship to them. It is this task that philosophers attend to within human societies; this is their role in the division of human labor.

WHAT IS PHILOSOPHY?

Before we turn to what distinguishes philosophy from other areas of study, some general points need to be observed. Philosophy is an activity, that is, something done by human beings and directed toward some goal. Like other fields, it involves scholarship and professionalism, as well as amateur interests and stages in between. It can be a well-executed activity, done with skill, conscientiousness, and discipline, or it can be done badly—carelessly, inattentively, or even without the needed respect. Its results, too, can be used wisely as well as in bad faith. These are very broad points, applicable to all sorts of human activities, including philosophy. As with the other broad categories of human endeavor—science, law, technology, business, and education—philosophy has a general purpose and it can be done badly or well.

Before we can even begin to think carefully about the general or personal value of some *particular* philosophical work, however, we need to gain some understanding of what philosophy is.   Even without knowing exactly what is studied in philosophy, most people know that there are many philosophies, schools of thought, and philosophical positions that are famous and quite influential.   It is also well known that philosophers often disagree among themselves and argue about practically everything.   Perhaps this is reflected popularly in the statement, "Now you're being philosophical." Often this means: "Now you're beginning to debate the fine points of this issue.   Now you're getting down to the nitty-gritty."

But there is much more to it.   Philosophy is something quite specific; it is a human activity of a certain kind, not just any variety of gabbing, speculating, or debating.   In spite of the many differences among various philosophies, the field itself is specifiable.   *Philosophy has as its purpose the identification and study of the most basic facts of reality and our relationship to them.*

From this abstract statement of what philosophy is we can now move on to fill in some of the details.   First of all it will help to give an example of what some philosophers have considered a basic fact, and to suggest how human beings might relate to such a fact in their lives.   Basic facts are rarely thought of in our everyday, normal experiences, since they are very obvious—just as on earth we rarely think about gravity, since it affects us always.

To characterize such facts, let us contrast them with the more ordinary kind.   We often make note of such facts as the moon is difficult to see in the daytime because the sun is bright, or it is raining very hard in the Midwest.   Such facts are of limited scope. Although they are simple enough to make evident, many other facts are required before these sorts can be understood and appreciated.   In the first case, for example, the facts of the moon's, the sun's, and the daytime's existence are presupposed.   Many such facts are encountered each moment, every day, and throughout a lifetime. But these are not basic facts, since they depend on too many other facts.

A basic or fundamental fact would be something different.   It would have very broad scope and would be evident on a very wide scale.   For example, let us assume that it is a fact that everything that exists must be composed of material substance, that it must have mass, dimension, and weight.   (See chapter 2 for a discussion of materialism.)   If what we are now assuming were correct, then anything that could exist would be composed of matter.   Such a fact, if it were a fact, would have the entire universe as its scope, and all other facts we might encounter would have to include it as a feature, as a "background" fact.

We, in turn, would relate to existence, to all of reality, in a way that would be directly influenced by this basic fact. Thus, when discussing whether something or other exists or could exist, the answer we would give would depend first of all on whether the proposed item is composed of matter. Suppose now that it is shown that what is proposed to exist is not composed of matter. Then if it were true that everything that exists is composed of matter, we could conclude that the proposed thing simply does not and could not exist. So the assumed basic fact that everything is material relates to human life as a sort of basic guide to what we should accept as possible. If materialism is true, then it is impossible for something to exist that is not composed of matter; therefore, we should not bother with any suggestions to the contrary (except as a curiosity, perhaps).

This is just one illustration of what basic facts might be, and of what sort of inquiries philosophers might conduct. We will consider materialism in more detail later. For now, the important point is that materialism is an attempt to identify a basic fact about reality. If it is correct, certain things follow about how we can, and maybe even should, relate to existence, that is, how we should live. The example should also make clear that the work of materialist philosophers, those who have concluded with something like the above idea about reality and our relationship to it, is a clear example of philosophy and indicates its purpose. To repeat, philosophy is the study of the fundamental features of reality and our relationship to them.

Such an enormous task involves innumerable adjacent purposes, just as the central goal of a drama group—an excellent performance of a play—must involve many related purposes. Philosophy is multi-faceted. Nevertheless, it is distinguishable from other fields for its primary focus on basic facts. And this is indicated, again, even in the casual use of the term *philosophical*. Another meaning of "being philosophical" is to rise above the *particular* issue one has been discussing—for example, having lost one's fortune or having found one's true love—to some more general facts about such things, such as fortunes are but changing goods, or rare is the person who is lucky in love.

In a comparable way, philosophy (figuratively) goes beyond or underneath particular issues to the fundamentals involved. For instance, when philosophers try to identify the most basic facts about human knowledge, they are not usually concerned with the mechanisms of perception or with how the brain works while people think or learn. Instead, they want to know *what it is that knowledge has to be*, that is, what are the most basic, or essential, features of knowledge. Philosophers do not focus on details. They want to investigate human knowledge as such, not your or my or anyone's particular problems of learning, nor the various psychological, social, and physiological facts that are involved in coming to know something. Philosophers often proceed somewhat in the fashion of scientists who want to know about the human heart, not your or my particular heart; or the helium atom and not any given helium atom. In the field of philosophy those who discuss knowledge, namely epistemologists, inquire about the nature of knowledge. Or, as some contemporary philosophers like to put it, they want to discover the criteria for correctly employing the concept (or word) *knowledge.*

Other philosophers are interested in the nature of human action. They are concerned with what human action is as such, not with this or that particular human being's acts. By discovering the basic, essential features of human action, it would be possible to distinguish the actions of people from the actions and behavior of other kinds of things (animals, plants, molecules, planets, and so forth). Here the philosopher's study borders on engaging in psychology, or even biology. But while psychologists and biologists study the mechanism and components of the phenomenon of action and behavior, philosophers want to define the very idea of "human action"; they want to find out what makes such a thing or event what it is. This task could be crucial for purposes of distinguishing between what people do (their actions) and what simply happens to them—for example, jumping off a horse versus falling off. Then, for example, if someone is accused of causing some harm, it would be possible to establish whether he or she was involved in the event as an actor or as a mere component of the passing scene. And the philosophical part is to discover whether there is a difference.

The above is an example of the point made earlier, that aside from studying the basic facts, philosophy involves the study of everyone's relationship to these facts. The point here is that once we learn some fact that is indeed fundamental, one that pertains to everything, next we become concerned with how it relates to human beings as such. Suppose that everything that exists in reality is indeed material—has mass, dimension, etc. What of it? Just how does this fact pertain to human beings? Can we, for instance, know it? Do we need to know it? What role, if any, would such a fact play in our lives?

Other fields besides philosophy involve work that pertains to these issues, but in philosophy the focus is directly on them, and other questions arise usually in connection with a concern for these fundamental issues. The main concern here is to find out how human beings per se—that is, all of us as *persons,* not as citizens or grandparents or doctors—relate to reality and to its basic aspects (or how we could and perhaps should relate to these facts). Thus, should we make much of the fact, if it is one, that everything is ultimately material? Does that have any bearing on people's lives? Or, again, suppose that God exists and His will gives direction to everything else that exists. Does this matter for anyone? Or should it? If so, why? Suppose, as another example, that criminals cannot help what they do—in fact, that none of us can help what happens, that what will be, will be, regardless of any choice any of us makes. So what?

Not only do philosophers deal with these matters outright, but they do so in painstaking detail. Their efforts to understand the questions being asked are often greater than the effort exerted to find answers. One would find philosophers engaging in rigorous examination of whether the above question—"So what?"—even makes sense if people cannot help doing what they do. In short, how could it matter? How could there be an answer to "So what?" if we cannot control our own lives?

The point of all the above has been to give several illustrations of what philosophy involves and to indicate what people in the field attend to in their divergent ways: the identification of basic facts and our relationship to them. Later more details will emerge, but it helps to learn first what has a place in philosophy and why. For now we should note that philosophy, like most other general fields of study, does not deal directly with particular events, or individuals, or things as such, or with your or my particular relationship to the basic facts of reality. However, since we are human beings, and since philosophy does examine relationships involving these basic facts and human beings, there are implications in these findings for each of us.   Philosophers are not personal advisors or counselors to people individually.   But they do produce understanding and wisdom that are important to human beings everywhere.

Just how important the results of philosophical inquiry are, exactly what it means for something to be important, whether it is even true that philosophy does and can produce such understanding—all these are issues philosophers tackle in their own work. Disagreements rage constantly on these matters, and later we will try to make sense of that also.   Philosophy has its own difficulties, aside from ones it shares with other fields of study.   This book aims to acquaint the reader with these, as well as with philosophy's accomplishments.

PHILOSOPHERS AND THEIR WORK

Philosophy's disputes, which are numerous, will be regarded as extreme shortcomings by some observers.   Why has there been so much dispute and so little agreement?   Why bother with a field that has such persistent problems?

In the final analysis these questions prove to be unfair.   They assume that other fields of inquiry do not encounter similar difficulties.   Yet, all in all, philosophy fares no worse, or better, than other fields of inquiry.   As with the rest of the activities people engage in, philosophy does as well or as badly as its practitioners do.

In any case, our primary concern in this book will not be with the dispute about the nature of philosophy itself but with seeing close up the arguments and ideas that engage philosophers in their work.   **Argument** as it is used here implies not a quarrel but a careful, well-developed inquiry.   When we say that philosophers engage in argumentation, we are referring to their development of well-reasoned, systematic theories and explanations, much like those we expect from scientists.   The numerous positions we will encounter in this book, mostly in outline form, are usually advanced with detailed arguments to give them support and to show that they, not others, are the correct way of understanding some topic in the field.   In philosophy, as in other careful scholarship, the task is to develop well-established answers, to produce understanding that can stand the test of close scrutiny.

Theories are usually advanced on a variety of topics, yet the ultimate goal of philosophical work is to provide an overall view of reality.   Sometimes philosophers reject the assertion that such a general, basic goal lies at the end of philosophical inquiry.   In the last analysis, however, even these efforts to deny such a goal amount to serving that goal. That is, the idea that striving for overall, comprehensive understanding is futile, that only piecemeal work is possible, is itself a comprehensive view.

The rest of what we will be doing in this book need not be prejudged to get an idea of the philosopher's work.   The philosopher's task is to investigate the basic facts of reality, to identify our relationship to such facts, and to carry out the variety of studies that enhance our efforts to understand these matters.   We can now consider very briefly what makes philosophy important and why it is of value to engage in philosophical inquiry.

THE IMPORTANCE OF PHILOSOPHY

Is there an important role for philosophy in human life?

One aspect of philosophy evident in the ordinary philosophical remarks cited earlier, as well as in all major philosophical systems and schools, indicates the answer to our question.   We can already detect the indispensability of philosophy to human life.   Recall that all of the statements listed earlier are very broad in their scope. They cover or refer to many things, many individual events, relationships, actions, institutions, or elements of whatever subject matter they involve.   When a person says, "Life is nothing but struggle," the meaning of that statement includes *all of life*, from birth to death, without exception.   "Words mean whatever one wishes them to mean" refers again to *all words*—even those used to make the statement.   "You made your bed so you must lie in it" refers, metaphorically in this case, to *all* those instances when a person chooses some course of action and is faced with the results.

If someone takes these thoughts seriously, and many do, it is very likely that such an individual's life will reflect what is meant by them. A person will most likely have an attitude toward, an anticipation of, or a regard for life that conforms to the belief expressed— or to the same belief held in silence. To see the impact of philosophical ideas we need to consider what will happen when a person takes such ideas seriously and lives by them.

It is most likely that those who take such ideas seriously will find their impact evident throughout their lives. This can be so whether the ideas are worked out in great detail or held as firm conclusions without close scrutiny. Even in what might be considered less reflective, less systematically intellectual cultures, there is clear evidence that ideas such as those we cited have considerable impact—in the form of myths, sayings, religious writings, and the like.

It should also be stressed that virtually everyone has some such general ideas. Whether explicitly stated, self-consciously believed, or merely accepted by habit, such ideas influence one's life. They sometimes govern entire cultures, even epochs of human history, as is evident today with Marxism throughout a considerable portion of the globe. In the last analysis, for philosophical purposes, the crucial issue is whether these ideas are *correct*. But their importance cannot be overstated.

If it is true that everything is relative, then it is open to demonstration and the philosopher is professionally responsible for seeking out the argument that will show it to be true. Many such ideas float around, but the crucial question for philosophical investigation is whether there is truth in them. If such ideas are true, and if we act on them, we would most likely be in harmony with the basic facts of existence. If our basic philosophical notions are false, we are very likely going to be out of kilter with reality. Even the belief that philosophy is of no importance—a view that has been advanced by some—can have serious bearing on human life, so that it is an issue deserving the attention of members of the philosophical profession and those interested in gaining philosophical understanding.

Here we find that philosophy is somewhat different from many other fields of study. With most other special areas of study, the understanding that is produced has less than the universal impact of philosophy. We can go through life without ever becoming involved with horticulture, astronomy, or international relations, since these apply only within a limited range and only intermittently (though, of course, widely and often enough when compared with some other concerns). But philosophical ideas, by their nature, apply directly or indirectly to the basic features of existence and human life. For example, the philosophical idea that none of us can help what will happen in our lives pertains to all of everyone's life! That surely is not a restricted scope, and if the claim is true, it can have considerable bearing on how we should understand ourselves and others—whether, for instance, we can ever meaningfully hold others responsible for criminal activity, credit ourselves or others with achievements, and so forth.

It is quite evident then, on a commonsense level for now, that philosophy is important for human life. As the most general field of inquiry, its concerns reflect on everything people think about and do. Philosophy touches upon virtually every aspect of life—directly, when someone consciously, knowingly decides to invoke philosophical ideas, and indirectly, when a person absorbs such ideas on hearsay or must deal with others who have done so.

It must now be emphasized that the view that philosophy is important does not mean that *philosophers* are more important people than, say, economists or plumbers. There are some philosophers who would argue this, but the view is not defensible. Being a philosopher does not prove a person a good human being, nor even a good philosopher. Often, the fact of being a philosopher gives no indication of whether what the individual does is of special importance and value.

There is a sense in which *philosophy* is more important than other branches of knowledge. Since it studies fundamentals, it has a claim to priority. We can appreciate this point by way of a simple analogy. The destruction of the foundations of a building will bring the entire structure down, whereas destroying the top floors or this or that wing leaves something intact. Without a well-developed, reasonably sound philosophy the rest of human knowledge and understanding will likely become disintegrated and shaky. Philosophy focuses on the essentials of existence and human life, whereas psychology, sociology, and biology deal with special areas of existence and human life. Philosophy is also concerned with understanding the relationship between the various sciences and the several different aspects of human life—art, education, law, science, etc. This, too, places philosophy in a position of its own. But this circumstance does not make philosophers special sorts of people, entitled to more power or wealth or status. Their work is of very wide significance, that is all.

Even though there is widespread debate among philosophers in every generation of philosophical scholarship, this has nothing to do with whether a philosophical position may be identified as correct. Just because people everywhere dispute that the earth is spherical, we cannot justifiably conclude that the earth is *not* spherical, nor that it *is*. Disputation is a fact in many fields and perhaps more so in philosophy than in others. The issue of whether we can arrive at a correct philosophical position has nothing to do with the existence of widespread debate. This is worth noting at the outset in view of many people's confusion on the issue.

WHY STUDY PHILOSOPHY?

Does it follow from philosophy's importance to human life that it should be studied by everyone? If *study* here means professional, in-depth study, then the answer is no. But there is a case for the view that everyone should study philosophy, where *study* means to familiarize oneself with. Let us spend some time on this.

During the better part of human history, most people lived under the guidance of a few others. (Never mind the quality of that guidance and how some attained their position of leadership.) If the few had a decent enough education, they managed their lives and the lives of others with tolerable wisdom. If they lacked in wisdom and whatever other virtues are needed for leadership, then the entire culture experienced the consequences of bad judgment and conduct. In elitist societies—those ruled by an allegedly superior group such as members of royalty, the clergy, clan, or tribe—education in general and philosophical scholarship were the province or unique privilege of just a few.

We are not concerned here with whether such situations were right or wrong; this will be considered with the discussion of political theories in chapter 6. The point here is different. When people do have the chance and take an interest in self-government, they are definitely going to benefit from education, including some study of philosophy. Citizens cannot be forced to gain philosophical under-standing, but it is quite possible that in open societies people *should* learn about philosophy. It is required for their existence as rela-tively free members of the culture. This may be true even if most people are unaware of it. After all, many of us are unaware that dieting, exercise, or being courteous is of value to us.

The point to be stressed is that for those who want to live an independent life, who want to be free of constant servitude to others' ideas and life plans, knowledge of philosophy's place in life can be of considerable benefit. And this is nothing extraordinary. Neither does it mean that we should all turn into full-time professional philosophers. What is meant is that a person should know about philosophy just as a motorist should have some understanding of an automobile engine.

For those who want others to make the crucial decisions in their lives such knowledge may not matter. But what of those of us who choose to live our own lives, at least to the extent that opportunity allows? Then it is best to be prepared for the occasions when the various branches of human knowledge relate to our own existence.

Philosophy's aim is to fulfill an important requirement of human life. Philosophy is not important just accidentally, just because people happen to be philosophical about their lives. Philosophy is crucial to human life as a matter of necessity. It is indispensable. If philosophy is addressed to the basic facts of existence and life, then we need it; philosophy is essentially important to our own lives because the knowledge of these facts is important to us as human beings. But why do we need to know about such facts? How could such knowledge be of importance to us, granted that individually we may not work out all the answers and would use it only as we learn it from others?

Let us take an example here, one already considered in another context. Is there a need to learn whether existence is always, every-where material, that is, whether everything that exists is constructed out of physical, material substance, having mass, dimension, weight, etc.? This is the sort of conclusion that can emerge from an inquiry in one of philosophy's branches. If it is true that everything that exists is material, we have learned something that could be very useful to us.   For example, using this information, we can consider embarking on the study of various particular things suggested to us, such as ghosts, moon rocks, the Loch Ness Monster, and subatomic particles.   We could begin by checking if what we are to study would indeed be constructed out of matter.   If the proposed or suggested subject matter of our examinations did not conform to this minimal requirement, namely, that it be a material substance, we would have all the justification required to dismiss the project right away.   In short, we would know that *nothing can exist that is not material.* Granted that we have here a fundamental fact about everything that exists, a proposed item that does not satisfy this requirement simply could not exist, and we need not bother with any further study.   It would be fruitless, given the truth of the basic fact in our example.

Another example will be useful here, one that is perhaps less hypothetical than the above (although many people do proceed along lines indicated there).   The great philosopher Aristotle held as one of the basic or first principles of all existence that a thing could not be a certain kind of thing and not that kind of thing all at once, in the same respect.   (See chapter 2 and chapter 4.)   Thus, if something *is* a dog today, then it cannot at that time also *not be* a dog.   This is a very widely accepted idea, so much so that people hardly notice that they abide by it.   When we discover that someone's statements could be true only if the above principle were false, we consider him either to be mistaken or to be lying.   This is true regardless of his topic.   In short, discovering that someone has *contradicted* himself tells us immediately that something is wrong with what he is saying.   It is in philosophy that this basic idea is defended and, of course, contested.   If true, however, it is obviously crucial to thinking and communication.   If false, then again it is indispensable that we should discover that.

One should consider this function of philosophy quite seriously, even if there is no intention of going further in one's philosophical investigations.   Do we need to know whether or not human life is absurd?   Must we learn if people can have knowledge of the world or whether, perhaps, this is an unattainable hope?   Do we not require knowledge of our ability to understand one another when we communicate—or of our inability in this respect, no matter what we might do?   It is quite clear that we must have some views on these matters to guide us through our own lives, however rarely we think about such matters on a conscious, explicit level, however rarely we discuss such issues.

DOES EACH PERSON NEED
TO PHILOSOPHIZE?

Obviously one can live without explicit philosophical knowledge or convictions. One can also live without strict attention to one's health. Even without crucial nutrients a person can survive for quite some time. Many of the biological, chemical, psychological, and other requirements of life can be neglected without drastic consequences. Therefore, if the issue is whether one *can* continue life without philosophy or some of its better contributions, then clearly the answer is yes. But this is not the issue, for one can live without many things that one *should* secure if they are even remotely possible.

Philosophy seems to be needed for a reasonably successful life because of some human characteristics evident to anyone. First of all, people depend on and must use principles. In driving, talking, riding, swimming, business, law, and whatever we do, we rely on them. We are also aware, especially near academic places, that all branches of knowledge teach principles—of economics, physics, psychology, art, law, etc. Those who want to engage in an activity on a regular basis will be helped by understanding the principles that underlie that activity. Professionals rely on the principles of their fields most directly. But laymen who depend on the expertise and work of the professionals also rely on those principles. Thus, even though I do not know the principles of auto mechanics, by depending on the work of the person who does, I testify to my reliance on those principles.

Unlike other life forms, we human beings must *learn* the principles that underlie our activities, especially the more complex the activities. Even when it seems that these can be "picked up" without explicit learning, in fact we simply are not aware that we have learned them. By our nature we seem not to live by instincts but must study, learn, and come to understand the world around us and how we can cope in that world. By understanding the principles that govern life, we can often predict events or prevent them. We can make things happen, invent, produce, and create. This is because principles are what govern existence and its numerous, probably infinite elements, features, and characteristics. By knowing these principles, we have a better chance of succeeding in what we do.

Now, since philosophy focuses on the most basic principles of existence, and on our (proper) relationship to them, its results are of importance to anyone who wants to live successfully. The results of philosophical work are not now at issue. What concerns us here is whether philosophy has a role in life and, if it does, whether the role is a vital one. It appears evident that philosophy has a role, and that the adequate fulfillment of this role is necessary if we want to do well in life. A human being simply must use concepts, ideas, and principles. These are the mental tools for learning and for guiding ourselves through reality. Philosophy, when sound, identifies the most general principles about existence and our relationship to it. Such a sound philosophical system would enable us to base our thinking and ideas on correct basic principles about existence. I would like to make it clear, however, that living with the benefits of a sound philosophy will not *guarantee* success in life. The best techniques and ideas about swimming will not overcome all dangers of drowning! The basic principles are not enough. Many things must be faced in life for which neither philosophy nor any other general framework can be one's full answer. Personal resolve is needed for almost every situation, and even then surprises—fortunes or misfortunes—can arise.

Without a general plan, however, it is difficult to get going, to take one's bearings. Among all of the branches of knowledge and inquiry from which benefits can be reaped, philosophy pertains to everyone because everyone has a concern with reality as such. Philosophy can pay off in the sense in which the field's own original name indicated: philosophy comes from the Greek word meaning "love of wisdom," a love that surely must contribute to human life. It may sound like a slogan by now, but Socrates did make the point well when he remarked that the unexamined life is not worth living.

After these comments on philosophy and the individual person, let us now take a quick look at the possible connections between philosophy and the human community.

PHILOSOPHY AND HUMAN COMMUNITIES

From the earliest times that philosophy occupied mankind's attention in a more or less systematic way, it has been closely tied to the concern people have for their communities. It is not the case that all philosophers want to rule society, but most philosophers do believe that their ideas should be given serious consideration. Because of their attention to fundamental issues, philosophers would be able to help solve the large problems typically faced by communities.

The philosophical enterprise is concerned with the broadest possible issues that confront people. Existence, God, knowledge, mind, matter, truth, virtue, beauty—all these concerns are basic. Whatever the consequences of a philosophical investigation of these issues, their philosophical treatment will have a bearing on many aspects of human life. Just as the ideas formulated by earlier philosophers are now embedded in our language—ordinary and technical—so the philosophical thinking of our times will have its impact on the future.

It is not yet crucial what these ideas may be. If they are sound and people make use of them, they can be helpful for communication and progress on many fronts. Plato, for example, tried to discover the essential features of things (the nature of knowledge, virtue, beauty, justice) so as to be able to evaluate human affairs. Suppose he actually did discover these facts. Would knowing them not help in coordinating community understanding and activity? Would it not be important to have answers to such questions as what is the basic human virtue, what renders a society truly just, and what is it to know something about such issues? The answers could help us as our bases for sound judgment in many areas of concern, but most assuredly in the effort to live together in peace.

Having identified some very general principles will not guarantee harmony among people, for their interpretation of these principles may not always be equally accurate or relevant. But the chances for mutual understanding are far better when citizens live with a common philosophical framework that is basically sound. Nor would such agreement on fundamentals destroy those elements of individuality and distinctiveness that are usually valued—just as the common influence of gravity does not make all movements toward the center of the earth uniform and identical.

The institution of the law, for example, assumes a common basis that most of us will at least tolerate if nòt fully subscribe to. Thus the basic rights of the United States legal system serve as a unifying framework within which more than two hundred million human beings coexist and interact with some degree of continued success. (It might be argued that the inconsistencies in that basic framework produce the bulk of the difficulties we experience.)

Consider, finally, that almost all major philosophers have proposed political theories: Plato and Aristotle, to name but two of the ancients, and John Locke and Karl Marx, among more recent contributors. Each had different philosophical ideas but shared with the others the conviction that philosophy matters for human community life.

PHILOSOPHY AND SCIENCE

A persistent obstacle to taking an interest in philosophy arises from the widely held belief that the sciences are the only areas of inquiry in which reliable knowledge can be produced—the reliability being due to the *methods* of science. Many think that in the humanities— arts, philosophy, law—one cannot gain firm understanding of anything. Many freshmen come to colleges and universities with the belief that science is the only road to truth and in all other fields one opinion is as sound as any other. This impression may develop in high school years, when a somewhat naive view of the sciences prevails and many treat the humanities like a huge rap session, or it may arise from a somewhat lopsided view of technology. Most people tend to give full credit for technological achievements to the hard, physical sciences, whereas in fact technological progress is due to a combination of many aspects of human life, including politics, law, education, art, commerce, and philosophy. Lack of appreciation for this has led many to assume that only science—and no other field—can yield knowledge and understanding.

In general it is a simplification, if not an outright mistake, to think that every science uses the same method of inquiry and that in other areas of life nothing like the scientific method can be employed and thus the results must be inadequate. This view is itself the result of a philosophical theory that has been prominent during the last hundred years. It emerged from the doctrine that all knowledge must be achieved by relying exclusively on sensory input. (See chapter 3 for a discussion of empiricism.) In the physical sciences such reliance is considerable. It is then often accepted that only in these sciences is knowledge obtainable. This view has led to much controversy in all other fields, and many of the social sciences have adjusted so as to accommodate this standard of being scientific by ignoring anything not strictly physical in human and social affairs.

Before a person commits himself to one view of the relationship between philosophy and other fields of inquiry, he should take a look at philosophy itself and examine what various philosophical theories have to say about that relationship. It is in philosophy that the relationship between fields of inquiry is examined. The various theories we will examine in this book, especially when we investigate theories of knowledge, aim at identifying the proper relationship between the sciences and other fields of scholarly activity.

For now it will help to understand this issue as controversial and subject to philosophical examination. On a commonsense level it is safe to suggest that fields with differing subject matter will employ somewhat different means and methods of inquiry. (See chapter 3 for a discussion of contextualism.) Philosophy studies basic issues, whereas the sciences study special areas of reality. It makes sense then to expect important differences between the ways these fields approach their tasks. The types of arguments used to support their claims may differ considerably. These differences notwithstanding, there is a major feature that unifies the various fields of inquiry—which ought to be emphasized more often than it is. Rationality, objectivity, care, and attentiveness are of equal importance in all areas of research and inquiry. What exactly will be the most rational means of dealing with a specific topic should not be prejudged; logical consistency and clear awareness of pertinent facts and theories are crucial.

OBJECTIVITY—
A CRUCIAL LINK

In everyday life we understand by **objectivity** a quality of judgment or of attitude. Those who are prejudiced are chided because they lack objectivity; they prejudge rather than rest their beliefs on facts. (See the discussion of prejudgment in chapter 4.) In the context of such concerns, objectivity means paying attention to the relevant evidence in forming judgments, opinions, and attitudes. For example, the racially prejudiced individual lacks objectivity because in judging someone he invokes considerations that have nothing to do with the person's character. To reject someone as a moral equal because of color is to blame that person for something no one can help, namely, one's color at birth. It is generally recognized as unjust, something that comes from not taking an objective view of human beings.

Objectivity also has importance in describing the world around us: are we exaggerating, are we being comprehensive enough, do we trivialize the issue? The idea of being objective in these respects stands in contrast to the idea that descriptions are a matter of personal, subjective judgment. (See chapter 3 for a discussion of subjectivism.)

From these familiar ways of being objective, it emerges that objectivity amounts to a serious regard for truth, accuracy, and relevance. To examine something, we need to sort out the evidence carefully. We must make sure that our own concerns do not lead us to inject material that is unrelated to what we are dealing with. Generally, but with many exceptions, it is assumed that people can be objective. Therefore, in courts it is a requirement for juries to make objective assessments of the guilt or innocence of defendants, to ignore comments or testimony that has no bearing on the issue. None of this is to say that objectivity is always easy to achieve and maintain. Yet, this does not prove its impossibility.

Sometimes being objective is equated with being heartless, cool, or insensitive, and it is then thought of as a negative quality. Yet this is probably a mistake when generalized. Consider the surgeon who approaches an operation in an emotionless, methodical fashion. Simply because he does not allow his emotions to interfere with his work and focuses on the facts and methods of surgery, he would not be open to criticism—there is nothing heartless about remaining objective about his work, including the illness which it is his task to cure. During the performance of his task it would not be appropriate to indulge in the display of emotions, even though we can assume that any good surgeon and physician appreciates the emotions and concerns related to making people well. That is one reason for the existence of medicine, even though while at work it is crucial that the physician's emotionalism not be allowed to interfere with the objectivity needed for doing a good job.

In philosophy, as in many other fields where we seek knowledge and reliable guidance for conduct, we need to be objective. We need to be able to assess our own arguments and those offered by others, to determine whether all that is relevant to an issue has been considered in reaching a conclusion. We need to know if criticism has been handled with justice and objectivity, rather than without due regard, that is, arbitrarily or with prejudice. Depending on what is being studied in the field, we must learn how objectivity should be achieved, what will make it possible and likely, and what will make it difficult. In this respect philosophy is like the sciences again, or like the law. But it does not follow that we most employ the specific standards of objectivity used in physics or some other particular field as we assess a philosophical point of view, a philosophical argument, or a philosophical conclusion.

Scientifically oriented people sometimes criticize philosophers for not being objective, for expressing only "their own point of view," or for claiming "what is true only for them." Such critics must be asked to explain what they believe philosophers should do. If they claim that philosophers are not upholding the same standards of objectivity demanded in some field of science, the criticism must be rejected: philosophy is not committed to such a task, any more than scientific creativity is committed to following the form of creativity found in literature or poetry. If philosophy were so committed, it would not be philosophy; instead, it would be science, which is absurd. It constitutes an obliteration of differences evident in human affairs.

PHILOSOPHY AND COMMON SENSE

Common sense is not a very precise term. Sometimes when we call some viewpoint "commonsensical" we mean that many people hold it. Other times we mean that simple people hold it. Or it can refer to what those not specialized in some field of study believe about the subject matter at hand. It is important for those who are just about to examine philosophy to consider what sort of relationship might exist between their commonsense beliefs and philosophy. Many philosophers have had something to say about this relationship.

Generally speaking, philosophers consider "common sense" to indicate the views people have of uncontroversial issues in their un-reflective moments. (Sometimes philosophers call these intuitions—when they say "intuitively I would hòld" or "on first intuition.") It is a matter of common sense that when you call someone on the phone, the person who answers really exists and has not been created by your mind. Common sense would have it that when people leave your sight and go on about their own business they continue to exist even if they are unseen for some time after. Common sense would have it that when a person asks for something, he really wants it. These are all commonsense beliefs. But there are even more complicated ones. We believe that TV sets cannot work as washing machines and that puppies cannot give birth to kittens. It is also common sense that playing a piano must be learned and does not simply come to us out of the blue.

Many of these beliefs, even when some turn out to be mistaken or only partly true, are central to getting along in life. Common sense is, to most of us, a sort of layman's philosophical framework. Furthermore, the traces of any philosophical position can be detected within commonsense ideas.

Yet, however important common sense is for us, we can find some of it problematic. It embodies many confusions. For example, people tend to believe both that they have control over their lives and that their backgrounds cause them to be what they are. Both beliefs are incorporated in common sense. So, if we insist on common sense as our final court of appeal, it can lead us into much confusion and even prevent experimentation and development in human knowledge. Although our common sense tells us that horses cannot give birth to rabbits, it seems that some horses did manage to bear something like donkeys. Scientists at times demonstrate problems with common sense. Reliance on common sense is challenged by the possibility of ESP, plants that respond to human attention, reincarnation, and so forth.

Philosophy never sets out to deny or affirm common sense. It must, however, start by paying it some heed. It is from the common opinions we form (quite unaware that we even form them) that we begin to wonder, to question, to try to make better sense of existence and our relationship to it. However much we might later question our commonsense ideas, they are the first step on the road to philosophizing and all other intellectual and scientific activities. In addition to starting with common sense, some philosophers try to make sure that their views mesh with it. Others attempt to provide commonsense ideas with sound backing.

Yet, considering how many commonsense ideas have been overthrown by science (e.g., the belief that the earth is flat), we can ask why philosophers would be concerned at all with these beliefs. This question assumes, however, that *all* those things we take for granted in our daily lives will be explained away by scientists of the future, and such an assumption is misleading. Consider that all of the sciences start with daily experiences and commonsense beliefs. Science works from the surface to detailed knowledge of events, things, relationships, and so forth—for instance, from the objects we all deal with and know of, scientists start their investigations into the composition of such objects. The beginning for science, however, is the same as ours in philosophy—common sense. To believe that every feature of this beginning could somehow be overthrown by subsequent inquiry is to believe something that is quite impossible. If we start with some samples of what are generally recognized to be facts, our conclusions must accord to at least some degree with a few of these facts. Otherwise we would lose the beginning point of our thinking; we would, so to speak, cut off the branch that gives our work needed support. For instance, if a scientist becomes interested in the composition of some substance believed to be a metal and this prompts him to examine it in detail, he could not end up denying that the substance exists. He might conclude that what he began examining is not a metal, but he could not conclude that what he started to examine really does not exist at all. This is because his proof started with the fact that this substance exists. (Later when we investigate logic we will see why a proof that ends by denying the premises with which it starts can be used only for a very limited purpose, namely, to call into question the entire argument, not to demonstrate the existence or nonexistence of anything.)

Another important consideration is the context in which scientific and commonsense claims are made. For example, when it was common sense to say that the earth is flat, "the earth" very likely meant the ground in sight of a person. The statement was quite true—and in a sense still is. Only when we remove the context of the time and situation in which that statement would very likely have been seriously made, initially, do we find trouble with it. Therefore, science may be seen as expanding the context, and the problem is not so much with common sense as with generalizations from it. Common sense is quite appropriate so long as we realize that it is always to be used without dogmatism, that it must remain open to challenge, and that there must be no undue extension into areas not examined. If we heed these cautions, we can retain confidence in the commonsense approach to reality.

PHILOSOPHY AND RELIGION

The foregoing discussion has pointed out philosophy's differences from and similarities to science. Another area of human concern, even reverence, is also frequently discussed in connection with philosophy. Religion has great personal significance for many people, yet it deserves careful scrutiny. In philosophy we turn a critical eye upon religion, however uncomfortable that may be to some. It is best, in the final analysis, to form views about religion— its truth, its importance—on the basis of continued reexamination, not on the basis of habit or hearsay. Some points about the relationship between philosophy and religion can be indicated here.

The main issue of common concern to philosophy and religion is the existence, nature, and characteristics of God. But philosophy and religion have something else in common. They often conclude with similar or even identical statements about some areas of human concern: the meaning of life, human nature, the values we should pursue, and so on.   An important difference, however, is in their *ways of reaching these statements.*

In philosophy, acceptance of a conclusion is based on reasoning, reflective thinking, argumentation, and debate, whereas in religion, acceptance of a conclusion is usually or ultimately not dependent upon evidence and proof.   That is, religious beliefs are often said to be based on *faith.*   Since faith is a rejection of fact and logic as the necessary elements of proof, it is clear that philosophers attempt to avoid resting their conclusions on faith.   Of course, there are some who argue that we must end with some things taken on faith, even in philosophy.   But here, again, this is a philosophical argument concerning the nature of philosophy.   It is obviously treated differently from the manner in which people treat their beliefs in the goodness of God, the existence of heaven and hell, whether there exists one God or many, the immorality of premarital sexual intercourse, the unity of God and man in Jesus, the chosen status of the people of Israel, and so forth.   These are all accepted on faith by most people who believe them, while most would not hold that beliefs about other matters should be based on faith, at least not in the final analysis.   It is with those religions that hold up faith as the only correct basis for accepting whatever is important to the religion that philosophy is in disagreement, usually.

What is crucial is that philosophy insists on argument, rational reflection, clarity of thought—in whatever way these apply to its subject matter.   However the conclusions of a philosopher might accord with a religious doctrine, the philosopher is not praying or relying on divine revelation as he seeks philosophical understanding. He tries to convince with argument, even when what he argues is that arguments are futile!   If he believes in God he wants to demonstrate the sensible character of that belief, even the truth of it, without reference to personal revelations.   Or he wants to show that revelations are valid means to knowledge, and in trying to show this he offers arguments, not more revelations.   Even if some philosophers do not do this, philosophy as such does require it.

There are some who argue that religion is "infant philosophy." Others try to explain the existence of religion by way of psychology, anthropology, sociology, or economics.   None of these touches on the philosopher's crucial concern: are the claims of various religions true or false?   Even when philosophers affirm the claims of some religion, they usually treat these claims in accordance with this basic requirement: as philosophers they want to scrutinize the arguments involved, the evidence being offered, and the ideas about how one might come to have knowledge of religious matters.

Many of my own students have asked me whether their religious beliefs could be affected by their attention to philosophical debates about them. Certainly they could be. But behind this question lies the more serious one: *should* the conclusions of philosophers (for example, about God's existence) matter to a person? Whether one *should* yield to any convincing argument is a moral question; it concerns how one *ought to* live and guide one's life. Such questions must be thought through carefully by each of us as individuals so that their implications for our life can be fully appreciated.

BRANCHES OF PHILOSOPHY

Having offered some general observations about philosophy and having attempted to dislodge some prejudices I suspect many people have, I would like now to outline the several branches of philosophy. I must point out that this division is not one to which all philosophers would subscribe. Both the major and the subordinate branches are debatable. In this brief outline I will not even attempt to justify my own arrangement of the various areas of work done in the field. I think that what I offer represents the natural division of philosophy, except for several areas that are ambiguous because they are new and not yet fully developed. With some, of course, I am not familiar enough to be all that confident in assigning them a position. Here I rely on advice given by colleagues and teachers. The areas I describe, then, are metaphysics, epistemology, ethics, political philosophy, and aesthetics.

Metaphysics

Metaphysics was initially called (by Aristotle) "first philosophy"— the science of being or of reality as such. Not all philosophers consider this a viable area of study. Some think it occultish. But those who do accept metaphysics as a branch of philosophy contend that it aims at answering certain very basic questions about reality. Among them are: What are the basic facts of reality, of existence? What principles are true of everything that exists? Is there some all-pervasive fact that exists everywhere, throughout time? Are there some necessary facts, indispensable to existence itself? What is the basic substance or material of the universe? Must there exist anything at all?

From these questions it can be seen that metaphysics concerns the facts or principles at the foundation of existence. The task of the metaphysician, then, is to identify such facts or principles. The word *metaphysics* is itself a kind of indication of this point, although its exact origin is still debated by scholars. *Meta* means "after" or "beyond." *Metaphysics* means "after or beyond physics." Since *physics* originally meant "study of nature," this simply suggests that metaphysics studies what stands above, or transcends, nature. In fact, the evidence is that the term *metaphysics* does not have this literal meaning but derives from accidental circumstances. For centuries it has meant the opposite of its literal meaning—namely, the study of what is before, or prior to, physics or nature. The idea is that in this field those facts are studied that lie at the foundation of nature, reality, or existence, facts which the special fields (e.g., the physical sciences) would not study but would take as given.

But many philosophers, as mentioned before, deny that there are basic or essential facts of reality and that the facts or principles metaphysicians want to identify exist. The very idea of such basic facts is thought to be a confusion; nothing *could* be considered crucial or essential *to everything*. Others have argued that the facts that precede all other facts, the truths that underlie all other truths, are actually features of the human mind—admittedly basic, indispensable, and necessary features. This idea may be more familiar to nonphilosophers by way of the widely expressed belief that all of us are "caught" within a certain inescapable (human) point of view from which we look at and understand existence. Another expression of this belief is that human beings are "forced" to see the world from a certain perspective because we cannot get outside our own minds to check if the mind does not in fact distort, by *its process* of awareness, what actually exists around us.

Still, the traditional branch of philosophy called metaphysics has had as its main goal to identify what is fundamental to all existence.

There have always been those who said we *cannot discover* those basic facts or features or elements of reality. Others have claimed that we actually *impose* the basic features of the human mind upon a reality that we cannot know in itself, that is, as it really is. Still others have insisted that *each one* of us, separately, *imposes his own* mental presuppositions onto a reality that cannot be known without bias, or that we actually *create* reality and there is no reality outside what our minds create for us. Those who characterize metaphysics along these lines dismiss its original goals as impossible to achieve.

When we study the philosophies that have emerged in human history, we find trends that are more or less popular, dominant, pronounced, and emphasized in various periods. From epoch to epoch, emphasis has shifted from one branch of philosophy to another. In our time metaphysics is somewhat neglected, at least if one judges by the activities of the bulk of Anglo-American thinkers.

Epistemology

The second-most characteristic of philosophical undertakings is **epistemology,** the theory of knowledge. It is obviously central. Anything one might want to say of reality, or of any part of it whatever, can always be met with the following question: How do you know? And the central concern of epistemology is to specify what counts as knowledge. For something to succeed as knowledge, certain central characteristics must be present. Many things are said to be known by us, but in all cases where we actually have knowledge it is appropriate to inquire what makes it that—why is it knowledge and not just an opinion, hunch, belief, guess, illusion, or dream? Put in various ways, epistemology aims at identifying the essential characteristics of knowledge, or the defining elements of the concept *knowledge*, or the meaning of the term *knowledge*.

Epistemology has often been thought to address itself to the question, Is knowledge *possible?* The question is of special significance in connection with those who have held that we really cannot know the world, or ourselves, or anything else for that matter. Many philosophers deal with this issue under the rubric of epistemology, although very likely the question does not belong there; it is more appropriately an issue of metaphysics, since it betrays a more basic question: Is the world such that human beings could know it?

Here the question concerns the nature of reality. It might also be a question within psychology: Is the human organism able to know reality? While these are often of concern to philosophers, epistemology is best understood to be that branch of philosophy that concerns itself with the nature of knowledge, not with whether it is possible.

Epistemology involves itself in many subbranches, some of which are also subbranches of other major branches of philosophy. Among these, the philosophy of science, metaethics, metapolitics, the philosophy of language, and logic must surely be cited.

The philosophy of science includes epistemological issues when it attends to problems of justifying scientific conclusions, supporting and testing theories, choosing from among competing basic approaches to a given field of science, etc. The problem of induction—how to provide rational justification for a belief about something new by reference to earlier experiences with (allegedly) similar cases—is crucial to scientific reasoning. Do the methods of justification employed in one field of science provide adequate tools for justifying beliefs in another field? These and other problems are treated in the philosophy of science and in epistemology.

Metaethics studies the character of judgments, statements and reasoning about basic values, principles of conduct, moral virtues, obligations, and the like. Can moral principles be justified at all? Can we obtain knowledge of what is good, right, wrong, evil, etc.? Metaethics and **metapolitics** (the latter concerned with judgments about community affairs and the common good) are complex fields, of course, and often give rise to skepticism. Despite this one might want to tackle them, since their difficulties may stem from their being so closely tied to our daily lives and decisions, our own character, and the character of our community, not from their alleged inherent futility!

The philosophy of language is a subbranch of the theory of knowledge because language is the medium not only of communicated thought, but also, perhaps, of all thinking. At least beyond a primitive level of thought, language becomes entirely interwoven with thinking itself. This may not be true for everyone. Einstein held that he could think some of his most complex ideas without recourse to language (words, signs, etc.). But it seems evident that when I try to formulate my thoughts for purposes of making these points about the philosophy of language, without language I would be helpless. Even if I could think of all these things without recourse to language—which is very unlikely, for reasons discussed in the philosophy of language as well as in psychology—I could certainly not learn about them, discuss them, or defend them. This suggestion accounts for part of the interest in the structure of human language: might it not function, just as some think the structure of the mind itself might, as a distorting factor? Can we, for instance, say anything about the human mind, knowledge, reality, God, values, political principles, or members of other cultures and epochs with the confidence that these claims are free of distortions due to features of language? And if language indeed bars understanding, how would we come to know *that?* But if it does not, why do we have so much trouble understanding not just one another but ourselves?

We come to the most important but least evidently exciting area of epistemology, the study of **logic.** It must be emphasized that logic is not regarded by many as a branch of epistemology. For now, however, we would best regard it as such because it deals with the methods by which reliable conclusions should be reached and tested.

Philosophers rely a great deal on logic, and very often little other than logic, outside the examples they take from ordinary (or some special area of) life. In philosophy, logic is the most highly visible tool in producing results, although any branch of knowledge requires it. Yet philosophers do not have laboratories or special instruments. They attend to reality as they find it or as specialists present it, and they use the tools of logic to criticize and understand what they deal with. (Chapter 4 will be devoted to a discussion of logic.) The thing to be noted here is that logic, *the field concerned with the basic principles and methods of sound reasoning,* is very closely related to the issue of what knowledge is, as well as to philosophy's endeavors of criticism, understanding, argument, proof, etc. Thus it is usually philosophers who are logicians, and logicians teach in philosophy departments.

In logic proper one studies valid argumentation and sound reasoning. The standards of such reasoning emerge everywhere in our lives. Logic has an important role wherever and whenever thinking takes place, even if logic is used only as a sort of mental training to be adopted as a subconscious habit in daily affairs. Both the principles of sound thinking and the pitfalls of fallacious reasoning are investigated in the formal study of logic.

Outside of logic itself, philosophers study the foundations of logic as well as what is sometimes called **metalogic,** the field where the question of the status of logical principles arises—what sorts of things are principles and rules of logic anyway? Philosophers want to know whether logic itself has firm grounds. Why would we have to use logic in correct reasoning if this tool could be dispensed with easily enough? Aristotle, the founder of logic as a systematic field of study, seemed to think that the axioms or first principles of logic are also metaphysical facts, that is, basic facts of existence. Those who agree would hold that logic works because its rules reflect or express the structure and mode of existence itself.

Those philosophers who deny that metaphysical principles can be known or exist characterize logic quite differently. Some think logic is a Western approach to using the mind, a mere prejudice. Others consider it an indispensable feature of human thought, due to the structure of our minds. Yet others take it to be a convenient tool that we have picked up and found desirable through trial and error. Whatever their view of its foundations, most philosophers consider it necessary to learn logic, and it is arguable that everyone should receive training in logic at an early age.

Ethics

Ethics, or (as it is often called) moral philosophy, is the study of whether there are any values each and every person should pursue, whether there is a set of virtues or a code of principles of conduct for everyone, and what these are if they do exist. It attempts to answer such questions as: How should human beings conduct themselves? What general ideals should they pursue? What traits of character are virtuous? Ethics is also concerned with whether basic values are absolute, relative, subjective, culturally varied, modifiable, and so forth, and what it would mean for these values or virtues or ideals to have the characteristics just mentioned.

Some philosophers defend the idea that we can only *create* values, or opinions about them, for ourselves and that we can have no rational justification for thinking that any of them apply to everyone. Others hold that certain basic values or virtues or ideals have validity for all people and only their implementation varies from one place or time to another. Some argue that values are applicable only to acts that relate to other people or to God; others hold that in whatever circumstances people may find themselves, social or private, they should act to pursue certain values and follow certain principles of conduct.   There are those who claim that different values or ideals apply to people with different backgrounds, intelligence, social class, economic status, genetic makeup, knowledge of the world, and so forth.   Others would argue that ethical considerations apply to all human beings equally, by virtue of their being human.   But all in all, ethics is the study of problems that surround questions of right and wrong conduct.

Political Philosophy

In political philosophy the focus of attention is on human conduct within an organized human community.   The prominent questions here concern the relationship of individuals to the requirements of community existence.   What are the correct means by which to acquire authority to issue orders to others?   What should be the basic constituents of a legal system?   What is the standard of political or social justice?   Under what conditions are laws open to justified violation?   Do principles of community conduct vary from culture to culture; that is, are different principles valid or justified for different groups of people?   Under what conditions, if any, is punishment justified?   And, in general, what rights and wrongs pertain to human community life by virtue of the fact that it is *human* community life (as distinguished from its being twentieth-century, German, caucasian, or wealthy community life)?

Some philosophers argue that no universal (firmly grounded, lasting) political principles exist.   Some say that the sheer power to impose principles justifies itself, whatever principles are imposed. Others say that the principles of a human community are determined by certain invariable laws or forces of history (as these pertain to human community or social life).   Yet others defend the view that once laws are established and widely accepted, these laws are the only source of standards or criteria for identifying what is right and wrong in human affairs within the community in question.   There are also philosophers who claim that philosophy can only study the meaning of well-entrenched political ideas and ideals and connot say whether they should be implemented.   In the main, however, for those who consider political philosophy a valid field—and some do not—its subject matter is the values, ideals, or virtues of human communities—not what people believe these to be, but what they are, in fact, whether acknowledged or not.

Aesthetics

Aesthetics, or the philosophy of art, focuses on values and standards related to human artistic affairs: creation, appreciation, evaluation, criticism, and the like. Questions arise in this area about what renders some human creation a work of art. What, if anything, is the difference between art, craft, and design? Can the criteria by which something should be identified as a work of art change? Are there standards of beauty? Are such standards justifiable and do they serve to help us evaluate works of art? What, if any, function, role, or purpose does art have in human life? Are there certain things in nature, untouched by human beings, that may be works of art? Is art representational, expressive, symbolic, emotionally significant, etc.? These and related questions arise in aesthetics.

Some philosophers concerned with this branch of their field have argued that there are universal standards of art that anyone can discover. Others have said that art is just whatever one wishes to regard in some special way. Others have said that in appraising a work of art the only relevant consideration is its *form,* whether certain rules have been satisfied. But others argue that the *content* of a work of art can have a great deal to do with its aesthetic merits. Some want to defend the view that art must satisfy certain ethical or moral standards in order to be good. Others say that art must express certain political ideals in order to attain excellence. Still others see art as a psychological need, even a social force that contributes to the development of civilization. But aesthetics in general includes considerations of all these and related issues.

FUNDAMENTALS: THE PROVINCE OF PHILOSOPHY

Maybe it is not obvious, but in all of these branches and subbranches of philosophy the focus in on basic, fundamental issues. In metaphysics the fundamental aspects of reality come under scrutiny; in epistemology the fundamental features of knowledge are investigated; in ethics, too, philosophers are concerned with basic values, virtues, ideals, principles of conduct, etc.; in politics the same issues come under philosophical investigation; and in art no less is true.

When the civilization from which ours developed had just begun to record what people thought about the world and their relationship to it, almost every field came under the heading of philosophy—the love of, or serious concern for, wisdom and the understanding of nature.   But as the details of its study emerged, different areas of nature were identified and various special fields— astronomy, mathematics, physics, etc.—developed.   This differentiating process is still occurring.   Psychology and sociology were not long ago indistinguishable from philosophy.   Some people have actually concluded that with their breaking off into special fields, philosophy was left without a subject matter, that is, that there are no *basic* principles of nature and human life left to study.   Yet it would appear, even from this brief survey, that philosophy will always have its sphere of concern.   Even when people deny this, they turn out to be offering philosophical considerations and philosophical conclusions, including the paradoxical conclusion that philosophy has no subject matter.   Somehow that idea turns out to be part of philosophy itself—meager philosophy, mind you, but still not the concern of any special field.

Anyway, the view that reality is something about which basic discoveries can be made, existence something that calls for understanding just as it is, knowledge something that requires identifying, and so forth—all this makes it very likely that as long as there are human beings, philosophy will be one of the main concerns people will have.   Its significance for life, however remote and difficult to identify and trace within the particular lives of individuals and cultures, will also persist.   The main question is how well philosophers will carry out their work, and how eagerly others will seek knowledge of at least some part of philosophy.

QUESTIONS FOR DISCUSSION

1. What are signs of philosophical interest in the ordinary thinking that people engage in?
2. Why would we consider some ideas or claims *philosophical*?

3. What are some examples of ordinary activities, daily issues (simple or complicated) that involve philosophical topics?

4. Is there a reason why people ought to have some understanding of philosophy?

5. What, in general, could be concluded from the fact that philosophers disagree with one another as often as they do? What could *not* be concluded from this fact?

6. What appears to indicate the importance of philosophy in human life? What indicates that human beings need philosophy?

7. Why would anyone think—what reasons could he offer to justify—that philosophy is something we all need?

8. In what sense should we understand the claim that philosophy is concerned with studying fundamentals?

9. If philosophers do have as their goal the study of fundamental facts or principles, how does this emerge in the discussion of the various branches of philosophy?

10. Show how false philosophical ideas can have an impact, as well as true ones.

11. Is philosophy of actual importance to *you*?

12. What is your idea of the best way to obtain knowledge and can this method be implemented in philosophy? If not, why not? If the answer is yes, what reasons would you offer to defend it?

13. Explain whether philosophy and science differ concerning the matter of reaching agreement. What are your ideas on this, now that you have considered the suggestions offered in this chapter? Defend your ideas, even if they are still held tentatively.

14. Indicate why this chapter suggests that different methods of learning are required in different fields of inquiry. Use examples that would support the points made in this chapter and think of what might nevertheless count against those examples.

15. Compare the approach to reaching conclusions in a criminal (jury) trial with that used in some of the better-known sciences (choose one you know well enough).

16. Do you think there are what could be regarded as psychological factors that render treatment of certain topics more difficult? Do you think this would be sufficient to explain widescale disagreement concerning topics in, for instance, sociology? Why?

17. Describe what objectivity is and then indicate how it might be part of both scientific and philosophical inquiry. How would it manifest itself in ordinary life? Defend some objections to the claim that objectivity is possible.

18. Does science depend on common sense? Why or why not? What indicates that it does and what that it does not?

19. What does it mean to drop the context in a discussion? How could that mislead someone in thinking about various topics? Give some objections to the claim that omitting or removing or dropping the context interferes with sound thinking.

20. In what way (s) does philosophy differ from religion and in what respects are they very similar? Does the suggestion in this chapter concerning this matter seem right? Defend your answer by telling why or why not.

21. Why would the question of God's existence link religion and philosophy? Which branch of philosophy concerns itself with this issue and why is it this branch more than others (except for the question of how we might know that God exists, which is different from one in which we ask whether God exists)?

Metaphysics

2

In chapter 1 I gave some indication of the nature of metaphysics. It's the branch of philosophy that concerns the most basic features of what the world is like; it attempts to answer such questions as: What are the most basic and common features that are present in everything and anything that exists? By "basic features" or "basic facts" I mean facts that are prior to all other facts—those that would remain even if most of the facts we are familiar with were to cease, were no longer the case. These basic facts, if any could be found, would be what characterizes reality as such, just for being the reality it is. As we explore the various metaphysical theories, the idea I have tried to clear up here will come into greater focus.

My aim here is to make metaphysics a more familiar topic to the reader. My discussion will be sketchy, but once my outline of the various positions has been understood, the reader will be able to use this understanding as a stepping-stone to more advanced discussions.

One of the purposes of this chapter is to show how the subject matter of metaphysics is quite natural, that metaphysical questions have a clear place in our lives even when we do not directly ask them. Sometimes I will associate certain theories with specific philosophers, but more often I will outline a metaphysical position without tying it to any given thinker who gave it forceful expression.

THE POINT OF METAPHYSICS

Most serious fields of investigation develop because people have found that certain questions need to be answered in order for them to live successfully. Even pseudo-sciences like astrology and scientology last only because their practitioners believe or have persuaded others that the investigations undertaken and answers discovered are valuable. Even those who claim that many fields of inquiry are pure, and serve no interest, could only have in mind that no *specific* purpose is served by them. So-called pure research is often said to have no practical goal. In fact, its practical goal is the increase of human knowledge, which is certainly a most significant result.

To check if metaphysics has a purpose to serve it will help to learn what questions it aims to answer and why one would ask these questions in the first place. I have already indicated the sorts of questions that metaphysicians consider in need of attention. Later I will show what different metaphysicians have proposed as answers to these questions, but now we need simply to recall some of them. What are the basic facts of reality? What is the most basic thing (or kind of existence) in reality? What are some of the most significant types of existence? These and other questions are treated within metaphysics. But why would anyone raise them in the first place?

Examples of Metaphysics in Life

The following is an illustration of how metaphysical questions arise and become relevant. Detectives are trying to determine who broke into the safe at a bank. It is suggested to them that Mr. Perkins, the head teller, did it. But the break-in occurred at 5 p.m. on Tuesday—a known fact—and now Mr. Perkins proves to them that at 5 p.m. on Tuesday he was across town at a wedding. The detectives immediately reject the suggestion that Mr. Perkins broke into the safe. Why?

The detectives reject this suggestion because their common-sense metaphysics excludes the possibility that a person can be in two places at once. At least one cannot be in two places in the same respect, that is, bodily—although one could be at the wedding while "in imagination" be by the safe. If the metaphysical position that something cannot be in two different places at the same time in the same respect is true, then these detectives did well to reject the suggestion that Mr. Perkins broke into the safe. If they did not accept this position, they might press on with an attempt to prove Mr. Perkins's guilt, ignoring the dictates of the commonsense metaphysics. In this instance the commonsense metaphysics serves an important practical function: it limits possibilities and closes off options for consideration.

Or take a more controversial case as an illustration of the place of metaphysical concerns in ordinary life. Suppose someone claims that a ghost resides in his house. If one accepts the metaphysical position that everything that exists must either be, or depend for its existence on, a physical object, then one will not even consider the story plausible, let alone probable. Since ghosts are disembodied spirits, and the reported house guest is therefore to be something that is neither a physical object (that is what "disembodied" tells us), nor dependent on a physical object for its existence, our metaphysical position excludes its possibility. Here, again, the tenets of the metaphysical position serve as basic checks on what is to be taken as a serious possibility, as something that could really exist.

Basic Facts as Check Points

These examples are not very strange. But if they do not convey the point to someone, a slight change will probably do the trick. One might recall the many disputes about talking to the dead, communication with spirits, telepathy, sensing things without the use of the sensory organs, and so forth. Many of these debates have to do with whether what is claimed could be true, not with whether any particular claim is or is not. When the question is raised as to whether such things could exist, whether, for example, dead people could communicate, it is often someone's metaphysical position that dictates the terms. Thus, someone who believes that communication must involve physical materials will reject the idea that such "occult" claims could be true. Similar metaphysical ideas underlie debates about the existence (possibility) of miracles, God, angels, thoughts, time, and other purported beings, some of which are widely accepted as problematic and some of which are usually taken for granted.

These and similar concerns explain the relationship of metaphysics to everyday life. Not everyone would recognize these as metaphysical concerns. However, most of us do need to have some ideas on metaphysical topics, regardless of how we might classify these ideas, in our normal, day-to-day endeavors. We need to know something of these basic facts of reality so we can guide ourselves in our thinking and actions.

Metaphysics is not the only field of study that concerns itself with what is or is not possible. But the other fields are special realms of study. In these we deal with chemical, biological, economic, or psychological possibilities and impossibilities, and in these we rarely close the door to unheard-of possibilities. The issue of what could not be, what could not exist at all, is the concern of metaphysics. In our lives we make plenty of use of certain dominant metaphysical ideas—even of the idea that perhaps metaphysics is impossible, that we could not know the basic laws, facts, or features of existence.

Topics in Metaphysics

These familiar concerns are part of what occupies the attention of the metaphysician, but they are certainly not all. Within the many different but often overlapping metaphysical positions, topics of considerable complexity are investigated. Aside from considering the issue of the basic facts of reality, that is, what is the basic stuff of existence (e.g., matter, spirit, mind, events) and what kind of things can and cannot exist, metaphysics also asks less obviously relevant questions. What sort of existence do thoughts have, if any? What is the status of language in reality? Is there a given number of types of things that exist (e.g., temporal, spatial, mental)? What is the relationship between different types of things that might exist?

Then there are some familiar problems again, somewhat more restricted to human concerns but still frequently discussed within the field of metaphysics. Is man free or is he controlled by forces outside of or inherited by him? Could human beings act as causes of anything? Is everything in nature predetermined? Does God exist? Could man have a soul and could the soul exist separated from the body?

The plan of this chapter is to take up some of these topics later. First, however, I will discuss various alternative metaphysical positions and explain their answers to the most basic metaphysical questions: What are the basic facts of existence, and of what is existence composed? I will also explore some positions that reject the very possibility of answering these questions. These deserve some attention because in our own times the members of the philosophical community are quite divided on the issue of whether metaphysics is possible and whether metaphysics is a legitimate, fruitful field of inquiry or a sphere wherein only idle speculation could prevail.

ALTERNATIVE METAPHYSICAL POSITIONS

Metaphysical positions are answers to the questions that arise in the field of metaphysics. We have already mentioned some of these questions. To appreciate why there are so many different answers, it may be helpful to think of the metaphysician as a sort of detective. When detectives or police investigators are attempting to solve a murder mystery, they propose various theories, some emphasizing one thing and others thinking of different things in the same vein. All of them will try to explain how the event occurred, who caused it, how the pieces fit together, and so forth. There may even be some, perhaps certain interested laymen, who will claim that we do not understand murder well enough to worry about the problem and we might as well concern ourselves with the victim's family and friends or with the social consequences of such terrible situations.

Similarly, there are metaphysicians with different theories that aim to make sense of the area of concern we call metaphysics, emphasizing different points as more or less important. And there can be philosophers who simply find the entire field too confusing and inherently problematic and will ask us to leave aside this worry and turn to more fruitful areas of inquiry.

In this discussion of the various alternatives it will help to view the different theories along the lines suggested above. And each different theory is at once a challenge to the correctness of the others.

Idealism

There are different versions of **idealism.** In more detailed studies, at more advanced levels, these different versions will each be important to understand. Here we will consider one of the oldest versions, that which is often associated with **Platonism** and **Neoplatonism,** but this will be a sketch, not a faithful rendition of any philosopher's theory.

As the name suggests, idealism is the view that the ultimate features and elements of reality are ideas in their most perfect rendition. These ideas could exist quite independently of the human mind, or, in some versions, they might be mental entities either in man's or in God's mind. The basic argument can be put as follows:

We seem to know a number of things quite well, despite many disagreements. Even when we are shaky in our knowledge of particular books, chairs, or governments, we seem to have a good grasp of what a book, a chair, or a government is. Particular things change too much to be known well; they escape clear understanding and we are therefore uncertain about them. But *what* a table is, is quite well known. The "what" is not this or that table, but tables in general: the *essence* of tables, the *nature* of tables, what features distinguish tables from all other things. (See chapter 3 for a discussion of definitions.)

We seem to know this whatness of things, and yet it is not a quality the sense organs can come into contact with. Our general idea or definition of a table is in fact quite different from this or that table we sit by or build in our basement. Moreover, is it not clear that we can state what the nature of a table is, at least when we spend some time investigating the issue (as maybe only furniture makers would), with greater precision than we can describe any given table? Even after we have described any given table, we will generally have omitted many of the things about it, such as its material, the composition of the wood out of which it is built, its dimensions, the chemical components of the varnish and paint, and so forth. In addition, some of the features of the table change very rapidly; for example, its color may change as we move away from the light, or the table may be taken apart and the pieces used to make a chair. So we are left with nothing stable and firm at all, nothing that we can know for sure. Apparently, the only items about which we can have certain knowledge are the *ideas* about tables—what tables are or must be, what their basic dimensions must be, what sort of things they must be made of, and so forth. These are all ideas of things and relationships, none of them particular things.

Furthermore, we seem to require some idea of what tables are—what something must be like, in general, to be a table—before we can suggest that this or that thing perceived around us is or is not a table. Unless we have some idea, or a framework that suggests some idea, we simply cannot identify what exists in the world. Even our education appears to require that we be told what things are before we can actually organize our experiences.

Idealism suggests that the basic stuff of reality consists of ideas—not physical or material or any other kind of object, relationship, or power. It is the ideas of everything—of objects, qualities, features, colors, materials, etc.—that we seem to know. Only ideas exist; the rest are passing images or incomplete versions of ideas. (This appears to have been the view of the great Greek philosopher Plato.)

Some idealists argue that the world of ideas is in fact a perfect or an ideal world. In that world everything we ordinarily find around us but cannot really know exists in perfect form. Many of us are familiar with this notion in connection with mathematics and geometry, where we learn that there are no perfect circles or triangles in the physical but only in the theoretical world. In this ideal world we would find perfect mathematical principles or ideas, such as the perfect circle (i.e., what the definition of circle *describes*). So it is with everything else that surrounds us. This or that chair is changing, imperfect, unstable. But in the world of ideas there exists an ideal chair, the essential chair, which is not capable of change or destruction because it has no physical, material elements; it does not exist in time and space, in the realm of changing things. And some of us come to know these ideal things, as we shall see in chapter 3.

Idealism as outlined above is often presented as Plato's view. Whether or not this is strictly accurate is not important here. But to appreciate idealism it may help to consider what is meant by the phrase *platonic love*. It is supposed to be a very pure, beautiful, perfect, intellectual relationship that has no physical features!

For idealists the world of ideas is the only real world. For some there is a realm or world of ideas, ideals, or perfect versions of all physical things, relationships, or powers, and this realm exists apart from the world that surrounds us. For other idealists this realm is either the individual mind of any person or the collective mind of humanity itself. Yet other idealists will hold that this world of reality is the mind of God. This last position was held by the philosopher Berkeley.

One last point must be mentioned about the idealist doctrine. Idealist philosophers generally advance theories in several branches of philosophy. It is evident from the foregoing discussion that a good deal of the idealist philosopher's case depends on his doctrine of human knowledge. Indeed, idealism has a theory of human knowledge that is closely linked to its metaphysical position. (See chapter 3 for a discussion of rationalism.) This holds true for virtually all philosophies, even for those that end by denying the possibility of metaphysics and even for those that go a bit further and deny the possibility of theories. What philosophers conclude is generally tied up with their conclusions elsewhere, even if they themselves have only accepted but have not worked out these conclusions in detail.

Materialism

Like idealism, **materialism** is a very old metaphysical doctrine, dating back in recorded thought to ancient Greece. Its central contention amounts to the view that everything which exists, has existed, will exist, and could exist must be or must consist of matter or physical stuff.*

Unlike idealism, this metaphysical doctrine would seem to appeal to common sense. Most of us would admit that material things—the typewriter on which I am typing, the paper that bears the printed word the reader is reading, the rings on our fingers, the door, the key, hamburger meat, and the millions of things we deal with day in and day out—are just the sort of things that we can confidently say exist in the world. While disputes may surround

---

* I have been using the idea "stuff" on and off without dealing with it in detail. It seems to me that most readers take this idea to mean anything that things can be composed of. At any rate, it is a loose idea that most of us use when we want to indicate that we are thinking of the composition of something, the filling that makes up what is or what exists. This meaning is apparent when we speak of the stuffing in the turkey or the stuff that lies around in the basement. For the present its vagueness will be useful.

the issue of the existence of such things as governments, laws, friendship, happiness, God, ideas, and many other items that are not obviously physical or material, the earlier list poses little or no difficulty to common sense.

The promise of having found something stable, firm, and clearly detectable does seem to lie with materialism. We often dismiss material things as perhaps less important than others. Yet, when it comes to having confidence in our beliefs about what does exist, the material things and features of the world enter as ready candidates. It is understandable, then, that materialism is one of the most prominent and widely argued and defended answers to the metaphysical question concerning the basic component of reality.

Mind and Materialism.   An area in which materialism is not quite readily admitted as a successful answer, or from which examples are offered to show that it does not really succeed in the final analysis, is human mental life. The point is offered in the following way: Surely if everything is composed of matter, then we could detect the existence of everything by way of the human senses. Sensory awareness is rendered possible because many things are material and the senses are able to perceive material features of things, such as the colors of objects produced by their inner composition, their shapes, the sounds they emit in motion or in collision with other things, and the tastes they give off by affecting our senses through their chemical composition. But there are some features or facts of existence that we learn of without the use of the senses. Thus our dreams are not heard or seen or tasted or felt, nor are our thoughts, images, memories, and the like. But if the organs that serve to detect material existence are not needed to learn of the existence of certain things, then there must be some things that are not material, namely, whatever makes up human mental life.

Yet many materialists will argue against this and similar challenges. They will point out that even in the admittedly material world we do not rely solely on sensory evidence to make sure that certain things exist. Although the air that takes up the distance between the chair and the table is seen or felt, the actual *distance* itself is not. The weight of some object may not itself be experienced by some sensory organ, but it may be identified by complex calculations. Indeed, color itself seems to be all too changeable to be considered the same kind of material stuff that the thing having the color appears to be.   Then, again, consider that without denying materialism we would be quite willing to accept that the walk we are taking in the afternoon exists, even if all we can see is the legs, one in one place at one time and in another the next, and the same with the other leg.   But still we would admit that the walk itself exists or existed.

Materialism can admit that not everything is solid material stuff alone.   But everything must be either such material stuff or the relationships and activities of such stuff.   Thus, thinking, dreaming, memory, and the like could be fitted into some materialist frameworks by adding that these are simply aspects of material things, in this case our bodies or brains.   A thought, then, would be one of the many complex kinds of activities that we find the brain of a person to be involved in, just as the walk mentioned above is one of the activities the legs can be involved in.   Memories, feelings, and similar mental activities would be dealt with in the same manner. The materialist would not have any difficulty accepting the existence of love, either, despite the fact that this issue has been raised frequently as an objection to materialism.   Love may not be simply chemical reactions between people, but it could be complex neurophysiological relationships and activities of two fully material things.

By the above line of approach, materialism could incorporate the existence of not only ideas but also values and complex institutions, such as honesty, law, government, marriage, and friendship. Human affairs such as learning, vacationing, international conflict, and trade could also be understood as the complex existence of material stuff and its manifold relationships and activities.

Not all materialists would allow their position to admit of so many different sorts of material existence.   This is especially true in view of the fact that many of them claim that only one set of scientific laws governs the existence of all things: the laws of physics. (Scientific laws are statements of the principles of the actions of various kinds of things in reality such as chemicals, germs, cells, and societies.   An example is the law of gravity.)

This narrow version of materialism would hold that once we admit the more complex kinds of things such as justice, love, friendship, and international goodwill as existing (or possibly existing) items in the universe, we are making a mistake.   We must confine ourselves to admitting the existence of only those items that are governed by the laws of physics. Justice and the like could exist only if they are made up of material things.

Materialism of the narrow variety just described is generally referred to as **reductionism.** This is because reductionists believe that complex items must be *reducible* to simple ones; complex laws—those in biology, psychology, economics, and sociology—must all be tested for their validity and meaningfulness by making sure that they are really no different from the laws of physics. Their view is that the proper way to understand existence is to realize that everything conforms to one set of physical laws; only if something that is said to exist can be explained by reference to these laws are we entitled to conclude that it does indeed exist.

But not all materialists are *reductive* materialists. Whereas reductive materialists would argue that items other than simple material bodies are only numerically complicated, that is, composed of many simpler material things, other materialists would contend that *qualitative* differences can exist among various material things. That is, the complex organization of simpler material items can make the composite product qualitatively different from its parts. This position would imply that not all the laws of science must be translatable into the laws of physics, for example.

The Marxist system of **dialectical materialism** allows for qualitative differences among material things. The Marxist doctrine holds that one major, universal law of reality—the principle of dialectical development—governs everything that exists throughout time. However, this law renders it possible that various material things be qualitatively different, depending on their stage of development in time. Dialectical materialism is the view that everything in reality undergoes a recurring, triadic (three-stage) process of change. The first phase produces its opposition (negation) and the conflict involved produces a totally new stage (or thing, as the case may be), which is not simply a combination of the two previous ones. (This three-stage development shows up in society in the process of revolutionary progress, as we will discuss in chapter 6, Political Philosophy.)

In the next chapter we will see that certain theories of knowledge accommodate the materialist metaphysical systems. For now, the crucial point is that materialism states that everything is physical matter, or physical matter and its relationship and powers, or even that the world is composed of tiny, indestructible stuff.

Process Metaphysics (Occasionalism)

The position we will outline now, **process metaphysics,** is not necessarily in conflict with either idealism or materialism, but it is a theory that is less well represented in some familiar systems of thought. Even idealism is expressed by nonphilosophers when they sometimes tell us that everything exists only in the mind. Christian Science is very close to the idealist position. Materialism is a belief held by many people, especially in their daily, routine endeavors. In contrast, the metaphysics of processes is not so familiar.

Although the philosopher Alfred North Whitehead advocated this position and gave it its name, many other philosophers have accepted and still accept the most important tenets of the theory. For the sake of convenience I will refer to the position as **occasionalism,** because it holds that the fundamental items of existence are occasions, events, or processes.*

Occasionalism, unlike materialism and idealism, denies that entities or objects, mental or material, can constitute reality. Instead, the basic stuff is composed of events—a flux or process. This appears to be a curious view, since people would expect that events, processes, or occasions must involve entities or things. For example, when we think of an event such as the collision of two cars, we generally assume that such an event can be analyzed into participant (individual) things, such as the two cars and their actions, or movement. But occasionalism rejects this idea. It holds the view that ultimately the stuff that composes a complex event such as a two-car collision must itself be events, although more minute ones, of course. A bit of reflection will indicate the attraction of this doctrine, despite its conflict with common sense.

Consider that reality or existence never stands still at any of its manifestations. Everywhere one wishes to point, the things that exist are in motion. We may find it useful to conceive of various items of existence as if they could stand still, outside of the everlasting chain of events or occasions. However, this is merely a view we have derived from our way of thinking and speaking of things. We speak of that table, this chair, that person, yesterday's meal,

---

* It should be mentioned that another, usually unrelated theory has also been called Occasionalism. This latter theory is associated with the great philosopher René Descartes.

tomorrow's football game, so they appear to be stable and unmoving, but that is because of our way of regarding them and our habit of fixing that which exists within our awareness. We must reason about things as if they stood still in time; thus, as the syllogisms in the chapter on logic will illustrate, we think of all human beings as animals and all animals as mortal, and we conclude from this that all human beings are mortal. Both in our minds and on paper before us it appears that we are dealing with fixed items. But in reality these items do not stand still; they move on without stopping while we think about them. Although it helps us to regard them as if they were fixed, out of the process of time, in fact, as they actually exist, all the items that we think about are in motion.

It would follow, so the occasionalists would hold, that entities, objects, things, or whatever else we might call the stuff of existence, are fictions only. In fact, all that exists are events, moving processes, or occasions.

If this line of argument does not suffice to show the plausibility of occasionalism, there is another we can outline. Consider that our awareness of the world by way of sensory perception gives us bits and pieces of sensations or sensory impressions recorded by the senses. Our minds may store these away and unite them with one another to construct ideas of things. Thus we believe that there really exists that thing or this one—the woman who is our mother, the house that is our home, or the countryside that is our land. But these, too, are constructed by us. The stuff out of which we build these fictions does not remain still at all. The sensory stuff itself always moves, passing into our field of awareness and out of it, without stopping to support the conclusion that reality is in fact composed of fixed, stable items.

Moreover, when we turn to some of the older sciences, we find them resting on laws of nature that seem to avoid dealing with entities or objects. Physics, for instance, used to assume the existence of objects, but even when this was done, the laws of physics concerned motion, not bodies as such. And most of us have heard of the law of universal causality, which is usually stated as the undeniable fact that every *event* has a cause which is itself an *event* that came before that which was caused. Not only in physics but also in the social sciences we find scientists producing laws about events. Behaviorism, the school of psychology that is accepted (in one or another of its versions) by many psychologists who consider themselves scientists, considers that the basic units of its realm of study are behaviors, that is, bits of events involving human beings. These units are processes, occasions, or episodes of human affairs. Economists, sociologists, political scientists, and other social scientists often exclude discussion of objects or things and focus exclusively on events.

Perhaps the reader will argue that this is just the problem with the social sciences—the individual person is ignored and only the events in the environment or the person's history, or in someone's biological makeup or brain, are given attention. Perhaps this is so. But we should consider that one of the most advanced fields of science, modern subatomic physics, rejects any consideration of entities or objects. In fact, a widely accepted theory of subatomic physics, quantum theory, rejects the assumption of classical physics that there are any particular entities or objects. In quantum physics the very idea of individual subatomic particles has no place. This follows, in part, from the theory of the famous physicist Werner Heisenberg, who taught that particles cannot be individually identified at all. We simply cannot, in fact or in principle, isolate particles so as to identify them as individual things. In quantum physics there can be no concern for the individual. Only probability statements about groups or aggregates can be produced from this most advanced field of science. Any concern about the position and velocity of some particle at any given moment—that is, what would be required to deal with individual particles—is impossible in terms of this physical theory.

True enough, physicists still argue about this issue, and Albert Einstein himself thought that this conclusion must be provisional, forced upon us by *our (technical) inability to record* what an individual subatomic particle consists of. Others, however, hold firm to the view that quite apart from our recording devices or methods, the nature of reality itself is such that no individual entities can be made sense of, however much we may insist that eventually this will be possible.

Interestingly enough, the idea that nature is composed of processes or events was already advanced by philosophers in ancient Greece. And the idea is even more potent today. Objects, things, and even people like you and me must, accordingly, be viewed as sometime convenient fictions, no more. Existence itself is composed of events. The debate goes on, of course, and the reader who is interested can pursue it to its more technical levels, as with any of the doctrines we are examining throughout this book. It will be clear from some of the later discussions that these somewhat remote topics have a direct bearing on what can be held to be right in terms of more immediate human concerns. Thus, such issues as freedom versus determinism, the existence of God, whether knowledge is possible, and even whether individualist or collectivist political positions are correct have much to do with which metaphysical theory is correct.

Dualism

In the earlier discussion of materialism and idealism I could have mentioned **dualism** as a sort of merging of these two metaphysical positions. Dualism holds that reality is composed of two separable parts: (1) the material and (2) the ideal (or mental or spiritual). Both idealism and materialism are *monistic* rather than *dualistic,* for they hold that reality is fundamentally made up of only one kind of thing, ideas (in idealism) or matter (in materialism).

For almost every dualist, the physical and the ideal, or mental, are related or connected in some way. There are dualists whose metaphysics encompasses all of reality, so that in any aspect or feature of reality we will find two radically different but connected modes or ways of existence. On the other hand, there are dualists with a narrower focus who argue for a dualism only with reference to human existence.

In both cases the dualist's main thesis is that there is a realm of being or existence that is material (or is uniquely dependent on material reality), and a realm that is mental or spiritual. The former is characterized by its capacity for study and understanding by the various sciences; in other words, material existence can be measured, experienced by way of the senses, controlled and thus subjected to experimental investigation, and usually put into the service of human needs. The latter, in the most clear-cut form of dualism, is just the opposite: it escapes scientific study and understanding, it has no measurable aspects, it cannot be controlled, and it is quite different from that which is related to our natural, biological existence. For example, the first realm includes planets, molecules, plants, animals, and the human body, whereas the latter is composed of our thoughts (or those of God's), our beliefs, the theories we construct, the intentions, wants, and purposes we have (or God has), and so forth.

In the more restricted type of dualism we find the well-known and widely accepted idea that human nature is composed of two radically different stuffs: the mental and the material, soul versus body, mind versus brain, spirit versus flesh, the rational versus the animal, etc. This restricted dualism is noticeable in many areas of study, especially in such fields as psychology. But in ordinary life, too, people often refer to the conflict between their reason (mental or spiritual being) and their passions (material being). In a somewhat more complicated way we find ourselves contrasting theory with practice, ideas with things, analytic sciences with experimental or empirical ones, theoretical entities with real or actual things, and so forth. However well or ill justified dualistic metaphysics turns out to be, even our commonsense consideration of reality indicates that something important is captured with this position. So it may turn out that even a metaphysical position that rejects dualism such as materialism will contain features that aim to do justice to what dualists are concerned with. For example, the position called **dual aspect theory of mind** attempts to deal with the dualist view in relation to the mind / brain issue. The idea is that although mental entities and processes are not the same as brain states, they are aspects or powers of brains. The **mind,** which is the concept we use for human conscious brain activities, is thus supposed to be a radically unique but still not a separate feature of the world.

Dualism has its impact upon the theory of knowledge, also. The problem of whether other people's *minds* can be known or known to exist when all we really perceive is people's behavior or bodily movements is prominent in philosophy. It was pointed out as a problem by one of the major dualists in the history of philosophy, René Descartes (1596–1650). It is still frequently discussed by philosophers.

ON THE PROBLEM OF THE EXISTENCE OF GOD

Theism is belief in the existence of God. **Atheism** rejects this claim as either false or unsupported. **Agnosticism** holds that the issue is fundamentally undecidable—we can never know whether or not God exists.

Here, again, it is important to note that hundreds of varieties of these three positions have been proposed within the literature of philosophy and theology. Still, the three positions are best characterized as above at our stage of investigation. It is appropriate to introduce the problem of God in the section on metaphysics because God's existence or nonexistence would, at least for most believers, have fundamental significance. Clearly, if God existed and were anything like what most believers think God to be, then the very character of reality, everything included, would be affected. That is, we would have to look at the world in a fundamentally different light as believers from the way we would look at it as nonbelievers.

Widely Known Ideas of God

Ordinarily, in most religions God is regarded as all-knowing, all-powerful, all-good, everlasting, etc. Omniscience, omnipotence, omnibenevolence, and similar characteristics are generally attributed to God.*

The problem of God enters the field of philosophy when it is contended that God's existence is provable or evident to any thoughtful and aware person by some means accessible to all of us. This way of treating the problem of God is philosophically relevant because we can submit claims about God's existence or nonexistence (or unknowability) to scrutiny without having to be in some special state such as being "graced," "faithful," etc. To refuse to consider the issue of God along philosophical lines is, in effect, to reject the importance of gaining a reasoned understanding of reality.

Preliminaries

We will look at some of the more well travelled arguments for God's existence, for the nonexistence (or lack of any proof) of God, and

---

* In this discussion I shall be capitalizing "God" so as to conform to tradition. Within the Christian and Jewish religious traditions "God" is taken to be both a name and a word. It is the name of an individual and a word that means a being of a certain kind, for instance, divine. To spell God with a capital "G" is somewhat of a bias against polytheism, the view that many gods exist. Most of us are best acquainted with **monotheism,** the doctrine that there is just one god, so the word is capitalized as a name would be.

for the impossibility of deciding the issue—for theism, atheism, and agnosticism. First, some general points will be cleared up, and then the arguments will be presented and commented upon. One reason for the somewhat detailed treatment of this topic is that many readers will probably consider it important and most philosophers have spent some time on it.

When the question of God's existence arises in most philosophical discussions, a certain general idea of what God would have to be is already spelled out. It is widely held that if there is a God, it would have certain fairly well described characteristics. A God without these would not appear to deserve the considerable attention people have given this issue. Clearly, most people will admit that if we are concerned with the existence of God, we are concerned with the existence of a unique, unfamiliar, perplexing entity. It is not that "the works of God" would be strange, but only that whatever God is would be something not usually encountered—something unlike trees, walks in the field, eggs, flowers, or fatherhood. Perhaps it would involve all these things, but this, too, would make it quite unusual to start with.

These points need to be made so that we do not misunderstand the issue involved. In trying to prove the existence of God, it is clearly not enough to prove the existence of Red China or my grandfather's grave. In short, we are trying to prove something quite extraordinary. Even when someone wishes to prove that "God is love," usually the idea is not that God is just the sort of love that we human beings experience for one another. If this were the case, we would have only exchanged one word for another. We would have advocated that "God" be substituted, at least now and then, for "love." But this would not have demonstrated the existence of God; it would only have shown the occasional usefulness of making the above word switch.

To put the matter somewhat differently, by trying to prove that God exists, some people are trying to prove that something very important and unique exists, something that is or has a more important being than anything else, an entity of great significance, power, etc. God is supposed to be even supernatural and transcendent (i.e., above and beyond the natural world and what exists in it).

Argument from "First Cause"

As the first argument for God's existence, let us consider a view that is very famous among those interested in this issue, not merely among specialists in philosophy and theology. The argument may be stated in its simplest form, even though far more complex versions of it have been produced throughout human history. Here is the argument:

> All that exists is caused by something other than itself, and
> the universe exists, so
> the universe is caused by something other than itself;
>
> whatever caused the universe is greater than the universe, and
> God is the only being greater than the universe, so
> God caused the universe.

The idea here is that God, being the kind of thing that we earlier noted he would have to be if he existed, is the only being with the power needed to cause the universe; therefore, if everything requires a cause, and since the universe is certainly something, only God could have caused the universe. This argument infers the existence of God, the kind of (supreme) being capable of the greatest of powers, from the fact that without reference to God the existence of the universe could not be explained. God is here identified as the creator of everything, the being or cause that ultimately explains everything.*

Objection. Criticism of this argument will begin by claiming it trades on a confusion. Once the confusion is removed, the argument will not be valid and the conclusion will have to be considered ill supported. (See chapter 4 for a discussion of validity and truth.) Accordingly, when the point is made that all that exists is caused by something other than itself, what is generally meant is some *specific* event, action, or thing such as the destruction of a building or the

---

* In more advanced discussions of this issue, technical terminology could turn out to be very important. This is crucial. (However, if the introduction of technical terminology is not justified, then the arguments presented by relying on it will suffer.) In any case, as we consider the original statement of the "first cause" argument for God's existence, no technical jargon will be introduced.

forming of a contract.   On the other hand, when we have occasion to talk or think about the universe, what we have in mind is not some specific event, action, or thing but the *collection and structure* of all things that exist—everything, reality itself, existence as such. The universe, when so understood, is not one of the things that may be ranked alongside the rest of the events, actions, or things we know and mean by *all* the things that exist.

With this distinction, the argument is not valid.   The claim that the universe exists is already assumed in the claim that all the things that exist have causes.   The appropriate meaning of the second statement in the argument would be that things exist or that existence exists.   "The universe exists" means only that there are things, that there exists something, whatever it is.   "The universe" is precisely all that exists, not something that is *part of* what exists.

Reply.   Here we encounter one objection to the first cause argument. Those who advance the first cause argument might reply that the criticism makes an arbitrary distinction.   That is, they would maintain that there are *no good reasons* for making the critic's distinction between the various individual elements of existence and existence itself.   Existence itself could be a thing that exists, but in this case the thing would be the totality of all that exists.

Counterobjection.   In answer to this reply the critic would repeat his point that the argument rests on a confusion, since there is very good reason indeed to distinguish between the totality of what exists and the elements of that totality.   Unless we admit this distinction, the first premise of the argument would already state what the conclusion does and therefore prejudge the entire issue.   By saying that all that exists has a cause, we would already be stating, by use of a different *word,* that the universe has a cause.   Yet the second premise requires the distinction between elements or things in the universe and the universe itself.   So the critic would reiterate that a confusion exists and the distinction is not arbitrary.

Additional Discussion.   Assuming that the critic's point has merit, could it not be held that just as individual elements or items in the universe have causes, so the totality of all of these requires a cause? One problem with this suggestion is that the first premise asserts only that the individual items in the universe require a cause for their existence.   It says nothing about whether the totality of all things itself requires a cause.   We would need another premise in the argument.   While it seems quite true that all individual items in the universe require a cause for their existence, it is not so obviously true that the collection itself requires a cause.   Perhaps the universe itself, in some form or another, existed always and did not require some cause to be brought into existence.

Now the argument could be revised again, and it turns out that many who have proposed this argument did revise it to meet these and similar objections.   Sometimes, for example, it is assumed that "cause" must mean something like a previous fact or event that can be used to *explain* the fact or event in question.   So the first premise is then taken to mean simply that all facts require and indeed can be given an explanation.   And if this is accepted, we can then ask whether the process of explanation could go on forever.   Surely if it could go on forever, nothing ever would be explained sufficiently.   There would be no final or complete explanation of anything.   But perhaps this is unacceptable.   To bring the matter to a halt, therefore, we must invoke the final explanatory fact, namely, God's existence—something that needs no explanation.

Again we can put forward an objection.   When we consider the idea *cause,* we find that it is developed in the context of a study of this world, the framework of the many things and events that exist around us.   Thus, when we consider that something might have caused something else, we find that the kind of cause we are referring to is intimately tied to what occurs around us.   In short, we generally deal with causes *as they occur in the universe.*

In the above considerations of the first cause proof of God's existence, the idea *cause* is suddenly applied in a manner that is very different from the usual, familiar way.   That alone does not prove that other causes could not exist.   But to claim that, from the fact that there are causal connections *among* things *in* the universe, we may suppose a casual connection between the universe and something very different from the universe—this claim faces problems.   What are we to understand by this assumed causal connection?   The sort of causal relationships that obtain inside the universe, so to speak, are assumed to obtain between the universe and something outside or apart from it.   To accept this possibility we would first have to accept some new view of what causes could be.   But there is no reason offered to support this new type of cause.   So the argument fails on account of equivocating between two radically different meanings of the term *cause* used in it.   Equivocation occurs when two ideas that are quite different from each other are made to appear the same by simply calling them by the same term.   A simple case is reasoning that since all rats are ugly, and my brother is a rat, my brother is ugly.   But obviously here "rat" is used as if the ideas meant by the terms in the two premises meant the same thing.   Of course, they mean very different things, despite the use of the same term.

Ontological Argument

Let me now turn to a very different argument for God's existence. The **ontological argument** is called that because it considers the *type of being* God presumably is as central to the proof of his existence, and *ontology* is the *study of types of being*.   To see how the ontological argument goes, let us look at a rather simple statement of it.

First, we should recall the point made earlier about the most prominent idea of God that people have entertained, namely, that God is all-knowing, all-powerful, and all-good.   This idea has also been expressed by saying that God is a perfect being.   The ontological argument begins by noting that only the confused or ignorant would deny that God is the most perfect being there could be.   In other words, everyone but the fool would accept that God, if he exists, must be the greatest, most perfect being possible.   This amounts to the belief that God is, by definition, the greatest or most perfect being.   With this in mind we can now sketch the ontological argument:

> God is the greatest or most perfect being conceivable, and anything that is the greatest or most perfect being is something that exists (otherwise it would lack something and fail to be the greatest or most perfect thing conceivable), so God exists.

The position of the theist starts with the observation that all sensible people can conceive of God and that their idea is that God is the most perfect being possible, one that surpasses in greatness anything else.   But once this is noted, we are told that part of the idea of such a being is that it exists, for if this were not so, it would be possible to conceive of something more perfect and great—namely, something that does not lack existence and is in all other respects the most perfect and greatest possible being. As such, it is clear that God, who is this most perfect and greatest being possible, must exist. It would be contrary to the idea of God that it should not exist, and since that idea is meaningful, the idea that is part of it, namely, that it exists, must also be realized when we conceive of it. God would not be what we all conceive him to be if he did not exist.

Objection. To this argument I will raise only one objection and then point to what may be wrong with that objection. It is objected that by this argument we can prove the existence of the greatest and most perfect version of anything whatever, including the greatest and most perfect table, government, or painter. Does this not indicate that the ontological argument permits that we simply establish the existence of various things by first forming an idea of them? And clearly this would be quite impossible to do. Why allow it then for the attempt to establish the existence of God?

Rebuttal. But those who defend the ontological argument have a point when they remind us that the idea of God is not an idea of some ordinary thing, but of a great and most perfect entity of some kind. The idea of God is an idea of a unique type of being, namely, the greatest or most perfect being possible. This is just why the argument is called the ontological proof—to point up that no ordinary being is meant by the idea "God." So the objection may not hold after all.

Of course, the argument continues beyond this point. Some of the most sophisticated modern logical approaches have been utilized by philosophers and theologians both in support of and in opposition to the claim that the ontological proof is sound. For present purposes the discussion of this famous attempt to establish the existence of God has come to an end.

Atheism

There are basically two approaches that atheists have taken. First they have argued that God *could not* exist. This is the constructive or positive case for atheism since it attempts to prove the impossibility of God's existence, not simply to show the inadequacies of alleged proofs of God's existence.

The idea is that what God is supposed to be could not exist, somewhat as a square-circle could not exist. To prove this position the atheist examines the various definitions of the concept *God* and attempts to show that the characteristics identified as necessary for such a being could not coexist.

As an example one might want to argue that it is impossible for something to be all-good and all-powerful at once, as God is supposed to be. It seems quite clear that anything that is both all-good and all-powerful would employ this power and goodness. When we consider what goodness involves, just on a commonsense level, we must note that it conflicts with the existence of evil, injustice, cruelty, malice, and the like. So when we imagine that someone might be all-powerful and all-good, we immediately suppose that one clear result of this would be the elimination of evil from the world. In short, an all-powerful and all-good or benevolent God would not permit the presence of evil in the world. Even assuming that it would be good for those who are evil to suffer evil, it clearly is not good for those who are innocent to suffer evil. It is evident, though, that many innocent individuals are suffering at the hands of evil people or are experiencing pain and misery that anyone capable of eliminating without doing greater harm should eliminate. A God that exists and has both perfect goodness and absolute power as characteristics simply would not allow such injustice and misery. There simply could be no being such as God is supposed to be, for the evidence speaks against it throughout human history.

In this way the first atheist approach tries to find contradictory features in the idea of God and, having found some, concludes that, since contradictions cannot exist in reality, God does not exist. Accordingly, the line of approach taken by the atheist who argues that God cannot exist would challenge the ontological argument. Contrary to what proponents of that argument claim, not only the fool but also any rational person would reject the meaningfulness of the idea of a greatest or most perfect being.

The atheist would also argue that perfection is something we apply to things that could be less than perfect. For example, knives, marriages, tennis serves, circles, summers, and the like are perfect or not so perfect. So the idea of a great or perfect something is meaningful only on a continuum. These ideas, when applied to things that could not possibly be less than great or perfect, are meaningless. It would be like talking about the middle of a spherical surface or the end of time. "Middle" makes no sense unless there is a beginning and an end. The end of time makes no sense because time itself measures the duration of something that exists; it cannot itself be something that exists in time, since it would have an end. Whatever is perfect could only be something that could be less than perfect, and so with greatness. Therefore, the fool is right to reject that idea of God as the kind or type of thing that he is supposed to be in terms of the ontological argument.

The second type of atheism does not have a positive case against God's existence. This form of atheism amounts to holding that the ideas of God usually advanced are either self-contradictory (or are simple equivocations) or lack sound arguments in their support. But this atheist would hold that someone could perhaps invent a new use for the idea *God* in the future, a use that might even be fruitful. However, the burden of proving that this term is meaningful and that something called *God* should be so called and does exist lies with the future proponent of this novel form of theism. This atheist holds that the existence of the God that people now discuss and believe in has never been proved, so there is no reason to believe in God. But this second type of atheist is a bit more cautious than the first and does not wish to assert that no legitimate use for the word *God* could be found in the future.

Many atheists and agnostics have theories about what people could be driving at when they seek to show that God exists. Not all of them view the "search for God" as entirely pointless or foolish. Some believe this search expresses an insight that must be clarified and should be purified of its theistic overtones. Thus, some atheists would suggest that a possible meaning of the often confusing idea of God is that something firm and unchanging exists, namely, reality itself as identified within a certain metaphysical framework. The idea of God is here viewed as a prephilosophical, undeveloped, and personalized reference to the totality of existence, with all of its complexities, including human life and thought.

Alternatively, some atheists have argued that the idea of God represents our own idealization of ourselves. After all, God is conceived as all-knowing (something that is an extension of a human capacity), all-powerful (ditto), and all-good (once again something partly manifest among us). So, by seeking for God and affirming his existence, people have in fact been showing their reverence for and their hope of the realization of human ideals.

What is noteworthy in all this is that atheism is often combined with an attempt to provide an explanation for the importance of theism in human life.

Agnosticism

Agnosticism is in one respect radically different from atheism. The agnostic does not deny that God exists, but he refuses to take a position on God's existence. His view is often related to the more general position of skepticism about human knowledge because he holds that it is impossible to ever know either that God exists or that God does not exist. The case for agnosticism consists of a demonstration of the success of both proofs for and proofs against the existence of God. By this the agnostic wants to prove that human reason is unequal to the task of settling the issue of God's existence.

DETERMINISM AND HUMAN FREEDOM OF CHOICE

The problem of God has been discussed as one of the more specific issues usually considered within metaphysics. Other issues have received detailed treatment in this field as well, and among them we find one of philosophy's most important problems, the conflict between determinism and human freedom of choice.

Here we will outline some of the main arguments on the various sides of this issue, for indeed there are not just two of them.

Very broadly put, the doctrine of **determinism** asserts the view that whatever occurs in nature must have a cause; that is, everything must be *determined* by something. Determinism is thus also called the principle of universal causality. Let us see where this issue fits within familiar human concerns.

Hardly anyone could have failed to come upon the topic of human freedom of choice, often expressed as the problem of free will. Are people responsible for any of their actions? Can people help what happens to them? Are criminals not simply determined to commit crimes? Are not the factors in our past, our biochemical and environmental conditions, what cause us to act as we do?

In ethics and in law these are extremely important questions. In our private lives we may treat people according to the answers we have accepted and given to them, and our institutions reflect how those involved in forging them have answered the same questions. Current policies, debates, and even a great deal of the political ferment surrounding us concern the dispute between those giving conflicting answers to questions about determinism.

Freedom and Reality

The question of human freedom of choice belongs, first of all, to metaphysics. Whether or not people can initiate what they do is discussed in this area of philosophy because it is a question of what kind of things human beings are, and whether or not it is meaningful to conceive of human beings as having freedom of choice. The issue here is not whether some particular person is free, or even whether people are free, but whether anything free could even exist. First, we need to see whether the kind of thing that might exercise choice is even a possibility in nature; then we can consider whether we are or are not that kind of thing.

In ordinary life we do accept now and then that people could not help what they did. In criminal trials, defendants often claim that they could not help themselves. The "insanity plea" refers to this kind of defense. Elsewhere, we question whether success was achieved by someone or whether it resulted from factors beyond the individual's control. So, in ordinary life we accept that some of us sometimes cannot control our own actions. But this does not exclude the possibility of our making genuine choices. In fact, by picking out people who cannot help themselves, we make it clear that they are unusual, that ordinarily we expect that people can govern their own conduct, make genuine choices, and take the responsibility for what they have chosen.

Sometimes, however, we hear it argued that none of us can ever help what we are doing, that other people or events in our past, or some other facts, are fully responsible for what happens to us.

This kind of thinking is usually identified as the determinist position. We will briefly consider several variants of determinism. The first may be the most familiar to those outside of philosophy because it is based on what science is supposed to have discovered about human nature. Often the idea that the principle of universal causality excludes the possibility of human freedom of choice is associated with science.

Freedom and Science

As a starting point for the view of scientific determinism, let us consider that most, if not everything, that exists may be studied by the methods of science. The scientific view proposes to show that the subject matter of its varied branches can all be treated systematically. That is, the various sciences have identified laws or principles of behavior. These govern the actions of whatever is being investigated within the science in question. However incomplete some sciences may be now, we appear to have every reason to believe that eventually all of nature will become susceptible to scientific treatment. This includes human affairs.

From this it would be most reasonable to anticipate that the sciences of human affairs will discover the laws that govern human behavior. These laws, and those we have already identified in the various other sciences, can be expected to govern all of human existence—personal, economic, social, political, artistic, religious, etc. While we may not have the details down, any other supposition would be unreasonable.

In line with the above reasoning, there is no justification for assuming that human beings could escape the conditions that prevail in the rest of nature. Thus, no matter how certain we are of our control over our own lives, the contrary is the most sensible assessment of the situation. Human freedom of choice is not real. It might be a convenient, pleasant, or even necessary illusion. Perhaps, as with many other ideas developed by people throughout history (e.g., belief in the existence of devils, voodoo, and witchcraft), the idea of free will served as an explanation only so long as we were basically ignorant of what actually affects or produces our behavior. But since the idea of freedom contradicts science, the only rational conclusion is that human beings are governed by incontrovertible principles that will eventually be fully identified.

Objecting to Antifreedom "Science"

Whatever one may think of the line of argument sketched above, clearly many people accept it fully, especially in the social sciences. To understand the prospects of these sciences, and to assess their contribution to an understanding of human life, one must come to terms with some of the issues just raised.

The first point to be noted about the position is that it is not the product of science itself. Social scientists, for example, do not *discover* that human beings are not free. It is generally their idea of what being a scientist requires, what they should *assume,* that leads to their denial of human freedom. The underlying argument is not scientific but metaphysical, a widely accepted position about the nature of existence accepted as needed in order to carry out scientific studies of human affairs.

The metaphysical position that is usually presented to support this line of argument is reductive materialism, and its success will have a bearing on the soundness of the determinist position just outlined. Occasionalism, too, is a standard position given in support of the view that human freedom is impossible. If the basic stuff of reality is events, and if every event that occurs in nature must be preceded by a previous event, *ad infinitum,* then no individual *thing* such as a person could cause anything to happen. At any rate, a good deal of what is argued on grounds of what science requires has very little to do with scientific discoveries and a lot to do with the philosophical framework that is held to be required for science.

There are problems with the argument, and we will now examine those objections that are unrelated to its metaphysical underpinnings.

Freedom and Social Science

The social sciences, which have for the most part accepted the view that human affairs are governed by laws that govern the physical world (the view called reductive materialism), have not really fared very well in providing some intellectual order concerning human affairs. In these fields the goal has been to understand and often to control human affairs, and seventeenth-century social scientists promised almost fantastic results with the reductivist approach. But this approach was not scientific at all. It consisted of borrowing methods from other sciences (mostly physics) without proving that these methods fitted the study of human affairs. For example, social scientists saw that the ideas of good and evil had no role in the hard sciences. Therefore, many inferred—or jumped to the conclusion—that these ideas *could* have no role in the sciences dealing with human affairs. But what if, as it seems, human affairs are different and these ideas do have a serious place in dealing with them? It is not scientific to assume otherwise without proof. After all, there is ample evidence to suggest a substantial difference between human affairs and the behavior of the planets, for example. Why assume the identical method for studying these admittedly natural things?

As with the issue of values, the presumption about free choice might also be a questionable one. Granted that rocks and molecules do not exercise choice, so the sciences dealing with such entities need not take account of freedom. In human affairs, however, it seems we have evidence of freedom; at this moment every person who considers the issue would think that the next moment's affairs related to him are in his control, at least to some significant extent. The writer could stop writing and the reader could stop reading, both *of their own free will*. Should not science then consider this, and not reject the idea simply because it has no role in chemistry, anatomy, or geology?

Considering the relative confusion in those social sciences that have aimed at copying the hard sciences, as well as the apparently dogmatic adoption of the methods of hard sciences by social sciences, the case for determinism based on the requirements of "science" would appear weak. If we add to this the arguments against reductive materialism, we see that perhaps this is not a very compelling thesis. All in all, any determinist position relies on numerous other positions developed within various branches in philosophy, just as this is the case with the position that rejects determinism or considers it compatible with human freedom of choice. Thus, philosophical ideas about causality, nature, mind, and God will usually have a bearing on the problem of determinism versus free will.

Soft Determinism

Outside of this rather straightforward deterministic position, in terms of which no free will could exist and thus people could not choose what they will do in any important sense, there are some less harsh deterministic views. Thus, a position sometimes referred to as "soft determinism" has been advanced as well. This is the view that although human beings do possess a will, a faculty used to make decisions, choices, and the like, this faculty is under severe influence from outside factors such as one's background and environment. This position is still deterministic. However, the process by which actions are determined is thought to be more complicated than in what is called "hard determinism," the position which was outlined before.

In hard determinism all events are fixed by the natural laws that have always governed reality. In soft determinism these events are less strictly governed by such laws. A good deal of laxity is accepted within this view, so that while free will is impossible, the choices and decisions people make are not fixed from the outset. They are developed gradually, under the influence and control of complicated psychological, economic, social, and other laws, some of which are statistical, probabilistic, and imprecise.

The soft deterministic position is equally embedded in complex philosophical ideas. Here nature is viewed as a less firm, more flexible system of events and entities, and its laws are viewed not as precise, unalterable governing principles but as more or less regular occurrences from which we can formulate probable generalizations. While prediction and control from knowledge and technological skill would be possible within this view of nature, too much uncertainty and flexibility is considered present in nature itself to offer us the kind of hard determinism advanced in the earlier position.

In the end, however, the soft deterministic position would collapse into the "hard" version discussed above. This is because soft determinism seems to emphasize a lack of fully reliable knowledge. Although we cannot learn the laws of nature as precisely as hard determinism seems to require, it is still fair to assume that in the world as it is (not as we inadequately know it) hard determinism would hold completely. So, too, the objections advanced against hard determinism would be applicable to soft determinism.

As we go on to consider the several positions advanced in support of free will, it will be possible to make an initial appraisal of the strengths and weaknesses of these views, all of which have a direct bearing on how we think or should think of ourselves and the world in which we live.

Dualistic Freedom of Choice

The first position in support of human freedom flatly admits that the rest of nature is fully determined to proceed as it does, but it exempts human beings from this deterministic process. This view holds that we have ample evidence for both—that everything in nature aside from people (and perhaps a few groups of more intelligent animals) is governed by unalterable laws, and that human beings are fundamentally distinct from the rest of reality precisely in their capacity for choice. It appears fairly obvious that trees, rock formations, the growth of a calf, and so forth are all subject to principles or laws of existence and change. Therefore, learning about them renders it possible for us to make good predictions about the future of each. Clearly, pebbles do not choose, nor do flowers or ants. With more complex entities such as cats and bears the laws become more intricate, but by now scientists have shown that these too behave in accordance with laws that involve precise (enough) causal links. Predictions can be made, and control over development can be exercised by those knowledgeable and willing to do so.

Yet it is also clear enough that people—you and I and the rest of humanity—have some area of freedom that cannot be denied. Even under the most severe restrictions, the most drastic bondage, human beings can engage in creative, original activity. People can develop themselves. They produce yet-unheard-of events and things. Even their languages can be used by them to do what is entirely novel. Art, science, education, politics, law, and the rest of the well-known human institutions and endeavors have not ceased to develop from the many original, creative contributions added to them by generations of new human beings. This unique aspect of human life could not be accounted for without the fact of free will— the capacity of individuals to choose, to step out of some regular process and forge a new one.

By this view human beings are not simply unique in comparison to animals, as animals might be in comparison to plants, and plants to rocks. Human beings are entirely different from all these things. They, unlike the rest of nature, can make themselves what they will be; they can create their own nature! In short, other things have a nature and are determined to be what they are, whereas human beings determine themselves to be what they are (or what they fail to be, in cases of neglect or severe restrictions on their freedom).

Evidently we have here another complicated outlook on human life, one that rests on numerous philosophical ideas. Earlier we discussed dualism. Here we see a position on the issue of determinism versus free will that draws considerable intellectual ammunition from the dualistic metaphysical viewpoint, for it holds that there are two fundamentally different elements in reality. The case for this view must therefore meet the objections dualism has to face. But a few questions can be raised even without going to the foundations of this defense of human freedom of choice.

Objections. Without denying a great deal of difference between people and other things in nature, does this position not overstate the issue somewhat? Are plants not really quite different from rocks, so that plant life in nature may qualify for the unique position claimed for human life, were human life not present to push it into a less distinguished place? Consider animal life, even the life of a mosquito. Surely it is so different from the existence of a pebble that without human life it could claim total uniqueness. Clearly, human life has much in common with the existence or life of other kinds of things. People can tumble down hills just like rocks. People can break a leg just as horses can. Their skin can be burned, just as the leaves of trees can be. So what ground is there for the drastic dualism advanced above? It is not that we need to deny a great deal of difference, but to argue for a virtual separateness seems unwarranted.

If the case for human freedom of choice depended on this position, it would not appear to be very strong.

Chance and Freedom

We can now look at yet another way of handling the free will viewpoint in a favorable light. Perhaps free will consists in the fact that some events in nature are completely *random*. It is not that we are *unable* to discover the causes of such events or to make predictions involving them, but that these events are by their very nature unpredictable, or random. They occur by pure chance.

Exactly what these indeterminate things are is not agreed upon. Some philosophers argue that certain tiny atoms or other particles in nature act randomly, so that it is impossible to determine what they will do next, no matter how much information we obtain about them (their past, environment, etc.). Others maintain that it is only human action that is random. In the case of human life there could exist a great deal of chance; it often seems that the bulk of what we do is unexplainable. The failure of the sciences to develop adequate accounts of human affairs, and their inability to predict the future—this and the rest of what we refer to within the domain of free choice—is due to the *inherent* unpredictability and indeterminacy of certain aspects of reality. Some philosophers think such indeterminacy characterizes all of nature, but those who argue for the existence of free will usually restrict it to the realm of human action. The essence of the doctrine here is that freedom is a manifestation of nature's inherent randomness.

Objections. This position flatly denies universal causality, sometimes not just in human affairs but as a general condition of reality. Thus, it faces problems on account of that denial alone. Moreover, it is doubtful that it provides for one of the essential elements of the free will position, namely, that human beings can control their own affairs. If some things happen randomly, and among these is human behavior (at least now and then), then surely people have no more control over their lives than if what they did were controlled by forces outside them. Random is random—out of control, haphazard, full of chance. This position seems to advance not free will but universal chaos.

Self-determined Choices

Among those who think that human freedom could exist we find metaphysicians who hold that reality consists of entities of various kinds, some of which participate in one sort of action, others in different sorts, and so on. Thus certain kinds of things could only participate in a series of mechanical interactions, for example, as the movement of a switch causes a current to flow through a wire, which causes the illumination of a lightbulb, and so forth. The lightbulb is not the sort of thing that can turn itself on. On the other hand, according to this metaphysical position other sorts of things could exhibit the capacity to participate in self-generated but relatively simple activities, such as animals finding food or watching out for predators. Yet other things could not only engage in self-generated activities but also be able to direct such activities toward far-off goals or purposes.

This metaphysical viewpoint would link the principle of causality to the more basic principle of identity. Then the kind of causal interactions and actions that something can be involved in would depend upon the sort of thing something is. This position would not assume that there can be only events or entities or processes or ideas in nature. Many varieties of things could exist, from subatomic particles to international treaties. Some of these would exhibit certain causal principles, others different sorts, with each to be discovered by the field of inquiry focused on that realm of existence. The law of universal causality would hold, but it would be exemplified by several kinds of causality instead of only one. In fact, an infinite variety might be possible, given the infinite possibilities as the universe evolves.

Within the framework of such a metaphysics, human freedom is at least possible. Such freedom would not contradict the fact of universal causality because free action would be an instance of causality, for example, a human being causing—creating—a musical composition.

In terms of this view, human freedom of choice would be possible. But whether such free will actually exists would have to be argued in addition to the argument for its possibility. That is, given that different kinds of things can participate in different kinds of causal relationships, it would still have to be shown that human beings are the kind of things that can initiate activity and not simply be moved by other forces. Criticism of the idea of free will is often based on the very impossibility of freedom, not just on its alleged absence. So this position would open up the prospect of proving the existence of freedom, even if the position does not prove the existence of freedom.

Objection. In objection to this view, one can turn first to the arguments for determinism and other metaphysical theories which deny that anything in existence could be free. Thus, if occasionalism is right, and there could only exist events or processes in nature, then the idea that some particular *entity* could be a cause of something would have to be abandoned. When ultimately everything is a process, then only processes could be causes in the final analysis. That would imply that apparently causally efficatious human acts really must be analyzed into the composite processes. When someone is said to have caused something, the correct rendition would be that not the person but some event in which he is involved must be the real cause. Not Mozart but, for example, the event of Mozart's having been brought up in a certain way must have produced the compositions Mozart is usually given credit for.

Another objection to this metaphysical possibility of human freedom comes from the view of science held by many people, including philosophers. This is that science presupposes that whatever is a part of nature can be subject to physical (or material) explanation and therefore to control or manipulation. Since, by the doctrine discussed above, it could be possible that some human activities (e.g., creativity, thought) are not open to outside control, the doctrine would have to be considered incompatible with a sound understanding of the nature of science. Furthermore, any basic conflict between a sound view of science—including what it presupposes about nature—and another viewpoint would have to be resolved in favor of science. This would preserve the basic idea that nothing in nature can be in basic conflict with anything else in nature—that nature is a coherent system, not one filled with internal contradictions and conflicts. So, if the view of science that prohibits freedom is right, then the metaphysical view that permits freedom cannot be right.

Final Note

We can now leave the issue of freedom versus determinism.   The several solutions of this problem we have examined have appeared in the philosophical literature in modified form over and over again. Clearly, this problem, which is treated mostly within philosophy, has a direct bearing on the way we can and should act concerning ourselves and others.   Some theories associated with this issue would require that we assign to people no responsibility for their actions. Some hold that it is possible to view people as active agents, responsible for what they do.   Yet others hold that human action could be free, but only in the sense that it is random and cannot be accounted for by any means.

MYSTICISM

Mysticism pertains to metaphysics since it bears on the nature of reality, as does the possibility of freedom.   This position proclaims that although an ultimate, fundamental reality exists beyond what we experience in daily life, it is rationally incomprehensible, incapable of being understood.   Reality, according to mysticism, is a basic, fundamental mystery, not just a mystery for the time being. It denies that a systematic study of ultimate reality is possible.   All we can realize is that nature is at heart mysterious.

Words and Experiences

Some people think that mysticism is the doctrine that we cannot state our experiences of reality in words.   People will often say that they have had experiences that they could not put into words, feelings they cannot express by language, and so forth.   This is often taken to mean that human knowledge and language suffer a shortcoming.   Yet, what this amounts to is only that the feeling itself, for instance, one's joy or sorrow, is not the same thing as the ideas or words by which we talk of it.   "Joy" is an idea (and a word when written or spoken), whereas experiencing joy is not.   One is wrong to ask of words to contain and impart the experience they are used to think or talk about. To complain that they cannot do this is not to complain about words but about those who, when they are told of one's joy, respond with little effort to imagine, empathize with, or *feel through* the experiences and feelings that the speaker communicates.

Mysticism does not argue that, for example, words are not feelings; anyone can figure that out, even if sometimes we forget it. Mysticism states that our experience of ultimate reality cannot be described, that there are no ways to form ideas and words that mean or refer to those experiences. This is because ultimate reality, though it does exist, is beyond human reason. It cannot be characterized or explained, and trying will only lead us astray!

The only means of learning about ultimate reality—although not learning but a kind of encountering is really what is at issue— would be by some drastic experience, some state of consciousness that is superrational, or *mystical*. Such an experience is so overwhelming and unique that only having it can bring one to acknowledge its existence. The mystical experience is unclassifiable and ineffable (not capable of being expressed in language). And the reality with which such an experience brings one into contact is itself a total mystery except to someone having the experience. Unfortunately, that individual could never explain it for some other person's benefit, regardless of his desire to do so.

It really does not help to try to say very much about mysticism, although surprisingly many mystics—those claiming to have had mystical experiences and, thereby, contact with ultimate reality— write volumes about it. Whether or not extraordinary experiences exist need not be doubted, although just what these are and whether they might be explained by way of psychology, chemistry, or the like is a different issue. As to the claim that there exists a reality that is fundamentally, unalterably mysterious, that proposition is difficult to handle. It seems that mystics, by their own announcements, have eliminated any chance for a rational consideration of their claim. It is by definition impossible to investigate the meaning of that claim, since its meaning, if it means anything at all, is totally beyond human (rational) understanding. What understanding is available here? Mystical understanding. But this is itself beyond rational understanding. Yet that is just the point of mysticism, so it is useless to press the issue further.

Philosophical Mysticism

One point to be raised about mysticism is that many metaphysical doctrines that begin with a concerted effort to explain the nature or basic character of reality have ended in a variety of mysticism. Many Western philosophers have concluded that underlying the world we can study and experience there is (or, for some, may be) a we-know-not-what substratum. Those who have arrived at these conclusions have, in their own way, contributed to the case of the mystical metaphysician. It would not be unfair to say that many contemporary thinkers even equate mysticism and metaphysics. (Some occult bookstores call various expository works displayed on their shelves metaphysical works.) The philosophers of the early twentieth century who wanted to provide philosophy with a scientific basis pushed all metaphysical questions and suggestions into the realm of the mystical. Since these questions and statements could not be given a meaning that could be checked out by sensory observation, scientifically minded philosophers consigned them to the domain of the mysterious.

Life and Mysticism

There is a common question that mystics are asked and it will be useful to consider it. Mystics are often asked how human life could exist if mysticism were really taken seriously and people abandoned respect for reason, science, objectivity, and so forth, only to turn to intuition, meditation, and other types of subjective experience. After all, technology (including transportation, medicine, etc.) makes sense within the philosophy that considers reality capable of being understood by human beings. Would we not need to dispense with such valued things if we construed ultimate reality, the truly important aspect of things, incomprehensible?

There are many answers given in response to this line of questioning. One should realize that mystics do not all agree on just what mysticism implies about human life. Some will say that within their mystical doctrine plenty of room is left for a modern, technologically progressive life. They believe in a hierarchy of values, and they counsel only that when we aspire to reach goals, we should put things into the proper perspective and pursue spiritual, mystical experiences, not material well-being exclusively. This answer is not really so different from the idea of some Western thinkers that the intellectual, emotional, and biological life of a person must be well integrated.

On the other hand, there are some mystics who advocate that life must be given up to the full pursuit of mystical experience. These mystics renounce worldly goods, enjoyment, and pleasure and hold them in contempt. Only the spiritual life is important, however impossible this is to understand. When asked to explain themselves, these mystics will often become impatient and show that we simply do not want to believe. They contend that those who refuse to follow the mystical paths are not ignorant but abusive toward an idea they do not appreciate.

Such thinkers will admit that the isolated life of a mystic, as with the Western monk or nun, is in one sense empty. The pleasures and joys of earthly existence are missing. But they quickly add that this loss is insignificant. When it is compared with the incredible, indescribable, overwhelming experience of the mystic, even if that experience is only occasional, the mystical experience overshadows earthly concerns; anyone who turned to the mystical life simply would not think of giving it up for earthly enjoyment.

Some of this is intriguing, of course, especially when one notices that many mystics live in "Oriental" luxury, enjoying greater wealth than most American millionaires. But the fact that some people use the words of mysticism to deceive others and themselves about what worth their lives have is not important. There are mystics who are indeed poor but totally devoted. And their approach to life is one of the many alternative philosophies and metaphysics that we find wherever human beings are trying to cope with existence. Some of the followers of Eastern thought have brought this serious mysticism onto the Western cultural scene. (I do not have in mind the transcendental meditation movement, although traces of the most sincere and involved version of mysticism may be found in many such movements.) Neither is it quite sound to hold to some radical difference between the way of life of Orientals and those within the Western philosophical and religious traditions, even if as approximations to the truth it does make sense to speak of two significantly different cultural climates.

The last point to be made here about mysticism is that in a certain respect such an approach to human life is antiphilosophical.

Philosophy as a branch of knowledge—even one that consists in seeking to obtain ultimate knowledge of some matters—presupposes considerable confidence in the capacity of the human mind to know reality, however difficult it may be to achieve that goal. Mysticism rejects from the outset the possibility of the kind of knowledge that we usually need and seek. The only kind of "knowledge" it professes is incommunicable, ineffable, and completely private. The mystic's "knowledge" is not achievable except by the loss of one's human *identity* and a communion with the object of knowledge— that is, by a mysterious, inexplicable union of what we usually take to be the beings of the knower and the known.

As such, mysticism, even if it were possible in some sense, does not belong within philosophy but must be laid alongside religion— the concern with the nonnatural or supernatural.

ANTIMETAPHYSICS

The view that we cannot possibly know any basic facts of reality and that metaphysical explorations and investigations are therefore necessarily fruitless has often been advanced in philosophy. One very prominent defense of this position, called **antimetaphysics,** will be sketched here, but others are also available.

Blocks to Clear Understanding

Most of us have heard the claim that people's upbringing influences the way they look at the world. This position is also expressed by saying that the perspective or framework we take toward reality is determined by the ideas taught us at an early age. Some people argue that the environmental conditions, or our membership in racial or social or economic groups, determine the way we see things.

There are others, however, who say that *as human beings* we all have a very specific, conditioned way of viewing reality. By being members of the human species, we are limited in our viewpoint by the structure of the human mind. Since it is impossible for us ever to escape these limitations, it is impossible for us to ever *know* reality as it actually is.   We can only know the way that it looks to us, with the kind of perspective human beings can have on it.   Thus, while we can make pretty good sense out of the way things appear to us, adequate even for developing scientific understanding, we can never attain knowledge of the basic facts of reality.   What reality is as such, completely free of influence by prejudices, preconceptions, and other obstructions, cannot be known.

This seems at first to be a theory about human knowledge.   In fact, however, it is a theory about what kind of things we are and what kind of reality there is.   It is an antimetaphysical position; yet, paradoxically, it has a sort of metaphysics.   It holds that reality is such that the human mind is unable to know it, and that our minds are such that they cannot know reality.   The rules of thought, the principles of understanding, and the ideas that figure into our thinking and knowing at once prevent us from getting a clear picture of what reality really is.   To overcome this limitation we would have to do something impossible: step outside of our minds and examine whether our minds' *perception* of reality and what reality *is* coincide with each other.   Barring this impossible achievement, we will never know the nature or essence or basic features of reality.   Although we *may* in fact be right in what we think reality is like, we can never know it and could well be wrong.

Self-exempt Status

According to the position we have just outlined, metaphysical knowledge is plainly unattainable.   But there are obvious difficulties with the view.   Although it appears to be sensible when presented in the above way, even in our sketch there are some puzzling elements. For example, there does appear to be a purported knowledge of metaphysical facts implicit in the view.   Because it holds that reality is such that it is unknowable, it appears to lay claim to *knowing* something about what is supposed to be *unknowable*.   This is an unacceptable position, since it amounts to a contradiction, something that could not be true because it ends in nonsense.

It also appears that this view treats knowledge as if to know something amounted to imposing certain characteristics on what is known.   Yet there is no reason to think that this is the case with most of our knowledge. Even if many people allow their ideas to color their attempts to understand and perceive reality, this need not be the case. Actually, unless it were possible to avoid it, we could not discover that it is happening. We can tell that prejudice, bias, preconception, and the like exist because we can identify ways of understanding things without these. For the suggestion that we cannot know reality as it really exists to even make clear sense, we would have to have a pretty good idea of the way to achieve the opposite, the way to learn of reality as it truly is. If we could not achieve this last, our conclusion that we cannot know reality as it is would be highly suspect. How is it that we can know this about reality, about the reality that is the condition of the human mind? And if we can, what prevents us from knowing more?

FINAL NOTE

These and similar objections can be raised against the critic of metaphysics. Indeed, much of the work of philosophers involves debating these issues. The reason is, ultimately, that human beings want to have a good idea about their relationship to reality, including how well they can know the basic facts of reality and how likely it is that they can answer their metaphysical questions. In a certain respect these issues touch each of us very closely, for they are concerned with the human mind, the faculty or tool by which we must all make our way in reality. Is it a good instrument; is it capable of yielding results when we make careful use of it? What sorts of results are we entitled to expect of it?

Metaphysical knowledge could well provide us with something that we often yearn for. It could give us a clear idea about the sorts of things that are possible in reality. It could guide us to exclude certain suggestions from consideration from the start. If such knowledge could be obtained, we would be richer for it by far. If we discover that we cannot obtain this knowledge we remain without any guidelines of the sort promised by metaphysical knowledge and must make our way by different means concerning these issues. In either case we have a considerable stake in having the work of the metaphysician carried out competently, and each of us can benefit from knowing a little bit about what that work involves.

QUESTIONS FOR DISCUSSION

1. Identify any metaphysical views you or someone you know outside of philosophy accepts. Make sure that these are in fact best characterized as metaphysical views.

2. What sort of problems would most likely prompt you to turn to metaphysics? Why?

3. Is there a difference between studying existence and studying some particular thing that exists? Justify your answer.

4. What approach would you have to use in order to establish the truth of some metaphysical position? How does it differ from other widely known approaches to reaching truth?

5. What answer would you give to the question "What is the basic component of reality?" and why does this answer seem best to you now?

6. Give the best arguments you know for and against the proposition that existence does not depend for itself upon the human mind. Evaluate the two cases and select the strongest case on the basis of this evaluation.

7. What evidence for idealism do you find in your own experiences? What supports materialism? Which of these positions should one consider more sensible? Why?

8. Try to defend mysticism and then criticize this position.

9. If you are a theist, defend the claim that God exists by the best argument you know (never mind your *feelings* for the moment); if you are either an atheist or an agnostic, defend these positions. Entertain objections and respond to them.

10. What connection, if any, do you see between mysticism and theism? Why do you think the connection exists?

11. Are there elements of dualism that are compatible with theism? Why or why not?

12. What arguments would you offer to support the dual aspect theory of the human mind? Are these convincing?

13. Give the best answer you can construct to the following question: "Why is there something instead of nothing at all?"

14. Do you think that metaphysics has any impact on human life (other than having to face discussions of it in philosophy courses)? Why or why not?

15. Now that you have some idea of what a metaphysical position amounts to, try to search your own thoughts and outline your own metaphysical views in a few sentences. Then give reasons why these, and not the ones outlined in the text, are best suited for purposes of understanding reality.

Epistemology

❧3❧

In this chapter we will take up one of the central issues of philosophy. Unlike metaphysics, which is at present somewhat neglected, epistemology is currently the most prominent field being investigated by philosophers. As with our previous topics, it will help to explain first of all why epistemology is important and how its subject matter emerges from ordinary human affairs. After that, some of the more prominent problems of human knowledge will be introduced. We will canvass the arena of epistemological theories and examine competing answers to the questions asked within this branch of philosophy. We will then discuss some of the arguments that attempt to prove that knowledge is impossible or at least highly unlikely. Finally, we will close this chapter with a discussion of some special topics within epistemology.

OPINION, BELIEF, AND KNOWLEDGE

Hardly anyone is without opinions about one thing or another. An **opinion** is usually a statement or judgment that something or other is thus and so. "People are not to be trusted" is an opinion that some people have and often voice. It is an opinion because it is rarely, if ever, defended with care and precision; it is simply proposed as one way to view the situation in question, namely, what people are like. "Inflation will continue for a long time to come" can also be an opinion when it is simply asserted, without serious substantiation. Opinions are usually held less firmly than beliefs; they are often put forth in casual discourse with less commitment than beliefs. When a question arises about why Johnny isn't reading so well, even after several years of schooling, someone may suggest that Johnny could have a vision problem. The person who makes this comment is offering an opinion unless that statement has been preceded by serious preparation on the subject and an examination of Johnny.

From Opinions to Beliefs and Knowledge

Even without these hints most of us have a fairly good idea about what opinions are. The fact that people have opinions suggests something very important. The very possibility of understanding that something is an opinion—just your opinion, merely an opinion, only his opinion—suggests that we can go further than having and offering opinions about various topics. (Of course, not all opinions are *just* opinions, but many are.) We realize soon that although opinions are important, an opinion is not enough to get a grip on a subject. It is fair to observe, then, that where opinions are possible there may, with more work, be well-founded beliefs and, eventually, knowledge. Before we get to knowledge, let's consider beliefs. The difference between opinion and belief may not be precise, but we seem to accept some important points that make the two different.

If an acquaintance tells us that she believes something to be thus and so, it is quite a reasonable next step to ask *why* she believes it. A belief, if we have reason to suppose that one holds it seriously, requires some (however feeble) support. At the present time I believe that my next-door neighbor is at home. This is not just an opinion I have. Yet I certainly do not *know* it. I believe my neighbor is at home because not long ago I walked past his house and saw his car parked in front, his living room lights on, and people moving about the house. Clearly, since the time I saw all this he could have left the house. However, my belief is not without support. Usually when at this late hour I find these things in evidence, I have also found my neighbor at home upon going over to chat with him.

It is not a mere opinion of mine that most of my students will show up at the test that I am giving in one of my classes tomorrow. However, I clearly do not *know* that they will do so. Even more importantly, when I reflect on whether some of our political leaders distort or report candidly on their own activities, I believe that some are deceitful, whatever their motives. Again, this is not just an opinion, but I certainly do not have knowledge about their truthfulness or deceit. (Therein lies our general practice of taking a person to be not guilty until *proven* to be guilty, however much we *believe* his guilt after reading reports in the newspapers.) Our beliefs, when we treat them seriously, are well-supported conclusions about things; they are not just opinions, but neither do they qualify as knowledge.

Yet, here again we already accept that aside from believing something to be thus and so, we are prepared to grant that it is possible to know that which we believe to be thus and so. *By "know," we commonly mean that we have a belief that is true and we have good, even conclusive, reasons for believing what we do.* Of course, philosophers debate a great deal about what knowledge is. But usually their efforts to show that something is knowledge take for granted the above commonsensical view. There is obviously much discussion and theorizing about what "true" means and how much reason is good, conclusive reason. It is within the branch of philosophy called epistemology that these issues are thoroughly explored, debated, developed, challenged, and otherwise discussed.

Why is all of this important? Why worry about the matter at all? Why should anyone pay attention to a field concerned with identifying the nature of knowledge and exploring what it might take to obtain knowledge? Only some sketchy suggestions can be offered here, but hopefully these will make good sense to the reader for the time being.

Ordinarily, on a commonsense level, and granting many variations even at that stage, we consider the possibility of human knowledge as vitally important. This is because in living our lives successfully, we have to make decisions and select from alternatives before us. To make these decisions with some promise of success, we need to have reliable information about the world. Opinions may suffice about many issues. For instance, my opinion that most magician acts are relatively simple tricks—this is how I would express it should the topic arise—matters little to me. I really do not have much confidence that this opinion is actually right. I do have hearsay evidence, and quite enough of it, to give some support to my opinion. Yet it is, as we usually understand the term, just an opinion.

In the philosophical discussion of this issue, opinion is often used as a synonym for belief, but this is not how we use the terms ordinarily. I believe now that my mother is alive and well in Europe. I also believe that my car will be in good running condition this weekend when I have to drive it several hundred miles. I believe that I am in reasonably good health. For these and similar items of belief I have very good evidence, although it is clear also that much could be presented to me that would change my mind. My reasons in support of these beliefs are far from conclusive, since I haven't had a letter from my mother for four weeks, my car has often acted up quite unexpectedly, and my age and general physical condition are such that it could easily turn out that something is not functioning well without my being aware of it.

On the other hand, as I drove to work last time I knew when the light turned green at the first intersection. Here belief would have hardly been enough. Whatever knowledge actually is, whether it is in fact possible, I certainly needed what we would call knowledge in order to make it safely to my place of work.

Complications

Of course, the above cases are relatively simple. Far more complicated matters arise in human affairs and to be able to cope with them we usually require knowledge about many things. We clearly need at least well-supported beliefs about the matter. Unlike most, if not all, other animals, human beings do not appear to possess inborn guidelines for behavior. Puppies seem to be able to swim without learning how this must be done, and so do kittens and grown cats. But a child must usually learn what to do in order to stay afloat. And this is a relatively ordinary matter, an activity engaged in not just by man but by most animals. When we consider the complexities of human life and the thousands of questions we must answer in order to live with some measure of success, we clearly see that we have no automatic, built-in program to guide us. We must learn, and learning involves acquiring well-grounded beliefs and, quite often, outright knowledge. Without at least some knowledge, human beings could not live. This is at least a commonsense idea that has merit, however the detailed investigation about the nature of knowledge and its possibility for us turns out in the end. It is in terms of this commonsense idea that we can understand reasonably well why the branch of philosophy called epistemology—discourse about or the study of knowledge—is important. This is the general motive underlying its existence, whatever the individual motives of those who engage in this field of inquiry.

We can put the matter differently, also, even though that will amount to assuming certain facts that have not been touched on at sufficient length in this book. Yet, if we consider that human beings are the sort of animals that possess the capacity for rational thought and awareness of things in terms of abstractions, it is clear why we need to understand what knowledge is. Knowledge is the distinctively human approach to coping with reality. Only human beings, to the best of our knowledge(!), use abstractions and need them to guide their actions. The quest to understand what knowledge is can be regarded as an effort to understand one of the crucial aspects of being human. Emotions, urges, drives, and similar characteristics we can share, at some levels, with other animals. But knowledge, especially complex theoretical understanding, is something that only human beings appear to be able to gain *and* to require for their existence. And epistemology inquires about this uniquely human affair.

Opinions and Knowledge

It will be useful to return now to a consideration of what having opinions indicates about human knowledge. I have previously made the point that studying the nature of knowledge is important. This is one of the tasks that is treated within philosophy; it is perhaps among the most important, and one that comes to light in many ordinary and special human endeavors. Clearly, the issue of whether something we affirm is in fact something we know to be so

has a very serious place in human life.   It is obvious that in some
fields, for example, medicine, we want to make sure that what is
being affirmed is not just an opinion, nor even just a belief to which
some people have committed themselves.   However hard it may be
to obtain, it is knowledge that is usually desired in fields such as
medicine, horticulture, physics, and aeronautics.

At this point, however, it will help to indicate what sort of
considerations give rise to the idea that we can obtain knowledge
of reality.   Obviously, we believe we can know many things—at
least, most of us act as if this were the case.   But what argument can
be offered to suggest the availability of knowledge to human beings?

One strong hint, as I suggested above, emerges from a consideration of what opinions are.   Serious opinions and beliefs appear
to suggest that we can obtain knowledge of reality.   Why does this
seem so?   Professor Leo Strauss gives us the clue when he relates
how Socrates, the great Greek philosopher, considered the issue.
He tells us that

> . . . Socrates started in his understanding of the natures of things
> from the opinions about their natures.   For every opinion is based
> on some awareness, on some perception with the mind's eye, of
> something.   Socrates implied that disregarding the opinions about
> the natures of things would amount to abandoning the most
> important access to reality which we have, or the most important
> vestiges of the truth which are within our reach. . . .   (*Natural
> Right and History,* Chicago: University of Chicago Press, 1953,
> pp. 123–124)

Opinions are a clue to something else.   They are a clue to
what things really are.   As mentioned in our discussion of common
sense in chapter 1, we have to start with opinions—the more serious
sort, at least—in order to make headway toward obtaining knowledge and understanding.

But even the possession of opinions gives us something.   Even
when we go no further than forming opinions, there is a suggestion
in this of the possibility of something more than opinions.   The
fact that we have opinions, something evident enough to all of us,
suggests that we could gain knowledge.   Otherwise, we would be
on very shaky grounds about regarding anything as an opinion.
This is because we often admit that although we do have opinions,
having them is not enough.   We expect, seemingly quite reasonably,

that more could be achieved.   Unless we are in a frame of mind to entertain universal doubt—doubt about everything, even the prospect of learning anything—we expect that we can obtain knowledge of reality.

This shows that the field of epistemology has a basis in ordinary life, in our commonsense appraisal of the situation.   Later some objections to this expectation will be considered.   For now we will begin our inquiry into the field of epistemology.

MODELS, STANDARDS, AND THEORIES OF KNOWLEDGE

To begin with, some remarks are warranted about what epistemology is not.   This will help to avoid misunderstandings so easily acquired about any area of human inquiry.

First, epistemology is concerned with what knowledge is, not with the processes of the human organism (e.g., the workings of the brain or of the eyes) required to gain knowledge.   Some attention is usually paid to these processes by epistemologists.   Today, however, physiology, neurology, psychophysics, neurophysics, psychology, and even sociology, along with several more specialized sciences, have entered the more technical areas related to the mechanisms or processes involved in knowledge, learning, perceiving, sensing, and so forth.   However closely these areas may be tied to a detailed investigation of human knowing, they are not what the epistemologist is concerned with in the final analysis.

It could even be argued that before these other fields can get under way, the epistemologist's work has to be well under way, perhaps even to the point of offering some sensible conclusion about what knowledge is.   Unless there is some reasonably sound answer to the question of what knowledge is, the special, more technical research about the processes and mechanisms of knowledge cannot proceed.   These are processes and mechanisms *of knowledge,* and if we have no sensible notion of what knowledge is, how would the special researcher even begin to focus on the processes and mechanisms *of knowledge?*

Our second preliminary point is more germane to the actual epistemological project. It is the idea that most theories of knowledge, or attempts at a correct characterization of what knowledge is (the nature or essence of knowledge), assume a model that the theory must ultimately measure up to. In other words, even before a philosopher tries to answer the question, What is knowledge? he or she will accept some standard that the answer *must* meet. The answer to the question will generally be thought to be satisfactory only if *certain standards of what a right answer must be* are fulfilled. Very often the philosopher who attempts to answer the epistemological question assumes without stating it explicitly what knowledge would *have to be* even before proceeding with his inquiry.

This is a very important matter. I have said earlier that metaphysics is a field that must come prior to any other because it is in metaphysical investigations that we try to answer the question, What is it to be anything, to exist? Without answering this question, those who try to answer a more particular question (e.g., of what it is to be knowledge, what is the nature of knowledge) would not have a standard for making sure that they have indeed come up with an answer that can be right—that is, that they have actually identified a fact of reality, something that exists or can exist, for example, knowledge.

Philosophers who work in the field of epistemology sometimes disregard this matter and pursue their work outside of a metaphysical framework. At least they would not admit to having one. However, we will see that most answers to the questions of epistemology do assume metaphysics.

It must also be realized that the above points are highly controversial and that here it is my own view about the relationship between metaphysics and epistemology that has been made evident. It simply makes good sense to me, however, to point out this matter, whatever objections may be raised against it in a more detailed investigation. Certainly if I am correct, the empistemological enterprise would have to take it seriously.

I have stressed the point before that philosophy has often been considered a systematic endeavor where all the branches of the field should be coordinated. In this case the point would be that those who investigate epistemological questions should pay attention to other areas in philosophy and make sure that their conclusions contribute to a comprehensive, systematic understanding of all of reality. But this is not the only view. Students of the field need to carefully consider whether or not the systematic approach is indeed appropriate. Many philosophers consider it full of traps—mainly the one of dogmatism. The idea here is that working out various problems in terms of a system may cut off the opportunity to look at some problems with a fresh, unprejudiced attitude. On the other hand, if the system within which one considers various problems is itself constantly checked out, this kind of danger can be overcome.

If the systematic approach is appropriate, we would have to conclude that epistemology could not be considered a valid field of study without first admitting that there are things to be known, that there exists a world about which knowledge can be obtained.

We can now outline some of the main theories of knowledge. Remembering that to know would involve having beliefs that are true and well supported, even conclusively proven, we can examine various attempts to explain what is needed for knowledge.

Empiricism

Empiricism develops the commonsense idea that knowledge must be achieved by basing one's beliefs on experience. Most of us are familiar with the term *empirical* even before we come in contact with philosophy. We know the popular saying: "I'm from Missouri —*show me!*" The idea is that if you do know something, it must also be demonstrable, verifiable, confirmable, provable by "showing me"—by reference to sensory experience or evidence. This is what "empirical" means.

The attractiveness of this idea of what knowledge must be should be evident to most people. Most of us take for granted that when someone knows something, this is so because he can point out what he knows for anyone to detect or to verify by attending to it with the sensory organs. The theory that knowledge must be based on empirical evidence is clearly widespread in common opinions on the subject of knowledge. This itself should suggest that the doctrine deserves serious attention.

Let me now outline the strictest version of empiricism. Basically, this version states that the very possibility of some belief's constituting knowledge depends on whether the content of such a belief is capable of being supported by our senses. The statement or content of our knowledge, for instance, that Johnny has a cold, must at least be capable of empirical verification. This means that the ideas in terms of which the claim is made—namely, "Johnny," "has," "a cold"—must have empirical content. "Johnny" must refer to something we can sense. "Having" and "a cold" must also be capable of sensory specification. More precisely, each of these names and ideas must be capable of being used *to refer to contents of our sensory experiences* or groupings of sensory input.

Consider whether under this view the idea "ghost" could ever be used in expressing what we know. Take the claim or belief "There was a ghost in my attic last night." The idea "ghost" is generally understood to mean a being without physical character- istics, a disembodied soul. But such a being has no properties or attributes or characteristics or whatnot that we could experience by means of our senses. This being the case, the empiricist view would be that the above claim could never be successfully used to say whatever a person may know to be the case. Ideas such as "ghost" cannot be tied to reality!

More importantly, consider the idea "mind." "His mind was on his upcoming wedding." Unless we are able to specify the meaning of "mind" by reference to sensory evidence that we could possess, this claim could never be used to express knowledge. The idea "mind" cannot refer to anything in reality! This, incidentally, is one reason that many psychologists refuse to talk about the *mind* and choose, instead, to speak of the *behavior* of human beings, for instance, their verbal behavior. Behavior is something that we generally admit to be capable of being experienced by way of sensory awareness.

Any field of investigation that takes the strict empiricist theory of knowledge seriously—and many fields do just that—would have to exclude any sort of supposed thing that cannot be experienced by way of the senses. This is usually stated in terms of the require- ments of verification and confirmation by way of (sensory) obser- vation. Only those things exist that can be observed. Put in terms of epistemology, we can only know that which is observable.

We should restrict our beliefs, and the ideas we use to achieve mutual understanding, to that which we can all take part in. And this is clearly that which is capable of sensory detection. Anything else would be unavailable for (public) inspection. How far could we get with beliefs and communication that did not permit of such public availability? We would never be able to indicate what we are talking about, let alone find out whether someone who says he knows something does indeed know it, unless we accept the strict empiricist approach.

These are the main features of empiricism, and clearly the view seems to be powerful enough. There may be those who care little about knowledge, however much you and I might think that they are therefore mistaken. For anyone who does care for knowledge, the empiricist theory of what knowledge is—namely, a belief confirmed by sensory experience—promises a good deal. Nevertheless, a few difficulties with this view must be indicated shortly, for in the history of the concern with the issue of knowledge, empiricism has met with formidable opposition, to say the least.

The empiricist theory of knowledge requires that any successful claim to knowledge be fully confirmed or verified by sensory experience(s): We *know* that Johnny has a cold only if our belief that this is so is supported fully by reference to what we are aware of by way of our sensory organs. But just exactly what are we aware of by way of our sensory organs? What are our sensory experiences? In short, what are we asked to appeal to in support of our belief?

The most important empiricists (among them John Locke and David Hume in modern philosophy and several others before the times of Socrates, Plato, and Aristotle) answer by specifying something like sensory impressions, sensations, or sense data. These may be better understood if we imagine them as bits of input "fired into" our sense organs. When we see, our sense of sight encounters bits of visual sensations. Usually these bits are very small and come in groups. It is believed that when these groups of bits of sensations occur together more and more often, we associate them with one another. Thus, we receive such groups of sensory bits, sometimes grouped together by way of different sense organs, and we call them by such names as "table," "chair," "human being," or "city." The copies of these groupings, that is, certain images or ideas that linger after the actual experience is terminated, are our meaningful ideas that we can use to make meaningful statements. Any ideas not so constructed have to be treated with great suspicion, to say the least. (Only special ones are meaningful—usually those that refer to relationships between the meaningful ideas gained by way of sensory impressions. Thus "similarity" is a meaningful idea because it refers to relationships between several meaningful ideas gained by sensory experiences. But the similarity is between ideas, not between things.)

Criticism of Empiricism. These views are empiricist, even if no single empiricist has made them clear in just this way. The general idea is accurate enough for us. Now we can turn to some criticism —with caution, so that when slightly different versions of the position are advanced, we must be ready to reconsider some objections.

It appears that according to empiricism all we can know is sensory impressions, not the things of which we may get a sensory impression. Do we know that Johnny has a cold? No—we know sensory impressions that have been labeled "Johnny," "cold," "having," etc. Ordinarily we care about Johnny, not about some internal sensory impression we have that supposedly came to be labeled "Johnny." Within empiricism we never seem to be able to know anything about reality; we know only about some sensory impressions that may or may not tell us about reality. We may gain a type of knowledge, but it is knowledge of something we did not set out to know.

In the last analysis it appears that what we know is always a part of our individual minds—or, more accurately, what *I* know is my own mind, and nothing else. Beyond it I cannot know anything. This is **solipsism**—the view that only my mind exists.

Consider a case to illustrate this. We can pose the question to the empiricist: When a person sees a boat, does he actually see a boat as a boat; is "I see a boat" true in that case? It is clearly something we ordinarily, commonsensically accept. Seeing a boat would then amount to something more than having certain varieties of sense impressions that we have labeled "boat." We claim that we saw a boat, not that we have seen all sensible parts of it. In other words, we go beyond what we may consider the sensory material received from the boat—which is very likely sensory material from only one side of the boat—to the boat itself. We have, of course, sensed something: impressions, data, or whatever. But what we claim to have seen is not these discrete impressions but the boat, something that is much more than its strictly visible parts. If seeing the boat really amounted to having sensory impressions we have called "boat," then we could not mean that we saw the boat. The same would hold for anything else we see, hear, touch, or feel. In all cases we receive sensory impressions of parts, surfaces, sounds, and the like, not the whole nor every feature of the thing that has these parts, surfaces, sounds, etc.

If, on the other hand, to know something would really amount to knowing the sense impressions and nothing more, then we could not know boats, people, cities, or any other objects or events. We could, by the empiricist theory, know only sensory impressions, or what may be indicated in commonsense terms as the experiences of surfaces, textures, sounds, and other features registered by the senses. The objects, events, situations, and all of what we commonsensically accept as features of reality would drop out; we would be left with sensory impressions in our minds and the copies (ideas) constructed out of them. We would, in a way, know only the insides of our minds.

It turns out, it seems, that the theory that promised that we could finally latch onto something real, firm, and common to us all leaves us with only our own minds' insides (the sensory impressions) as real.

The empiricists, or some of them at least, argue that it is a mistake to ask for knowledge of the independent things, objects, events, causes, or effects we usually take to exist in our world. It should be enough to have the materials in our minds and to then act *as if* the world contained corresponding objects. Some argue that we will act as if the world contained such objects because we are habituated, or instinctively disposed to do so. But we should not delude ourselves and think that we *know* any such things. Because we will not at the same time have direct, final, and doubtless knowledge of all parts or features of the things we see (as in the case of the boat on the lake), we may not claim that we know of boats or other things.

The fact is that having seen the boat just as we usually do (without obstructions limiting our vision), we would appear to be entitled, ordinarily, to claim that we know there is a boat out there on the lake. Yet, if we demand of knowledge that we have direct sensory experiences of everything involved in what we know (the boat), we should have to accept that we can only have "beliefs"— defined by some empiricists as the anticipations of these sorts of sensory experiences based on the past occurrence of sensory impressions like these. In other words, by the empiricist theory we may be allowed to *believe* that the boat is "out there on the lake," but all we could *know* is that we are having certain sensory impressions.

Here, as elsewhere, the reader should recall that the topic has not been fully explored. It will be a wise policy to suspend for a while even tentative judgment about it. Only after we have presented some of the major alternatives among theories of knowledge will it be advisable to form a provisional judgment concerning which one is most adequate. (Just how this must be determined is not an easy matter. Some of the earlier remarks dealing with the relationship between metaphysics and epistemology should provide the clue as to how I would establish the standard of adequacy.)

Rationalism

The term that designates this school of thought derives from "rational." The emphasis of **rationalism** is on the role of reason in achieving knowledge of things. (Empiricism emphasizes the senses, whereas rationalism emphasizes reason.)

As with the previous theory, there is ample evidence from ordinary life to support the initial plausibility of the position. Hardly anyone could get far without the process affectionately referred to as putting two and two together. Thinking, reasoning, applying one's rationality to problems being faced each day clearly has something to do with whether we succeed in solving the problems and making the best decisions. Not always. But one cannot deny that careful thinking contributes a great deal to learning about life and how to live it with some success. Even the wildest mystic relies on some degree of logical, rational thought. Even the most devoted worshipper of the doctrine of living-by-pure-faith makes use of his mind by thinking while driving to the house of devotion. Even those who propose that man lives by instincts alone and that reason is just a myth, produce their theories to this effect by some rational effort.

But the rationalist's further argument that knowledge must ultimately rest on some purely rational principle, that is, a belief arrived at by unaided reason, does not derive from these common-sense realizations. He, like the empiricist, is more systematic. One of the most famous and influential rationalists in the history of philosophy gives us the following case, which I will only sketch. René Descartes's own presentation of his case is clear enough, however many subtleties it actually contains when examined over and over again.   This case is the *Cartesian* argument in behalf of the rationalist approach to understanding knowledge.

We find that by relying on perceptual evidence we can be fooled.   Mirages, hallucinations, illusions, and the like have often led us astray.   When we base beliefs on such evidence we could well be mistaken, so it cannot be relied on for knowledge.   But even if we bring to bear the rest of our mental faculties on some problem, we can be in trouble.   Is it not clear that some of our dreams resemble perfectly lucid, normal, daily experiences?   We dream and then we are awake.   But which is which?   Often we dream that we have awakened.   Sometimes we cannot tell whether what we remember is a dream or yesterday's event.   So, relying on careful attention, putting evidence beside evidence, and the like still will not assure that error has been completely avoided.   By the extraordinarily high standards of knowledge the rationalists impose upon us, this is clearly no way to obtain knowledge, however much we may believe otherwise in our ordinary goings on.   (Descartes himself did not deny that we can obtain knowledge, but he denied that we can acquire it by carefully attending to what things and situations we perceive and believe to exist.)

The general line of argument used here to arrive at one of the major rationalist positions on knowledge is not what all rationalists would use.   However, it does illustrate the kind of considerations that could lead one to arrive at the rationalist position.   The next step in this argument is to consider whether using logic and mathematics might not allow us to attain knowledge.   Perhaps the conclusions arrived at within these rigorous sciences would qualify as knowledge.

The response here, again outlined by Descartes, is that it is at least imaginable that a powerful but malicious being, an evil demon, has distorted logic and mathematics for us.   As when in the movies false fronts make it appear that an actual city street is being filmed, so such an imagined demon could have set up the false fronts of mathematics and logic, which we take to be actual studies of certain aspects of reality.   With this bare but imaginable possibility we must once again reject that certain knowledge, the only kind believed to be significant, is possible.

What is left?   Doubt, thinking—*these are certain for us!* Throughout this entire exploration we have been engaged in doubt; we have been thinking, questioning, considering what might be true, what we could justifiably call knowledge. And now we have dismissed everything but the fact that we have been doubting and thinking. By this route the argument led to the conclusion that the foundation of knowledge, that is, the one thing we can justifiably consider knowledge, is a principle or belief we apprehend by pure thinking alone. This principle is (to put it correctly but somewhat strangely): "I think, therefore I am." This famous phrase was offered by Descartes as the clearest and only ultimate piece of knowledge, expressed in the famous Latin statement: *"Cogito, ergo sum."*

According to the rationalist, our knowledge must be founded upon and have the characteristics of indubitable, absolutely firm truths, something like the metaphysical first principles that are held to be true by some philosophers. Once a basic principle has been identified, the rationalist would require that everything else we know be directly derivable from such a principle—on the model of mathematical theorems and principles. As with the empiricists, who take it that the ground of our knowledge must be absolutely unshakable, the rationalists also believe that knowledge must be grounded on some unshakable foundation and directly derivable from it at each point at which we in fact know something. It may make the matter clearer to distinguish the empiricists from the rationalists by reference to the kind of foundation necessary for knowledge in the case of each. Empiricism requires that knowledge be based strictly on sensory experience, whereas rationalism requires that it be based strictly on intellectual experience—a clear and distinct idea, a doubt-free intuition, or a basic principle that reason has fully confirmed to be true.

It bears mentioning that this important epistemological theory has a crucial metaphysical significance—that is, relevance to issues touched on in metaphysics. Thus, this argument locates the foundation of knowledge—the first and central fact we know—within the mind itself. Instead of locating the basic fact outside the human mind, in the outside world (so to speak), rationalism finds the mind itself to contain this fact. In different versions, this aspect of rationalism occurs in several philosophies that have been called rationalist in epistemology and idealist in metaphysics. Yet, as we saw, it also appears to be a feature of strict empiricism—where the most reliable facts, or items of knowledge, are sensory impressions.

Criticism of Rationalism. Some critical points about rationalism must be considered now. As we mentioned earlier, the argument calls into doubt the reliability of perceptual evidence on grounds that we can make mistakes by such reliance. The first stage of the argument rests mainly on our capacity for making mistakes. But has it also been shown in this argument that we can never rely on our perceptual information, even when we make a thorough check? No. From the general capacity to make mistakes it does not follow that on any occasion we are, in fact, making one. On a specific occasion we might have made sure enough and a mistake is out of the question! Although this situation may be rare, the argument does not prove its impossibility. From the general capacity to make mistakes it does not follow that a mistake has been made on some particular occasion. So the argument may be flawed from the start.

In the next phase the argument begins by distinguishing between dreams and conscious experiences but ends by denying that we could ever make such a distinction. The premise of the argument therefore asserts something that the conclusion denies, or at least in the premises it is assumed that we can do something that the conclusion states we cannot do with sufficiently good reason. There are at least some questions about proceeding in this way, so that in the end we may not have to accept the view that led to the rationalist conclusion.

It seems equally problematic to suppose an evil demon who can distort everything, including the very principles of clear thinking. If our reasoning could not be fully relied upon ever, then the reasoning by which we thought up the idea of an evil demon, even its mere possibility, could not be trusted. Thus, the argument could not be taken seriously if its conclusions are accepted. In general, arguments that invoke a mere figment of the imagination, even clever imagination, and thus lead us to distrust our ability to use our minds, should be viewed with grave suspicion.

Two points must be raised as general objections to the method of argument used to reach the rationalist conclusion. First, when it is argued that it is possible to be deceived by perception or that it is possible to mistake dreams for reality, we have an apparent confusion between two uses of the idea "possibility." On the one hand "possibility" means capacity—as in "It is possible to do 120 miles per hour in my car"—and on the other it means probability—

as in "Quite possibly it will rain tonight." These two meanings are quite different. Second, the rationalist takes a standard of knowledge applicable in certain limited domains (e.g., mathematics or, more plausibly, metaphysics) and imposes it on all domains. Thus, in order to know anything we are required to have it as firmly grounded as what we know in these few areas, which do themselves seem to concern grounds or foundations.

At this point we can move away from the argument that led to the rationalist conclusion and attend to what the conclusion involves. The main idea here is that we can know something without recourse to anything outside ourselves, without experiencing or perceiving or having sensory evidence of reality outside of our own minds. Not even our own bodies are accepted as something that exists; the conclusion implies (and Descartes states) that "I exist as a thinking being." The version of rationalism we are considering starts from what is often called an *innate idea,* a truth that we find within us, independent of anything else, in the human mind itself.

The objection to this position is that in order to doubt, it may well be necessary to have something to doubt. Must we not doubt something or other before we can understand doubting itself? Must we not be aware of something or other as existing before we can understand having an opinion? These questions suggest that even before we can make sense of our own existence, or at least at the time when we make sense of it, we must also make sense of the existence of something other than ourselves. This point is not about what comes first *in time.* It is a point about what idea is presupposed in understanding some other idea. Just as the idea of "male" is presupposed in understanding what the idea "bachelor" means, so the idea of "thinking" or "doubting" may presuppose "something to think about" or "something to doubt."

With just these brief considerations it appears that the rationalist view that knowledge must be founded on some truth discovered by unaided reason runs into serious difficulties. The mind of a human being does not seem to be able to know anything without the prior existence of something that can be known—however badly this something is understood, perceived, or identified by that mind. This appears ever so sensible, one might add, because the human mind, including human reason, is very likely best understood as a faculty used primarily for attaining and containing knowledge. It can contain knowledge only after it has engaged in the *activity of obtaining knowledge*. Then we can begin to learn about this activity, which is the function of the mind itself.

These and other objections can be raised against the rationalist theory that knowledge emerges from within the mind itself. Just one more point needs to be mentioned before we continue with some other theories of knowledge.

Empiricism and Rationalism Compared

The empiricist theory, which was presented earlier, is often thought to be in radical opposition to the rationalist position. This is because empiricism seeks the foundation of knowledge in sensory experiences, whereas rationalism seeks it in intellectual experiences.

Despite this difference, empiricism and rationalism share an important idea. This is that whatever foundation knowledge has, it must be certain beyond a shadow of a doubt. Whether it is intellectual insight or sensory impressions, it must be immediately evident to the person. Both theories go on to require that we infer or arrive at the beliefs we have from these immediately evident foundations. Only in this way can we justify the claim that these beliefs constitute knowledge instead of mere opinion or prejudice. Yet, strict empiricism does not appear to allow for arriving at such beliefs. Furthermore, rationalism gets to them usually by introducing some outside help, such as God (the existence of which would cancel out the possibility of an evil demon) so as to avoid its problems.

Of course, each theory has its modified versions. These are less strictly empirical or rationalist, allowing as they usually do for a considerable mixture of pure reasoning and pure sensory experience to provide human knowledge. In such diluted versions of these theories the model or standard of knowledge is far less demanding than in those we have looked at thus far. It would seem sensible that not all knowledge must amount to such absolute indubitability as the strict empiricists and the rationalists appear to require for it.

Subjectivism

When someone remarks that a true statement is only true *for him,* he is giving expression in simple form to the doctrine of **subjec-**

tivism. This idea comes in several forms and we will look at two. First, we will briefly consider **individual subjectivism,** and then we will explain **transcendental subjectivism** in greater detail.

Individual Subjectivism. The main idea about subjectivism is that knowledge is significantly determined by the subject of knowledge— the person or persons who know. It is one of the most forceful and widespread views. Its forcefulness does not derive from evident soundness but from its widespread attraction to people. Just why this view is attractive is not itself an issue to be taken up here. It can be suggested, however, that in its plain version subjectivism permits virtually any knowledge claim to have as much "meaning" and "truth" as its proponent desires. Very often this license about what one believes and says is seen as desirable in the face of what some call *absolutist* ideas about knowledge. **Absolutism** in knowledge is the view that once a belief or judgment is shown to be true, nothing else could or need be added to it, not now *or anytime in the future.* Clearly numerous perfectly meaningful and true statements appear to permit eventual revision, especially within the many sciences. This problem of absolutism appears to encourage people to go to the other extreme and claim that anything anyone wishes to claim as knowledge could be accepted as such if seriously affirmed. It is also a widespread belief that absolutism leads to authoritarianism—if I do in fact have the absolute truth, it is thought to follow that I should impose its implications on those around me. These and many far more complicated ideas about absolutism and subjectivism, as found among many who have never even heard of philosophy, could explain why subjectivism is attractive.

In philosophy proper, subjectivism plain and simple is more often a threat than a promise. In other words the fact that a philosophical theory of knowledge is suspected of implying subjectivism is taken as a serious threat to its success. If a theory allows that a person who says the earth is flat and another who says that it is not flat (without different meanings of the terms) are both saying something they *know*, the result is unacceptable by any rational standard. The one belief is the clear negation of the other. If both beliefs could be knowledge, then, by the commonsense notion of what knowledge must be, the earth would at once and in the same way have to be flat and not flat. But this amounts to absurdity!

Every theory of knowledge must preserve the essential distinction between truth and falsehood, between knowledge and error. By this requirement the subjectivist theory here considered implies that knowledge is impossible and that there are no true beliefs with conclusive support but merely your, my, his, and everyone's beliefs—each equally true just because it is believed by someone.

There are few philosophers who advocate forms of subjectivism that could be classed with the personal, individualist subjectivist position sketched above. The view is often voiced by nonphilosophers, however, when they say that anything is so if one believes it to be so—in other words, that beliefs are true for the person who believes them. Since serious advocacy of this position is rare, I will not spend more time on it. Those who think that believing something proves it so make it very difficult to engage in discussions about their views. How could one ever show them to be mistaken?

Transcendental Subjectivism. **Transcendental subjectivism** is a far more prominent philosophical position than the form of subjectivism just described, and it has an influential epistemology. One way to get a handle on this position is to recall that many people believe that individuals with varied backgrounds "see the world" differently. (We will consider this when we get to *relativism.*) It is often said, for example, that someone from India must view things differently from someone who lives in America, that women see things differently from the way men do, or that people from a ghetto must perceive the world quite distinctly from the way those do who grew up in a suburban community.

The idea expressed in these claims is that different groups of people are conditioned to perceive in certain ways. This is often put by saying that things are relative—usually relative to one's background, race, national origin, or sex. Now, if we move from the above position to the view that as human beings we must perceive the world in a given way, the transcendental subjectivist position comes into focus. "Transcendental" here refers to the idea that knowledge does not hinge on individual or group influences but on the *human mind* as such. Accordingly, the requirements for some claim to be knowledge proper derive not from the will or wish or background of an individual or a group but from the nature of the human mind. To transcend is to go beyond or above the individual or group. The transcendental subjectivist position, then, makes knowledge dependent upon the structure of the human mind. This view, which is found most prominently in the writings of the German philosopher Immanuel Kant (1724–1804), has had considerable impact.

The theory of knowledge involved can be outlined as follows: While the empiricist is correct to assert that from outside the human mind or consciousness we obtain only sense impressions, he is wrong to think that this is all we have to go on in what we can be said (correctly) to know. In fact, we do not simply find groups of sensory bits around us. We find tables, chairs, governments, love, marriage, books, the discoveries of the sciences, the facts of history, and a whole lot more. The empiricist viewpoint cannot make sense of this. It leaves us without an answer and urges us to go on with beliefs that we develop from habit or instinct—beliefs that are at best shaky probabilities and at worst inventions left rationally unjustified and unjustifiable. To make sense of our scientific achievements and everyday confidence in what we have learned, we need to explain why we are aware of chairs, tables, and all the rest, and why we are perfectly confident that we do know about some of these things quite frequently.

The explanation lies in the philosophical discovery, so the theory suggests, that the human mind is so constituted (not the human *brain* but the human *way* or *form of being aware* of reality) that it can only consider reality in a fixed way. We are aware of things in a way that is distinctly human, and this way is just as the nature of the human mind determines it. This notion may be clarified by thinking of the mind as a computer that is strictly programmed to handle its input in specific ways. By the time our sensory input is formed into ideas, the complex mind of man has formed this input into meaningful and orderly shapes, so to speak. By its very nature, the mind of a human being must impose its structure on the input received by the senses. The mind is both a means of being aware of and a way of filtering through or even conditioning or determining what the senses receive.

The structure of the human mind, or its "program," consists of certain fixed and unalterable categories (or forms or principles). When these connect with the material of the senses, we are aware of what we can know. This is not a feature of just your or my mind but of the type of mind that human beings have. It is *the* way of human knowing.

The particular judgments or statements of this knowledge are divided into various types and each requires different ways of being established so as to reach the status of knowledge. These different ways are nowadays widely invoked both within and outside of philosophical circles. It will be useful to point them out and show how they appear to serve some well-known commonsense divisions among the various sorts of knowledge we possess.

According to this view, certain judgments are called **analytic a priori.** An analytic a priori truth is a judgment (or statement) whose truth is knowable without our having to check the world for particular facts so as to confirm it, but merely by analyzing those ideas that make it up, at least some of which were learned on the basis of experience. For instance, we know that a thing is what it is by just considering what is meant by this statement. Analyzing our *ideas* will yield the judgments that are said to be analytic a priori.

Certain other judgments are called **synthetic a posteriori** because these are known and knowable to be true only after (a posteriori) we have become aware of various representations of facts (through our senses) and have put our awareness into order (synthesized them). For example, that the ink with which these words are printed is black is known by inspecting and organizing the results of inspection.

Finally, there are judgments called **synthetic a priori.** These are not discernible in the analysis of the ideas involved, as are analytic judgments. But they are a priori—knowable as true without checking the judgments against the world. The "machinery" of our minds, functioning as it does, shows that this kind of judgment is true. In addition, since that machinery fixes any possible representation of the world, it involves this type of judgment, necessarily, in all possible true descriptions of the world. Anything that could count as true knowledge presupposes these types of judgments; they underlie the very possibility of arriving at true judgments about the world. In this, the most controversial of the three types of judgment, we do not learn the truth of a judgment by analysis, but our minds, structured as they are, give support to it. For example, any scientific principle, a judgment about the general, uniform laws governing activities in some area we inquire about, qualifies as a synthetic a priori judgment.

These three types of (true) judgments considered by the present position to constitute human knowledge may be viewed in the more familiar way as (1) knowledge of the relationships among ideas that are basic to human thought, (2) knowledge of individual (or groupings of individual) facts that are apparent to us, and (3) knowledge of laws of nature, of the conclusions of basic scientific inquiries. (More often than not, philosophers and other theoreticians accept the first two types and believe that the third is really better placed within the second. Thus we are familiar with the distinction often made between judgments of theory—ideas, concepts, etc.—and judgments of fact—what we can confirm via the senses.)

Again, the influence of this position upon the general intellectual environment of the last 150 years cannot be overemphasized. Of course, this position is not new in all of its elements. We could trace many of its features as far back in the history of ideas as Plato's writings. Many others have provided it with intellectual help. In the form outlined above, however, the position has achieved considerable importance in philosophical and other intellectual areas.

Criticism of Subjectivism.   Some problems with the view may now be hinted at. By the provisions of the theory we appear to achieve far less than we would ordinarily expect in our efforts to make true judgments about the world, that is, to obtain knowledge. With each of the judgments outlined we seem to be unable to obtain *knowledge of reality.* All that we seem to be able to reach is knowledge of the nature of the human mind and of what appears to be reality to us. To put it another way, we would seem to be able to know only our minds and *what reality appears to be to us* (not *what it is*).

Clearly, the position allows for much more than does the subjective knowledge we spoke of before, at least on first inspection. This theory tries to avoid individual subjectivism. Yet the view allows for no more than a different, more complicated form of subjectivism—that kind of "knowledge" that is uniquely possible to members of the human race. This form of subjectivism transcends, or goes beyond, each individual. What we know by this theory is not put there by each one of us or even by groups of us. It is not conditioned by our individual minds nor by circumstances shared by groups. It is, however, determined by the forms of understanding that characterize the human mind as such.

Why does this constitute a limitation? Because, as the theory maintains, we could never *prove* a judgment about what things *really* are. Why not? Because we can never learn whether our judgment is free of the conditions constraining it, or whether those conditions are in accord with the way things really are. According to this theory, knowledge of reality itself would be possible only if we could escape the structural limits of our human type of minds. We can never take an independent position to see whether or not our judgments really fit the facts, whether or not we possess objective knowledge!

This idea is common enough. Recall what was said before: We are often told that people from different cultures must understand things in radically different ways. We are told that people from different socioeconomic, ethnic, and racial groups see the world from a viewpoint that others cannot share. The present theory just takes this view to the extreme, that is, to the conclusion that as human beings we are limited to viewing the world in our human way. This sounds plainly true, at one level. How could we know things in any way other than as human beings?

But as the theory would have it, the structure of our minds compels us to be aware of reality not as it is but as it appears to exist to us, so that reality might be different however carefully we have investigated it. It is as if our eyes actually made it impossible for us to see clearly regardless of how good our vision is. The most careful and detailed efforts of the human mind could nevertheless be accompanied by a distorting feature. Of course, we might be correct, but this we could never know. To know it we would have to escape our human mind in order to check whether it is indeed aware of reality without a distortion. Since this is impossible, we can never know that we have in fact learned about reality rather than a false representation of it.

Here we can recall the discussion of antimetaphysical views presented earlier. The idea was that knowledge of the basic features or principles or facts of reality is impossible. The theory of knowledge here being discussed leads to that view. (The theory does not say that our beliefs could not be true, only that we can never prove them such.)

Another objection to transcendental subjectivism is that it leads to individual subjectivism. If all knowledge is determined according to the structure of our minds, our knowledge of this structure is also determined. What reason could any of us have for the claim that there are others with such a mind as our own? Our own minds condition what we know of human minds. If we cannot know about what things are but only about what they appear to be, then we could only know what the human mind appears to be. Thus, the supposed structure of the human mind would seem to be no more than the apparent structure of the human mind as it is conditioned by our own (individual) minds. How could we know anything more? It then would turn out that all we can know is that our own minds are structured in certain ways—or, more accurately, that my own mind has a certain structure, while the human mind (the minds we all have) merely appears to me in a way determined by my own particular mind.

Reply to Criticism. In answer to this last objection one would perhaps be able to argue as follows: In the appearance of things as I perceive them, I have evidence that supports the existence of beings that at least appear as I do. With this evidence (of things that appear to be similar) I can proceed to suggest other features these have in common. Then one could perhaps argue that, like me, these have a certain kind of mind, which, however, is limited by a structure.

Pragmatism

When related to epistemology—the study of knowledge, truth, belief —pragmatism is the systematic expression of a very common idea. It is said often enough that however nice or good some idea may be, it is useless unless it works. In other words, a true belief has to be workable; it must succeed in our practical endeavors. The central idea that distinguishes pragmatism from other views concerning what truth is (i.e., when it is fully justified for someone to consider what he believes as knowledge) pertains to the role of the practical consequences of one's ideas, beliefs, theories, etc.

There are, as with other positions, several versions of pragmatism. The philosophy is one of the few American "products" to this date in the history of this field, although its tenets can be traced to elements of Kant's philosophy, as well as others. For our purposes two versions of the pragmatic notion of knowledge will be considered.

In the first, any judgment is true if it achieves results that *satisfy* the person who made it in ways the judgment would have suggested it. If one believes, for instance, that someone is powerful and then if one acts on that belief and finds that these actions succeed—for example, the person actually demonstrates great strength by lifting or pushing things and otherwise showing power —one's belief is true. This version of pragmatism is concerned with personal satisfaction in how things turn out in relation to one's beliefs. Thus, a famous idea of the prominent pragmatist William James was that belief in the existence of God is true if living with it is satisfying to the individual who holds it. For the results of one's actions to be satisfactory is to have them turn out as one's belief would lead one to expect.

In the second version, more widely held among pragmatists, a judgment is true if it achieves results in practice that satisfy the expectations of society—or at least that part of it where a concern exists about the issue being judged. Thus, a scientific judgment is true when the community of scientists is satisfied with the practical consequences of the idea. (In an even more refined version, it is not necessary to have the current group of scientists be satisfied, so long as it is likely that in the future all the scientists will find the results of the practical application of the idea satisfying.) The pragmatic notion of truth—of when a belief constitutes knowledge— applies to all fields, not just to science. In art, politics, or ethics, as well as in ordinary commonsense concerns, it is the practical consequences of an idea that determine whether or not it is true.

One crucial aim of pragmatists is to divorce a concern with truth from a concern with absolute certainty. As pointed out when we outlined empiricism and rationalism, the model of knowledge to which many philosophers have tried to tailor their theories requires that whenever one knows something, one must be absolutely certain. Either the ultimate grounds or, more often, each instance of knowledge must meet this requirement in these other theories. This demanding standard has led to a streak of failures. Pragmatists argue that the only hope lies in rejecting the absolutism required of theories of knowledge. The evident changes in the history of human knowledge suggest that knowledge, truth, and the soundness of a (scientific) theory do not require a strict standard such as absolute certainty. What counts, instead, is short- or long-term practical applicability, that is, whether an idea, a belief, or a theory will work.

Of course, pragmatism is not some flimsy notion that any idea that is acted on is all right when those who act on it say so. In the numerous treatises written by pragmatists we find elaborate schemas by which we can establish whether an idea, a belief, or a theory does indeed work in practice. Nevertheless, despite the care many have devoted to making pragmatism a sophisticated theory of knowledge, the term *pragmatic* is often used to characterize a flimsy, crude regard for immediate payoffs or expediency. (Any theory can be cast into crude versions that make it appear completely false or even dangerous. Therefore, it is unwise to judge such theories by their caricatures in common discourse.)

Criticism of Pragmatism. One criticism of pragmatism is that the position appears to allow for either personal or social arbitrariness. One reason other theorists have always aimed at finding some absolutely fixed benchmark—innate ideas or sensory impressions, for example—is that such firm ground would serve as a reliable guide in inquiry. But if what we know need not be demonstrated by reference to some unshakable standard that will support a conclusive proof regardless of whether anyone is satisfied, then have we really obtained knowledge? Individuals can obviously be self-deluded about the practical applications of their beliefs. The worst ideas have had champions who went to their deaths proclaiming loyalty to what they believed, claiming it worked for them. Even large and influential groups can suffer from illusions, or persistent wishful thinking. For years certain types of programs to solve social problems have been supported in America. Monies were spent on these efforts that kept failing, yet millions of people, including academicians, members of Congress, and experts in various areas of government, refused to concede failure. Instead they blamed incompetence, lack of good will on the part of administrators, etc. as grounds for practical unworkability. So it seems that numerous ideas can satisfy large groups of people even after the practical applicability of these ideas showed results that seemed (by the few rebels or, perhaps, honest observers) to have gone astray. Even in science, there are periods when entire communities of scientists are deluded, with only a few stubborn mavericks opposing the trend, only to find in the last analysis that the loners were right. So for an idea to be satisfactory when applied (as judged by members of groups concerned) does not appear to yield reliable guidance to whether it is true.

In general—and these are only a few points of criticism—pragmatism rejects absolutism in all areas at the peril of ending without any objective guidelines to determining the truth of ideas, beliefs, and theories. Pragmatism appears to be more a theory of the social acceptance of ideas, not about how one must make sure that one's ideas, beliefs, or theories are correct. In its efforts to relax the unreasonably rigid standards in various areas of knowledge, pragmatism eliminates every possible area of certainty, even logic, metaphysics, and, worst of all, itself (as a possibly correct theory that does not depend on widespread satisfaction).

Reply to Criticism. The pragmatist will reply that what he considers knowledge is clearly distinguishable from hunches, opinions, and widely but carelessly accepted beliefs held by concerned groups. These are different from the carefully conceived ideas that have been verified in practical application by those who are not slipshod when testing ideas, theories, policy recommendations, etc. Once in a while a mistake lasts for a long time without anyone catching it, but even the critic must admit that it is only through practice that we come to realize that various social practices, governmental programs, personal habits simply do not work. In sensitive areas there is more difficulty in getting an honest report—too much vested interest lies in proposals that do not work, so that wishful thinking, even outright lying can subvert the methods pragmatism proposes. But from the fact of occasional failure it does not follow that we cannot rely on the pragmatic method when it is conscientiously carried out.

In addition, the pragmatist refuses to offer any fixed anchor to reality because he believes that it is a fraudulent offer, a guarantee that cannot be filled. He suggests, instead, that by following his advice to conduct meticulous tests of practical applicability with any important idea, belief, or theory, we have the best chance of staying in touch with reality, of reaching truth and knowledge.

Moreover, the pragmatist argues that he is perfectly willing to submit his own pragmatic theory to the tenets of his position. He is not threatened but encouraged by such a test, since that is, after all, how he came to hold his own position. Virtually any reasonable person follows the pragmatic principle. If ideas of child rearing, physical fitness, personal relations, or international peace are proposed, don't we test these ideas in practice and then weed out those which are unworkable? That is all that the pragmatist insists upon, so abuses notwithstanding, we should accept his position. There is no hope in the idle dream of a fixed, independent, absolute bottom line on which all our knowledge can rest without fear of challenge. The very idea of such a bottom line should be rejected by anyone who is concerned with progress, discovery, and a greater understanding of reality. As the first major pragmatist philosopher Charles S. Peirce noted, that kind of absolute principle would be a bar to expanding inquiry, a virtual censoring device.

Operationalism

This theory is somewhat more technical than pragmatism, although historically the two are closely related. To appreciate it, we must consider a new notion in this book, something we have not mentioned thus far.

It is evident that whatever human knowledge may be, it always involves ideas, general notions, or as philosophers often put it, **concepts.** These are variously thought of as mental entities or tools, the sort of things that human beings use in thinking—thus we sometimes hear of *the concept of motion, the concept of government, the concept of furniture,* etc. In thinking about a human being climbing up a mountain we use the concepts "human being," "climbing," "up," "a," and "mountain."

Thus far we have not discussed concepts, but the term itself could have been used when ideas or notions were mentioned, since these mean practically the same thing. All the theories of knowledge discussed in this book deal in one way or another with the nature of concepts—how to tell whether they are meaningful, how they are formed, what guides us in their formation, etc. Theories of knowledge attempt, in part, to identify how and why we can use concepts to learn about or organize the impressions we have of reality. Thus, we might know on some occasion that human beings are climbing up a mountain. How and why could this be known with the aid of the concepts we use (that are signified differently in languages other than our own but are essentially the same, barring some strange cases)?

As we saw, empiricism holds that ideas about the things around us are copies of certain sensory impressions we encounter; rationalism holds that concepts of things around us derive from certain basic insights; subjectivism suggests that they are produced by one's own or humanity's mind; and pragmatism proposes that concepts must always conform to successful or satisfying actions we have undertaken with their guidance. Briefly and very incompletely put, this is as far as we have gone.

With *operationalism* we must mention a certain special aspect of ideas, namely, their definitions. Sometimes a definition of an idea or concept (e.g., "love," "courage," "government") is required. Many people start books by defining their terms. The same is done in debates, arguments, and, especially, in legal documents (where a lot hinges on whether people share an understanding of the concepts used). Definitions commonly serve the purpose of setting the limits on (or specifying the range of) a concept's applicability. If *love* is defined as "admiration expressed intimately," then *only* when we find relationships involving these elements are we justified in identifying them as love. If *God* is defined as "perfect, all-knowing, all-powerful, all-benevolent being," then only upon finding an entity like that are we warranted in believing that (a) God exists. Of course, with different explanations of what concepts are and how we come to form them, we generally find different characterizations of definitions—that is, definitions are often defined differently! Some theories do not even distinguish between a concept (or idea) and a definition of it; others deny that definitions are possible to identify clearly (because, for example, some hold that there could be no limits on when to use a concept). There are also those who consider concepts and definitions a myth, holding that all we have are physical events (movements of the lips, writing on paper, sounds), but none of these dubious entities in the mind can (be shown to) exist.

In the doctrine called operationalism the emphasis is placed on definitions, although other theories deal with definitions too. Drawing a good deal from pragmatism and empiricism, but applied mostly to scientific knowledge and truth, this view holds the following: A word or an idea must be defined by reference to the operations we perform as we act on it. An *operational definition* is one that states the procedures (operations) carried out as we make use of the idea being defined. (When restricted to concepts—by those who do not differentiate between concepts and definitions—the same applies to concepts alone.)

For example, if *love* means "admiration with intimacy," then both admiration and intimacy, as well as their connection ("with"), would have to be something we find operating or occurring whenever love takes place. A simpler case is the definition of the concept *knife* as "hand-held and causing sharp separation when pressed against soft objects." Both "hand-held" and "causing sharp separation" are operations we can be involved in directly or indirectly. "Pressing against" and "soft object" can be further defined in terms of operations (e.g., "involving pushing" and "experiencing little resistance when pushed").

The ingredients of the definition are the operations we can perform on what is being thought of. Operationalism specifies that definitions which do not specify such operations, activities capable of being carried out on something, do not allow effective employment. Without referring to such operations, how could one ever specify a precise enough standard for the correct use of the terms being defined? There is no other, especially scientifically, more successful approach than what operationalism offers. This is one reason why many scientifically and technologically oriented individuals insist on operational definitions even out of their field of work. They are often rather impatient with humanists, people concerned with literature, poetry, music, or philosophy, because in these fields it seems that ideas are used without concrete operational meaning!

Criticism of Operationalism. A problem arises with the operationalist position in several fields, especially those just mentioned, as well as in the areas of social relations, politics, humor, etc. Here much more appears to be involved in the ideas that are used rather than the clearly tangible, measurable, concrete procedures of the physical sciences and technology. The method of isolating what is being considered—the important aspects of the subject matter of concern—does not seem to yield to measurement and detection, methods common in physics or horticulture. Such ideas as "harmony," "equality," "friendship," and "distrust" are quite meaningful without yielding to operational definitions. Certainly no strict specifications of physical operations or processes apply for purposes of understanding these ideas, when they can be used correctly, and when they do not apply. Furthermore, the ideas used to explain operationalism do not involve definitions that are themselves operational. Operationalism also seems to lead to the paradox that knives, friendships, international treaties, and whatever else exists amount to no more than our *own actions or behavior* involved in our awareness and treatment of those items. For example, it seems that only hand-holding, pressing against, and cutting exist; knife itself is not specified or indicated by the definition of *knife*.

Reply of Operationalist. Since the concepts cited are enormously difficult to define—indeed, there is no end to the haggles about what beauty, love, equality, justice, friendship, and similar sorts of things *really* are—we are well to give them up or to attempt to explain them in more manageable operational terms. When concepts such as "witch" and "demon" were invoked, those with power and authority could apply them to what they wished because there was no way to prove what they meant. We have finally given up such ideas, at least in serious discourse, and it is time that we start giving up others that present enormous, insurmountable difficulties.

As to finding operational definitions for ideas used in explaining operationalism, we will simply have to wait and see whether operationalism is capable of yielding certain operations that are clear and unambiguous. It is evident that operationally defined concepts are useful in the sciences and engineering. When matters take a more scientific, rigorous form in other areas of life, we may find operationalism vindicated by very specific operations.

Contextualism

Contextualism is proposed less frequently in philosophical circles than are other theories of knowledge. A number of philosophers have recently defined their views as contextualist. There are elements of pragmatism and operationalism in this view, but with significant differences. The position will now be considered.

Context means any portion of reality or some subject matter of belief and discourse that has bearing on some purpose or goal. For example, telling the truth applies in the context of communication. "Charge" means one thing when used in the context of a military operation, another in a court of law, and still another in a department store where credit cards can be used. Cross-examination occurs within the context of an adversary trial system; artificial respiration is used in the context of reviving someone; morality emerges in the context of facing the question, How should we live as human beings?

Contextualism proposes that it is crucial about knowledge that there are many different kinds and types of things that could be known. For a starter, common sense shows not only that such different things as tables, chairs, and desks exist, but that broader groupings such as physical objects, plants, and mental entities are necessary. True, chairs differ from tables, but both differ radically from plants or memories.

Contextualists argue that the criteria for having knowledge about these different types of things (or events, actions, aspects) of reality could vary enormously. What constitutes knowledge of a chair, knowledge of the nature of chairs, knowledge of furniture, knowledge of the human mind, and knowledge of mathematical theorems would differ in important respects. For example, introspective knowledge could be crucial for purposes of learning about one's feelings and memories but not useful for purposes of learning about one's cracked bones or acid indigestion. In contextualist theory it is regarded as possible to use mainly logic and extensive abstract thought for purposes of studying philosophy and obtaining philosophical knowledge; however, for learning about the weather such methods are not regarded as promising.

Broadly speaking, then, contextualism holds that in different areas of inquiry different standards of what could count as knowledge—including different methods of obtaining knowledge—may apply. Although some very general requirements unify all of what counts as knowledge, satisfying these general requirements does not by itself suffice for knowledge. It is true that when someone knows some fact of reality, the person had to have identified that fact correctly; this holds for all cases of knowledge. But what will count as "correct" depends upon the kind or type of thing about which knowledge is sought.

Empiricism appears to prejudge that all knowledge must come down to sense experience, whereas rationalism seems to prejudge that all knowledge must emerge from a process of derivation from first principles. Contextualism does not prejudge these things but leaves it open to discovery what will count as knowledge in different areas of inquiry. It is possible that some things in nature can be understood only by minute, detailed observation, other things by flawless deductive, formal reasoning, and still others by various combinations of these. True, when one knows something, it must be possible to prove it, but contextualism holds that the standards of proof can vary. That is one way to explain the existence of so many different fields of inquiry and the futility of trying to make all conform to one method. Contextualism has the additional virtue, it seems, that values—what is good, evil, right, or wrong— could also be known. Here, too, the subject matter could require very special ways of proving what one claims, but that is not grounds for disqualification under this theory of knowledge.

A point is due here on why contextualism is not, on its face, a form of pragmatism or even of relativism. The contextualist does not deny the possibility of absolute, unalterable truth or knowledge. That is an open issue. Perhaps in some areas of inquiry, attentive to certain aspects of reality, such knowledge is possible. All that is required is that we have identified reality correctly, and just what being correct amounts to will depend on the standards appropriate to the field in which we seek knowledge. A conclusive judgment or a proof that shows we are correct in one field may be different from that in another. It is the context of the inquiry and the aspects of reality at hand that will determine what counts as knowledge within that area, not some standard used elsewhere. Unlike relativism or pragmatism, contextualism holds that it is the facts of reality that determine the context as well as the standard of knowledge, not one's desires or background.

Objections to Contextualism. After this sketch of the contextualist position some objections will be worth raising. Does this view confuse knowledge with what we are justified in believing? Based on well-developed standards of demonstration in some domain we may believe something, for example, that a certain mineral can heal a person who has malaria. But some rare, idiosyncratic condition in that person could prevent the healing effect. Thus, while we have every reason to believe, we might nevertheless be wrong. Surely if knowing involves a correct identification of reality, then having a well-supported belief, given the standards of this field, does not suffice for knowledge when the belief is contradicted by reality.

Furthermore, the contextualist appears to undermine his own position. Perhaps the best-developed standard in epistemology supports the contextualist view. Is it therefore correct? Does it succeed in concluding something true about knowledge? That would depend on getting something better than a well-supported theory of knowledge—it would require a true theory, one which states what in fact knowledge is.

To this the contextualist would very likely reply that his central point has been missed. Well-developed standards of demonstration are just those in terms of which we can tell whether some belief is true. There is nowhere else to go to check. The supposition that we could have a judgment that is supported fully in terms of the highest standards in a field, and yet is wrong, is meaningless! "Wrong" would mean simply "not fully supported by reference to the highest standards." The challenge would make no sense. The ideas of true and false, right and wrong in what one claims, of correct and incorrect in one's identification of reality, do not work outside the contextualist framework. To pretend that they do is to invent a nonexistent, nonfunctional theory of knowledge to which a challenger has no (logical) right.

To the charge that the theory leaves open the possibility that the theory itself is wrong, the contextualist would say that this is quite true, but what of it? Any theory, being a product of human thought and research, *could* turn out to be wrong. But because of this possibility, *nothing follows* about the actual merits of the theory. Contextualism does not say that it can guarantee against the possibility of failure. Nothing can do that. It merely advances itself as the best theory, the one that most satisfactorily achieves standards we have a right to impose upon a theory of knowledge.

SKEPTICISM

Among the well-known problems that are handled within epistemology, the first one to be taken up here is also the most persistent.

In the history of human thought and philosophy, skeptics have always been given close attention. Few people endorse **skepticism** —the denial of the possibility of knowledge. But many take the view very seriously.

At first glance skepticism appears to be an impossible position, one that could not be true. It is perhaps true that very few people understand what knowledge is, and even that few of us know anything very well. But to deny that knowledge is possible would seem to go too far. How odd that someone asks us to accept as a fact something that makes it impossible for us to know any facts. Is the possibility of knowledge not just what supports our confidence in some people who may wish to have us accept what they claim? But if none can have knowledge, why would we accept what anyone says; why would we treat it as if we could be confident that it is true? More simply put, if it is a fact that we cannot know facts, knowing this would be knowing at least one fact. And then why not more? And more?

In fact, skepticism is usually put forth to show that a certain way of conceiving of knowledge will not work. Thus, any one of the theories discussed before might be criticized by showing that *it* leads to the impossibility of knowledge. Furthermore, the skeptics generally assume some very demanding, ideal standard that any theory of knowledge must satisfy—a basic model of what knowledge must be—and show that it is not satisfied in many instances when a theory allows that we know something. Thus, what appears at first to be a good account of knowledge comes to nothing in the end.

Some skeptics, however, go much farther. They argue not just against some theory of knowledge but for the general view that knowledge is impossible. When their point is resisted in the ways outlined earlier, they respond with a complex approach. The sophisticated skeptic holds that although we may know some things, we cannot know that we ever do know something. So we can never tell whether what we have is knowledge, although it may be. When a person believes and says that there is a book on the table over there, he may be saying something that is true but he will never be able to determine whether what he says is true. To put this in a different way, the sophisticated skeptic holds that we can never apply the concept *knowledge* with confidence, with rational justification, even though sometimes we might have such justification without being able to identify it.

Perhaps by this time the reader will think that this skepticism issue must be an mere academic exercise. Surely only crazy philosopher-types would go to such lengths worrying about the matter. Surely we know well enough many things we need to deal with, so why all the fuss? Those things about which we are doubtful—well, those we will worry about. But why go to such extremes?

Yet in the lives of many of us there are moments when doubt seems more than a mere mundane affair. Once in a while we can practically feel the force of doubt through our bones. We seem unable to find a fixed point that can give support to us and to our beliefs, ideas, and ideals. Since such feelings are unique to each individual, it is difficult to convey the sense of these moments here. However, a little reflection should enable any reader to imagine going through such a trying moment.

The skeptic takes that moment very seriously and wonders if it is not really the true, permanent condition of life. Of course, we act as if we could know, as if we did in fact know on various occasions. But we often act as if we could do something, or even pretend to do it, when we cannot and do not. Perhaps we behave this way about knowledge. Some philosophers will defend that such is our general condition. What we can do is accept the fact and realize that we face a bottomless pit of uncertainty. Some philosophers deny that we could even have probable knowledge. How serious they are about this one cannot tell without knowing them better. But they do write as if they were serious, and when we read what they say we should probably take their purpose seriously.

But here a problem arises. When, in a book or an article, a philosopher wants to explain to us that we cannot know anything or even believe anything for better reasons than we might have for believing something else, it is difficult to read on. What could one learn from such a book? If the skeptic is correct, we can learn nothing. Learning is impossible. If the skeptic is wrong, well then, why not go on to more fruitful endeavors?

The answer here could be that it helps to know the best objections to the prospect of reaching one of our most important goals. It helps to know what some careful philosopher has to say against the prospects of obtaining knowledge. This will put us on our guard against overconfidence and carelessness. It should make little difference in one's philosophical education what motivates someone to develop a powerful argument for or against some position, however much one might be justified in wondering about that when the problems themselves—in this case, the problem of how best to demonstrate knowledge—are no longer the focus of attention. Practically every idea that has been advanced by human beings has had some philosopher give it a full run for its money. Granted, of course, that ideas have consequences and some bad ones have very bad consequences. As philosophers it is important to omit that from consideration for a while and inspect the idea for its possible merits. Then, after such an exploration, we can mount our opposition.

Skepticism is an idea that can lead to drastic lapses of human confidence. It can lead entire nations to turn to mythical sources of salvation, promised by some divinely inspired leader, and to abandon control over life and country to service of this figure. But it can also produce careful reflection, caution, patience, and the realization that in many instances knowledge is very difficult to obtain, even though it is not impossible.

One of the reasons skeptics have had so much persuasive power is that many philosophers have been absolutists and have set too high (impossible) standards for what knowledge would have to be. To appreciate the skeptic's position, we will benefit from discussing absolutism.

Absolutism versus Skepticism

Absolutism is one road to skepticism. People are called absolutists if they believe that what they claim to be true holds for all times and places, independently of their circumstances, their way of thinking, their use of the ideas needed to express their beliefs. An absolute truth must hold true, unrevised, forever.

It is of no concern here whether any statement one could make may or may not be true absolutely, in the sense just characterized. Even if some such statement could be made, the trouble arises when one says that all true statements have to be true in this sense, absolutely.

The point may be understood better by considering scientific statements. Certainly many of them are offered as true ones. Even when a scientist's research and inquiries lead him or her to assert a claim as only probably true, others sometimes hold it up as the

absolute truth.   At times, scientists themselves will go on to proclaim their discoveries as absolute truth.

But when scientists start talking about what makes statements
true, they are no longer speaking as scientists.   This is important.
When they explain what supports their statements, what demonstrates the facts they put forth, then they work as scientists.   However, when they start discussing what makes a statement a true one
in general, they are not unlike most of us, relying on common sense
or on prominent and widely accepted philosophical positions about
truth, knowledge, and the like.

There have always been thinkers who have argued that they
have achieved the goal of stating absolute truths.   Perhaps few
serious scientists have said this, but not all famous scientists are
always serious.   Outside of science, for example, in religion (as
when the Pope speaks for the Roman Catholic Church) or in art,
absolute truths are often attempted.

In the face of such claims of being able to produce absolute
truths, especially when they have been derived from revelation,
papal authority, or mystical insight, critics have tended to go the
opposite direction and deny that truth itself is ever possible.   Thus,
even when people no longer characterize truth in absolutist terms
but accept that what is a true statement today may have to be updated or modified tomorrow in the light of better knowledge, there
are those who insist that no truth is possible.

There have always been theories of knowledge that have held
that what people know must be *absolutely* true in order to qualify
as knowledge.   According to these theories we rarely ever *know*
any scientific conclusions.   All we can obtain are probable judgments, estimates, and approximations.   Because the subject matter
of the sciences (e.g., atoms, planets, plants, people) undergoes rapid
and frequent changes, there really are only very few topics about
which knowledge is possible.   But with the aid of a few absolute,
stable truths we can generate a good deal that science by itself
would not be capable of providing.

The model of absolute truth has usually been the type of
knowledge achieved in mathematics, geometry, and formal logic. In
these fields demonstrations and definitions are precise, clean, and
unperturbed by the confusion of concrete reality.   These abstract
sciences offer absolute truth, or so the story would have it.   Some
philosophers have held that without obtaining this kind of knowl-

edge in all fields, knowledge is impossible there. Skepticism is in full agreement with this view, except that it takes it further by arguing that not even in the abstract fields is knowledge of reality possible. At best here we have knowledge of stipulated ideas and how they relate to each other. For example, if we define "2" as a certain number, and "4" as another number, then when "+" is also defined by us, "2 + 4" will mean something quite precise. After we define "=" and "6," we can say "2 + 4 = 6" and be quite precise, but only because we have made up definitions with which we could, of course, do whatever we pleased. After we have made up these definitions, it seems as if these fields produce absolute truth. But there is nothing we can learn with these truths that we did not ourselves invent. In short, absolute truth about reality is impossible, after all.

Since many theories of knowledge have promised this kind of truth, skepticism has served as a powerful debunker of pretentions. For example, both empiricism and rationalism seem to demand that knowledge produce such absolute truths. The empiricist, it will be recalled, hopes that sensory impressions will qualify, while the rationalist thinks that pure, clear, precise ideas will achieve that goal. When the skeptic shows that neither is possible, that neither yields (absolute) knowledge of reality, it appears that skepticism is correct and knowledge is quite impossible to us.

Mitigated Skepticism

There are those who reject both the extreme skeptic's and the absolutist's positions and opt for mitigated skepticism: We may not know anything for certain, but we can have cautious confidence in many of our judgments. Thus, although I could never know that I left my car at the garage to be fixed, it is not wrong that I have good enough reasons for believing that I did.

The earliest version of this variety of skepticism is called probabilism. This term signified that although we could not obtain conclusive knowledge of reality, we could obtain estimates of probability, of what will probably be so and so, what is probably the case, and the like. As mentioned earlier, some scientists insist that this is all that their efforts can produce. In ordinary circumstances we often admit to having only an adequate estimate of what is going on, rather than the full truth of the matter. My having left my car at the garage this afternoon is not indisputable, since I might have dreamed the whole thing. It cannot be established beyond a shadow of doubt that I did leave my car there. Yet, there are good reasons to accept that I did so: I remember it clearly, it isn't in my garage now, my keys are not with me, etc. But this gives us only the probability that I left my car at the garage to be fixed.

The mitigated skeptic's view has problems. One function of the term *probable* is to distinguish beliefs that have at least *some* degree of support in their behalf from beliefs that have *none* and those that are *fully* supported, confirmed, and certain. Mitigated skepticism destroys the validity of this distinction. Nor does it explain the standing of the grounds for probable judgment. Are they, too, merely probable?

If this is so, then the radical, strict skeptics have their way. Their view is that not just knowledge but also *well-founded* beliefs are impossible. If the well-founded beliefs can only have other well-founded beliefs that never connect up with some firmly founded beliefs, why consider these well-founded in the first place? If all I have is hazy memories about where I left my car, and hazy memories about whether I have a car, and hazy memories about what a car is, and so on about everything, I simply have no well-founded beliefs at all. With one or two hazy points I would not be in very bad shape. With all of them hazy, however, there is little hope, if any. Similarly, if *all* my beliefs are only probably true, then it is quite doubtful that I am entitled to have confidence in any of them, even in their probability. In the end I must admit that I know nothing and have no good reason to believe anything. This is exactly what the pure skeptic believes!

Some other types of beliefs about knowledge appear to invite skepticism, of course. We have seen that absolutism appears to invite the skeptic's wrath. There is another position, often heard of in nonphilosophical circles, which appears to run into skeptical problems once fully analyzed. The idea that everything is relative is often heard from people. It usually means something akin to "What you and I believe and take for granted is really nothing more than a colored perspective, something we have been conditioned to believe by our circumstances." There is a fairly cohesive theory of human understanding and knowledge that is called *relativism.*

Relativism

The term *relative* is used often in in discourse, mostly with little philosophical significance. We know of relatives we or others may have, for example, and know that they are called "relatives" because they have a special relationship to the person in question, certain ties others lack. The nonphilosophical idea used in the above context is useful for purposes of understanding what is meant by epistemological **relativism,** that is, the doctrine that knowledge must be *relative to* the knower in some specified way.

Relativism is the broad view that knowledge is always something that stands in a significant relationship to features of the knowing person or group. More specifically, the idea is that when we know something, we must know it *as* it relates to certain conditions that are involved in knowing, that is, certain features of the knowing mind or situation. Transcendental subjectivism may be considered a form of relativism because knowledge is thought to be firmly related to the permanent, fixed, unchanging conditions of human awareness. In relativism as such, with no reference to its origin, the conditions involved are not specified. Thus, varieties of relativism exist and there are relativist views not just in epistemology but also in ethics, politics, and aesthetics. (Sometimes advocates of relativism are also determinists, that is, those who hold that human beings do not have freedom of choice. As such, they hold that because they determine our knowledge, knowledge is relative to certain conditions. Many theories presented in the various areas of philosophy and other fields are not always different in all respects —there are many overlaps!)

Relativism tends to appear odd when considered from the point of view of common sense. We act as if the position were false because we take it that the facts we know are what they are and are not usually influenced by our knowing them. We are aware of something being the case, but whatever is the case is not a function of our being aware of it.

In other words, when Harry's mother is ill and Harry knows

this, we ordinarily accept that Harry's knowing that his mother is ill has no influence on that fact. Oddly enough, relativism requires that we view the situation *very* differently: When Harry knows that his mother is ill, his knowing this fact is supposed to be influential on the character of what he knows. His processes of knowledge are determined by various factors such as his nationality, ethnic origin, genetic makeup, and economic circumstances. What we would think are facts with an independent status are really conditioned and influenced by his processes of knowledge. This is sometimes expressed by saying that Harry's mother's illness is a fact *to* Harry—or that the methods of medicine used by witch-doctors are right *for* those who accept witch-doctoring.

Relativism is best recognized in reflecting on situations in which people say that someone believes in something because he comes from a certain culture, and what he believes is true *for* him. The expression "It is true for you but not for me" states the result of this position reasonably accurately. The result is explained by reference to people's different backgrounds or other factors.

Often it is argued that people with different backgrounds must perceive or know the world differently (rendering the world itself different to different people) because of influences exerted upon them by various unique forces and situations. For example, it is sometimes argued that essentially conflicting beliefs about what will cure certain ailments could be equally correct—as when medical science in the United States conflicts with "primitive" medicine practiced in some parts of Africa. The processes of identifying what will cure an illness differ because of different circumstances, and the facts, though quite possibly contradictory, as to what will cure the illness will also be different.

While even saying this seems very odd—how could two facts both obtain even though fact A is a denial of fact B?—both ordinary ways of discussing such matters and some philosophical approaches to the issue advance the relativist position. There are even philosophers of science who argue that different scientists are influenced by different factors (preferences, background, aesthetic tastes, etc.) and these influences can determine the theories they will accept as true. Thus, the facts identified within the frameworks of such different theories can conflict with each other. For example, within certain theories of physics it is possible to travel faster than the speed of light, while within other theories it is not.

Ordinarily, relativism is suggested on grounds that languages of different cultures vary greatly, or that many value systems are treated as equally valid by different people at the same time. Not all these doctrines emphasize cultural differences. Some hold that sexual, racial, and economic factors are of crucial importance. The number of factors to which one's knowledge could be relative is probably infinite within the framework of relativism.

Objections to Relativism. The problem of self-reference always faces a position such as relativism. If what we know must be relative to certain factors about us which we cannot control, our "knowledge" that knowledge must be relative must also be relative. (Relativism, as knowledge about knowledge, is then said by some to apply only for some people, not necessarily for all. Without this admission, which would reject universal relativism, it is not clear whether the truth of relativism can be articulated from within the position itself.) Does relativism accurately state the facts about human knowledge? The position denies that anything could be known about that. All we could have is a piece of "knowledge" that was forced upon us by conditions we cannot control or escape.

Furthermore, if we take the position to be true, we end up with a result that is even more difficult to imagine as sound. If the theory is true, then it is highly doubtful that we are right to regard anything we believe, prove, and demonstrate as knowledge. It would do grave violence to common sense to regard something as knowledge that excludes the possibility of objectivity and of a standard binding on all who claim to know. In short, if my knowledge that it is evening is compatible with your knowledge that it is morning (when we are together talking about the time of day), then our idea of knowledge allows every claim, even diametrically opposed ones, even the most absurd, to qualify as knowledge. Though such examples are not usually used by relativists, they are not essentially different from the supposition that a primitive tribesman's knowledge that some stone is a divine being and my knowledge that it is nothing but a colorful rock are both valid. And if both are truly knowledge, then the concept of knowledge is useless for purposes of distinguishing certain kinds of things in reality from others, for example, mistakes, errors, and myths. Difficulties such as these lead to the conclusion that relativism in a theory of knowl-

edge is impossible and that such theories must lead to skepticism—
the view that knowledge is impossible to us.

Pure (Dogmatic) Skepticism

If absolutism is the pipedream of some theorists concerning knowledge, pure skepticism is the stubborn resistance of some to any
promise of a theory of knowledge. This kind of skeptic minces no
words on probable truth or the like. He flatly denies that knowledge is possible. He points to the hopeless attempts of mitigated
skeptics. (This, for him, includes various types of subjectivists,
relativists, and pragmatists, all of whom merely try to erect inadequate substitutes where a pipedream has been put to shambles.)
He argues that we have no support for the reliability of any of our
beliefs. He points to the widescale disagreements that permeate the
history of human thought and to the constant changes in science,
ethics, politics, and, most of all, in philosophy. He sees failure
everywhere. He tells us that instead of rejecting the ideal goals of
knowledge, we should simply admit that those are the appropriate
goals, but unreachable by us. To God or to some infinite being,
one that could be everywhere and everyone at once, knowledge
might be possible. Such a being could avoid error and succeed at
certainty. But for us, we should realize our limitations, since this
will, perhaps, lead to good. (Perhaps intolerance, piety, vanity, and
conceit will be reduced when we all acknowledge that we cannot
obtain knowledge of reality.)

This skeptic is rarely a constructive theorist himself, except in
cases where he is asked what might be done once the possibility of
knowledge is rejected. Then he may discuss whether we should
trust great leaders, the social customs, our instincts, our intuitions,
or whatnot. But these are not epistemological theories. They are
mostly psychological and sociological recommendations about how
to cope without the prospect of ever knowing reality.

However, there is one clear sense in which the skeptic is (im-
plicitly) a theorist. He has a theory about the human mind and a
theory about reality. Concerning the former he theorizes that we
cannot correctly identify reality and concerning the latter he
theorizes that it cannot be known by the human mind. The full-
blown skeptic, then, is a theorist. This is where his troubles begin.

The Skeptic Trapped?   As a theorist the skeptic asks us to regard some of his conclusions as true.   Certainly he wants to have us accept them, judging by the fact that he argues for them in books and philosophical articles.   He tells us, perhaps without saying so directly (but that is not always necessary), that he has learned something about human beings and reality.   *He knows!*   The human mind cannot identify reality; reality is unidentifiable.   The question is: why should we accept these views when accepting them would, at once, amount to rejecting them, also?   If accepted, with justification, as not just a likely story but a true one, then these claims would pose as knowledge about reality.   Moreover, the two claims would conflict: if we can know something about the human mind, then we can know something about reality.   At least we can know about one feature of reality.   But then why give up on trying for more?   This is the problem faced by the skeptical positions considered above, also.

Finally, the pure skeptic must cope with another problem, assuming that he is interested in solving those that are naturally developed from within his views.   By denying that knowledge of reality is possible, the skeptic also denies that we can know the basic principles of reality, that is, metaphysical facts.   If, however, metaphysical facts or principles, whatever they are, provide the standards for judging whether some hypothetical phenomenon, event, or activity exists, then the skeptic has robbed us of the very prospect of proving that knowledge exists.   While he appears to be waiting for us to come up with a proof for the existence of knowledge, he is actually dogmatically clinging to the impossibility of knowledge, by denying that such a proof is possible.   In short, the skeptic does not simply deny the possibility of knowledge; he denies the possibility of demonstrating or proving the existence of knowledge.

By this move the skeptic loses the opportunity to fault some proof of the existence of knowledge. He lacks the standards for criticizing such a proof.   The skeptic seems to be in a much worse position than someone who does not deny the possibility of knowledge but simply fails to see the value of a demonstration of knowledge.   The skeptic cannot, by his own doctrine, reject a proof for the existence of knowledge because, according to his own beliefs, no standards for rejecting or accepting anything could exist.   To put the matter even more bluntly, the skeptic holds that he cannot know what knowledge is and he therefore cannot know what he is talking about.   He could not, by his own position, recognize an adequate theory of knowledge.

The Skeptic Replies.   Most skeptics would probably answer the above line of criticism by drawing certain distinctions.   Simply put, skeptical claims about knowledge cannot be understood as claims about some real entity or event like the human mind or the world. Instead skepticism pertains to an idea and concerns whether this idea can be made meaningful and applicable to anything.   This, then, is a matter of knowing something not about reality but about ideas.   The skeptic will invoke the distinction (discussed earlier) involving analytic and synthetic judgments.   When skeptics deny the possibility of knowledge, they are making an analytic a priori judgment; by the attempt to analyze the idea of knowledge, skeptics have discovered that it is inapplicable to anything and incapable of being used.   Thus they have discovered, by way of analysis, that knowledge is impossible—something akin to discovering that square circles are impossible.

Returning the Fire.   This reply has its own problems, however, and critics have pointed them out.   We might just note that invoking a distinction developed from a complicated philosophical system is very risky for a skeptic.   Such a philosophical system requires for its foundation some premises that are known to be true. Only if this foundation exists could the system be considered sound and its results be utilized in defending some conclusion.   But on skeptical grounds no such foundations for the system could be identified, so the conclusions of the system are not available for use to skeptics.

History and Skepticism

Another viewpoint that both philosophers and laymen give voice to is called **historicism.**   It is a viewpoint that gives strong support to skepticism about human knowledge.

The idea is that knowledge is relative to the historical period in which it is obtained and held.   (Note that not just the statement of what one knows is colored by the influences of one's special situation but whatever is known is itself supposed to be subject to such coloration.) Historicism is a version of relativism, one which has recently acquired considerable significance.   Several well-known theories about humanity and its relationship to reality can be considered historicist.   Among them the most famous is Marxism, which is often called historical materialism or **dialectical materialism** (where "dialectical" indicates that what happens is determined by specific movements throughout history).   Another well-known historicist theory emerges within the philosophy of science.   This view argues that scientific theories are sound or correct relative to certain historical circumstances.

Most generally, historicism is the view that what we know is valid for the historical period within which we live.   The world itself is different in one historical period as opposed to the other—not just in the obvious sense that things will have changed but in the more radical sense that the nature of things, the nature of reality itself, *must* change.   Historicism is not the view that reality is basically stable but our knowledge of it grows.   It is instead the view that what we know—our knowledge *and* the subject matter of it—is indistinguishable from the circumstances of knowing something.   Since the latter is under the influence of the times in which we live—our way of thinking is influenced by our education, the subtleties of language currently in usage, and so forth—the former, reality itself, is also influenced accordingly.

To get this point quite right, let me reiterate that historicism is not the common idea that there are changes in the world and in our knowledge of it.   Instead, by its tenets the principles and laws that govern nature, those that philosophers and scientists aim to identify, actually differ from one historical period to another.   Other viewpoints admit that our *statements* of these laws will differ in different historical periods, or that we will have *learned more* about reality (and so can identify it better) as history progresses.   Historicism makes a different point.

One way to appreciate the importance of the historicist position is by considering a possible instance of it as it applies to ethics.   It is sometimes argued that whereas slavery is an obvious evil today, when it was practiced in earlier times it was perfectly acceptable.   Here the idea is that the practices that people should respect and observe change from one historical period to another.

Concerning knowledge the situation is not very different. We could take the case of slavery to illustrate the point. Should someone have said that slavery is wrong, it could not have been "knowledge" in an earlier historical period, whereas in our time it could be that it is something that someone *knows*. The point is that what is knowledge is determined by the historical situation.

In science the position applies as follows. One might argue that when Aristotle proposed his theory of motion, he could very well have been quite right about the topic, even though later, when others proposed radically different theories of motion, his theories no longer could be considered correct. Newtonian physics could have been absolutely right for Newton's own times but today it is Einstein's view of the universe that describes what is our world. Not just theory, but also the world has changed.

Historicism maintains that this is the case about everything and anything. Other theorists may accept the view that some claims considered most sensible in an earlier era can no longer be viewed as the best idea on a topic, without saying that this must be so with respect to anything of concern to us. Historicism is the view that anything that could qualify as knowledge must be subject to the forces of history. And always the latest stage gives rise to valid knowledge.

Different versions of historicism are often distinguished by reference to (among other things) the way in which the changes occur in what we know. For some the changes in knowledge must be gradual, that is, evolutionary; for others it must be drastic, or revolutionary; yet others argue that it is random. But this element of the doctrine is not central for our purposes. It simply points out the fact that there are many varieties of historicism, often heard of in casual conversation. We often hear talk of revolutionary changes in knowledge, references to how the laws that govern human psychology today are different from those that held true in another epoch, the different values necessary to accept in ethics, aesthetics, and politics, and changes in the principles of economics, international relations, communication, and so forth. Talk of this sort comes close to giving expression to versions of historicism, although not all who accept the possibility of radical changes in what we know would accept the possibility of radical changes in *all* of what we know.

Criticism of Historicism. When we consider criticisms of historicism we find that the most forceful charge is that it leads directly to skepticism. Based on what we would take to be a good commonsensical notion of knowledge, historicism seems clearly to fall short of satisfying the most rudimentary requirements of what knowledge has to be. Such requirements include that at least some of what we know, perhaps the standards of what counts as knowledge in various fields, or perhaps the basic statements of reality that limit the possibility of what *can* be true of reality, remain unchanging. Unless some common, objective standards that do not change can be identified, it is difficult to see what makes some claim, including possibly historicism, knowledge. Assuming that a system is accepted in some historical period, and assuming that in that system some statements are well supported—we can still ask whether the system itself deserves to be accepted, whether it is the right system for purposes of correctly identifying the feature or portion of reality with which some field is concerned. In other words, an entire system of thought, not just individual claims that fit within such a system, can be subjected to the question, Is it correct, is it sound? If so, historicism cannot answer this inquiry either affirmatively or negatively. According to historicism, some elements of a way of perceiving and dealing with the world are historically determined, changeable but beyond rational challenge. Systems from different eras cannot be judged by us, who are determined by our own historical circumstances.

It appears, then, that historicism is a denial of the possibility of knowledge as we understand it in common sense—knowledge that rightly states, describes, and identifies the facts of reality. This undermines the truth of historicism, for if the historicist position is true, then there is at least one system of thought that is true independently of historical circumstances, namely, historicism; so it must not be true.

Historicist Replies. To these objections very often historicists will grant the point and simply hold that at least historicism might be true, whether we could ever know it or not. By this move historicism admits to the charge of skepticism. It therefore belongs among those theories of human knowledge and understanding that lead to skepticism, though this may not disturb the historicist at all.

Skepticism: Concluding Remarks

We have now considered skeptical arguments as well as varieties of theories of knowledge that seem clearly to lead to skepticism. As a matter of fact, one of the major strengths of skepticism has been that so many theories of knowledge seem to lead to it. In short, in the effort to explain what knowledge is and how we might obtain it, philosophers have tended to propose ideas that have allowed others to show that these ideas would render knowledge impossible. If we were to accept the view of knowledge proposed by these theorists, we would have to conclude that knowledge is impossible for us to obtain.

In justice the skeptic should abstain from concluding that knowledge is impossible. He could, however, conclude that knowledge as proposed by the various theorists he has considered is impossible. When he advances to argue that knowledge is impossible, he runs into difficulties. He is faced with the problems we have cited earlier. He robs himself of the tools needed to make out his case because he rejects that anything could be known, including what would make his argument a good one. As soon as he declares knowledge to be impossible, his subsequent remarks are difficult to consider. If we take him seriously, we will stop reading what he has to offer since we know that it could not be knowledge—at least we have no way of ever learning whether what he says is true or not. If we do not take him seriously, then we have two alternatives: either we can read on and hope that he will point out some areas of difficulty in our idea of knowledge, even if he is overstating his case, or we can dismiss him and turn to constructive theorists in the hope of arriving at a sound understanding of such matters as the nature of knowledge.

Many people have argued that skepticism is nothing more than an antidote to human pride. The skeptic aims only to warn us about getting too complacent and too arrogant about our achievements so far. He wants to point to our weaknesses or failings so that we do not go too far with our achievements.

It is possible that some people require this kind of subtle warning about how far they should go with what they have achieved. It is possible that occasional cautionary remarks are good for all of us, once in a while. Yet there is an element of self-righteousness in a skeptic who takes himself to be our guardian angel, the person who believes that his warnings are needed to put humanity in its place. Many skeptics are not at all interested in such crusadings. They are quite convinced of and mean what they say, or at least wish to say something true and important when they claim that we cannot know anything. When we appreciate that knowledge has often been understood as a kind of absolute, final certainty in need of no improvement, and that those who thought they knew or actually did know some things have often believed that they were thus entitled to force the rest of us to comply—then we can appreciate that the skeptics had more in mind than sanctimonious warnings.

The importance of the issue of skepticism cannot be overestimated. It may be argued quite convincingly that it is the most important question about our relationship to the world: can we know that world, can we be right about reality—or must we consign ourselves to groping in the dark, with no serious prospects of ever achieving what seems clearly to be our greatest need, self-understanding and understanding the world?

We have not covered the issue of skepticism in its many technical details. But from the foregoing discussion one can appreciate its philosophical and general import, as well as its intricacies. We will close the discussion of skepticism at this point, although much more could be said.

TOPICS IN EPISTEMOLOGY—
ANCIENT AND RECENT

Aside from the various more or less complete theories of knowledge, it will be helpful now to look at some of the specialized issues in epistemology. These will not be elaborated upon beyond making the issue clear so that newcomers to philosophy will have an idea of what the numerous specialists attend to. As in other fields, in philosophy there are problems of various scope and depth. The topics considered here will indicate what kinds of discussions occur at more technical levels of inquiry.

Definitions

When we ask for a **definition,** as we do quite often in ordinary and technical endeavors, what is it that we are asking for? Perhaps the best-known figure in the history of philosophy introduced this issue as central to his philosophy: Socrates spent a great deal of time inquiring into the definitions of various concepts, and he proceeded to ask, also, what exactly it is to offer a definition. To this day the problem of definitions is prominent among philosophers. Nowadays the question may be put somewhat differently. For example, some would ask: "What is the criterion for employing the word 'mind' or 'pain' or 'understanding'?" Others ask: "What are the necessary and sufficient conditions for the correct use of the concept 'law' or 'love' or 'alive'?" Yet others inquire into the nature of knowledge, justice, and government and have pretty much the same issue at hand. The nuances involved in distinguishing the precise meaning of these questions and problems can be very important, but in each case the inquiry belongs in the same ball park.

What then is the problem of definitions? One way to get an idea of it is to recall that we have encountered elements of the problem at earlier junctures throughout this book. In several places we have asked questions about the nature of knowledge, for example. We also use the phrases "the *nature* of logic" and "the essence of art." In these cases we are concerned with the issue that at least several theories take definitions to refer to. For example, when we discussed idealism in chapter 2, I started by noting that according to that theory it is more likely possible to know the nature or essence of a chair than any particular chair that we might come across. The general idea here is that while there are admittedly many thousands of chairs, and there have been millions of others since people started to make them, there might be just one essential chair; that is, the nature of a chair might be just one thing, whatever it is. (In idealism it is identified as an idea or a form; in other theories the possibility of definitions may be denied or they may be conceived of very differently. But most theories say something about the issue.)

A definition is a judgment or, when articulated, a statement that we use to identify the nature or essence of something. The nature or essence of something is, in turn, some set of properties, qualities, forms, or whatever that unites that something with others of its kind. The nature of a chair is what "makes something" a chair—not the carpenter, of course, but those features or attributes of chairs by virtue of which they are chairs and not something other than chairs.

There are philosophers who believe that each item in nature contains within it its essence, or nature, so that, for instance, underlying each chair or tree or government there is its essential nature, which it shares with others of its kind. The individual items are very different, of course. One need but think of the many varieties of chairs, trees, and governments, and the fact that each individual of these is itself quite unique by virtue of its different location in time and space. But all are *what* they are because, supposedly, they share each other's nature or essence. And definitions are the judgments or statements that identify that nature or essence.

This should not be very difficult to appreciate, since all of us ask for definitions now and then. We ask: "What is a crocodile?" "What is tort in the law?" "What is an electron?" "What is philosophy?" Here we are not asking that someone show us each instance of these items. We want a sort of summary, a statement of what something is essentially, in its crucial respects—what makes these what they are.

Other theories of definition hold that it is a general idea or image that has developed in our minds in consequence of having encountered many things with similar features. After having had these repeated encounters, we find ourselves with these ideas, these lingering images that we state when we define what something is.

When some theorists speak of the criterion for using a concept, they refer to what clues one must keep in mind so that the concept is correctly employed in thinking about various things. These clues are the essential aspects of what is to be thought of.

The necessary and sufficient conditions for using some word are those conditions that make what we are saying applicable in successful ways—mainly because the thing for which the word stands or is used in discourse conforms to those conditions. If those conditions obtain, then we have indeed found such a thing, we have found what it is essentially.

These are quick characterizations, and sometimes powerful reasons are put forth to argue that talk of definitions, essence, nature, and the like might better be avoided. But in each case the problem of definitions is being attended to. In each theory of knowledge some views are offered that bear on the problem of definition, even if only in a destructive way, for example, so that the possibility of ever stating or finding the essence of something is ruled out.

It is also helpful to keep in mind that when we consider definitions, we take the epistemological view of the issue, but when we consider essences or natures we could be making a metaphysical point. Sometimes it is argued that the essence of something is an independent entity, just as the particular thing is, in other words, that the nature of something is itself a thing, even separable from the particular items the nature of which it is. But other times we could be facing a theory that argues that the definition or nature or essence of something is epistemological—a result of our own activity of distinguishing various things from each other on the basis of sensible qualities they may share, purposes they may have in common, or even their origins. The definition of the concept "triangle" could be a statement of what shape some things have in common; the essence of a chair could be identified by reference to the purpose it serves in human life; and the nature of government may have to be identified by reference to what gives rise to it in society.

A short treatment may give the impression of minor significance. Definitions are of no small import in our lives. As one theorist put it, they offer us the inestimable advantage of knowing what we are talking about.

Truth and Knowledge

Truth is not the same as knowledge, although the two are closely related. This is obvious from a mere cursory reflection.

If some statement expresses what a person knows, then it is a true statement. But a statement could be true even when the person who makes it does not know what is being asserted. Thus, Johnny may know that his mother is ill, and his statement "My mother is ill" would be a true one. Johnny may not know (but simply guess) that his mother is ill, and yet when he states, "My mother is ill," it could well be that he is making a true statement.

A statement can be true even if the person who utters it does not know the fact or whatever else in question is being expressed by it. Someone else could know that Johnny's mother is ill and thus could identify the statement made by Johnny as quite true. Truth is necessary for knowledge of the fact stated, but knowledge is not necessary for stating something true. (It has also been argued that at least someone must know that Johnny's mother is ill for that statement to be capable of being true. Some have even argued that the idea that a statement is true is without clear meaning when no one could possibly know it as such.)

The distinction between truth and knowledge can be of importance when we want to understand the difference between what we say and what is on our minds without saying anything. Language, which is the means by which true statements can be produced by us, is not the same as the knowledge we have that language helps us to express. It is also likely that without language, which makes thinking and communication so much easier by virtue of its economy, knowledge itself would not extend very far—beyond the most simple facts we can be aware of. Some of our ideas are very complicated, but language seems to make it possible for us to think by using these ideas because we can have a kind of shorthand way of considering them. Despite all this, however, knowledge and truth are distinguishable.

Facts and Knowledge

There is considerable debate about the nature of facts. Some say facts are indistinguishable from true statements; some say that knowledge itself consists of facts; and yet others hold that facts are what is independent of anyone's knowing anything or having said anything that is true. This last idea seems to be correct, although there will not be space here to defend it in full.

The idea is that facts are what the world consists of. That the sun is a certain kind of entity, whatever it is, and that it has had a certain history, whatever it has been, would be *facts* of reality whether anyone could ever know of them or not. The knowledge of these facts is a different matter entirely. What knowledge we have of reality depends on how well we have been attending to the facts (or the absence of facts, where that is important), but the facts themselves do not depend on what we know.

This distinction between knowledge and facts is considered by some philosophers to be unjustified or very questionable. Since our characterization of facts occurs in terms of the ideas we have formulated about reality, it is sometimes argued that the facts themselves could not be what they are without first having been characterized by us in various ways. It may be difficult to understand the possibility of the existence of facts independent from our knowledge (and characterization) of them. Without so understanding the situation, however, unresolvable paradoxes would arise. The idea of discovery, that we may discover what is the case, presupposes that something exists that could be discovered. If facts come into existence by the emergence of human knowledge, then the idea that we discover the existence of facts, that some state of affairs could exist without anyone having yet discovered it—all this must fall by the wayside.

There are, to be sure, philosophers who argue against the "dualism" of the knower and the known, a "dualism" that admits of the difference between what is knowledge and the facts that are known (and that are not known, for that matter). They argue that this dualism (i.e., the view that two different aspects of reality are accepted as equally real) leads to the estrangement of man from reality.

To this, those who admit to the difference between what knowledge is and what fact is, would very likely reply that there is no estrangement involved here at all. The knower is as real as what he knows, but there are distinctions to be drawn on the basis of recognizable differences between different kinds of things that exist in reality. Some things, for example, human beings, can know other things, whereas others, like mountains, cannot know anything. There is no conflict between these; there is only a difference that we are better off acknowledging than denying.

Contemporary philosophers of science have been engaged in vehement disputes about the knowledge / fact distinction. There are those who hold that when different basic worldviews or general frameworks (e.g., Newtonianism, Einsteinianism, etc.) emerge within some field of science, the facts identified in that field also change. It is these frameworks (or paradigms, as one theorist calls these) which determine what the facts are. The facts do not have an independent, objective existence that scientists become aware of and try to understand and explain by way of their theories.

A response to this general idea (which is given here in a bare caricature at best) would have to be that, whereas the facts scientists deal with, from individual and momentary events to the broadest laws of nature, exist independently of our knowledge of them, our way of characterizing them can change, depending on numerous factors, including our goals, the degree and care of our understanding, the capacity of our tools and instruments to deal with details, and the level of sophistication of our theories. A great deal can hinge on how carefully and judiciously our scientists have gone about identifying what they study and expressing their findings in words. (A good deal of misunderstanding about the relationship between science and the facts studied by scientists may stem from the eagerness with which some observers of science have extended the modest findings of scientists to seem much more than modest findings!)

At any rate, the distinction between what exists and the knowledge we have obtained of what exists appears to be sound. Denying the distinction also appears to lead to the impossibility of even identifying our proper relationship to reality, since such an identification would then come to little more than a new invention, certainly not a discovery.

True Belief and Knowledge

Quite often we may find out that a belief we have held was true all along while we were not fully convinced of it. Indeed, we act on many beliefs we only take to be true and never would claim to know for sure. For example, most of us believe many things about the history of the United States that we have not studied and therefore could not justly claim to know. Yet it is very possible that these beliefs are true. That is to say, when asked what John Adams believed about slavery, we could answer by saying what he indeed believed about slavery and yet it could well be true that our idea of Adams's views on slavery could not be considered something we know.

Knowledge does not require only that someone happen to be— even have fairly good reasons to consider being—right. Knowledge, as most thoughtful people would admit, requires something more. We would have to be ready to give adequate grounds for holding what we believe is indeed the case. Only if we are able (even if not willing, for various reasons) to come up with such a demonstration and proof of what we believe, carefully checked to satisfy

standards that apply in the context, could we earn the characterization that we actually *know* the point in question.

There is every reason to believe that such fine distinctions as
indicated above are appropriate in understanding the numerous
ways in which we can be aware of reality. Our law courts, for
example, make considerable use of such distinctions when evidence
in some case is evaluated. In those circumstances, of course, much
depends on a correct evaluation of the evidence, so people will tend
to be very picky about how some piece of testimony is characterized.
Someone may well be right in what he believes about some topic,
but sometimes it is not sufficient to merely have a true belief, known
as such by others, to proceed to act. Certain kinds of actions should
be taken only when the agent knows the situation fully. Hearsay
may well give one the correct information, but it does not serve to
justify some kinds of action. Even in personal relations we tend to
distinguish between the propriety of acting on rumors in certain
circumstances, even when later we find out that the rumor is true,
and acting on knowledge.

Aside from the distinction between true belief and knowledge—
one that is not just important but often puzzling—there are many
others worth observing and thinking about. The difference between a so-called intuition, a hunch, a feeling, a well-supported
notion, and the like can become crucial in our assessment of theories,
stories, or responsibility for conduct. So when philosophers interested in human knowledge and understanding concern themselves with these issues, one should understand that they are not
just spinning wheels for purposes of amusement (however amusing
their spinning may at times become).

Sense Experience and Knowledge

We have already discussed empiricism, a theory of knowledge that
gives prominence to sense experience. At this point some of the
commonsense reasons for considering a close link between sense
experience and knowledge will be mentioned.

Just the briefest reflection will indicate to most people that the
contact we have with reality through our senses has a great deal to
do with what we know and whether we know anything at all. If
my wife asks me where the latest issue of the *American Economic*

Review is, the very possibility of my knowing the answer to her question seems to depend on whether I can see (or hear, in case someone told me). We know our friends in part by sight; we can recognize a symphony by sound, what is cooking by smell, the fabric of a suit by touch, and so forth. When we know something about these sorts of things, we know it in part (at least) because we have had sense experiences of certain kinds.

Yet it also seems clear that sense experiences are insufficient for the purpose of obtaining knowledge. When we drive through our city, we have many sense experiences that do not give us knowledge. Lights, colors, sounds, smells, and whatnot fill the environment. Yet, if traffic is heavy and we must watch carefully what we do, it is possible that we learn nothing at all of the things that produce or possess the sensory qualities we have experienced. Most likely, for example, millions of tree leaves have given off sensory qualities that we could have noticed but did not. However one might put the matter in a correct analysis of the situation, it seems clear that the sensory qualities of these tree leaves did in some sense strike our senses. Yet we could not say that we know what leaves surrounded the streets we traveled.

One need only multiply the above case to appreciate the puzzle about the relationship between sensory experiences and knowledge. No doubt, some of these puzzles are not philosophical at all—they relate to perceptual psychology, physiology, and other sciences. But it is clearly of interest to epistemologists to determine just how sensory experience, the fact that the senses have had some kind of contact with whatever has sensible qualities, relates to human knowledge.

The idea may be considered that human beings must pay heed to the qualities they could sense in order to use them as data in their effort to learn about the world. It could be argued that there must be an active involvement with the world on the part of a potential knower so as to produce knowledge. Mere exposure to sounds and sights is not enough for purposes of knowledge and understanding. It is possible that attempts to explain knowledge merely by reference to people's being exposed to reality will always fail. Knowledge may well involve a sustained effort to attend to reality, to organize what one becomes aware of by way of sensory experience in terms of principles. Therefore, efforts to explain knowledge by reference *only* to principles of thinking (rationalism) *or* to sensory impressions (empiricism) must remain insufficient. Both the principles and the sensory experience are probably required to obtain knowledge of reality, at least in the initial stages.*

Certainty and Knowledge

Very often knowledge is intimately linked to certainty. This link was discussed in part when we considered the model of knowledge that many theories invoke. Thus we noted that many theorists seem to believe that we have knowledge of something only if we know it in the way in which we know mathematical truths, truths that most of us would consider the most certain truths there could be.

Yet even when we do not require that our knowledge have the quality of certainty associated with mathematical truths, we seem to ask that some form of certainty be present. If I know something, it would be very odd to suggest at the same time that I am not certain of it. Sometimes this is possible, as when we may know the full list of presidents of the United States but not be certain of them (because it has been a long time since we thought of the issue). Yet here, too, once we have recited them, we will mostly say in the same breath that we know them and are certain of them.

The connection between knowledge and certainty is not a simple one, in part because there seem to be different kinds of certainties. There is the *feeling* of certainty, or sureness, we have sometimes when we believe something. I am certain that it is the young Paul Newman who appeared in that early movie I was watching last week. This feeling of certainty is one kind of certainty we seem to be referring to when we use the term. But there is also the certainty that we attach not to ourselves, not to how we feel, but to something we believe. Thus, when we have carefully researched some topic and conclude that such and such is the case, we may claim that this conclusion is itself certain.

In this last case we often distinguish between certainty and probability. Also it seems quite likely that we are talking about something objective here and not the subjective feeling we have.

---

* It seems to me that the story of Helen Keller could be read fruitfully in the above light. In her case, because so many of her sensory organs were impaired, the attention to the little sensory evidence she could count on had to be ever so great in order to produce ideas and, through that, knowledge and understanding.

We seem to be talking here about the strength of the evidence, the force of argument that lies behind our conclusion. Whether or not evidence is conclusive and the argument sound is not a matter of how we feel. (No doubt, upon reflection some people may say that the strength of arguments is only a matter of how one feels about them, but that usually comes from having been disappointed with attempts to support a different characterization of the issue.)

Probability, in turn, amounts to the degree of strength between nothing and complete. Thus, when we arrive at a conclusion that is probably true, we have reached one that is well enough supported in terms of some standard but not enough so as to warrant the judgment that it must be right (in terms of that standard).

Of course, in all these cases we may obtain a sense or feeling of certainty, confidence, uncertainty, and so forth, on the basis of what we have discovered. But the plain fact is that people can obtain that feeling from different sources as well. Our feeling of certainty about some conclusion or idea may stem from our extreme trust of someone who has told us of it. That, in turn, may be entirely insufficient for purposes of evaluating the conclusion by an objective standard. Our desire may be satisfied by the emergence of some conclusion and, despite the weakness of the evidence or argument, we may jump to a conclusion and feel certain without justification.

It seems to be a wise policy to be cautious about the use of the term *certainty* in light of the above considerations. Because of the term's significance in theories of knowledge—only that is true of which we can be absolutely certain!—philosophers have paid very close attention to it. In discussions of the problem of human knowledge, certainty will be one topic that will very likely get coverage.

Justification, Demonstration, and Proof

These terms, like so many others we have dealt with so briefly, are used in several senses, and I will only suggest some useful distinctions for purposes of relating them to epistemological problems.

A **justification** is often thought to relate to what we do when we back up a statement we think to be true or very likely true. We often say that we can justify what we have asserted, or that we can give a justification for what we have said.

However, it is perhaps better to leave this sense of the term to the related idea of *establishing* the truth of some claim, statement, or assertion. Justification seems to be something we should ask for when we want to learn whether or not a statement was made on rationally acceptable grounds. In other words, we may be asked to justify *having asserted* something but not the assertion itself. I may yell "Fire!" in a crowded theater and be asked later to justify my having done so. The request may well be satisfied even if there was no fire in the theater. One is often justified in making a mistake. I may be able to justify my having yelled "Fire!" by reference to my having smelled smoke from someone's smoldering cigarette and my associating the smell with a sudden flash of a bright red lamp near me. A few seconds more and I could have discovered that there was no fire anywhere at all. The conclusion that there was a fire was clearly unwarranted. Yet I may well have been justified in what I did.

Often we are asked to justify an act that amounted to having said something. Justification is ordinarily called for when one does something that has questionable consequences, so it seems to be a wider notion than one which might be tailored to the treatment of conclusions one accepts, believes, etc. Yet in philosophy there is an entire subbranch of epistemology called justification theory, one in which one studies the attempts to provide backing to what one believes, the highest standards that may be achieved in such attempts so as to have one's belief qualify as knowledge. This subbranch is now coming under close scrutiny, and the reader should not be surprised that there exists much controversy in the area just now, since much of the field is being examined from bottom up.

Demonstration is most frequently used in science. It is when someone proposes a theory (or a hypothesis) that a demonstration of what he thinks is so and so will be required. (Of course, "demonstration" has other meanings as well, as in demonstrating for a cause, demonstrating one's powers, etc.)

Demonstrations are often required in any effort to establish the truth of some claim, even outside of the fields that we consider the sciences. Thus, in a courtroom the prosecution or the defense is frequently called upon to provide a demonstration of the various elements of its case supporting the guilt or innocence of the accused. It is mostly when we want to obtain knowledge of some fact (that relates closely to a conclusion we are asked to accept) that we ask for a demonstration of the fact in question. It is to show that something is the case, to bring something to light without actually presenting it to the interested parties (i.e., without producing the fact itself), that demonstrations are offered. A demonstration aims at establishing some fact as a fact. It is not statements that are demonstrated but facts. However, this does not mean that we cannot understand what a person means when he speaks of having demonstrated a truth. Yet even there, it is the truth of some claim, the fact that it is true, that is demonstrated. (There can be many kinds of facts of reality, including facts about certain statements— namely, that they are true or false or probably true, etc.)

Finally, we need to say something about **proofs.** A proof is what we offer when we proceed logically, by the method of valid argumentation, from various statements to others that these statements imply. (See the next chapter on logic.) The statements that can be used in proofs may themselves be proved; others are what can be true simply because the evidence supporting them is there, before us, consisting of the facts we are either aware of directly or remember well when we make reference to them; other statements state principles or laws that have been established or may need only reflection to learn about (e.g., principles of atomic reaction or the laws of logic). For a proof to succeed in showing that a statement is true, the premises that state the facts or principles or evidence required have to be true. (But we will later discuss that there can be good proofs without true premises, in the sense that *if* the premises were true, *then* the conclusion would have to be true.)

Not all statements require proof; clearly, not all *could* require proof. This is because any proof requires premises, and a proof that succeeds in establishing the truth of a statement must have true premises. But if every statement did require a good proof for establishing its truth, the process would go on *ad infinitum*. And then nothing could ever be proved true. If, then, good proofs can be offered for purposes of establishing the truth of a statement, then some statements could be established as true without requiring a good proof itself. (Indeed, the statements of the laws of logic could not themselves be proved as true *ad infinitum*, since then we could never have grounds for accepting these laws.) In other words, although many beliefs and statements can use a good proof, some do

not require it.   These are called obviously true or *axiomatic* statements; that is, they are indispensable for purposes of saying *anything*
meaningfully.

With these brief comments on three very important ideas usually
discussed in connection with theories of knowledge the chapter on
epistemology must be closed.

CONCLUSION

Philosophy, including epistemology, does not arise out of the blue
and its problems involve problems we all face now and then.   But
these problems are distinguished from others because all of the
special areas—science, art, ethics, law, trade, love, and so forth—
involve them at some point.   The problem of human knowledge
is a philosophical problem because virtually everything we do and
think and feel is tied up with our knowledge of things.   It is, in
short, a *fundamental* problem or issue of reality and our relationship
to it.

The problem of human knowledge is extremely significant to
all of us.   It is perhaps the uniquely human problem of philosophy,
if we are to consider seriously that any person must cope with life
by way of the mind, the organ of knowledge.

QUESTIONS FOR DISCUSSION

1. What reasons could be offered for the contention that having
   opinions suggests the possibility of knowledge?
2. Psychology often discusses and studies aspects of knowledge.   Why,
   nevertheless, does epistemology also concern itself with knowledge?
   Is there a case for a role for both of these treatments?
3. What could be the function of a model of knowledge?
4. Give some examples of the uses and abuses of models in various
   areas of investigation.
5. What are some of the reasons that may be offered in support of
   empiricism?

6. Are there any crucial similarities between empiricism and rationalism? If so, what are they?

7. What is the relationship between ideas and sensory impressions in the version of empiricism discussed?

8. What are some of the problems with the empiricist theory of knowledge as discussed here?

9. What is the argument that was outlined in support of rationalism and what difficulties may it contain?

10. What are the two subjectivist theories discussed and in what important respect do they resemble each other?

11. What are the crucial elements of transcendental subjectivism and what reasons can be offered in support of this view? What objections could be offered against it?

12. Outline the main features of pragmatism. In what important respects does it differ from the other positions presented here?

13. What are some examples of operationalist definitions?

14. What is the relationship between a concept and a definition?

15. What are some examples of definitions that would not be acceptable to an operationalist?

16. What arguments could be offered in support of contextualism? Does contextualism solve some problems other theories do not? What objections could be raised against it?

17. What is the central point raised by the mitigated skeptic and how does it differ from the pure skeptic's position?

18. Describe the various ways in which the skeptical position could result from others we have discussed.

19. What arguments could be offered to support or reject the claim that the onus of proof lies on the skeptic to prove his case?

20. What reasons could be offered to distinguish truth from knowledge and fact from knowledge?

Logic and Reality

4

WHAT IS LOGIC?

To provide an answer to the apparently simple question, What is logic? we should say something about the commonsense understanding of logic. This will establish a link between the familiar view and specialized, scholarly conceptions of the topic.

Logic in Common Discourse

Most people have an idea of what logic is, so they know what it is to be logical or illogical in various circumstances. In arguments and debates, people who do not make sense, talk beside the issue, and fail to link different segments of discussion into a coherent whole are called illogical. When good sense is being followed, the result is usually considered a logical presentation or performance. It is by reference to how people perform in these endeavors that they are called either logical or illogical. By paying attention to people's thinking, talking, writing, and the like, we discover whether or not they are logical.

Several fields of study which are now well established have the term *logy* affixed to them. Disciplines such as psychology, sociology, and biology are cases in point. The ending *logy* indicates the fact that people engage in *discourse* on a certain range of topics within these areas of study. *Logos* is Greek for language, discourse, or thoughtful study—and the term has come to characterize careful, organized, coherent discourse when used in ordinary situations.

History

People have made use of logic since the time human thought and communication began, but not until the philosopher Aristotle set out to study it did logic become a special focus of scholarly attention. Ever since then, logic has been an independent subject matter, even though in practice it is never separated from various areas of discourse.

Aristotle thought of logic as a kind of *instrument* to be used in gaining and testing knowledge. His treatise on the subject matter is called an *organon*, which means "instrument." He also viewed the basic principles of the system of logic as basic truths about reality (as we have discussed in the chapter on metaphysics). According to Aristotle, logic is an instrument for gaining and testing knowledge *because* the principles of logic characterize the way reality itself must be. The Law of Noncontradiction and its corollaries (e.g., the Law of Identity) would on this view be both basic facts of reality and fundamental principles of logic by which our thinking and communication should be governed. It is because logic is so wedded to reality that it can serve as an instrument for sound thinking and correct reasoning. Without that initial link, logic (in the Aristotelian approach) may well help to put order into our thinking. However, such order would quite possibly be without significance for purposes of obtaining knowledge of reality.

Although the work Aristotle performed has always been regarded crucial, not all logicians share Aristotle's view of the relationship between logic and reality. Recently, in fact, some thinkers have considered it necessary to expand the scope of logic far beyond Aristotle's work. Yet he is acknowledged as the pioneer in the field. Moreover, his conception of logic is once again becoming prominent among professional students of the field.

Crucial Features

We can now get a closer understanding of what **logic** is. It is a method, an instrument or "tool," used in thinking and communication. It serves the purpose of obtaining and testing knowledge. It is a system of principles that is often viewed as reflective of the basic structure of reality itself. It can be studied apart from how it is usually applied—namely, in various special areas of discourse (e.g., psychology, anthropology, and physics). The pioneer student of logic as a distinct field of study was Aristotle. And it is evident that people are familiar enough with what logic is to make use of the adjectives *logical* and *illogical* in many circumstances. Even when they would not be able to explain the details of this valuable method, people can use it in thinking about the world.

As we reflect on the distinction between what is logical and what is illogical, it is clear that in most cases the former is considered valuable and the latter, destructive. (Later we will consider objections to such a view.) Giving a logical argument is generally admitted to be superior to giving an illogical one. Except for critics who wish to disparage our "excessive" reliance on our minds, most people believe that being logical is valuable as we engage in thinking, arguing, etc.

More precisely, however, logic helps us in formulating arguments that possess the virtue of **validity!** Valid arguments are good, whereas invalid ones are bad. A valid argument is one in which the belief that the premises are true gives conclusive reason for believing that the conclusion is true.

Valid arguments are those whose *structure* is such that if their premises are true, their conclusions *must* be true. A **premise** is an independent statement or assertion about something in an argument, so that, for example, if the separate statements "Bavarians are German citizens" and "German citizens are Europeans" are true, then it must be true that "Bavarians are Europeans." If we (mistakenly) believe that Bavarians are French citizens and (correctly) believe that French citizens are Europeans, we must also conclude, by logical thinking, that Bavarians are Europeans.

Arguments can be valid even when the premises are false. Remember that the validity of an argument has to do with its structure. What matters for validity is that *if* the premises were true, *then* the conclusion would also have to be true, whatever in fact is the case.

Logic alone will not enable us to reach true conclusions. But if the facts are known by us, logical thinking enables us to learn more, and to reach true conclusions from what we already know. In most cases, then, logic is necessary but insufficient for making sure what we believe is true. (It may not be required in cases of *self-evident* truths, assuming there are such.) Sometimes, of course, logical thinking is almost automatic—as when an experienced detective quickly "puts two and two together." But more often logical thinking serves to test our less rigorous thinking so as to make sure we have proceeded correctly, by the rules of validity!

Logic Misused. We can stop for a moment to reply to an often-voiced comment about logic. Some people decry that we too often insist on logical thinking. These are not at issue here—we will face them later. But there are those who correctly lament that sometimes logic is used without purpose. Emotionally distraught people often do not need argument but sympathy and comfort. Then, again, being logical about an issue that is in fact beside the point would be an obstacle to learning. When people accuse others of being "coldly logical," it is these misuses of logic they must have in mind. Only those who view clear thinking as inevitably opposed to freely experiencing emotions will consider logic always objectionable—even though to find out about this would itself require a logically conducted inquiry. It seems evident, then, that logic is indispensable.

Summary

By our more precise characterization of logic, beyond our common-sense view, logic is the system of principles of reasoning used to test whether our beliefs are well or badly supported. It is an instrument to be used in an effort to obtain knowledge. We can believe many things that may or may not be true, but with logic we can test some of these beliefs. (We also need evidence, of course. But more on that later.) In our efforts to make sure that we believe what is, in fact, true, it is the method of logical thinking that enables us to attain our goal.

Of course, more is needed. For example, the meaning of our ideas must be clear. When we think about something, we need the best, clearest ideas with which to do this. When we discuss logical arguments, we will see why these issues are important. Everyone realizes that in the law, for example, a good deal of stress is put on clearly defining one's terms. That is because when a topic is important, we should know what we are talking about. Only when our ideas are clear will logical thinking help us reach correct conclusions. (Ordinarily we do not have problems with the thousands of ideas we use; however, in complicated matters disagreements and confusions can and do arise. At this point we need to discover the best way to grapple with an issue, however difficult this turns out to be.)

Without knowledge of the various factors that are relevant to a certain investigation, we simply will not be able to use logic, since the method of correct thinking requires understanding a few matters with which the thinking must begin. Without that beginning the method cannot be employed.

EXAMPLES OF LOGICAL THINKING

There is no one who knows nothing of logic, since it is used by all of us in virtually every moment of our waking life. (In fact, one way people have characterized the distinction between dreams and actual experiences is that in dreams things are incoherent; they follow *no logical pattern!*) This is why we could say a good deal about logic thus far without giving detailed examples of its various features. But at this time it will help to present some simple cases of logical thinking (of course, *written out,* not simply thought of).

Let us consider the case of Harry, who knows that all Republicans are American citizens. Let us accept it as true (as a matter of law) in the United States. Now, after having taken some interest in party politics, Harry learns that some Republicans are conservatives. These two facts are both known to Harry, but at no point did he consider them together until a visitor from a foreign country remarked that unlike Europe, America appears to have no citizens with a conservative political point of view. At this stage

Harry objects, and he makes the observation that some American citizens are conservatives. When asked to prove this, he proceeds as follows:

> *1. All Republicans are American citizens, and some Republicans are conservatives; therefore, some American citizens are conservatives.*

It is now easy to imagine that our European friend would wish to make certain that the argument does in fact establish the conclusion (the last statement). For this he would have to learn whether the premises—the statements about all Republicans and some Republicans—are true. This comes first. Assuming that he could be convinced of this, he could then go on to ask if it is enough to know those facts in order to demonstrate that some American citizens are conservatives. Since this is a rather straightforward, even uninteresting argument, however, one hardly needs more than basic good sense to see that it succeeds at its task. But we can use it to indicate how one would make sure that thinking or arguing in the above fashion does succeed. In short, why is the above a good argument? Why does it yield a true conclusion if the premises are true?

Validity

To understand why the foregoing argument is a good one, we need to know a little more of what the facts of the discussion amount to. All Republicans are American citizens, which amounts to the fact that *everything* that is a Republican—that is, each person who belongs to that political party—is also an American citizen. Being one involves being the other, in this case as a matter of legal statute. That some Republicans are conservatives amounts to the fact that, among all of the Republicans, *at least one* accepts the conservative political viewpoint. But if this is so, then could it be that no American citizen is a conservative? Those who are Republicans are American citizens and some of the Republicans are conservatives, which is to say that some who are American citizens are conservatives. If the conclusion above were denied, we would now have to say that the (at least one) conservative who is a Republican, and by law has to be an American citizen, is *not* an American citizen. And this violates the Law of Identity—a thing is what it is. In this case: an American citizen is an American citizen. If we deny the conclusion of the argument we are discussing, we are claiming that an American citizen is not an American citizen!

Now let us change the situation somewhat. Let us assume that unbeknownst to our friend Harry, Congress changes the law involved, allowing some foreigners to join political parties in the United States. Instead of the fact that all Republicans are Americans, we now could very likely find that only some, even if most, of them are. So the case lines up as follows:

> 2. *Some Republicans are American citizens, and some Re-*
> *publicans are conservatives; therefore, some American citizens*
> *are conservatives.*

Taking it that the first two statements are true, does this line of thinking demonstrate the truth of the third statement? In other words, given the facts provided, do they serve to support the conclusion; are we justified in claiming the factual status of the third statement? Let us examine this now.

To assume the fact that some Republicans are American citizens is to assume that there is at least one Republican who is an American citizen. Beyond this we do not make any assumptions. But we do accept here that at least one Republican is an American citizen. That is all that we can work with as the case is presented. We also accept that some Republicans are conservatives, which is to say that at least one Republican is a conservative. The conclusion states that at least one American citizen is a conservative. Yet, if we deny this we find that we are simply saying that it is not the case that at least one American citizen is a conservative. Since all we start with in the above case is that *some* Republicans are American citizens and *some* are conservatives, by denying that some American citizens are conservatives we are merely saying that no American citizen is a conservative. While this may not be so, we do not *know* from the information given that it is not so. That is because from the information available it is quite impossible to tell whether or not the same group of Republicans who are American citizens are the ones who are conservatives. It could well be, given what we here know, that those Republicans who are American citizens are not conservatives and that only the foreign Republicans are. There is no contradiction here between asserting the truth of the premises and the falsity of the conclusion.

Let us check out another argument, very briefly, to get a better grip on what arguments amount to.

> 3. *No rocks are animals, and some stones are rocks; therefore, some stones are not animals.*

Obviously, the premises in this argument differ from those in the foregoing arguments, not only in their subject matter but also in the kind of statements being offered. But it is still an argument and we can investigate whether it is a good one. Let us test it by denying the conclusion. If we deny that some stones are not animals, we are saying that all stones are animals. (This sounds strange because we are sure that no stones are animals. But for the sake of the example let us stick to what is given above, no more.) If we now still accept that no rocks are animals and some stones are rocks, can we also assert, without contradicting ourselves, that all stones are animals? If we could, the above argument would not be a good one.

So, we have as our premises that no rocks are animals and some stones are rocks. If this is so, then nothing that is a rock could be an animal and since some stones are rocks, some stones could not be animals. But the denial of the conclusion of the argument above says that all stones are animals. We do have a contradiction. Therefore, the argument is good.

These considerations should enable us to appreciate the function that logic has in testing our thinking. Of course, we don't always have to say only what we *know for sure*. We often say what we believe but do not know. Mostly we have reasonably good evidence for our beliefs, or at least we have testimony to back what we think. We often say, "I think some American citizens are conservatives" or "It seems quite certain . . ." or "most likely. . . ." We do this to indicate that we have not tested our conclusions rigorously. (Or because we don't *want* to bother with proving our point.) And sometimes no one has definite knowledge of some topic, even when many have an intense interest in it. (Gossip is usually like this!) Thus, to go back to the earlier argument, if we had been told only that *very likely* some American citizens are conservatives since the majority of Republicans are American citizens and *quite a few* of them are conservative, the situation would have been different. These claims are not definite, so we should treat them with due regard for the caution with which they are expressed. But that is not the way the example went, so we were right to dismiss the conclusion as unsupported by the premises.

To see how the above points may be used, it will help to simply check them out on the following argument. If the argument is valid—a logically good argument—then the denial of the conclusion should contradict the conjunction of the premises, that is, their combined truth. So just make this a test:

> *4. Some courses are not boring, and all boring (things) are hard to follow; therefore, some hard-to-follow (things) are not courses.*

Or the next one:

> *5. No soldiers are gentlemen, and some gentlemen are polite; therefore, some soldiers are polite.*

It is important not to expect that the conclusion of an argument alone informs us about the validity of the argument. A good deal must be learned about arguments before we can go about constructing them successfully. For the time being, however, the only thing that is crucial is that we can find out whether an argument is valid. This can be done by denying the conclusion and determining whether this denial contradicts the conjunction of the premises. If it does, then the argument is valid, since validity involves *necessary* coherence.

Terms

When looking at the arguments above we see that each of the statements (premises and conclusions) contain terms. These are the words or phrases by which we express what is being spoken of and what is being said of it. "Soldiers" and "gentlemen" are such terms, for example. The statements also include quantifiers—"all," "no," and "some." These specify whether every (or no) one (of what we are talking about) or only some are being talked about (are all, no, or some soldiers gentlemen?). ("All" and "no" both specify the entire class!)

The first term in the statement is called the subject and the second the predicate. In argument 5, for instance, we are saying that no *soldiers* (the subject) are *gentlemen* (the predicate). Every argument of the kind we have been considering is called a **syllogism,** which means, from the Greek, that thoughts are brought together.

When logic is studied without regard to the content of arguments, we can employ (and most logicians use only) symbols. The simplest kind of symbolism with which most logic courses begin involves the *quantifiers* ("all," "no," and "some") and symbols ("S," "P," and "M") in place of the terms. Thus the structure of argument 5 would be represented as follows:

6. *No* S *are* M
   Some M *are* P
   Some S *are* P

Notice that "*M*" replaces the term that occurs twice above the line, in the premises, linking the two statements to each other (bringing thoughts together!). "*S*" stands in place of the subject and "*P*" in place of the predicate as these occur in the conclusion! In such symbolic treatment of logic it helps to have a very economical way of referring to all standard logical argument forms. Four symbolic notations that occur in standard syllogistic arguments are "All *S* are *P*," "No *S* are *P*," "Some *S* are *P*," and "Some *S* are *not P*." These are generally referred to as the A, E, I, and O *propositional forms.* Even more briefly, these are written as follows: *SaP* (A), *SeP* (E), *SiP* (I), and *SoP* (O).

Much more would be explained and studied in an introductory course on logic. The aim here, however, is to make the topic familiar and to indicate how it relates to life in general.

VALIDITY AND TRUTH

Validity is what is good about good arguments. A valid argument is one in which *if* the premises are true, then the conclusion *has* to be true. That is why when the conclusion of a valid argument is rejected or denied, a contradiction will arise between this denial and the conjunction of the premises.

In ordinary discussions people sometimes make a *valid* point or offer a *valid* objection. This relates to the strict use of that idea in logic. The idea in both cases involves what is carefully reasoned, well thought out, logically defensible.

Soundness

Arguments may be valid without being sound—that is, their premises could be false and yet their conclusion would be true *if* the premises were true! In sound arguments the premises are true. In the following

> 7. *All Bavarians are French citizens, and all French citizens are Europeans; therefore, all Bavarians are Europeans.*

we have a valid argument that is *unsound* because the conclusion is based on at least one false premise. It does not matter that the conclusion is true; the point is that it rests on shaky foundations. But the argument is valid! *If* all Bavarians were French and all the French were Europeans, *then* all Bavarians would have to be Europeans.

We can easily turn to a person and say, "Your argument is quite valid, but unsound." That is because a valid argument could have false premises and a false conclusion, whereas the sound argument must have true premises from which a true conclusion will follow, thus yielding knowledge. We can arrive at a true conclusion in an unsound argument, but we will not be able to establish that conclusion from *facts*. And knowledge requires this as a minimum, *when we reach it through argument.*

An argument is valid *if the assertion of the premises and the denial of the conclusion produce a self-contradiction.* We have seen this where the test used involved the Law of Identity in checking out the arguments' validity. Another way of putting this characterization is to say that an argument is valid if, assuming that the premises are true, the conclusion would have to be true also. We saw earlier that some of the arguments had conclusions that, when denied, did not conflict with the premises. Any such conclusion is not the product of a valid argument.

Enter Truth

Thus far I have simply said something about validity as a feature of arguments, quite independent of the issue of truth. How is it possible that an instrument whose main purpose is to lead to knowledge will allow for the following use?

> 8. *All men are monsters, and all monsters are great swimmers; thus, all men are great swimmers.*

The argument is valid—simply test it as I suggested before. But it surely has little if anything to do with truth, except for one thing: it is quite true that *if* all men are monsters *and* all monsters are great swimmers, *then* all men are great swimmers!

Truth and validity are distinct but they cannot be divorced from each other. At least validity requires the idea of truth, since only by first understanding what *true* means can we understand what *valid* means. This is evident from the fact that to understand the concept of validity we must understand truth. An argument is valid if, should the premises be true, the conclusion would have to be true. Valid arguments could have false (i.e., not true) premises, of course. But we have to explain validity in terms of arguments whose premises might be true.

Whenever some idea is understood only by reference to another, it is necessary to admit that if *this* idea is meaningful, the other one must be. We can say at least that for logic to be a meaningful enterprise, for validity to make clear sense, we must have an idea of what truth is. Whether having an idea of what truth is also means that some of what we think has to be true, that we know something and can make true statements, is another matter. There is much dispute about these things and it may help to discuss the issue more.

TRUTH AND LOGIC

Logic is a method or instrument for gaining knowledge, for making sure that what one believes is true or right. The connection between the instrument and the goal consists in the basic axioms of logic. Aristotle argued that the Law of Noncontradiction—that is, nothing can both be and not be something, or never A and not-A—is a law of reality as such. As the basic laws of physics or biology apply to all the objects and events within the domain in question, so the basic laws of reality apply throughout existence.

Basic Law of Logic

To those who would ask for a demonstration of this law, Aristotle answered that such laws cannot be demonstrated because everything depends on them, *including demonstrations.* That is how funda-mental such laws are. Any discussion, proof, or demonstration—in short, all intelligible, meaningful discourse—requires that this law be admitted as binding, or applicable for all existence and so for the discussion and study of everything. Aristotle noted that even those who tried to deny the all-pervasive, universal character of the law actually had to invoke it whenever they wanted to make sense of what they were saying. This is because the words we use cannot have a definite meaning if the law does not hold in the case of what the word is used to mean. If we use *apple* to mean something that can both be an apple and not be an apple at once and in the same way, then the word is useless and communication with it is im-possible. If something can both be what it *is* and be what it *is not* at the same time and in the same respect, then we can never fix it in our minds for purposes of understanding or communicating about it.

Furthermore, the law implies that by both affirming and deny-ing the same thing at once, we *must* be saying something false. In other words, saying "X is an apple and X is not an apple" must be wrong! To deny this has the consequence that we really could both deny and affirm the law. If the Law of Noncontradiction is denied, then both "X is an apple" and "X is not an apple" could be true. But this would also hold for the law itself. Denial of the law lifts all constraints on discourse, even concerning the law itself; therefore, it, too, could be both true and false. Then total nonsense is the result.

In **Aristotelian logic** the laws of noncontradiction (not both A and not-A), identity (A is A), and excluded middle (either A or not-A, not both) are fundamental principles of reality. And these laws are required for productive thinking, although it is we who have to do the thinking in which the laws can help us to be productive of knowledge and understanding.

Applying the Basic Law

That the main law, the one Aristotle identified, is crucial in everyday life is not difficult to see. It not only helps us in science, math, and all other rigorous fields of study but also serves to guide us in our thinking whenever we are a bit doubtful about how well we are doing in understanding things. With the aid of the Law of Noncontradiction we can detect serious errors in thinking. When lying occurs, we detect it by showing that what the liar says is in basic conflict with the true statement of the situation. In courtrooms the entire encounter between prosecutor and defendant, through their representatives, hinges on effective use of this law. Even more general is the occurrence of simple logical thinking we witness among tradesmen, professionals, and other ordinary people. In such cases "logical" means something less rigorous than what we find among professional logicians when they develop technical arguments. But essentially the same thing is at issue: clear, unambiguous thinking and conduct guided by it.

The important connection between truth and logic is that to identify the facts of reality correctly, that is, to arrive at true conclusions, it is extremely important in most cases to use the rules of logic to check how carefully we have reasoned. This care begins with using considerations here being spelled out.

LOGIC AND PHILOSOPHY

Earlier we dealt with the difference between standards of successful treatment of various branches of knowledge and various fields of study of reality. It should now be noted that in the bulk of what philosophers do, logic plays a very important role. Philosophers disagree about many things, and a great deal of what they disagree

about concerns just how reality can be known. Philosophers propose various methods for learning about what things are. When we
looked at theories of knowledge in the previous chapter, this was
quite evident. However, almost all philosophers utilize logic in
their construction and criticism of theories. Logic is for most philosophers a well-accepted tool. Whatever else philosophers accept
as appropriate in our efforts to obtain knowledge, the majority of
them admit that the laws of logic must never be violated.

But philosophers do not always agree on the relationship between logic and reality. We have reviewed Aristotle's views on this
subject, but his position is not accepted by all philosophers. Even
those who admit that Aristotle made the definitive, most fully developed contribution to the study of logic do not accept all of what
he believed about this issue.

The Source of Logic

The most controversial feature of Aristotelian logic is its source.
What are logical principles? Why are they principles so widely used
and taught? Are they laws of reality or laws of thought?

In everyday concerns such worries are expressed when people
protest the need to be logical in their thinking, when they ask why
thinking carefully and sensibly is important anyway. After all,
what reason is there to believe that logic has anything to do with
living a human life?

These questions are raised quite often, and by philosophers in
particular. Nevertheless, most philosophers agree that logic is necessary for evaluating the merits of their own or others' positions.
This testifies to the widely recognized fact that whatever else philosophers may use in putting forth their own ideas and criticizing
others' views, they must conform to the principles of logic.

This is also where some of the problems arise and it indicates
why the question of the origin or source of logic is so important.
Although most admit its necessity, few agree on just what this
necessity itself implies. In other words, admitting that we require
the use of logic may or may not amount to admitting other things,
however much we might like to affirm or deny this.

Suppose for a moment that admitting that we need to employ
logic does commit us to some other claims. In short, suppose that
recognizing the need for logic presupposes that certain beliefs are

also true, or that there are certain facts one simply cannot deny. (I earlier argued that this is so.)

Now, if the above is right, it would appear to require that someone who sees the need for logic accept certain facts. Yet it is very often just about what facts should or should not be accepted that philosophical disputes ensue. When we argue about things logically, it appears that we are presupposing certain beliefs. Yet is it not the main purpose of argumentation to prove our beliefs? Would it not be a case of prejudgment to believe some things from the start, even before the argument gets off the ground?

If logical thinking is a tool to be used to gain knowledge, how could logic require that some facts be known already? If the Law of Noncontradiction does not have to be proved by a logical argument, then why can't there be other facts that require no proof? On the other hand, if this law does require a logical proof, don't we go around in circles forever? These and similar criticisms are often advanced against the very idea that logic is universally important and is required for knowledge.

An Undeniable Source

The Aristotelian answer to this is that some facts stated by **axioms** are simply undeniable, as pointed out earlier. They are not demonstrated as particular facts must be because they are so fundamental that they could not be proved by relying on yet some other, more basic facts. To try to derive the most basic fact of all from other facts would be to misunderstand what a basic fact is. To ask for the foundations of the foundation is to fail to understand what it is for something to be a foundation, or to be fundamental. What could be done is to show that these are fundamental facts, and by showing that they cannot be denied without rendering even the denial nonsensical one can show that these facts are undeniable. (One can utter the denial in words, of course, but this will not make it sensible, just as one can utter the statement "I am not speaking now" without making it possible to make sense of it, but simply to see how it could possibly be true.)

Some thinkers have argued that the Law of Identity is a basic feature of human thinking and inherent in the mind. Others have argued that these laws are invented conveniences. (These criticisms will be discussed later.) There are even some who reject logic as harmful. In the process, however, they use it to explain themselves and to prove, incredibly enough, the alleged fact that logic and knowledge are worthless. So even here, in making sure that logic is not very important, even harmful, we seem to rely on logic to find out about or demonstrate the matter. It is notorious how many people who attack logic or thinking and intellectual effort in general carry out very complicated logical arguments! Even more notorious is that many who deny the significance of conceptual knowledge (that is, abstractions, or theoretical inquiries) and advocate relying solely on instincts, habit, and custom spend volumes trying to produce *this* piece of knowledge.

Logic with Presuppositions

We are here concerned with the narrower issue of whether accepting logic requires acceptance of some other matters. It is a fair answer that admitting that logic is indispensable requires the admission that some other things are indispensable also. But some philosophers hold that this is not so; they claim that one can concede the importance and usefulness of logic and still deny that anything else could be known. Views along these lines were encountered in the chapter on epistemology.

As noted earlier, logic is characterized by valid argumentation. The idea of logic—that is, understanding what is crucial about it—requires the idea of validity. (Some will hold that a branch of logic, inductive logic, does not require validity. This objection should be remembered for future reference.) And we have already seen that understanding validity requires understanding at least something about the nature of truth. To characterize validity requires that we know what the idea *truth* means. It appears now that anyone who admits to understanding validity must already understand truth. But when we look closer, some difficulties emerge.

By "understanding truth" some philosophers have in mind knowing only the meaning of the idea *truth*. Furthermore, they argue that one can know the meaning of an idea even if nothing ever could be characterized by that idea. Thus, they would hold that we know the meaning of *witch* or *pegasus* or *ghost* even if no such things ever existed. So even if we know the meaning of the idea *truth,* it may turn out that there exists no truth at all.

It is difficult to avoid involvement in these issues at some length, so at least a brief comment needs to be made about the matter here. It will not finish the topic but settle it for now!

We may know the meaning of *witch* or *mermaid* even if no such thing exists because we have some idea of what it would involve for them to exist. We find such entities in stories and myths. We can imagine them, mostly in the vague, incomplete way we can imagine flying elephants, ghosts, or good tyrants.

If for certain things to exist witches or mermaids would also have to exist, we would have to reject the idea if witches or mermaids could be shown to be impossible. Unless truth were at least possible, validity *could* never obtain either. Therefore, if we define validity in terms of the idea of truth and we claim that some things (arguments) are valid, then we must admit at least·that some things (premises) *could* be true. Now all we need to ask if there is any straightforward and adequate idea of truth we can identify.

Despite the persistent controversy about the nature of truth, we have a good grasp of what it is in our day to day conception of the meaning of the term: A statement or belief is true if its content, that is, what is stated or believed, is a fact; if the statement or belief is false, it fails to state or contain a fact.

As understood here, some statements or beliefs are clearly true even without a proof of their truth. For instance, sometimes the denial of a belief would render it plainly impossible for us to make meaningful and true statements. In that case, we are in· possession of a basic truth, even when we don't reflect on the matter. The Law of Noncontradiction is such a true belief, presupposed in any meaningful discourse, and when we reflect on it we can learn of its truth explicitly.

Without further work on the details, we have here a crucial (although clearly very obvious) true belief, one that is true but not *proved* true (as other beliefs would have to be so as to have their truth established). This indicates that some facts could be known prior to anything we might learn through our use of logical arguments. Little knowledge of this sort is likely to be readily available —we must obtain the rest by the usual methods of scientific research, theoretical analyses, and ordinary experience. The few we can identify before we require logical thinking are accessible because they are so basic that they stare us in the face everywhere. Not only must we have ideas of truth in our understanding of logic, but we must possess true beliefs as well at the outset, so we can begin our logical thinking from some foundations.

IS LOGIC LIMITING?

A few objections to logic can now be presented. Some think that sustained use of logic—a commitment to rationality in one's thinking and conduct—must suppress the emotions, limit freedom and creativity, and stunt natural growth. Does logic prohibit all spontaneity? Must it stifle human nature? How can we enjoy the freedom needed for creative action, especially art, when we confine ourselves to the strictures of logic?

These sorts of objections are available in both highly sophisticated and rather simplistic versions. As for the latter, we have all heard of those who proclaim their disdain for any organized thought, live from moment to moment, and never give anything serious consideration. (This may be what characterized the Yippie movement.) On the other hand, a respected and accomplished individual such as Albert Einstein, the great physicist, characterized some of his creative thinking as free, uncontrolled inventiveness. Einstein and others have remarked that guessing is the most important part of scientific creativity—so much so that the greatest scientists always use it and the most important achievements require it. The notion that artists think little but feel always, very deeply and profoundly, is widely accepted. Mathematicians, engineers, accountants, logicians, and philosophers (in the Western world) are often expected to be stuffed shirts without spirit or the capacity for natural emotion.

Logic in Its Place

It may be worth giving some indication why and how logic and emotions are not only compatible but in natural harmory.

Obviously not only those who have logical acumen have made worthwhile creative contributions. Logic is simply not *sufficient* for creativity, in art or in science. Properly invoked, however, it satisfies a requirement that is not in natural conflict with other values and desires.

Logic is one method for identifying reality and obtaining reliable knowledge of it in all sorts of circumstances. It is involved mainly in thinking, especially deliberate thinking. That is why the emphasis in teaching logic rests on invoking it when we test our beliefs, hunches, theories, hypotheses, and other kinds of judgments.

Thus, logic applies to an area of human life that has a definite role, however wide-ranging it may be. It is used in the area of critical and constructive thought: in learning, analyzing, predicting, planning, calculating, examining, investigating, detecting, diagnosing, explaining, and understanding. This is generally considered the domain of the intellect, the life of the mind. Of course the mind pertains to emotions, feelings, moods, and impulses as well, and we will see how these may relate to our intellectual endeavors.

One can say that logic's place is in the proper ordering and use of our ideas or concepts. Thinking conceptually is something only human beings are known to do, especially at complex levels. We have seen this in the epistemological discussions where philosophers showed their concern with the nature of concepts as the most crucial ingredient of human knowledge. Some monkeys, dolphins, and even certain kinds of birds have been found to make use of simple ideas—usually when people prompted them. But human beings are thoroughly immersed in them. They write novels, develop scientific theories, make plans for entire cities, discuss highly abstract philosophical issues, conceive of elaborate artistic projects, and entertain doubts about all of these. To our knowledge only people are aware of the world by means of ideas or concepts. We may experience reality in many ways, but we know of our experiences in terms of the ideas we use to think and talk about them.

Reason and Emotions

If this is where logic has its function in human life, why would it ever conflict with emotions? Why would anyone think that our diligent use of logic must be unnatural or pose an obstacle?

One reason sometimes given is that other animals appear far more wedded to nature than do human beings and, with minor exceptions, they simply do not make use of logic. Human beings are rational animals, and they appear to have a much more difficult time of it than do other animals. Animal life appears to most people as something utterly harmonious, unproblematic, almost idyllic, whereas human life is clearly filled with horror, mayhem, and misery.

Such ideas, combined with others such as original sin, divine touch, or fundamental misplacement in the world, tend to encourage views that question the value of reason, logic, science, technology, and other uniquely human aspects of our lives. By these sorts of reflections anyone can come to accept that the human mind, this logical tool, is a nuisance and clearly a severe stifler of the emotions. Is it not, after all, the "up tight" businessman-technocrat who is incapable of feeling, who cannot show emotion? Does this not indicate that the use of logic is bad for us? And are not so called primitive, "backward" people much more natural? Does this not indicate that our culture, built to a large extent on reason and logic, is out of touch with nature?

The following observations should give an initial answer to these queries. They will help to suggest how and why logic, human reason, and the rest of our capacities (e.g., for enthusiam, joy, love, sorrow, spontaneity, excitement, and compassion) can coexist in full harmony, even if such coexistence is rarely evident.

As noted before, logic and reason pertain to learning, knowledge, and science. These are not the concern of the emotions. Their function is different, but not necessarily conflicting. Emotions are responses to the world, including to ourselves. Reasoning is often a deliberate matter: we can take our minds off something and turn to something else, we can attend to something or not at will. Feeling sorry or joyful, excited or anxious, angry or in love are things we cannot *decide* to do. It would be easy otherwise. A bad mood could be willed away, just as we can take our minds off philosophy by closing the book and turning to another task. Instead we are subject to good and bad "moods," often without the slightest idea why and unable to help it. Other times we have a sudden craving for pizza or ice cream, or feel an abiding desire for good company. It seems evident that emotions and desires are not decided on by a person.

On the other hand, we cannot deny a connection between reason and emotions. Our feelings often conflict with our judgment—we may feel nausea at the sight of our best friend's spouse yet will decide not to act on it and force a smile; or we may wish very badly to sleep on the morning of the philosophy test, yet will discipline ourselves to act on our judgment that yielding to this wish would be very costly. Such cases could be multiplied. How might we make sense of this conflicting relationship?

We are not born with our complex emotions and desires—how could we when we have no idea before birth what there is to desire, to fear, to be anxious or joyful about? Children have the potential to develop feelings of romantic love, remorse, anger, friendship, or hatred, but as infants these are not yet present. At most they can feel good or bad, gradually developing complex emotions and desires.

It is also evident that later in life people can like or dislike the wrong things. Some can crave tomatoes, others heroin, and while the former is normally of benefit to a person's health, the latter is harmful. There are those who want quick, effortless affairs with the opposite sex, while others desire a patiently, gradually developed relationship. Some people wish for hasty riches, even if their work brings them misery, while others are pleased by a challenging occupation or career despite only moderate, even uncertain, income. Whatever one picks as good or bad about life—pollution, war, drugs, religious devotion, blackmail, or medicine—some people desire good things while others desire bad ones. They feel responsive to one sort or the other as they carry on with life.

How did these complex emotions and desires, both wise and unwise, come about in someone's life? There is a detailed history about that for all of us. The idea that may make general sense of the entire process is that much depends on how we have kept our minds focused on reality in our early years. If we have done so, if we did not daydream all the time or have our elders scare us away from using instead of encouraging us to improve our heads, we could come to understand the world clearly enough. By our commonsense use of reason and logic we could come to learn what is important and good, as well as what is potentially dangerous or harmful. Our feelings then could evolve accordingly, so that we fear the dangerous and desire the valuable. Simply put, we must know what is to be feared in order to experience the emotion of fear in the appropriate manner. Similarly, we must know what is valuable and good in order to find that we are responding with good feelings to such things. That this could be achieved was Aristotle's view. But we cannot deny the rarity of those people who are, so to speak, in such harmony within themselves so that they desire what their mind can demonstrate is in fact worthy of desire and detest what is actually detestable. By the above considerations, this is due either to a lack of sustained effort to understand one's world and life or to various obstructions in the process of gaining such understanding. All kinds of obstacles can enter and people can develop serious discords between the sort of things they think are good, true, and accurate, and the feelings they have for these.

Abusing Logic

Logic itself *can* be misused. After all, even lunatics can use *some* logic in their lives just as they are engaging in the most destructive activities. They can senselessly believe what is entirely false and reason from it to various conclusions. In such cases, and they are numerous, not logic itself but its very selective use can damage a person severely.

The same can occur in the more complex areas of science. Initially unwarranted generalizations can limit a person to seeing possibilities only within a narrow range. Although these limits may now follow logically, the trouble is not with logic but with its inappropriate use. Even the maddest of scientists can make use of some arguments, just as a pathological liar can on occasion tell the truth. Also, there are stubborn people in any field or in ordinary life who insist on following logic but only within their limited perspective. Think of those who seem extremely reasonable and proper but who consider issues from a viewpoint that has no logical support, only unquestioned habit or history, to give it backing. Still others make very good use of logic without regard to the truth of the premises they have accepted on the basis of wild speculation. (High school debaters often exhibit considerable logical acumen; yet, in their arguments they rely on unexamined studies or on "expert" opinion that has not been scrutinized. Interestingly, these debates rarely end in agreement. Yet, surely the goal of a serious

debate is to gain mutual understanding, even if some do confuse
debates with horse races—another kind of engagement entirely.)

Clearly, then, logic can be misused, and whether or not it limits
us properly or unnaturally depends on what it limits us *to*. If logic
limits us to the truth, by our using it in arguments with true
premises, so much the better. If, however, it limits us to prejudices
or wild speculations, it is these unfounded opinions that must go,
not the method used (in this case) for purposes that do not justify it.

Creativity and Logic

Would artists and great scientists be limited by practicing logical
thinking? The purpose of art is not to achieve knowledge. So logic
would pertain to artists only in obtaining their skills and conceiving
of their presentations, not in making sure of facts. Even if we
accept Einstein's point about free inventiveness in science, it has
to be understood that Einstein may have been misleading when he
said "free" inventiveness, meaning by it something that is unlimited,
random, or haphazard. That would lead not to great discoveries
but to cheap fantasies. Einstein and most other great scientists do
fish for ideas without a systematic method, but usually only when
all else has failed. Then it can help to let a trained mind roam for
answers. But the qualification of "trained" is important. Although
amateurs may make valuable contributions at times, who knows
how much better they could have been with some systematic study
prior to going out on a limb. In art, too, it is possible to achieve
fame and fortune overnight, even without the slightest bit of work
with the tools of the artform—especially when painting and poetry
are at issue. But this is more often illusion. If architects and
composers failed to learn how to achieve their ideals but charged
ahead anyway, the result would be disastrous to the eye and ear,
respectively. Yet, since the object of these human activities is not
primarily to obtain knowledge of reality but to create versions of it
for admiration, excitement, empathy, or a sense of tragedy, finding
logic somewhat in the background should not be surprising.

However, we need to repeat that there *is* a limiting aspect of
logic, as when logic impels us to move from true premises to true
conclusions by its correct use. For example, knowing that with a
few drinks at the party I am not able to drive carefully, and that
this is a likely source of catastrophy, logical thinking would limit me

to a position outside the driver's seat. I *can* reject these limitations; I am free if I do not wish to be limited. I can reject logic and evade the consequences, even though a little effort could have brought to mind what they would most likely be. But we might want to consider that these sort of limitations may not really be that at all. Calling them so misses the point. They are guidelines, perhaps, or clues to sound conduct, just as traffic lights are such clues, despite their occasional inconvenience and unpleasantness. With this point of view, it may be appropriate to characterize the situation by noting that logic does not limit one's liberty; it merely indicates, at its best use, where it would be wise to venture.

ONE LOGIC OR MANY?

Some of the controversial issues surrounding logic have already been mentioned here. There remains one dispute that flourished recently concerning both the character of logic itself and the ways in which logic could be used.

Some philosophers have challenged the idea that fundamentally there can be only one system of logic. Originally Aristotle identified the basic axioms of logic as those true claims that state the basic principles of existence (or being). The laws of noncontradiction, identity, and excluded middle had at one time been widely thought of as both first principles of being and axioms of logic. Gradually this connection was considered less important. Students of what is now called traditional logic later agreed that only one logic exists, but the connection between the basic axioms of logic and reality was left pretty much indeterminate. In other words, granted that logic is the system Aristotle constructed, the issue of whether its axioms also expressed basic principles of existence was left open.

Starting in the modern period and developing in the nineteenth century, an idea of logic quite different from Aristotle's became prominent. In this development logic was held to be "purely formal" and completely independent of any possible metaphysical system. This meant that the connection between the axioms of logic and first principles of reality had been denied, not just left indeterminate. (It is very likely that other developments in philosophy, for example, the prominence of antimetaphysical ideas, precipitated this result.)

As an alternative to conceiving of logic as dependent on certain metaphysical truths, some began to think of it as dependent on the structure of the human mind. The idea that logic consists of the laws of thought became prominent. Because the human mind has a particular structure—that is, each person's mind has this structure—certain principles of reasoning were held to be appropriate.

Subsequently, the idea that the human mind has a particular structure came under severe criticism. Different ways of thinking about geometry, for example, were identified, so that it was found that Euclidian geometry is not the only geometrical system. It appeared plausible to suggest also that the original logic is not the only system of logic appropriate for human beings. Some philosophers argued, very persuasively, that the axioms of logic originally identified by Aristotle and his followers were not necessary for a system to be a logical system. The axioms of logic were considered legislated principles, or laws human beings could decide to impose on their ways of thinking and develop from there. But we need not be bound by the laws of the original system of logic, so these thinkers held.

Defenders of the original system replied by contending that such a view could not be maintained. They argued that any process of thought, to be even minimally productive and cogent, required the basic elements of the original Aristotelian system. It was argued, for example, that in the attempts to symbolize the non-Aristotelian logical systems one could not dispense with the Law of Noncontradiction or with the Law of Identity. To use the symbolism that is so common among logicians everywhere, consider the symbols "A" and "B," or "p," "q," and "r." To make successful use of these symbols in the highly formal elaborations of the rules of different logical systems, one must still accept that p is p or A is A. Otherwise, extreme confusion would result and no rules or laws or entire systems could even be discussed. And reliance on the repeated use of such symbols demonstrates that the axioms Aristotle identified are fundamental and indispensable.

The dispute goes on, of course, and it will probably last as long as human beings are around to consider these issues. We have here seen only one of the more radical objections to the idea that Aristotle's logic is the only true fundamental logical system. Other disputes could be mentioned but they could be discussed in full only in a detailed treatment.

To these and other challenges some answers have been suggested in the present section. We can reiterate that logic can, of course, be thought of independent of its role, namely, to obtain knowledge of reality. We can think of colors separated from what has those colors—that is, we can *distinguish* colors from the objects colored. But in reality these are *inseparable*.

It appears that this is true of logic, also. Accordingly, if this is so with logic, then there would exist a very firm connection between it and some facts, namely, those that are most general, most basic, and indispensable. It is in view of this connection that logic enables us to gain knowledge by its use in so many different areas of investigation. Whereas other methods suit only unique purposes, logic suits the most general purpose of achieving knowledge of reality. Formalists, the response would be made, make the mistake of confusing complete generality with something they call pure formality. But such pure formalism is impossible—even in the most symbolic, abstract discussions of logic and mathematics. Form cannot exist without some actual or possible content. Geometry, the study of physical forms in mathematically precise ways, would not exist without some actual objects that could be shaped or formed as the geometers investigate.

This much should be understood about how logic fares within philosophy today, even by someone only a little interested in our topic. It should be remembered, however, that this much knowledge is not a great deal, and that to believe otherwise can obstruct further inquiry. But used well, as a guide to further inquiry or for future reference, this knowledge can serve the reader well. What is left now is a brief discussion of the more common logical fallacies and widely exhibited errors of thinking. Some of these are quite obvious but others can be quite subtle. Anticipation of these will help one to face all sorts of discussions and attempts at arguing for something—whether in newspaper editorials or in great philosophy books.

COMMON LOGICAL ERRORS

The purpose of this discussion has been to indicate the importance and status of logic and to spell out its most basic features, no more. For anyone who would attempt to make use of logic in more than very simple cases of reasoning, a detailed treatment is indispensable. Most of the time our common sense suffices to identify the usual errors people make, and the same serves the need we have for clear thinking in ordinary circumstances. But as soon as cases become somewhat complicated, the reasoning required can involve complex rules, ones we would have to follow quite deliberately, without just relying on what some call our intuition, or our common sense. For such purposes formal training and study in logic are a must.

Fallacies

The more technical topics in logic include the rules of validity, the various types of argument, the kind of errors most frequently made, the different kinds of statements that arguments comprise, formal means of validating arguments, and the numerous methods that enable one to translate verbal arguments into manageable symbolic form. Aside from the formal aspects of logic, one would usually find it helpful to examine some of the errors in reasoning that arise from extralogical sources (e.g., problems stemming from ambiguous use of words, equivocation between alternative meanings for the same word, confusion of tenses, etc.). There are several very common mistakes in reasoning and argumentation that have been given names, and some of them deserve mention even in this brief informal discussion.

Ad hominem arguments aim to win a point simply by attacking the person whose views are being questioned. Of course, sometimes it is quite legitimate to seek knowledge of someone's character so we can tell if the person is trustworthy. However, when we are engaged in an argument in which the issue of trust does not arise, attacking someone's character is an inappropriate tool for making our case.

Argumentum ad ignoratium consists of defending one's point on grounds that it has not been proved false. What happens here is that ignorance about the truth or falsity of a claim is taken to be ground for its truth. We often meet with this type of thinking when people ask us "Why not?" or "Why shouldn't we?" The idea here is that if you do not know why not, then go ahead—even though no good reason exists to go ahead, or agree to some point. In the same vein, people often ask us to believe something because it might be true, although of course it might also be false. But nothing follows from the fact that something might be so, except that we cannot rule it out. Here, too, mere ignorance about some issue is used to gain support for it. It might be so (i.e., we don't know whether it is or not); therefore, it is (at least probably).

The *genetic fallacy* occurs in arguments that aim to disprove an idea on grounds that its source is defective. For example, a businessman is advocating some reform, so it cannot have merit; it could not be sound. Or a communist made the claim, so it must be wrong. Or, since the advocate of a position has a personal stake in whether it is true or false, it could not be true. More than that must be proven in order to discredit an otherwise well-supported idea, yet many people approach discussion in this fashion.

Then we should mention the common *fallacies of composition and division*. The former is involved in arguments in which one takes it that because members of a group possess some characteristic, the group as a whole does also. Thus, Americans want food on their table but America does not want food on its table, even if this kind of talk is often used as a shortcut to making a valid point. Care must be taken, however, because it can be very misleading to speak, for example, of America's purpose and the public's interest as if these were individuals who have purposes and interests. The fallacy of division is the reverse of the above. Here the characteristics of a group are ascribed to its members. Because America is thought to be prosperous, it does not follow that each American is prosperous.

Finally, a very frequently committed error in reasoning is designated by the Latin expression *post hoc, ergo propter hoc*. It involves thinking that because one thing *followed* another, it was *caused by* it. Quite likely many believers in the occult, faith healing, telepathy, and superstitions base their convictions on reasoning that involves this fallacy. Coincidences that have great impact on a person's life are often viewed as signifying a causal relationship— so when a mother experiences a sharp pain in the chest at the moment that her son is killed hundreds of miles away, this is accepted as causally linked.

Conclusion

This brief sketch of informal fallacies does not bring home the numerous contexts in which they occur. To get a good grip on the nature of these fallacies, as well as on some that involve formal errors, one should examine the discussions in the recommended logic books listed in the Bibliography. Our examination can be useful in helping one learn how to scrutinize the presentations of various viewpoints in editorials, articles, political speeches, and similar expositions. Individual efforts in defending one's beliefs or in discovering that one may be wrong will be enhanced by a closer study of fallacies of logic. To acquire logical skills used in many sciences, one needs far more study than is possible from the foregoing!

More comprehensive logic courses will usually examine a mode of reasoning that is called **induction.** Such reasoning is often involved in scientific research and discoveries. In deductive reasoning the conclusion of a good argument must be true if the premises are true. In inductive reasoning a good argument may have true premises that do not guarantee that the conclusion is true, although the stronger the evidence for the conclusion, the greater the likelihood that it is indeed true.

An illustration of inductive reasoning we are all acquainted with is weather forecasting. Here the forecaster knows numerous facts about current weather conditions, meteorological principles, and the like. From these he or she infers by inductive reasoning that the future holds rain or sunshine in store.

What we accept on the basis of inductive reasoning has often been challenged. If the conclusions are uncertain, can we regard them as knowledge? But if not, and most of our scientific and day-to-day information and thinking is tied up with inductive reasoning, are we not a great deal more ignorant than we would normally care to admit? (The reader will recognize that this was discussed in treating various epistemological positions.)

Finally, aside from the type of argument we have examined very briefly in this chapter, namely, the syllogism, there are many others we have not touched on. In effect, we have only looked at features of the arguments made up of rather simple propositions. But some arguments involve strings of propositions, conditionals, hypotheticals, and various modalities. We use these very often in everyday discourse, as when we say something like, "If Mary went to Germany, and Harry went to France, and if it rained in France but it did not rain in Germany, then, if Joe could not get to Germany . . . etc." Logicians have developed complicated tools by which to analyze such arguments, and scientific or legal theorizing often relies heavily on these tools to make sure its often very elaborate procedures are logically sound. Here, again, someone with even the slightest connection to science or law, where arguments such as these abound, would do very well to investigate logic in greater detail.

QUESTIONS FOR DISCUSSION

1. What is the relationship between the commonsense use of the idea *logical* and the more technical, special meaning of it?
2. Show how logic would assist one in obtaining knowledge. Why did Aristotle think knowledge could be achieved by making use of logic?
3. What is the distinction between practical, everyday uses of logic and the role it can play in testing our beliefs and hunches? What does it mean to use logic deliberately?
4. What reasons were offered in this chapter to support the view that logic has a role in even simple human activities?
5. How would scientists make use of logic?
6. Give some valid arguments and show why they are valid. Offer some invalid arguments and show their invalidity.
7. What are quantifiers? Which term in an argument is the middle term?
8. What reasons were offered in support of the view that logic is possible only when we understand what truth is?
9. Define a valid argument.
10. Define a sound argument.
11. Give some of the views of logic offered by philosophers.
12. What reasons have been offered to defend the compatibility of logical thinking with creativity and emotional openness? Discuss this matter critically.
13. What arguments are offered to support the claim that there can be many different logics? What objections to this view can be raised?
14. Give examples of some of the fallacies of reasoning briefly discussed in this chapter.
15. Discuss logic on the basis of your reading and your personal experiences, indicating how it relates to some of your own concerns.
16. Point to some fallacies of reasoning you have encountered in platitudes, prejudices, commercial or political pitches, etc.

Ethics

$$\approx 5 \approx$$

PRELIMINARIES

Ethics, or morality, concerns itself with the proper goals and principles of human conduct. It does not involve the customs, mores, or conventional etiquette of some group of people, even though these may be influenced by what the members of such a group consider to be ethical or moral. Instead, morality pertains to what is good and evil, right and wrong concerning human beings as such, by virtue of their being human. And it concerns what is open to their choices, not what happens to them because of factors outside their control. In this chapter we will consider this subject matter and it will be referred to by both terms, **ethics** and **morality.**

Why Ethics?

Why there is a role for ethics in human life must be the first issue on our agenda. The discussion below will offer some grounds for an answer that seems to me to be correct. However, as with all these issues, philosophers have given very different answers, some denying that anything like morality applies to human life at all.

Some of these positions will be touched on later.   For now I will offer what I consider good reasons for the pertinence of ethics and morality to human life.

The basic idea is that human beings are free.   We, unlike other animals, can make genuine choices between alternatives.   However, as animals we also face some very basic common alternatives. Animals are equipped by their nature—that is, by their particular characteristics as animals—with inborn means for making the selections required for them to achieve the results that are good, self-serving, and valuable for them.   Animals do not have to choose what they will do, even though they suffer harmful consequences if something interferes with their normal development and behavior. This is not the case with human beings.   Our nature does not equip us with such automatic guidelines.   Some clues to what our existence requires are provided, of course, by our biological system, most of which we share with many other animals.   Like other animals, human beings also feel pain and pleasure.   These sensations provide us with indicators as to whether we are well or ill, at least physically.   To engage successfully in the business of human life we need much more than the simple awareness of pain and pleasure.

The need for ethics arises because human beings have no automatic guidelines by which to live their lives.   "How should I live?" This question requires an answer, and ethics is that part of philosophy that examines, clarifies, and tries to answer, in very general terms, this question.   Its answer must be in general terms because, obviously, it cannot do it for each person individually, in his own circumstances—that is what each person himself must do.   It thus considers the question, How should human beings live?

The purpose of ethics, then, is to discover the most general, universal principles to guide human conduct.   It enters the province of human life because the fact that we need to answer certain questions applies to all human beings except those crucially incapacitated.   We all require some knowledge, some answer to the question, How should I live? or What should I, a human being, do?

How Is Ethics Possible?

Some elements of human life are optional—whether or not bridge playing is part of life is such an optional issue.   Some institutions of life are optional—whether or not we have amateur athletics is probably optional. We explain the existence of these optional features of life by reference to desires or wishes people happen to have but could also trade in for others without much consequence to human life as such.

Ethics is not an optional feature of human life. As some philosophers put it, everyone must play the moral "game" and even trying not to play it is playing it, probably badly. But to prove that ethics is indispensable requires that it be explained as integral in our lives. Aside from explaining what gives rise to the existence of ethics, we must also ask what makes it possible.

First, ethics requires that we can exercise some genuine choices and that we have the capacity to initiate some actions. If this were impossible, the idea that we should act in such and such a fashion would have no application in life..

Second, ethics requires that some principles that apply to conduct be identifiable. Unless we can learn some general principles, ethics has no place in our lives. It consists, after all, of very general principles indeed, pertaining to all human beings. Principles pertain to action, how we should conduct ourselves, and on what basis we should choose or select what we will do. If we could not identify principles, we could never make a sensible selection from among alternative courses of conduct. But, in fact, we can make principled choices, as we do in connection with less universally human tasks in our business and personal lives. Depending on what we aim for, we can identify the principles that will enable us to reach our goal. Thus, it seems that this second requirement of ethics, that we can identify principles of conduct, might be satisfied.

Third, for ethics to be possible there must be some very general, universal, or common goal human beings all share. Principles or standards of conduct are identified in terms of some goal. Unless human beings as such faced some goal(s) in common, universal principles or standards applicable to them all could not be identified and general standards of conduct (moral principles, virtues) could not exist. Ethical systems propose standards of conduct for human beings as such—not for students, women, Caucasians, or some other subgroup. The requirement that ethical positions be universalizable expresses the point succinctly. (Exceptions include the crucially incapacitated, but exceptions are likely in all fields.)

The common goal that is required for ethics is living life well. It is both what makes ethics necessary and what makes it possible— a natural part of human life. The goal of living life well or properly is shared among all things that live: plants, animals, and rational animals. But in our case we need to find out how to live well or properly. Ethics is the branch of knowledge involved in answering this question.

Facts and Values

Values are what a person seeks out (the concept *value* is used to mean whatever people strive for) and ethics is the field concerned with, among other things, basic values, that is, those crucial for human life.

Often the concept *value* is used in circumstances when ethics or morality is not involved, as when we speak of valuables, the truth value of some statement, or economic values. But the concern here is with basic values, that is, those which pertain to human life as such—those we call moral values.

A prominent topic in philosophy as well as in ordinary life is the similarity and/or difference between facts and values. Sometimes people argue that concerning values any opinion is as valid as any other, whereas concerning facts we have clear standards of what is and is not so. If this sharp dichotomy is justified, then ethics as an intelligible, nonmysterious field of inquiry is impossible. By this distinction we must admit that values could never be objects of knowledge. It is impossible to *know* something if all different opinions of it are equally correct. (See the discussions of relativism and subjectivism in chapter 3.) If values are not a species of facts, then we cannot have knowledge of them and the entire enterprise of ethics is left something undecidable, indeterminate, and even illusory.

The kinds of ethics we will consider here are ones that reject the fact / value dichotomy and hold that values, including moral values, are a variety of facts, albeit very complicated ones. Therefore, the answer to the ethical question, What should I, a human being, do? can be a factual statement of the form, People should act so as to achieve some goal. This answer is not different in type from answers to more simple ones such as the following: What should I, a carpenter, do? and How should an airline pilot live? We could easily consider the following answers factual: Learn to excell with your tools and produce quality furniture, and Never make long-range social plans in one location.

Later in this chapter I will indicate how those who deny that values could be facts in any sense still advance theories about what is right and wrong. But strictly speaking, any ethical theory or system that aims to be on the same footing with other nonmysterious, nonoccultish fields would have to view values as a variety of facts. For us to obtain knowledge of moral or ethical values, these values would have to be a kind of fact in the world; it would have to be possible to distinguish between correct and incorrect identification. If we could not provide objective standards to tell the difference between correct and incorrect value judgments, the kind of ethics we are here considering would be impossible.

Facts of morality would, of course, differ from such facts as Richard Nixon's resignation of the United States presidency in August 1974. Yet nonmoral facts are not everywhere the same kind. Two plus two equals four is a fact. Socks are worn on feet is also a fact. But these two facts both differ considerably from the fact about Nixon's resignation!

WHAT IS MORALLY GOOD?

Earlier we saw that one sensible explanation for the existence of ethics is that human beings need to learn the principles by which their lives should be guided, which will enable them to live well as human beings. Moral philosophers engage in the inquiry that explores the related issues and may even yield a correct moral position. Those philosophers who advance ethical positions aim to clarify and provide an answer to the moral questions human beings ask.

Many competing moralities offer answers to the main ethical question: How should I, a person, live my life? We will examine some of these by first outlining their idea of what is the highest good, or the main goal to strive for in human life. We will deal only with those ethical positions that provide an argument in support of their answer to the basic ethical question. Others reject the very idea of arguing for such an answer and offer the vehicles of revelation, special intuition, mystical insight, and the like as means for obtaining answers to moral questions. We will touch on some of these later in the chapter.

Hedonism

Most of us have heard of people who believe that the proper goal for us all is the pursuit of maximum pleasure. Sometimes such people have in mind increasing the existence of pleasure as such (measured either by reference to degrees of intensity or amounts). Sometimes not all pleasure, including those of nonhuman animals, but only the pleasure of human beings in toto is viewed as the proper goal. And for others the pleasure of the individual actor or agent is the only relevant goal to be pursued.

In this discussion we will consider the ethical position of **hedonism,** which holds that we should aim at the *maximum amount of pleasure for ourselves, for the individual actor.* First, however, a few comments should be offered about the version of hedonism that proclaims the *maximum amount of pleasure of humanity as the proper moral goal for everyone.*

According to the form of hedonism that declares the maximum possible amount of pleasure as the proper moral goal everyone should pursue, pleasure is a good in itself. It is not the pleasure of some individual person but pleasure as such that is considered good. (This is often referred to as the view that pleasure has *intrinsic* value, independent of its value *to* someone or something.) That pleasure is good in itself seems to be evident—if one *feels* good, that is what pleasure amounts to, plain and simple. And the goodness of good feelings is clearly self-evident. We are just the sort of beings who welcome pleasure and resist pain, at least under normal circumstances. Therefore, the theory that pleasure itself is intrinsically good has considerable appeal on the basis of our experiences with pleasure and pain.

It is not so evident that we should increase the amount of pleasure—regardless of whose pleasure is involved—just because it is normally preferable to pain. Of course, it may be possible to calculate whether our actions will increase the amount of pleasure for us and those near us, so that we can identify principles of conduct that will accomplish this limited goal. But calculation of the amount of pleasure in the world is not possible for any one person embarking on action; therefore, one *cannot* learn the answer to the ethical question, How should I act? if that answer depends on whether some action will be a significant contributor to the pleasure that exists in the world. Remember that one of the requirements of an ethical theory is that the moral goal(s) specified must be reachable.

The best we might do in defense of this form of hedonism is to consider that it may evolve into a different form, one we will consider next. It seems possible that the very idea of the maximum amount of pleasure is confused; thus, it would seem best to abandon it and consider the type of hedonism that deals with increasing individual pleasures. On the other hand, it is also clear that something like the idea of maximum pleasure or "welfare," understood to indicate the satisfaction of desires, governs much *social* or *public* policy. When social planners allocate the resources put at their disposal, they often think in terms of whether a certain distribution scheme is more or less likely to increase the satisfaction of existing human desires in the community. This will be dealt with in more detail in the next section, on utilitarianism.

More traditional is the hedonism in terms of which one ought to act so as to increase one's own pleasure. Hedonism considers pleasure to be measurable. Both the intensity and the quantity of pleasure are open to determination. Some hedonists make a very sharp distinction between the finer pleasures possible to human beings and the simple pleasures other animals can experience. Others see no basis for that distinction and believe simply that each and every person has as his or her proper goal in life the accumulation of as many pleasurable experiences as possible. In turn, the principles of conduct we should all invoke in making decisions about what we should do are those most likely to lead to the attainment of the above goal.

It should be noted that this doctrine has the correct form of a moral point of view. We are to do something we are capable of doing (namely, choose to increase our pleasurable experiences) and we are to live by principles that we can identify. This does not yet show that the doctrine is correct. It shows only that the doctrine, as described, can be a *candidate* for the best moral position for human beings. It appears to be a plausible answer to the ethical question, How should I live as a human being?

Criticism and Answers.   There are some difficulties we should point out, however.   These challenge the view that hedonism is the best answer to the moral question.   We can raise some of these challenges and postpone for later whether they are decisive.*

An internal problem of hedonism is that by pursuing pleasure, we often find ourselves undecided about what to do.   Many pleasures are of equal force.   Going to the movies and staying home to watch television could be equally pleasurable.   It would appear that to decide which should be done requires some standard other than that of maximizing pleasure.   Moreover, by pursuing our personal pleasures we frequently find ourselves in conflict with what other people want to do.   If someone would be pleased to have my company but I would not be pleased at having his, one of us would then have to give up on pursuing pleasure.   Thus, the goal of pleasure is often inapplicable to everyone involved because not everyone can pursue it.   We cannot be responsible for doing what it is impossible to do.   And in the community of others it would be impossible for all people to pursue pleasure—some would have to abandon their goals.   A moral position that results in frequent conflicts between people is impossible to generalize for everyone.

Finally, as a criticism of one form of hedonism, it is very likely that physical pleasures are not the only ones we are capable of feeling. Human beings have a more complex emotional makeup than other (even "higher") animal forms.   This is due, probably, to our advanced form of consciousness and our sensitivity to factors other than the physical.   The restriction of pleasures to physical ones because these are more likely to be measurable could be artificial.

Also, we may find it possible, eventually, to measure at least the intensity of other experiences.   Then their goodness or badness could become possible goals to be pursued.   However, these more complex varieties of pleasure, such as feelings of emotional satisfaction, are products of learning and opportunity; they are not inherent in human nature.   These complex pleasures or satisfactions are thus not universalizable.   Not all people could refer to them and the possibility of conflict within oneself and among different

---

* Many critics of moral positions simply assume that some things or courses of conduct or goals are morally good and then argue that the theory being examined fails because it fails to accommodate these assumed notions.   This is not a valid approach, however, since it presupposes that these ideas of what is good are correct.

people increases considerably when they are taken as goals that we *all* should pursue.

The hedonist will have replies to these objections, of course. The merits of these replies will not be discussed—readers will benefit from trying to assess for themselves whether they have any. For example, concerning pleasures of equal force the hedonist could argue that under such circumstances a flip of a coin is as good a device for coming to a decision as any other. About the conflicts between the pleasures of different people, which may cancel each other out and effectively render the pursuit of pleasure impossible for all concerned, the hedonist could claim that limitations on what people can do will exist no matter what their proper goal is. One must simply realize this and calculate the maximum attainable pleasure accordingly. Concerning more complex pleasures the hedonist may admit that they are more difficult to calculate but urge that we do the best we can with what we know. Hedonists may reply to those who deny the possibility of universal pleasures (because of different education and circumstances generating different pleasures) by the following: Pleasures may come in many forms but they are all pleasures and can be measured as such. It is one's duty to increase the amount of one's pleasure no matter what kind of pleasure it is. The objection is irrelevant.

The idea that it is our moral responsibility to seek pleasure for ourselves is not widely proclaimed except perhaps in *Playboy* and similar magazines. Yet in ordinary life most people do seek out many pleasures. Spectator sports, parties, vacations, eating, drinking, and, of course, sexual experiences are widely pursued. Some people pursue these pleasures diligently, some even systematically. Often we view such conduct as the result of inner drives we do not really choose at all. In that case the conduct would have no moral significance, since choice must be possible for morality to even enter the picture. But for some of us the pursuit of pleasure is indeed a serious undertaking, something to be learned and cultivated, not at all inborn. The idea that experiencing the maximum possible amount of pleasure could be *the moral goal* all human beings should strive for is not obviously absurd. Certainly some very prominent philosophers (e.g., Jeremy Bentham) have argued with great complexity and ingenuity for just this position. One who is concerned about what is good and what human beings ought to do will benefit from a close examination of these ideas, however unpopular they might be within our culture.

Utilitarianism

It will be evident in this section that **utilitarianism** is related to hedonism. From the name of this doctrine it appears that utilitarians emphasize what is useful. But this is just an appearance; the doctrine does not advocate that the good is that which is useful. Instead, the substance of the theory is that *the good is the greatest happiness of the greatest number.*

Happiness in this theory is not the same as pleasure, although it is related to the idea of pleasure. It would be more accurate to consider this view as the contention that the greatest welfare (well-being) of the greatest number of human beings is the good, and that we should do that which helps to achieve this condition.

We must first ask what this happiness or welfare is supposed to consist of. One of the main issues of utilitarianism is just the one we have mentioned here. What is welfare? Before we can examine the arguments for and against utilitarianism, we have to get a reasonably clear idea of what welfare is supposed to be within utilitarian theory.

In most utilitarian theories—and there are several versions in evidence—welfare is closely tied to the achievement of desired goals, the satisfaction of preferences, wants, and wishes. Whenever someone has his or her desires satisfied, we can justifiably hold that that person is well off and that the person's welfare has been attained, or so utilitarians would maintain.

Of course, utilitarians realize that some desires cancel out others, lead to conflict, and may even be self-destructive or destructive of society. Some qualifications are needed to make this a plausible theory. Some theorists hold that desires or preferences that limit the realization of the preferences of others do not count as significant in understanding welfare and what we should do to achieve it. Others make welfare depend on what are *healthful* or *natural* desires or preferences.

Utilitarian welfare or happiness is frequently identified with physical and psychological well-being (as these are characterized by the medical and psychological scientists of a community), instead of being left to subjective determination—desires, preferences, etc. Frequently the health and the economic well-being of (the population of) a community are picked as manifestations of such a goal. (In political theory this view comes to the fore in the doctrine of the *welfare state*.)

With these initial points in mind, we can now ask why the good should be thought of as that which fits the utilitarian definition. Why is the greatest happiness of the greatest number the proper goal we should all strive for?

Utilitarianism, like many other ethical theories, is tied to broader philosophical positions. One crucial philosophical underpinning of utilitarian ethics is that the good must be identifiable by means of direct observation. Otherwise, it would not be possible to know what is good, that is, what human beings are supposed to achieve. If we cannot know what is good—and thus have no way of learning how to achieve it—then it could not make realistic sense to hold ourselves and others responsible for achieving it. If only the perceivable, sensible things in the world can be known, and if there is a good we should strive for, it must be perceivable.

Historically, the epistemological base of utilitarian ethics is that we can know only that which we can identify by using the senses, that which we can measure so as to make sure it exists. There is ample plausibility to this view of human knowledge to accept it as a background for the sake of understanding the case for utilitarianism.

Given this point about identifying the good, the best candidate for what is the good or most desirable thing in human life is the combination of physical and mental well-being. The latter is difficult to identify, but the former would appear knowable, so utilitarians usually focus on physical welfare, which consists in having the basic human needs and wants satisfied. These needs include food, shelter, medical care, and protection from the elements and from disasters. Most obvious is the need for a certain degree of economic well-being—the capacity to obtain from various sources in nature and in society what one requires for a decent level of subsistence. The material conditions needed to maintain one's physical health and safety, and the requirements to sustain these— these are clearly identifiable as good for us.

Learning about mental well-being is not so easy. In utilitarian theory this problem is usually handled by leaving the matter to subjective understanding. In other words, the psychic welfare is best left to the individual for judgment—except in some drastic cases where psychological distress is clearly evident to observers. (In terms of this theory it is possible to deny that someone is mentally or psychologically well off, even when that person claims to be well off, but only rarely. Cases of involuntary mental hospitalization involve these exceptions.)

To summarize, utilitarian ethical theory is the view that the good is a state of physical and psychological well-being, the former identifiable publicly, the latter left to each person to judge privately. Right conduct maximizes the amount of what is good in the world, that is, increases to the fullest possible degree the physical and psychological well-being of people. The basis of this view is that it can be meaningfully implemented and it conforms to the requirements of a sound theory of knowledge; in comparison with other theories, utilitarianism is held by its advocates to succeed—it makes sense and it can be used to conduct one's life, whereas others fail on both counts.

Criticism and Replies.   Utilitarianism is not without its problems. One criticism is that utilitarianism is unworkable. It is impossible to know whether or not some action does in fact manage to contribute to the overall well-being of the membership of a human community, and it is even more impossible to know whether it contributes to humanity in its entirety. If it is impossible to guide one's conduct by reference to whether (the utilitarian goal of) maximum happiness is being promoted, then the theory falls prey to the criticism that no meaningful, implementable guidelines to conduct can be generated from it. Any ethical theory unable to provide such guidelines is unsuccessful.

Another criticism is that people could act in accordance with utilitarian ethics and have obviously nonutilitarian motives. An individual could contribute to the welfare of millions simply to achieve a good reputation, with no thought of the greatest happiness. Another could mistakenly believe that some act will benefit mankind, whereas it actually has adverse consequences. ("I meant well" is a frequent comment of those who are responsible for disaster, and sometimes it is quite true. Also, "He helped the poor a great deal, but he did it to satisfy his need for recognition" is a true description of some philanthropists.)

A further objection to utilitarianism is that it requires a centrally organized, dictatorial state. In order to satisfy the greatest welfare of the greatest number, a vast quantity of information is required, far more than any individual can obtain (as mentioned before). Everyone's needs and the total resources of the community must be known in order to learn what actions would maximize the benefit to be reaped from these resources.

But all this knowledge would be useless if whoever had it could not control the distribution of resources to those who would get the most benefit from them. (The utilitarian theory of justice is therefore often called *distributive* justice.) But all of this would require that select experts of a community—or, on a large scale, a fully centralized state—shoulder the ethical responsibilities that each person is supposed to fulfill in the role of a moral agent.

Such an arrangement would be moral paternalism, critics have argued. The responsibility for attaining the proper goals of human conduct would be taken away from individuals and political leaders would be the sole moral decision makers. This would make utilitarianism something other than an ethical theory, which requires human self-responsibility.

Finally, utilitarianism appears to violate certain commonsense ethical precepts. It is argued that by its tenets it would often be morally correct to lie, cheat, or even murder to facilitate the goal of the greatest happiness of the greatest number of people. Some persons achieve psychic well-being by being lied to (about their actions, health, looks, achievements, and so on). Promises might have to be broken in terms of utilitarian ethics, because keeping them would not contribute to the proper goal we should all pursue. For example, one could perhaps enhance the public welfare by violating a person's last will and testament or by reneging on promises made to those with no power to enforce their fulfillment. These and similar loopholes render utilitarianism suspect. Our commonsense ethical precepts may not be a complete enough ethical doctrine, but we need to beware of theories that violate them wholesale.

Now we can consider what utilitarians might say in response to these critical comments.

As to the unworkability of utilitarian ethics, there may be a way to escape this charge. It is not impossible within utilitarianism to identify general principles. In terms of these one could work to advance the overall happiness of mankind even without knowing how a particular act contributes to it specifically. This form of the doctrine is called rule-utilitarianism and it is contrasted with act-utilitarianism, which is widely admitted to be unworkable. If we were able to identify some general principles or rules of conduct that would aid us in supporting the utilitarian goal, then it would no longer be impossible to pursue that goal. For example, on the political level, by way of laws and policies, it is generally thought that following a certain course of conduct enhances the national welfare, even the welfare of the entire globe. In personal, individual conduct as well, one might follow the principle: "Whenever possible, pay heed to what people around you need." One's actions would thus be geared toward the general utilitarian goal everyone ought to pursue.

Concerning the problem that some people could further the good (of utilitarianism) without intending it as their goal, it is possible to view this as doing the right thing for the wrong reasons. The crucial fact is, according to utilitarianism, that actions are right because they contribute to the goal of the greatest happiness of the greatest number, not because they enhance the actor's reputation. Someone who acts from the wrong motives (i.e., wanting to be well thought of) may not be praiseworthy for his acts; however, it is another thing to deny the rightness of what he does. In this case we might recall the saying that hypocrisy is the compliment vice pays to virtue—so that even those with dubious motives are drawn to do what is right in order to achieve their goals with some measure of respectability. The occasional misuses of a good tool do not make the tool bad; the fact that people can do what is right by utilitarian standards, without meaning to, does not invalidate those standards. As for those who intend to further the utilitarian good but fail, for them it must be said that they ought to have paid greater heed to what needs to be done to achieve their goal. Meaning well is not enough. One needs to make sure that all that is required is being done to lead to success. So "I meant well" is not an excuse, although it points out that one did not do so badly as one could have (by not even trying but intending the opposite perhaps). (Even on a commonsense level we suspect that "I meant well" is often an excuse for negligence, not testimony of serious intent.)

It can also be contested that utilitarianism requires a centrally organized society. Let's recall that each person is the best judge of his or her psychic well-being. There is a great deal of psychic well-being involved even in what appears to be plain physical well-being. So decisions as to what will produce one's happiness would to a large extent have to be one's own. In turn, a utilitarian society would more likely be individualist than collectivist. Many utilitarians argue that it is impossible to engage in interpersonal utility comparisons—that one simply cannot weigh and compare the respective importance of different people's preferences, desires, and welfare, whether physical or psychic. Thus, the only way to secure the greatest happiness of the greatest number is by giving up on central economic planning and moral paternalism in general. Letting everyone engage in the pursuit of individual, personal happiness is the best road to the greatest happiness of the greatest number. (In this way utilitarianism might change into a form of egoism, a position we will look at shortly.) In terms of this reply one could also accept that the distribution of wealth for purposes of achieving the utilitarian goal is best performed in a free market economy. In such a system, if no one is permitted to use force on another, then desires, needs, and preferences can be satisfied in voluntary cooperation and competition. Since individuals know best what is going to produce their well-being or happiness (at least in the majority of cases), this arrangement—and not a centrally organized society—is best for purposes of living life in terms of utilitarian ethics.

Finally, the commonsense ethical precepts may not be sound, anyway; therefore, seeking mainly to adjust to them in a comprehensive ethical system could be a bad idea from the start. Even if these precepts do contain a kind of practical wisdom acquired in the evolution of human existence, it may not be true that they are contradicted by utilitarian ethics. Cases might be imagined in which utilitarian conduct would violate these precepts. It does not follow that realistically this would occur. It is quite likely, also, that if these precepts express practical (but nonsystematically developed) wisdom, they are the general rules utilitarians believe will promote the greatest happiness of the greatest number. Being honest, keeping one's promises, and even abiding by someone's last will and testament could be useful habits by which to ensure the furtherance of the utilitarian goal. Honesty, justice, integrity, and other virtues of wide acceptance would then be thought of as the correct means of achieving what utilitarianism holds to be the good we should all aim for.

Some features of utilitarianism will be touched on again later when we turn to political philosophy. For now, this brief discussion should suffice to acquaint readers with one of the prominent and philosophically significant ethical theories. Among Anglo-American philosophers it is perhaps the most widely discussed and respected ethical position today.

Altruism

Altruism is undoubtedly the most widely advocated, defended, and proclaimed moral position within human history and within our culture, as well. Among the many philosophically discussed moral positions, this one has achieved the distinction of gaining prominence within the language of nonphilosophers. Most people have heard that altruism is the moral code by which we should live our lives. The idea is now virtually synonymous with being morally good.

The term *altruism* was coined quite recently in human intellectual history, but its basic idea is very old indeed. This is that the moral goal of every human being should be the well-being or good of others. Service to *other* people alone, or to humanity in general, is the altruistic moral goal, and all the more specific principles of morality (or human virtues) must be geared to the achievement of this goal. The standard of morality consists in whatever *others* need for their well-being.

The argument for altruism comes mainly from the belief that unless people take their prime moral responsibility to be doing good for others, they would conduct themselves ruthlessly and cruelly toward their fellow human beings. Altruism stands in opposition to what its proponents believe is a very probable, if not inherent, inclination of people to take advantage of others whenever the opportunity arises. In a way, altruism is a viewpoint that takes as given the evil of selfish pursuits, considering these as leading to conflict among human beings unless restrained by morality, that is, the *obligation* to serve others, help them, and love them.

It is not unfair to observe that altruism views human nature as basically antisocial, as tending toward hurting others when this would satisfy one's pleasures and desires.* Altruism considers it

---

* The idea that man is tainted with "original sin," and will therefore be destructive both to his own and others' welfare, is well known. Although this is a religious idea, it has gained support from secular thinkers, also. We could cite many nonreligious theories in which human nature is considered at least partly base and opportunistic.

a central feature of morality to steer human beings away from inborn desires or inclinations for self-gratification, self-serving conduct, pride, vanity, and conceit. What human beings require for themselves is well enough provided for by these instinctual drives. To remove man from the realm of the jungle, the sphere of beastlike existence, to a higher, civilized, peaceful, cooperative stage, a morality is required to provide for suitable motivation. Our natural motives are selfish; this we share with other animals. Our human motives, cultivated by a recognition of the quarrelsome, hostile tendencies in us, should direct us toward the well-being and benefit of our fellow human beings.

Once it is accepted that motivation toward self-satisfaction is part of our natural, even instinctive constitution and inclination, it is a logical consequence that any viable moral position must direct us toward something outside ourselves, away from self-service. This is because, as we pointed out earlier, moral goals must be something we can choose to pursue. Moral principles must be chosen. Altruism directs us toward the goal of benefitting others or society or humanity (there are variations on this within altruistic positions). That is a goal we can choose; it is not automatic or innate. And we can all choose it, at least on first view. Therefore, it is a generalizable goal, one that can serve as the proper goal for human beings as such. Without the universal moral responsibility to pursue this goal, we would have no motivation to practice the virtues that can produce a peaceful, productive, just society. Why would we be honest, fair, and the like? Why would we pay our debts, keep our promises, respect others' property, fight for the security of the community, and defend liberty? Guided by the motive for sheer self-satisfaction, as we are by our animal nature or instincts anyway, why should we not cheat, lie, steal, murder, and neglect the welfare of the community? According to the altruist position, no reason exists for abstaining from such conduct unless the duty to serve others is accepted as binding on all.

Criticism and Replies. There are objections to altruism, in spite of its apparent superiority. First of all, it could well be false that people have inborn motives or drives causing them to serve their own well-being and take advantage of others when possible. Morality is needed for us to learn how to live well. Therefore, if morality applies to us, we do not have self-evident knowledge of what is to our or anyone else's benefit. We might, of course, be able to discover our own best interest more readily than that of others.

Second, it is not obviously true that we are geared by nature toward harming others whenever the chance arises. It is quite likely that all of us have the *capacity* for destructive action, yet this does not mean that we are *tending* toward it. If human nature did contain these basic drives, it is doubtful that ethical positions advanced by philosophers and others could escape the influence. It would be very likely that altruism itself reflects these harmful drives or tendencies.

It seems also that many people who have chosen to pursue their self-interest and self-satisfaction have not found that doing harm to others helped them to achieve these; to the contrary, many selfish people, concerned with doing what is best for themselves, engage in very productive and widely beneficial endeavors. Thus, it is very likely untrue, even at a cursory glance, that selfish motivation *must* lead to taking advantage of others (except, perhaps, in a mutually beneficial sense, as, for example, when we take advantage of the desire some people have for dancing, by watching them and so enjoying ourselves). Altruism assumes that it is in our selfish interest, more often than not, to hurt other people, to treat them unfairly, and to lie, cheat, and be unjust. This assumption conceives of human nature as benefitting from doing harm to others. This idea is not at all self-evident, especially without the assumption about the basically beastly or hostile innate drives of human beings. This idea of human nature, as tending toward mutual antagonism among people, appears to involve a view of nature in general as productive of freak entities, beings with mutually incompatible tendencies. (It is true, of course, that both theology and psychology have given us theories proclaiming just this kind of inner tension within human nature.)

Finally, altruism is not so evidently practicable as it appears on first inspection. Doing good for others requires that we learn what that good is. Yet others may not accept this judgment; they may be mistaken not to, but to do good for them will require acting against their own judgment. This could very likely result in open conflict—and the evidence from meddling mothers, meddling friends, meddling governments, and so forth, all supported by reference to good intentions, seems to bear out this prospect. A related problem is that if people in general do look out for their own interests as a matter of innate motivation, then the need or responsibility to do them good and to serve *their* interest (which they are already doing by nature) would be superfluous.

The altruist's answer to these critical points would consist, more than likely, of the following: History bears out the point about man's destructive nature. Some people may escape the force of this even without adopting the altruist position, but this is only by chance. Any sustained participation in social life requires altruism. (For those alone on desert islands morality does not apply.) The notion that people would themselves benefit from treating others fairly, speaking truly, respecting each others' needs and wants, and even helping each other out is perhaps correct for some occasions. But in times of danger or scarcity, people would most likely resort to anything if they were not bound by the moral duty to serve others first. Certainly, morality may not be needed under normal, uncomplicated circumstances. But when difficult decisions must be made, we can live right only by choosing the principles that do not come naturally, that do not simply accommodate our inclinations.

As a second reply, it is not at all odd for human nature to be somewhat freakish. Human beings are unique in nature; no other living creatures seem to have managed to create so much misery for themselves—so much internal conflict, agony, and tragedy. Human beings are the neurotic, psychotic, nervous, guilt-ridden, awkward, frightened, and similarly plagued animals. In light of this peculiarity of the human species, it is not unreasonable that human conduct should be constrained by responsibilities directing people away from themselves and toward others. Left without such guidance, human beings would have disappeared as a species long ago.

When we come to the difficulty of practicing altruism, the only response to be made is that care must be taken to make certain that what we do for others is for their good. Once this is accomplished, we can justify acting against others' mistaken judgment. After all, is it not better to help others even though they disagree than to tolerate their acting contrary to what is good for them by rejecting our help? What would millions of people do without the help offered by laws that prohibit self-destructive conduct? Even if those who are being helped do not know it, their being helped is still a fact—and that is what is important, not what they believe.

As to why we ought to help others even though they are driven to help themselves, the answer could be that by removing ourselves from our own drives we can be more objective, accurate, and successful in helping people in general, thus securing some measure of peace. In those cases where others are being helped, arbitrary feelings can be put aside in favor of careful judgment.

Egoism

In contrast to altruism, which enjoys widespread vocal support in both academic moral philosophy and the culture at large, **egoism**—concern for one's own well being—is a position in ethics with hardly any intellectual support. Of course, that is not what is important. What is agreeable to even the most renowned philosophers may still be very wrong. And the public sector of a culture is no less susceptible to error. However, when there is not enough time to study the various competing ethical positions, it is perhaps understandable that respectability and popularity become substitutes for independent judgment. The depth of the present treatment cannot overcome this problem.

Pseudo-egoisms. Egoism has several versions. A famous variety of egoism is definitely not a possible ethical position. This is the view that everyone always does what is in his or her interest. The view, called psychological egoism, lacks a crucial feature of any possible *ethics,* namely, the freedom to pursue or refrain from pursuing the right course of conduct. As stated above, it is obvious that psychological egoism is not a possible ethics, since there is no mention of what should or ought to be done, only of what is being done.

Several other often-discussed versions of egoism fail to qualify as possible moral positions. The subjectivist egoist, who claims that his and only his unique best interest has merit, fails because morality is by its nature a universalizable system. It cannot be something that applies to only one, unique entity.

The idea that all people should do what they as individuals feel, like, or wish will not succeed as a moral position, either. As with hedonism, what is liked, wished, or responded to with good feelings varies enormously and may not be universalized, that is, put into a consistent order for all to pursue. Moreover, these are not what one is free to choose. Only if learning to like something comes before liking could one attach moral significance to liking and doing what one likes. But then it must start with the process of learning, and liking, wishing, etc., could only be secondary. One can *learn* by choice, but one cannot *feel* the emotion of liking someone or something by choice. Emotions are responses to things, very likely based on what we have previously learned and decided about something.

Ethical Egoism.   The form of egoism that can be a *bona fide* moral position is one that avoids the problems cited above. The basic statement of this position is that each person should live so as to achieve his or her rational self-interest. This position does not assume that people will automatically do what is in their rational self-interest; it can be universalized to apply to everyone because people's rational self-interest is what suits them as human beings and as the individuals they happen to be, knowledge of which is available to anyone who cares to consider the issue.

The case for ethical egoism, or the morality of rational self-interest, may be outlined as follows: As living beings we need a guide to conduct. We require principles that will serve to provide us with guidelines when we cannot assess the merits of each action from the start. We could hardly act correctly if this last were necessary. As living beings we share with other animals the value of life. But life occurs in individual (living) things.

The value of *human* life, unlike animals' lives, cannot be pursued automatically. We must learn to do it. And the particular life we can pursue and about which we can exercise choices is our own. By understanding who we are and what we are, we can identify the standards by which our own life can most likely be advanced properly.

In short, the ethical egoist holds that human life is the value to be pursued with the aid of a moral code, and since one's own life is the only one a person can advance (pursue as something of value) in a morally relevant way (by choice), each person should live it successfully within that person's own context (as the individual one is within one's circumstances). Even more briefly put, people should pursue their own individual happiness, and the principles that make this possible are the moral principles and virtues suited for leading a human life.

The details of the egoist moral code, like those of the other moral positions we have considered, are not amenable to discussion.

The central virtue of the egoistic ethic is rationality, the uniquely human way of being aware of the world.   Success in life or happiness for any human being must be achieved in a way suited to human life. Virtue consists of being as *human* as possible in one's circumstances. Each person is a human being by virtue of the distinctive capacity to choose to think, to attend to the world rationally (by way of careful and sustained logical thought); therefore, to succeed as a person, everyone should make that choice.   For the egoist, rationality is the highest virtue, although other virtues, which must be rationally established (or at least capable of such establishment), are also spelled out in ethical egoism.

Finally, the goal, one's happiness, is something that should be sharply distinguished from pleasure, fun, or thrills.   Egoism of the sort that can be a moral position is not hedonistic—although it can turn out that for most people being happy will also involve having many enjoyable and pleasurable experiences.   Yet happiness is mostly a reflective attitude about how well one is doing in life and how well one is doing as a person.   This is because human beings, as reflective, self-conscious creatures, can benefit from doing what suits them, and knowing that they have been the cause of this benefit is a source of immense joy.

Egoism, unlike other ethical positions, considers the proper attitude in life to be *informed* selfishness—not, however, pathological self-centeredness (egotism).   Pride, ambition, integrity, honesty, and other traits that are by nature of value to any human life are considered virtues.   In turn, self-sacrifice and devotion to others as a matter of principle are considered morally repugnant.   But the worst, most reprehensible way of conducting oneself is to fail to think and exercise rational judgment, to evade reality and leave oneself to blind impulse, others' influence, the guidance of thoughtless clichés, and the like.   Since knowledge is indispensable for successful realization of goals, including the central goal of happiness, failure to exert the effort to obtain it—thus fostering error, misunderstanding, and confusion—is most disastrous to oneself and, hence, immoral.

Egoism is not advocated widely as an ethical code.   Indeed, it seems that those who use the term favorably often advocate a rejection of ethics.   Yet, many act as if they accepted egoism for their ethical system without being fully able to articulate its tenets. People strive to be happy, to succeed in career, school, marriage, and the numerous projects they undertake. Inventors are usually devoted to success, as are financiers, politicians, doctors, and most productive people. (There are some obviously mean-tempered people who also strive to succeed, but very often they try to achieve results without the work naturally required.) Even being rational is often acknowledged as the great virtue, as when people express dismay with unreasonableness and with their own failure to think —"Dammit, I didn't think!"—and with thoughtlessness in general.

Critics and Defenders. The critics have much to say about the egoist's position. They condemn it for its allegedly naive view of human nature—the idea that we are born without destructive impulses and that we should simply go about achieving our natural goals. They say that egoism leads to self-centeredness, *egotism*, the ruthless pursuit of gain, wealth, and power, prompted by the complex and often destructive motives that lie deep within us. (In a way, altruism is *the* criticism of egoism!)

On a more formal point, egoism as a moral theory is thought to disallow universal implementation. Suppose you are asked by another person what he or she should do and suppose that in fact it would be in his or her interest to marry the person you also want to marry. Could you as a consistent egoist give the correct advice to the person asking for it? If you do, you will have undermined your own self-interest. If you do not, you will have shown that egoism *cannot* be universalized to everyone. In general, when conflicts between the interests of human beings emerge, egoism appears to send people on a warpath because it lacks a coordinating principle that goes beyond the self-interests of the people in conflict. The criticism amounts, in fact, to charging egoism with generating contradictory plans of action: people both should and should not do certain things. Any ethical position found in this dilemma has to fail because it leads to the view that what one should do *cannot* be done!

A further objection is that all the talk about happiness really leaves us with very little to go on. Just what exactly should we pursue? What is this happiness, anyway? By saying that it is the awareness of ourselves as being successful at living as people—that is, rationally—this position prejudges that rational living will lead to something we ought to achieve. But is it not possible that something else besides this "happiness"—which seems very self-indulgent anyway—is worth pursuing? Could there not be far more important goals (e.g., political liberty, social justice, being a productive member of society) that overshadow happiness?

Finally, it does not even appear likely that rationality can produce happiness for a person. Many rational people, scholarly and artistic achievers such as scientists, lawyers, and writers, have been notably unhappy. On the other hand, some of the most irrational, whimsical, and haphazard people retire in luxury to Miami Beach to live out their lives in full bliss.

The egoist of the sort we have been considering will, of course, have responses to these objections. Again, the reader will have to assess both the objections and the answers.

In response to the charge that he is naive about human nature, the egoist could reply that he is concerned only with the essentials. What the critic sees as naiveté is what in reality is focusing only on the morally relevant aspects of every person, the capacity to freely choose to think. The misery, neurosis, cruelty, and self-destruction that often characterize human life are explainable in terms of people's refusal to think through the requirements of their lives and their willingness to meddle in the lives of others (always for others' good, of course). Were people to stick to doing good for themselves, much of the disarray would disappear. Moreover, such factors do not prove inherent conflict in human nature. As long as we can find some well-integrated people who live with peace of mind and are happy, this possibility is established for all human life.

The case about conflicts of interest, usually a conflict of desires and wishes, begs an important question, or so the egoist would say. If rationality is the first principle or virtue of egoism, then the appropriate course is to deal with the question, What should we do when what we want or desire conflicts? We should not conclude that a conflict precludes resolution. Of course, if the rational answer is to cheat and lie, then so be it—that is what then would be the right choice. (Sometimes cheating and lying at least seem quite right, as when we cheat against a crooked poker player to teach him a lesson, or lie to a Nazi SS officer about where our best friend, a Jew, happens to be.) But it is very doubtful that lying would be rational in cases like the one cited earlier involving rival suitors. Once the consequences are appraised—no one would trust another's advice any longer, and the beloved person would be deprived of a say in the matter—it could turn out to be irrational to lie. The rational course could well be to explain that both people are in love with another and let each make an honest attempt to earn this individual's love, and then let the chips fall and the best relationship come about. Certainly friends have done this before and are proud of it.

In general, egoism holds that each person should pursue his or her own self-interest, namely, happiness or success in life; furthermore, the common factor for all human beings by which this goal is attainable is discovered by doing something that is in everyone's self-interest, that is, thinking rationally. Self-interest, so understood, cannot be viewed as presenting necessary conflicts among good (that is, self-interestedly motivated) individuals. Conflicts between desires, wishes, and wants can be resolved by careful thought, which is in everyone's best interest. Only in periods of inattentiveness or irrationality—when one is impulsive and refuses to think matters through carefully—will conflicts be unresolved or resolved badly.

The difficulty of defining happiness is not a problem of ethics but of epistemology. This difficulty faces any complex system of ideas. It is enough to note, according to the egoist, that being happy does seem to be different from being satisfied, pleased, contented, thrilled, or fun-filled—it is the realization (and its corresponding feeling) of having carried on well in life and of having lived as a human being lives best. To be successful in the broadest sense means to do well at what people are uniquely capable of doing: guiding their lives rationally. No more skepticism is warranted here than anywhere else we deal with difficult issues.

Egoists grant that rational conduct will not guarantee a long and happy life; accidents can happen. The position holds that a rational life makes reaching success more likely than does any alternative. It is wrong, moreover, to compare one person's rational life with another's irrational life without making sure that the two people started from essentially similar points. True enough, some who have lived irrationally could be comparatively well off in contrast to those who live rationally but in extremely different situations. What is crucial to ethical egoism is that by living rationally each person would very likely be happier, and certainly savor a better self-concept, than by living irrationally. Egoists propose that this is what needs to be examined so as to learn whether living rationally is indeed the most promising method for achieving happiness.

This is as far as we can go here. Egoism is not widely defended, mostly because many people, among them most recent philosophers, conceive of the human ego or self in ways governed by other, non-ethical philosophical considerations. The human ego is viewed by many as a bundle of (prerational, even irrational) passions that some nonegoistic or antiegoistic moral system could perhaps tame. The last version of egoism I have presented rejects this view of the human ego. However, that rejection needs independent argument, which has merely been suggested.

Ethics as a Personal Concern

Ethical positions, unlike some other issues in philosophy, have a direct bearing on the personal and public problems people face day in and day out. It is an inescapable fact of the human condition that choices have to be made; even to leave things to the commands of others or to accept the view that choice is impossible is a choice! In metaphysical and epistemological questions most people tend to rely on common sense, at least in their ordinary activities if not in their professions. But in ethics they need to be alert in order to live with the conviction that they are meeting the challenge that is so uniquely human and often overwhelming. Questions concerning what we should do arise for us virtually every moment of our waking life. When we decide, do we do so according to sound standards, in line with correct principles? Do we choose our conduct, major and minor, long and short range, arbitrarily or randomly with no regard for why and for what purpose? Do we make at least our crucial decisions carefully, often relying on ethical notions we were taught but frequently mindful of the need to figure things out for ourselves?

Whatever we do, we are always confronted with the possibility that our decisions are ethically relevant, concerned with issues of general significance to living our lives properly. If ethics concerns the problem of living well or living badly as human beings, then being clear on how it bears on what we do can be of enormous importance to us. We may not always be blameworthy for not knowing what is right; sometimes it is not possible for us to identify the right course of conduct.   Yet maybe we need to pay more attention, at least in reflective moments (not obsessively, neurotically), to these issues.   As in the law, ignorance is not always an excuse; sometimes we should have learned about the right course instead of neglecting the issue as we did.   Perhaps today, in an age when philosophers who have been influential at educational institutions have not dealt with ethics very eagerly, each person needs to pay heed to the deeper, more basic issues of ethics.   All in all, the subject matter of ethics is of universal human concern, so it needs careful attention from us even when we might think that only specialists can handle it.

Theistic Ethics

It is fair to say that most people who think about morality or ethics associate these areas of concern with religion, and yet in the discussions above no mention of religion appeared.   The reason is that a sound ethical system must be shown to be such without recourse to factors that are fundamentally out of reach of human comprehension.   Most religions are essentially supernaturalistic, or mystical.   The few that are not tend to identify God with nature, with the universe as a whole, so for them the treatment above could suffice as adequate for purposes of understanding ethical issues.   Other religions do not pretend to base the moral codes they propose on arguments but rest their beliefs in certain ethics on faith.   Yet other religions hold that even though God is supernatural or transcends reality, the moral or ethical code that God designed for human beings can be identified by a rational investigation of reality.   These religions, too, would allow the possibility of treating ethics (natural law, moral law) in a fashion similar to what has been done above.

There are hundreds of different religions, but most of them would hold that the central duty of all persons is to achieve the salvation of their souls.   It is fair to say that this view, somewhat imprecise so as to allow numerous versions their own interpretation, characterizes the crucial feature of theistic ethics.   If we are to consider this view along philosophically appropriate lines, we must hold that whatever might be the salvation of our souls is something we could know and understand.   Since according to theistic ethics the salvation of the soul is achieved by fulfilling the will or purpose of God, this ethical position requires that the will or purpose of God can be known by all persons. This, in turn, requires that much of God can be known by us. Because no ethical position can apply only to some people, it is necessary that theistic ethics, too, be open to understanding by all (not crucially incapacitated) individuals.

This last point will strike many religious persons as somewhat unusual. It should be remembered, however, that not all religions hold that the correct ethical position can be proved correct. Many religions abide by various moral edicts as a matter of faith, at least faith in the authority of those who proclaim the religious ethical edicts. We are not concerned with such positions but with those that view their theistic ethics as open to philosophical scrutiny and demonstration.

The argument for such a position (which, incidentally, is a fair summary of most organized religious ethics) starts with the proof of God's existence. It proceeds to the description of God's nature, his creation of the universe and mankind, and his will or purpose—of what he wants us to do and how he wants us to live. Presumably by numerous means chosen by him, God makes his will known to us. The Bible and the words of prophets, ministers, the Pope, the saints, and others inspired by an awareness of God, communicate to people everywhere the code by which God's will can be fulfilled and, thus, the salvation of our souls be achieved.

As it turns out, there are many conflicting views on both the goal set for us by God and the virtues we must have to reach that goal. The idea that there are many religions—around 700 in the United States alone—and that therefore none could be right is, however, incorrect. People can be mistaken, for many centuries, about a number of things and still share some part of the truth within their mistaken views, be at least partly right, or eventually come to learn what is the case.

The various religious ethics at a fundamental level are not all that different from one another. Most of them are a variety of altruism; for example, loving one's neighbor as one does oneself (mostly more so) is a widely proclaimed ethical truth in the many religions throughout the world. Serving the needs of others, serving mankind, serving the poor, and similar well-known ideals generally make up a religious ethical code. Perhaps the one feature we can identify in most religions that accept the existence of an independent, objective God is that it is our duty to have faith in his design or purpose for us—that is, never to question the will of God. Indeed, this is one of the enormous rewards of religious conviction: God helps us when we are in doubt; he gives us guidance; the virtues required of each of us are just the virtues that make living a success instead of a failure.

Although all of the supposed truths of the (correct) religious ethics must be understandable and knowable to all human beings, clearly theistic ethics considers many people in need of guidance. This is especially true of those who accept that man possesses original sin or is basically flawed in character. The "fall of man" is a prominent idea in many Christian ethics. We have already touched on this in connection with other ethics, but in religious viewpoints the thesis of man's basic imperfection—that as a human being each of us is flawed—looms very large. In consequence, many religions have provisions for teaching morality to those who would not on their own search out or discover the will of God. The entire history of missionary service may be understood as the desire to give moral guidance to those who were unable to obtain it directly from God because they did not seek him out.

To a large extent, then, religious ethics is taught by clerics—priests, nuns, ministers, prophets, the Pope, church elders, and so forth. The mode of moral education differs from one religion to another, but certain matters remain basically similar. Parables serve in many cases to convey the essence of the good life.*

In summary, then, theistic ethics accepts God as a planner and holds that we are duty-bound to learn and fulfill the part of God's plan that applies to us. In practical terms this often means trusting religious leaders, almost completely, concerning what virtues we should adopt. In many religions, however, these virtues are other-wordly in that it is only after (the) death (of the body) that the human soul shall experience salvation, the consequences of the virtuous life, whatever these are. In another respect these virtues are altruistic. God's plan is served not by me or you but by humanity, and our duty is to contribute to humanity's role, to further

---

* Sometimes even the Bible is considered a book of beautiful but not literally true stories. The apparent conflicts between the findings of science and religion are cleared up this way. The creation of the world in six days really means something on the order of six major stages; when Lot's wife turned into salt, that really signified the dreadful psychological and emotional consequences of doubting the will of God.

its well-being. (One reason most Roman Catholics oppose abortion and contraception is that they conceive of sexual experiences as serving a purpose beyond the pleasure and joy of the loving partners. This goal is the furtherance of humanity in God's service.)

Criticism and Answers.   One of the crucial problems of all theistic ethics arises not so much from considerations of the ethical principles but from the problem of God's existence. This issue was covered in chapter 2 when we discussed some proofs for God's existence. Let us accept for a moment that some attempted proof is successful. In short, let us take it that God exists and that we can know it.

The other problem that is not directly concerned with ethics deals with God's nature. If God is all-good, it is difficult to see why he would put human beings through the agony of having to make choices that could lead either to a good life or to a bad one. Why would an all-powerful, all-knowing, and all-good being create something that could engage in wrongdoing? In short, why would God permit the existence of evil in the world? Again, this is not, strictly speaking, a problem with theistic ethics but with the reconciliation of God's existence and the fact that good and evil exist in the world. Still, at one point the problem touches ethical issues directly. When a person considers how he ought to act, he may ask: "Is it not God's will that I do whatever I want to do, whatever that turns out to be (good or bad)?" If the answer is no, God never wills evil, then questions arise about God's omnipotence, his power to do everything, including to prevent one's doing evil. If it is yes, then the question of the necessity of *choosing* the *right* course of conduct faces us. If everything that turns out is the result of the will of an all-good and all-powerful God, why should one take on the burden of deciding what to do?

Another problem that emerges in theistic ethics is more strictly concerned with understanding human virtue or what it would take to be a good human being. For a number of theistic ethics it is impossible for human beings to be perfectly good. We are only created in the image of God and cannot achieve the perfect virtue that God possesses. In other words, each of us *must fail* at something that we must nevertheless all attempt to achieve—namely, perfect goodness.

The idea of being perfectly good is difficult to grasp.   Yet it may mean simply that someone does the best possible in the crucial areas of being a human being: someone is as virtuous as circumstances allow.   In the theistic ethics we are now considering this is not sufficient for perfection.   The ideal is itself unattainable but serves as a goal to be approximated.

As such, theistic ethics tends to make morality somewhat of a mockery of justice.   One should strive to be a good person, yet at the outset it is clear that one cannot achieve what one should strive for.   It may thus be argued that such ethical systems are internally incoherent, since they require human beings to aspire to something they *cannot* achieve; they are duty-bound to accomplish what *cannot* be accomplished.

As to the need to rely on the work of the clergy or ministry, we are faced with the problem of elitism.   This problem is not unique to theistic ethics.   Some philosophers have argued that there is a chosen group of well-situated people (e.g., philosophers) who can achieve excellence and must act as moral guardians of the rest. Theistic ethics have often been mixed with such nontheistic doctrines and it is possible that some of the views that have been used to justify the role of the clergy in various organized religions derive from such nontheistic doctrines.

One problem with the introduction of the necessity for the clergy as those who have access to God's will is that not everyone can be reached by them.   Each day some people are born who will never meet a priest, nun, or minister or read a book relating the parables.   Are they to be barred from the morally good life?

This objection cuts at the heart of those theistic ethics that rely on the knowledge of the few who have a clear understanding of God's will.   Since the basic virtues must be universally implementable, those who cannot be reached by the clergy cannot become virtuous.   And that renders this "moral" position impossible.

Finally, insofar as theists are altruists, criticism of the latter viewpoint applies to them as well.

Leaving aside the issue of God's existence, the first response will be directed toward the question of whether God's perfect goodness can be reconciled with the existence and possibility of evil in human life.   One way of answering this objection is to maintain that God's will is good, and the human struggle between good and evil, between living well or badly, is itself good. But to make possible this good, it is necessary to allow for the struggle and for the accompanying possibility of evil. Of course, mankind always has the choice to do right and to live well instead of badly. God does not make evil necessary, only possible! For good to be possible, evil must be possible, too. Thus, God's perfect goodness guarantees only that good *can* be achieved, not that it *will* be.

One way of meeting the objection that theistic ethics set impossible goals—virtue *cannot* be sustained by us—is to suggest the value of high *ideals,* that is, goals that are indeed noble but not fully reachable. Virtues such as justice, kindness, humility, charity, and so on should be guiding standards, somewhat as the mathematical ideal of a circle is when we draw circles. We cannot live up to these fully, but it is our duty to make a valiant attempt in every situation, however discouraged we might be from failure. The idea is to consider these virtues unreachable but essential goals to guide our conduct. There is nothing wrong with setting unattainable goals, provided the efforts we make get us close enough to perfection.

Concerning the possible exclusion of some people from the province of ethics, it can be argued that those unreachable are neither good nor evil in their conduct and lives. Like young children, who can make only limited choices, these people have no moral responsibilities and no moral faults or virtues. Only reasonably mature individuals have developed the capacities for the ethical life. Those people who are totally ignorant of the will of God but have never willfully turned away from God's teachings are like children; they are morally untouched.

Before closing this section it must be reiterated that not all people who believe that God exists think that morality is related to his will or plan. Some will argue that God created the universe with the best plans he could think of, but these would be best even if they existed independently, without God's coming into the picture. So what is right or wrong has to do with the plans, not with God himself. Natural law theorists, some of them pre-Christian philosophers, believed that the universe contains basic laws of existence, including laws to govern humanity—principles of the good life for all people. They thought they were able to identify, without reference to God, the moral principles by which we should conduct life, even though some of them believed that something like God exists.

There are also theists who conceive of God as the creator of humanity but not as one who had any special plans for us. How we ought to live is for us to discover, not for God to just decide. These ways of viewing the matter are, at best, a small minority position within theism.

Finally, there is a large segment of humanity that does not view God or ethics as a matter of rational understanding at all. For many people God is what they call a personal issue, which is not capable of demonstration or proof; it is not like other features of reality most of us consider open to knowledge and understanding by anyone with normal human capacities. In modern theology a current expression is that God is dead. This is a metaphor—a way of saying that the idea of God's independent existence is no longer a plausible one. Instead, God has to be viewed as the deepest concerns we have, our *ultimate concerns*. This general idea is found in those religious movements that preach that God is whatever one thinks God is. God "exists" *in* one's heart, soul, or consciousness—that is all. The ethical notions that emerge out of these views are also rather perplexing. What is right and wrong is not universalizable; instead, right or wrong is a matter of personal conscience, with no possible foundation in reality so that *all* of us can discover it. Right or wrong is what is dictated by one's own, subjective conscience, how one happens to feel about things very sincerely. It is to some of these views, not especially wedded to religion, that we turn now.

THE CHALLENGE TO ETHICS

At the outset of this chapter I laid out the case for the existence and function of morality as such, whatever particular moral position is correct. I also said that there are many serious objections to what was proposed in my introductory remarks. As with the issue of the basic facts of reality, or human knowledge, there are those commenting on ethics who argue that we must give up attempts to get it right. There simply are no answers to questions such as, What is morally good, right, wrong, or evil? The point is not that this or that answer is not right but that none *could* be right.

These arguments are not simply philosophical exercises presented to sharpen our minds about the topic. Everyone who offers answers to important questions will have occasion to search for a sound foundation for them, and skeptical questions are useful to make as sure as possible that one's answers are the best that can be given. We engage in this kind of discussion often, as when we debate whether there are exceptions to the answers we offer in our professional capacities, or when we consider that contradictions may infest the answers we encounter about psychology or the media. But sometimes the questions do not serve the purpose of sharpening the answers. Ethical skeptics are those who do not simply ask for a better answer to the question of ethics. They argue that no (correct) answers are possible, now or ever.

Ethical Subjectivism

One well-known antiethical viewpoint is hardly a novelty to anyone who might read this work. This is the widespread idea that what is right is only so for the person who is faced with the choice, that right and wrong are right and wrong *to* the individuals concerned, and that no one can say what is right and wrong except the person involved. This concept has been prevalent in all human societies. Perhaps the way this idea is expressed here is somewhat different from how others have put it. There are fine distinctions possible even in this general viewpoint. Some would say that anything is right that one *believes* to be right. Others would say that deciding or choosing to do something *makes* that action right. Yet others hold that right and wrong (or should and should not) are not even meaningful ideas but confused ways of saying that someone *likes* or *wants* or *prefers* what is said to be right or that someone dislikes what is said to be wrong. This general mode of viewing conduct, institutions, policies, projects, and whatever human beings can undertake or produce is called **ethical subjectivism.**

One argument for ethical subjectivism is that nothing can be invoked to prove that something is right or wrong. People are unique. They are all creative, developing free agents and share nothing in common aside from their liberty to do what they will. There is no human nature from which to glean principles to help in our choices. Each of us is burdened with the full responsibility to create ourselves as we will, not as some preestablished standard or code or set of principles would require. Even our understanding of the world may be entirely unique and unshared with others. We must face up to this. There is no right and wrong; there are only our choices to be this or that, to do as we will. Indeed, human life is the complex and confusing affair that it obviously is because we, unlike other things in reality, starting out as mere flesh and bones, create the unique selves that we all are. To pretend that some standards can be identified to guide us in our conduct is self-deceiving and is an effort to hide behind a pigeonhole instead of accepting ourselves as we are—free and on our own. (This is very close to the existentialist view of the human situation.)

Another subjectivist viewpoint is that we are not free at all. Thus, we cannot make choices, right or wrong, about our actions. We are *moved* by our innate constitution (e.g., instincts) or environment (e.g., the sensory or social stimuli around us from birth) to do what we will. We have desires and aversions, but these are given or acquired without our having a hand in their development or assessment. We are, like the rest of the animal population of the world (except for our greater biological complexities) moving about reality as dictated by the laws of physics, chemistry, biology, psychology, sociology, economics, and politics. As with all things in reality, these laws are the principles that govern how we behave. They are not easy to identify, granted, and much work needs to be done in science to be able to fully understand just exactly what does play a decisive role in human affairs. But there is no reason to think we are different from molecules, stones, planets, plants, zebras, and the rest of nature, all of which move in accordance with a predetermined, preexistent order. In short, we are but complex machines developed through evolution by the forces of nature. Considerations of right and wrong are mere prescientific confusion. We are well off to abandon these.

This form of subjectivism denies that we choose what is right and wrong. But it does allow that individuals (*subjects*) produce utterances such as "This is right" and "This is wrong." However, these mean no more than "I approve of or like this" and "I disapprove of or dislike this." It is because approval and the like are, by this view, conditioned by the individual's background that this is a subjectivist position. (Sometimes advocates of this position hold that the utterances involved can mean *"We* approve" and *"We* disapprove," etc.)

There are subjectivists who hold that however we came to develop our sense of values is not to be prejudged. Yet, values must still not be thought of as knowable. Here subjectivism simply rejects the possibility of universal values, identifiable by and for everyone. Instead, we can give expression to our feelings of approval, dismay, and the like; these we feel strongly and can express by such ethical phrases as "It is wrong to hurt little children" or "Everyone should tell the truth." Right and wrong are still no more than preferences, although no claims are advanced about what if anything causes them, why these are the preferences someone does or does not have. The issue of freedom of choice is left unsettled here, but the character of statements about right and wrong is still subjectivist.

Finally, a more positive yet still subjectivist position holds that it is possible to know what is right and wrong, but each time the judgment applies to a particular subject or a given individual. Thus, "Human beings should cultivate the virtue of integrity" will be rejected by this view, but "Johnny should cultivate the virtue of integrity" could be either right or wrong, depending entirely on Johnny's identity. In some respects this view belongs under the group of ethical theories termed relativistic, since the idea here is that what is right and wrong can be discovered only as matters *relate* to a given person. No general, universalizable standard of right and wrong is available in line with this approach, so it cannot be a *bona fide* moral position. However, each of us may be able to tell what is right or wrong for us. How can we tell what is right without some general standard? The answer would be that it depends on our goals and purposes. Here, too, in the end there is no standard by which to judge the goals or purposes, so although relative to them it is possible to learn whether some actions or policies are right or wrong, there are no common goals or highest good, so there is no way to appraise the merits of many individual goals. Thus, it would be possible to state that *if* we want to become wealthy, we *ought* to learn about domestic and international finance. But *whether or not* becoming wealthy is good for us is not answerable by this viewpoint.

Subjectivism criticized. The reader will benefit from investigating the various subjectivist views critically. Here we will deal with criticisms of only one subjectivist viewpoint, ethical subjectivism. The others have already been challenged, by implication, within the earlier ethical theories and our introduction to these. To see whether these answers work, one will have to do a good deal of independent thinking.

Ethical subjectivism poses two challenges to ethics. First, it holds that *human* nature is a myth—each person must create his or her own nature. Second, it holds that we cannot identify a standard of conduct. (A further point, but not so crucial, relates to the connection between a possible moral standard and human conduct. The idea is offered that having such a standard would remove the responsibility to face up to *choices*.)

One problem with denying the existence of human nature is that the theory itself rejects this very denial. After all, to say that human beings are just *the sort* of beings who must create themselves and that they are free to become what they want to be is exactly to say what *human nature* is. (The theory may attempt to argue that the *character* of each person may well have to be of his or her own choosing—that none of us is *made* into a certain quality of person. But this is not to deny that we are all human by virtue of some features we alone share.)

The challenge to this view could go on to claim that there is, in fact, a standard of right and wrong that the theory itself proposes, however much this is denied. Because we human beings are self-created, free, and undetermined, it is our task to carry out the activities *we can freely engage in,* to be creative as only human beings can be. To be individuals true to the requirements of our human nature is to be creative, ever-growing, ever-developing, never-stagnant beings within our own circumstances. Whatever our freedom consists in, whatever it is that we are ultimately free to do, is just what we ought to do and do well. So even without leaving the theory itself, we can challenge some of the conclusions that amount to subjectivism. Of course, noting that this standard *applies* to us all is not to note that we are all *compelled* to live by it. It is a simple matter for us to negate our unique freedom by failing to exercise it and by refraining from implementing the general standard within our individual circumstances. The means of implementation are not given by the standard. It is our own responsibility to make that determination.

To all this the subjectivist would probably say that the reference to human nature in the objection is misleading. We may all be free, but is this not to say that *what* we are is indeterminate. If we can change tomorrow, if we can even reject our freedom by escaping from it, if we can commit suicide, how could we have a determinate, exact nature? To call this indeterminacy our *nature* is to obliterate the meaning of the term as it makes sense when used in other contexts.

And what does it mean that we ought to exercise our freedom where this freedom manifests itself? Perhaps we are free in thought, perhaps in emotional capacity, or perhaps in whatever we do. All we can tell is that we are free. This is hardly enough to generate some moral position. It is to confuse morality—a set of reasonably precise guidelines to human conduct, as we all know from our homes, churches, commencement talks, novels, etc.—with the mere realization that we are responsible to act and to decide. When it comes right down to the wire, we have nothing to go on but our feelings, perhaps. No, escape from subjectivity, from the circumstances identified in the subjectivist's position, is an illusion. We are only self-deceived to think it possible.

As mentioned before, the subjectivism outlined here is closely tied to the philosophy of existentialism. However, the existentialist view is best stated by those who advocate it, and many of them are very critical of presenting their ideas in lectures and books. Therefore, the discussion here should be considered separate from the existentialist view and taken as an independent challenge to the possibility of ethics.

Relativism

In one respect subjectivism is a variety of relativism, for right and wrong relate to our subjective, private, unique characteristics. Egoism also is sometimes thought to be subjectivist, but in the classical egoist position right and wrong relate to us as human individuals, not as unique, isolated entities. We should not call an ethical position relativist simply because it permits some variation based on different circumstances, provided some basic core is firm and absolute.

Relativism is broader than subjectivism because it does not specify *to what* the issue of right, good, wrong, bad, etc., must be related, although it holds that it is or can be related to a variety of factors. People's economic situations, national or cultural origins, level of intelligence, or historical era could all be candidates for what would determine the answer to the ethical question. In each case the central point to be noted is that there cannot be an answer to the ethical question, How should I, *a human being*, live? According to the various relativistic ethics, only the following type of question allows an answer: How should I, a rich person, a poor person, a Jew, a woman, a twentieth-century poet, an Italian, first-century carpenter, or a genius, live? In other words, no fundamental *human* morality is available.

The relativist's argument also comes in several varieties. The argument rests mainly on the widespread realization that people live in very different circumstances and engage in such large varieties of practices, most held to be right or good by many of the people concerned.

More importantly, relativism emerges in response to the view that no objective, absolute standards of human conduct can be identified. When this is accepted, mostly in view of the widespread failure to produce successful arguments in support of such moral positions, relativism is advanced as an answer. Its specifics depend on the kind of relativism. But usually its form is that we are bound at least by the practices and codes of our culture, profession, age group, etc. The relativist's only absolute is the following: Each person ought to cultivate the ideals or virtues that his or her group —of whatever kind—accepts. Whether these are right in some ultimate, objective, absolute sense is impossible to know.

To some extent the famous American ideal, democracy, carries with it elements of relativism. When one accepts democracy as the highest ideal of a community, and no clear limits are advanced as confining the democratic process to certain issues but not others, then one accepts relativism about values: the fact that a majority of the voters support or oppose something is taken to be sufficient grounds for considering it as either good or bad. In a pure democracy, where nothing is binding except what the majority of the people choose, the standards of political propriety—the ideals and values to be protected and preserved by law—are relative to the decisions (or compromises of various decisions) of the majority of the people.

A form of relativism is offered by those who believe that people of different class origin (from different economic or social backgrounds) are forced by their circumstances to accept ideals or virtues suited to the advancement of their class. According to this version of relativism, touched upon when we discussed subjectivism (involving personal approval), the ideals or virtues we ought to cultivate are actually produced in our personality or character by the circumstances in which we live. The underlying view of human action, as being produced by our environment, actually eliminates the very possibility of ethics in the sense being treated here. If we are forced to behave as we do by our economic circumstances, the idea that we are responsible for what we do makes no sense, and thus ethics makes no sense.

Criticism of Relativism. To criticize relativism requires an investigation of whether it is correct to conclude that no basic principle(s) of human conduct can be identified. One or two points can be raised, however, independently of such detailed and in-depth consideration. (Our discussion of various moral positions should provide the contrast needed to see whether relativism starts off correctly.) For example, is it true that different societies, nations, occupational groups, and economic groups vary in all respects in their ideals? It seems clear that some thread of common ideals is evident in all cultures and groups of people; for instance, life appears to be of considerable value, as do property, family, etc.

Also, is it not possible that most people in some cultures or groups are morally corrupt? It is often argued that the bulk of those in Nazi Germany were corrupt. Some hold that the system and its supporters in South Africa are corrupt, while others hold that this is true of the Soviet Union. And many people believe that the United States of America is a culture with moral shortcomings. To take seriously the view that universal moral standards are impossible to identify (or that such standards do not exist), we would have to prove that none of the above claims could possibly be correct—that they express preferences, dislikes, or something equally weak.

Although moral standards or principles do not yield predictions in the way that scientific principles do, some ethical systems do admit that if we disregard the right moral principles, we will live a bad life in crucial respects (e.g., be unhappy, miss out on pleasures, incur divine punishment).

Some relativists get into difficulty by arguing against universal moral principles on grounds that identifying some would entitle people to coerce others into abiding by them. The fear of moral authoritarianism has given considerable support to relativism. Yet it does not follow from "A knows that B should do X" that "A should (or is right to) force B to do X." So this fear is unwarranted, except perhaps on grounds of some psychological assumptions that knowledge of morality tends to lead people to impose their judgments on others.

If relativism holds that people ought to act as their peer groups believe they should, this itself becomes a moral principle in need of proof. (We noted a similar problem with epistemological relativism.) Those versions of relativism that deny the idea of human nature escape this; the earlier discussion of human freedom versus its denial considers this form of relativism in some depth.

Again, ethical relativists will have answers, and one of them is that although morality may be applicable to those who accept no part of it, it is questionable that it is necessary if cultures can exist without it! How could we prove the truth of a moral system in human life if entire groups of people today or in other epochs could live without being subject to the evaluations of that system? The onus of proof lies on those who claim that there is a universal moral position. They must show that each society, group, or historical epoch requires at least some of the virtues that are part of a sound moral position. Without that proof, relativism is the most sensible view of the matter.

As to the main objection that relativism is inconsistent because it, too, offers an absolute moral principle, this is a mistake. Relativism does not offer a moral position. It reports a fact of life. The only meaningful sense in which "What should I do?" or "How should I live?" can be answered is by adopting the principles widely accepted in one's group (whichever, wherever, and whenever). This is not a moral position but a consideration of what we can better understand by the term *morality*.

Nihilism

Unlike the skeptical positions concerning the very possibility of ethics, **nihilism** is a viewpoint that opposes values explicitly.

The term *nihilism* has its etymological origin in the Latin word *nihil*, meaning "nothing." Basically the doctrine is an attack on the value of values, on morality itself. Most nihilists are actually fervent opponents of the values that are prominent or *dominant within their culture,* although more broadly speaking nihilism advocates opposition to *all* moral and political values. The very idea that moral (and political) values are to be instrumental in human life is rejected by the nihilist.

Since nihilism is a position that opposes values, it is usually based on certain theories about the uses to which considerations of morality and political theory are put. By and large, nihilists have a cynical view of human nature. They believe, in the main, that moral positions, especially those that gain prominence within a culture, are devices by which the creative forces (people) in a culture are made to serve those who are incapable of creativity, who lack willpower, and who are parasites. Moral values are seen by the nihilists as means by which the productive, imaginative, *genuinely* powerful elements of humanity are made subservient to its baser members. Consciously or unconsciously, moralists, according to the nihilist, are conspirators against the very best in human beings. By intimidation, threat of punishment, doctrines of divine retribution (e.g., the idea of hell and damnation in an afterlife), and the like, moralists foist upon people practices, systems, and institutions that destroy the life-sustaining features of the human race.

One of the most brilliant and forceful nihilists in Western intellectual history was Friedrich Nietzsche, a nineteenth-century German philosopher. Nietzsche's nihilism was in part an attack upon the philosophical ideas about morality prominent in his own times both in academic circles and in the culture at large. He rejected Christianity's conceptions about morality (e.g., doctrines about the supreme virtue of humility, self-sacrifice, and charity). He regarded such moral ideals as part of a slave morality. He also opposed the philosophical conception of the nature of morality developed by another prominent German philosopher, Immanuel Kant. Nietzsche thought that in his moral writings Kant deliberately removed values from our natural world and placed them in a separate theoretical or ideal world where values turned out to have the character of formal rules or mathematical principles. For Kant, values had little to do with problems of living such as the consequences of actions and the benefits or losses each person can encounter in life. Nietzsche thought that this position put human beings in a natural opposition to morality. Thus, morality itself had to be rejected.

But Nietzsche's nihilism can also be regarded as a call for the rejection of the *existing* conception of morality. He himself predicted that the twentieth century would see a return to nihilism. Then new values would be created—values suited to human life, not to human enslavement.

The nihilist's position, in general, is prompted by total dismay and disgust with what the cultural currents proclaim and represent as the morally good human life. This sometimes leads the nihilist to reject and oppose all actual *and* possible moral positions. But as with Nietzsche, it often leads the nihilist to sharply attack prevailing ideals and values only to cry out for new ones suited for human life. Yet, outside of their occasional call for new values, nihilists in general do not believe that values could be objectively demonstrated. Therefore, the new values would have to be relative, in some sense, to the characters of the willing individuals who may select them.

Objections to Nihilism. Nihilism is not very systematic. Since it is often necessary to give it a structure rather than find one within it, criticism of the position is difficult. Nihilism is more often a desperate (though brilliant, powerful, and even dazzlingly beautiful) call for protest than a philosophically careful argument in support of the truth of some viewpoint. Therefore, nihilists will most likely be dismayed with carefully drawn up, intellectual objections to their outcries. This would probably be thought of by the nihilist as meeting a call for protest and action with a *theory* about protests and acting. However, a few intellectualized points need to be made about the nihilist's outcry. It does contain theoretical features, it does involve assumptions, and it does make use of ideas that may, in the fervor of the nihilist's call, appear perfectly meaningful but turn out very difficult to understand when one examines them carefully. In short, if we are to take the nihilist seriously, we are entitled to hold up certain standards and scrutinize his position.

For one thing, in a basic sense, values are just what the nihilist is asking for. By opposing values, he proclaims some of his own. The strict nihilist tells us to abandon our concern with values and moral truth. However petty this may appear to him, that call must then itself be warranted or not. Is it true that we *ought* to give up a concern with values? Is this universally true? Will the quality of life be improved if we do this? The nihilist is apparently obliged to answer yes to all these. But then he is not being candid with us. He is not telling us that we ought to discard *all* values. He is advocating that certain moral positions are in fact wrong and destructive.   True, the nihilist is disdainful toward argumentation. And at times the polite exchanges of ideas among philosophers and theologians offend him to the point that he believes they are phoney and that they fail to acknowledge the importance and impact of their utterances for our lives.   But it will not do to abandon the arena.   The charge of phoniness requires demonstration!   Perhaps the philosophers who advocate a morality that is indifferent to human life have left reality behind.   Still it is possible that they are very sincere: To simply attack them as frauds and enemies of mankind will leave them hostile, feeling offended and entirely uncooperative about the issue at hand.

Nietzsche himself seems to have had ideals that he believed to be suited to human life.   Perhaps he did not think that during his own times it would have been useful to be constructive.   Therefore, he denigrated the existing moralists and moralities.   But it is not accurate to view even his criticism as the actual rejection of *morality*. Nietzsche, too, criticized from a moral point of view; he, too, argued for what should be done instead of what is being done.   And he foresaw a future time when proper values would be generated, after the improper ones had produced their destruction.

Finally, it is one thing to argue that dominant moral currents are destructive, but it is quite another to claim that morality as such is destructive.   Assume, for a moment, that a correct moral position can be identified, that there are some things human beings should do by virtue of their humanity, to live well instead of badly.   It is quite possible that privately, with little advertising and historical notoriety, many people have indeed practiced proper moral principles.   Notions of morality in a culture may become distorted by news media or by the pronouncements of politicians, religious leaders, or parents.   Nevertheless, morality may also manifest itself properly. Thus, while many Germans may have believed in the virtues of national socialism (Nazism), obedience to the leader, and sacrifice for the Third Reich, there were others who acted in accordance with sound virtues.   This is at least one possible way of viewing the matter. Nihilism perhaps misses a different point about evil: it rarely announces itself as such but puts on the façade of good.   As Shakespeare put it in *King Lear,* "Wisdom and goodness to the vile seem vile. . . ."

To all this the nihilist would probably say that we are merely playing into the hands of his enemies by trying to save morality. He will say that we are missing his point: morality *is* a fundamental mistake. We must reject it *in toto* rather than attempt to resurrect it. Whatever we put forth as the proper approach to human life, let it not be anything like morality. Let it be something basically different, a force so removed from the concerns of morality that using "morality" to characterize it would be like calling trucks station wagons.

Moreover, some nihilists (probably including Nietzsche) would protest that it is wrong to ask for principles of human conduct that apply universally. Humanity is not homogeneous. Different life-styles may be appropriate to different people; to pretend otherwise undermines life itself. Geniuses cannot be expected to live by a code suited to those who are modest in intellectual and creative powers. Making the moral principles and duties applicable to all human beings is stifling. So, however much it seems that the nihilist is calling for a different morality, he is in fact rejecting the idea of morality completely and asking for something radically different— the freeing of people from the shackles of codes, principles, and virtues!

RETHINKING THE FACT / VALUE DICHOTOMY

In contemporary philosophical circles the force of the fact / value dichotomy is very powerful. At the outset we discussed this issue from the point of view of the possibility of morality. Now we will consider the various ideas related to this issue within prominent philisophies of our time.

Nowadays the view that facts and values are fundamentally different is widespread. The several social sciences accept this view. Economics, sociology, psychology, and history are regarded by most scholars as "value free." This means that economists, for instance, attempt to understand human economic activities entirely inde-pendent of any consideration of what is right and wrong. Soci-ologists, political scientists, and anthropologists make frequent declarations about the arbitrariness of values and the need to disregard them completely in scientific discussions (except as facts about what people prefer, desire, or approve). Even psychologists and psychiatrists, who deal with individuals directly, often proclaim that they could make no moral judgments and to inject moral evaluations into their assessment of their patients' situations would only be something arbitrary. Although exceptions to this approach can be found, and changes in the popularity of the value-free stance can be detected these days, the cultural climate is committed to a predominantly value-free, or amoralist, approach to dealing with human affairs. That is also why it is so often believed that only religion should take morality into account in understanding human life, but here matters must be taken on faith in the final analysis.

"Value free" science usually goes hand-in-hand with rejecting moral issues as incapable of study and understanding. Within this position the phrase "That is a value judgment" means "That is just your personal, arbitrary bias—simply how you feel about it." As a feeling, a value judgment is neither right nor wrong, since we simply have the feelings we have (or do not). So when value judgments are viewed as feelings, they do not contribute to our evaluation of a situation. Thus, if I say, "Any president who lies to the people in the course of performing his job is irresponsible," this is a *mere* value judgment; it is a feeling or bias I happen to have about such things, conveying nothing that could be right or wrong, true or false. Similarly, if someone states, "It was wrong for the United States government to enter the Southeast Asian conflict," viewing this as an expression of a feeling will render the statement incapable of rational discussion. The idea is widespread today that such statements express feelings, even if we aim by expressing them at getting others to feel as we do about something. And it is also an idea that has been defended presistently and in detail by many philosophers.

The main issue is whether value judgments can be proved true, whether values can be known. If they are sentiments or attitudes, then they cannot.* But why would they be regarded as sentiments, attitudes, and so forth?

An allegedly correct view of what facts *must* be leads to the conclusion that values cannot be facts, so they must be something like feelings. This view is not an ethical position as such. Neither can it be classified as relativism or subjectivism, since the latter discuss

---

* Although one might say that certain feelings are unhealthy, certain tastes vulgar, and certain attitudes degenerate. But as soon as one would try proving these claims, those who advocate the above position would hold that those claims, too, are unprovable and no more than value judgments, expressing the person's feelings, tastes, attitudes about other people's feelings, tastes, etc.

the source of values, not why they could not be a variety of facts. (However, there are connections between those views and what we will consider here.) We seem to be dealing here with an area of metaphysics and epistemology.

Facts, Values, and Metaphysics

First, the issue of values concerns metaphysics because we are asking about the kind of existence that values might have. Many different types of things exist. Days are temporal things, distances are spacial, ideas are mental, and tables are material. So there may be room for what ethics or morality deals with—namely, values. It is thus sensible that the ontological status of values should be very carefully considered before it is concluded that values could not be a variety of facts. (By "ontological status" I mean the kind or type of existence of something—mental, material, temporal, etc.)

Second, this is an issue of epistemology because we are concerned also with what kinds of facts could be identified and known by us, and how. We do not learn of the existence of every kind of thing in the same way. There are some common elements to all our knowledge—what makes it knowledge—but it is very likely, for example, that the way we learn about the existence of electrons is different from the way we learn about a flat tire.

Nevertheless, it is clear that many philosophers believe in the impossibility of the factual nature of values. We can now examine arguments supporting this position.

Values and Empiricism

The epistemological position called empiricism is a very powerful position in our culture, especially where systematic investigation of reality (i.e., science) is at stake. Reliance on observation, experimentation that can yield observable results, studies that yield findings that can be observed and measured, and so forth—all this is accorded intellectual support by the empiricist epistemology. As discussed previously, this theory of knowledge holds that whatever can be known must be known by way of sensory observation. The ultimate foundation of human knowledge is sensory experience.

But if there were such facts as moral values, they could not be known by exclusive reliance on sensory experience even if sensory data might enter the (possible) realm of moral knowledge. Suppose that someone makes the following claim: "Each human being should seek happiness in life." First of all, there may be very little or no evidence that anyone actually does seek happiness in life. The claim is not that people *do* seek happiness but that they *should* do this. How could a theory that ties all knowledge exclusively to sensory impressions support the view that moral values such as the pursuit of happiness or the practice of honesty, justice, humility, or whatever could be known to us? There simply does not appear to be any way of doing this. Therefore, the idea that values could be known must be given up if empiricism is accepted as the correct theory of human knowledge.

If we take values to be the expressions of desires, feelings, or the like—that is, if we equate any value with the existence of some desire—we can easily identify values by noting whether something is being desired by someone. From the empiricist theory of knowledge it is not difficult to derive the position we are now discussing, which is that facts and values are drastically different things: the *existence* of independent or objective value is a myth based on a false analogy that valuing is like seeing that something exists, whereas it is really the possession of feelings, either pro or con. The analogy holds that when I see, I see a fact; when I value, I value a fact (which is a value). But this analogy is false, and values are not facts. So the empiricist would argue.

It should be noted that most social scientists do not say that feelings or sentiments cannot be known. Only extreme behaviorists, who accept the existence of bodily movements alone, would claim this. What social scientists (and many philosophers) believe is that the statements expressing these sentiments and feelings can never be true or false. These cannot contribute to our understanding of the world and our relation to it, although we could learn things about the person who makes them. So when someone tells us that it is morally wrong to enter the civil wars of foreign countries, this could not be a true or false statement, something that could state what someone knows. It is only a clue to someone's feelings.

The view considered here is a prominent one concerning the nature of facts and values, judgments concerning reality and supposed judgments about moral issues, within both our culture and the current philosophical mainstream (although changes in both are evident). But this tells us nothing about whether the view is correct.

I will not consider objections to this view at the present time. Criticisms of empiricism both at the end of our discussion of that theory of knowledge and by way of alternative theories are sufficient now for assessing the merits of this view. In short, the fact / value dichotomy is largely dependent upon the soundness of the empiricist view of knowledge. If that theory is false, the fact / value dichotomy is very likely a mistake.

Proving Values Knowable

Problems about knowing moral principles do not end by disproving empiricism. Even if empiricism should prove to be false, or at least only partly true—that is, if knowledge could require other than sensory means—the issue of moral knowledge is not settled. A successful, sound, positive theory is required. The various moral positions we have considered in this chapter, combined with foundations in other branches of philosophy, suggest such positive theories. The reader will now be able to pursue the search for an answer to the main questions of morality. Starting with the discussions presented here, it will be possible to carry forth the search with some hope of success.

The search itself is not easy to conduct. The various arguments against the very *possibility* of morality are not the only ones to contend with. There are other, more complicated objections. Their character has emerged in some of the challenges put to the specific moral positions covered here. For example, it is sometimes argued against a moral theory that it is incapable of being applied in many situations. That would mean that such a morality is inadequate. In the end if a moral position cannot be applied in various situations facing human beings, then it cannot be a genuine moral position. One must be *able* to do what one *ought* to do! If virtue or moral excellence requires the impossible, then virtue or moral excellence is itself impossible.

One way moral positions can be tested is to confront them with hypothetical situations. If the provisions advanced (as warranted or obligatory) by a moral theorist lead to incompatible, contradictory requirements, the morality is again shown to require the impossible.

Yet often the hypothetical examples are not acceptable. Some are very sketchy. One frequently used involves a desert island on which there are two persons, one with a cup of water sufficient only for one person's survival until help arrives. The question is: What should either party do? Various moralities are called upon to provide the best answer. But the example is very odd. Where did these people come from? Are both equally good people? Do they deserve equal concern from the moral point of view? Can the moral issues be handled without our knowing much more of the situation? The lesson to learn may be that frightful fantasies are not suited for testing a moral position. Thus, when the search for a sound moral position is conducted, it is important to make sure the testing ground is itself appropriate. Consider such questions as the following: "What should you do if you were in the fifteenth century with knowledge of what we now know and you found people starving because there was not enough food?" Well, if you knew then what you *now* know, then, perhaps you should build a factory to produce food by employing modern technology. But in the fifteenth century this kind of knowledge was not available, and the hypothesis is unrealistic.

Very often people pose challenges that may be called the "science fiction" cases for testing various theories, including moral positions. Underlying such challenges is a view of what a theory must achieve, which is to cover not only cases that can be understood in terms of current knowledge but cases that may be products of imagination. Although the proper way to test moral positions is hotly disputed, one is entitled to ask whether the methodology accepted for these tests is itself not beyond question. If it is a questionable approach, a moral theory that may not succeed by that method may yet be sound by some other. Neither in science nor in other areas of human inquiries can the impossible be required. And a successful moral theory may not have to settle *imagined,* fantastic problems.

CONCLUSION

Thus far we have focused mainly on alternative ethical systems and various objections to the possibility of ever identifying one that is universally binding, that is, true. Other issues have been touched on, but by no means have I considered all the problems that emerge within the branch of philosophy called ethics.

For example, aside from the question of which system of ethics is right, what the true principles of morality are, and the like, philosophers often examine the character or structure of moral principles, whatever they might be. That is, assuming that moral principles can be identified, what would they be like? Would they be principles of a tactical or strategical sort so that invoking them would be means for achieving certain goals? Or would they be principles such as those found in "formal systems" (e.g., mathematics), so that they are binding on grounds that might be called internal necessity? Or perhaps neither, or maybe both? The former conception of moral principles is usually called consequentialist or teleological (forward directed), whereas the latter is called formalist or deontological (inherently compelling). Some argue that such divisions are artificial and that moral principles are both forward directed and formal, both consequentialist—identified *by reference* to consequences—and internally binding—imposing the requirement of being *principled* about adhering to them.

Another issue moral philosophers investigate is the nature of obligations, duties, promises, virtues, etc. These are central moral or ethical concepts, whatever ethical system one holds to be correct. Their character needs specification in any case. Sometimes it is proposed that the central concept of any moral position must be "duty" or "obligation." This view is contrasted with that which holds "virtue" or "goodness" to be the central moral concept, overriding all others. In some cases philosophers claim that whatever is morally binding, it must ultimately be derived from a basic moral duty each person should act on, whereas in other cases the basic principle is held to be a central value or good each person should pursue.

Some argue that all moral edicts and judgments must ultimately be traced to an imaginary contract to which human beings are party. The idea here is that the best way to learn what human beings ought to aim for in life, how they ought to conduct themselves—or, to use the phrase some philosophers use, what the principles of justice are— is to imagine a contract that might have been drawn by people considering living together in a society. The "social contract" theory of law is well known amongst political philosophers and many others, but even in the broader area of morality some have approached the issue by way of this contractarian path.

Throughout this chapter I have tried to indicate in familiar terms some of the specialized topics in ethics. There are other ways to refer to these topics. The fact / value dichotomy is often referred to as the "is / ought" problem. In other words, the issue is whether arguments with premises that contain the connective "is" could be used to prove conclusions with the connective "ought to."

I have also made extensive reference to some basic requirements that any *bona fide* moral system would have to satisfy. For example, in each, human beings would have to be capable of choice, principles of conduct would have to be open to knowledge, and human beings as such would have to be able to identify a common reachable goal they share. The philosophical "slogan" that is used to refer to these requirements is "ought implies can." If people should practice a principle, various requirements must be met. Several other catchy phrases have developed within professional philosophical circles, but it is not crucial for one to learn these outside of the communities of those who have made this field their bread and butter. It is more important to know of the ideas that are captured by these "shorthand" references.

As with all fields of inquiry, in ethics, too, one can get involved with many important technicalities. Specialists have taken on the job of developing fine distinctions and nuances to facilitate their understanding of some of the less well travelled aspects of the field. These are not trivial within technical philosophy, just as legal technicalities are crucial for those dealing with the finer points of law. But they are not central for purposes of getting an initial familiarity with the field of ethics, one of the most crucial branches of philosophy.

In these last remarks on the subject matter of morality an often-asked question will be considered. Frequently people ask, "Who is to say what is right or wrong?" The point of asking this question is very interesting. There are many who believe that what is right and wrong is *decided* by someone (father, mother, church, state). In other words, many assume that what is right or wrong is something that someone is to decide, to decree, or to announce. The question above takes this for granted and asks about the authority behind morality.

Is it correct to think of morality as a matter of authority? In a sense there is no harm in it. Let us assume that morally proper conduct can be identified. Let us assume that there are good people around who have done this successfully. This might not be different from assuming that there are people who have managed to identify the correct medical principles, laws of biology, etc. Medical doctors, for instance, are among those fit to say what is healthy or not. Who is to say what is a well-running automobile engine? Well, automechanics are.

Perhaps the answer to the question is that some experts in morality are to say what is good or evil. But this is not quite right. Morality is everyone's business because if morality is an actual part of human life, it is part of everyone's life. So there are no specialists in this field. Everyone is to say what is right or wrong. Yet just *saying* it will not do. The more appropriate issue is who is to identify what is right and wrong. The answer is: everyone. We all participate in the moral aspect of life, which is unlike business, law, medicine, education, carpentry, farming, etc.

Even in the professions there are those who mostly study a field on a theoretical plane, those who are concerned with application, and all those who practice it. In law there are scholars, lawyers, and all those who carry out our activities within the boundaries of law. In education there are theorists, administrators of institutions, and teachers. Economists, managers, and businessmen and business-women who buy and sell make up the field of commerce. These divisions are not sharp and those in the various branches usually need to be familiar with the others.

In moral matters we may be in the same boat. Moral philosophers are professionally concerned with theoretical issues of morality. Educators, conscientious parents, and community leaders teach moral positions by example and instruction, and the rest of us participate in the direct application of moral principles. And here, too, no sharp divisions are possible. In law, the legal scholars would also know about legal technicalities and must certainly apply the law to their own conduct. Doctors, too, will have to concern themselves with health measures, aside from curing others who are ill and studying some advances in medicine. So the layman will have to apply moral principles but also check them out and maybe even decide whether morality has been ill conceived by those who are supposed to deal with it on a theoretical plane. On the other hand, philosophers of ethics must also carry on with life as moral agents, so they cannot bury themselves in books about morality and leave the matter aside as they walk out of their studies.

Great human beings such as Socrates, Jesus, Buddha, the saints, creative geniuses, statesmen, military leaders, artists, educators, doctors, and the like are often viewed as "moral authorities." That is to say, such people are often thought of as exemplifying the moral life, either fully or at least in some domain of human affairs. They are not simply examples of greatness within some special area but rather examples of what amounts to human moral excellence within the sphere of their concern. One could be a great pianist and yet a morally detestable person. It is more often assumed, however, that the *great* human beings—not necessarily the *popular* ones—are also examples of how to lead a good human life, given their own situation, of course.

In a sense, some people may indeed be the ones to "say" what is right or wrong. But they do not do this simply by saying what is right. They exemplify human virtue and thus inform the rest of mankind of what it is to be good. (And of course the most vicious, degenerate, and malicious people around exemplify human evil. They would not characterize themselves as such, of course. But by their conduct they show what evil is, at least within their own sphere of activity.)

There is another source of moral information, if we may call it that (on the model of medical information or the like). Literature and drama mostly deal with moral problems. Some of the greatest playwrights—Dante, Shakespeare, O'Neill, Rostand—and the greatest novelists—Tolstoy, Dostoevsky, Mann—treat moral issues with incredible force and clarity. Films, too, serve as exemplification of human moral existence.

In all these mainly the implementation and practical consequences of certain moral positions are being exposed or exhibited! The business of formulating the arguments and justifications for various moral positions, as well as for the skepticism about morality, belongs in the philosopher's domain. Yet, when philosophy fails to work on these problems energetically enough, when philosophy itself is in bad shape, so to speak, others may take up the task. So there is no permanency about who attends to the moral aspects of human life. And in contrast to other spheres of human activity, which may concern us only now and then, or never, or in small measure, the issues of morality cannot ever be left aside. No one escapes the need to answer the question, How should I, a human being, live? Whether to dismiss the question, or to investigate it so as to avoid confusion, or to make the effort to answer it—all of this is everyone's business to some measure. To rely on others to say what is right and wrong is a risky business. Seeking advice from trusted friends, from people who are themselves morally good and know how to explain what it is to be good, or from artists, educators, and others who communicate about such matters may itself be the morally proper thing to do. If it is possible to know what is right, it may also be possible to know who lives by applying a sound moral position. And we might be able to trust those whom we know to have been virtuous. Yet here, too, people can change. So ultimately we cannot renounce our own role of moral agent.

Perhaps no man is an island. But perhaps, also, in some matters one is always alone, ultimately responsible. Morality would appear to be the prime candidate for this realm.

QUESTIONS FOR DISCUSSION

1. Why does ethics arise in human life? In your own words, describe objections you would raise against the answer offered in this chapter.
2. What are the basic or minimum requirements for something to qualify as a genuine moral position? Why are these the basic requirements?
3. If morality is possible, what relationship exists between facts and values?
4. What is hedonism? Why could it be a moral position?
5. What objections would you raise against the morality of hedonism?
6. What is altruism? Egoism? What objections would you consider forceful against these moral positions?
7. What are the distinguishing features of theistic ethics? Discuss theistic ethics critically. (Offer objections, respond to these, and give an evaluation based on arguments.)
8. What arguments would you offer to support the subjectivist position on ethics? What objections would you raise? Discuss some well-known issues of morality—deceit, fraud, injustice, and the like—in terms of the subjectivist approach.
9. What arguments support relativism? List some of the relativist

positions on values.   Select one that you believe has the most merit; criticize it and defend it.

10. Although discussed apart from the various sections in this chapter, what would you consider the position about the nature of morality that we could call realist or objectivist or naturalist?   (Examine what these terms imply and then present the characterization of morality that fits them best.)

11. What is nihilism?   What are the best reasons for holding this position?   Criticize the position.

12. Outline, in your own words, the empiricist case against the possibility of morality or moral knowledge.   By recalling the criticism of empiricism offered in the previous chapter, construct a criticism of the empiricist case against morality.

13. Explain your own relationship to the subject matter we have called morality in this chapter.   Does the discussion of this book touch on how you conceived of morality before reading the above treatment of the topic?   What is the difference?   What do you think about this now?   Why?

14. Give some examples of what you *seriously* consider to be morally wrong conduct.   How would you defend your judgment?

15. Defend the view of morality you consider correct and then defend some position in ethics or show why none can be supported successfully.   (In other words, what is your considered approach to this general topic of philosophy and human life and why?)

Political Philosophy

M ost of history's great philosophers have had a serious, even
overriding concern for politics. Their concern was not primarily with party politics, office squabbles, or efforts to manipulate
people so as to gain and keep power in any and every area of human
life. They were concerned with the nature of what Aristotle called
the *polis*—the character and structure of a human community that
has as its goal the achievement of the common good.

PHILOSOPHY AND POLITICS

In this chapter we will consider politics in the sense of the nature
of the good human community, not in the sense in which we say
that someone is politicking, grabbing for power. There is a connection between the two uses of the term, of course. Often the
effort to develop a good human community involves obtaining and
exercising power. But we will focus on the issue of the right ways
of gaining and using power, not just any kind of power-mongering.
We will examine some ideas about the best political regime or order
for a human community. The details of how such an order might

be implemented and what procedures of government and law it calls for will not be our primary concern.

Persons and Politics

Ancient philosophers such as Plato and Aristotle held that human beings are by nature political animals. In that tradition, which had a great deal of theory to give it support, many other philosophers to our day have given considerable attention to the central questions of politics: What are the basic principles of proper social conduct? Such well-known philosophers as Machiavelli, Hobbes, Locke, Marx, Dewey, and, in our time, Sartre, Marcuse, Rawls, Nozick, and Hayek developed elaborate philosophical systems in support of principles they believed would give us the answer to that question.

   The idea that human beings are political animals means more than that they are socially inclined, not naturally suited to live alone. Rather, it means that human beings live their lives best in a good human community, not in some haphazard, mediocre assembly of other people.

   From the early days of recorded history, philosophers have attempted to identify the sound, suitable principles for a good human community. For example, Plato wanted to identify such principles, and much of his philosophical work was directed toward that purpose. Many others, including those named before, were similarly motivated in their philosophical endeavors. The conclusions these philosophers reached were quite different in most cases. But their goals, or at least announced purposes, were similar.

   It is immediately apparent that the question dealt with by most political philosophers required an answer that would state a value. It would specify what the good of the community is. The right ways of organizing a human community would rely on some understanding of the common good, that which is the good of (all members of) the community.

   Thus, we are dealing with value-laden issues. A basic premise of the bulk of political philosophy is that it is possible to identify what is good and right in human communities. Commonsense reflection also appears to embrace this premise. Indeed, most political institutions and activities are based on some degree of confidence in our ability to know the common good.

Skepticism and Politics

In recent times, however, much philosophical effort produced the outlook that it is impossible to answer the questions that are raised in such value-laden political inquiry (just as it is supposed to be impossible to answer questions in ethics). By this we can see clearly how the various branches of philosophy relate to one another: If empiricism is right in epistemology, so nothing can be known that is not directly sensed, and if statements or judgments of value do not directly refer to sensory evidence, then fields concerned with values cannot produce knowledge. In metaphysics, too, if human nature is conceived of as passive, so that we cannot govern our own conduct, then to believe that principles of what we *should* do could exist is a mistake. The problems of values would be dismissed and the area would be left for the social scientists to understand. (This is just what seems to have happened!)

Other examples of the influence of philosophy's various branches on political philosophy could be demonstrated. For now let us realize that one reason for the hard work political philosophers devote to other branches of philosophy is that they need to prepare the ground for their work in politics. Without such preparation, their answers in political philosophy cannot be given convincing support. If a philosopher leaves the issue of free will versus determinism untreated, there will be trouble in the areas of ethics and politics. These latter areas tend, in the majority of cases, to require that human beings be capable of certain genuine choices. Otherwise, the view that they should behave in a certain way or institute a certain legal order can make little sense. If they cannot help what they do, it is impossible for them to choose what they should do. Generally, the idea that someone should do this or that assumes that it is possible for the person to choose between doing it or not doing it.

Controversy and Politics

However much some philosophers may have worked to show that political philosophy is impossible (and to leave its so-called problems to the social sciences), the questions of politics arise in each epoch.

It is evident in every age that people have strong feelings for or against certain kinds of conduct and certain institutions and policies in their communities. Furthermore, many believe that these sentiments are not arbitrary but well founded, even if they cannot provide the arguments in their support. During the Vietnam conflict many students had strong views about the role of the United States in Southeast Asia. Most could not produce well-developed arguments to give their views intellectual support. However, since it seemed to them very natural and appropriate to have views on the subject, they usually persisted in demonstrating their opinions and feelings.

Recent Revival of Political Philosophy

It is fair to suggest that students and young thinkers were mainly responsible for revitalizing political philosophy during the 1970's. Many saw that dominant philosophical positions could not address the pressing questions of political philosophy. Such issues as whether the war was unjust or not, whether or not certain kinds of conduct were justified in wartime, whether young people should be drafted into military service, whether or not military expenditures should continue for purposes such as those in Vietnam—all these and many others required attention. But both prominent philosophical approaches and renowned philosophers could not oblige with answers, and many held that right answers were impossible to find, since in these issues what is right and wrong could only be a matter of one's feelings or cultural upbringing.

After the years of turmoil, which were often most evident on college campuses, many philosophers returned to a concern with politics and the philosophical issues related to this field.* For the immediate future we can except widespread renewed interest in political philosophy in our society. This chapter discusses several different political philosophies, including the frequently influential political theories and systems that emerge from these philosophies.

* Elsewhere in the world there is a good deal of political thinking, although often very one-sided because it is dictated by the government in power. For instance, Marxism is not only widely accepted throughout the world but is also the position many governments support both by excluding or censuring other views and by propaganda.

ETHICS AND POLITICS

I explained earlier that ethics (or morality) has a role in human life because we can choose different courses of conduct in our personal lives, and not all are equally correct or good. The most general principles that could guide us best in living are those of the best ethical or moral system. If we could not make choices between alternative courses of conduct, then there would be no meaningful place for ethics. Many thinkers have argued exactly this: People are moved by forces over which they have no control, so there is no room for any concern with what they should or should not do.

The same general points can be made about politics. If the principles of a good human community, that is, the laws by which we and our political leaders should act, have a place in life, then we are the sorts of things that can make choices. In politics, as in ethics, if we should do certain things and if doing something is right (or not doing something wrong), then we can do these things. (It is possible to get oneself into a bind where what one should do is no longer possible. But in principle one's responsibilities, duties, obligations, and virtues must be within one's power of performance.) In this way we are significantly different from animals, since they carry on pretty much automatically. People, not other animals, are praiseworthy or blameworthy. Dogs and the rest might be given support or discouragement when they do what we want or like, but it makes no sense to consider them responsible. This, at least, underlies both ethics and politics.

Thus far ethics and politics seem very similar, but differences definitely exist. The question of politics is how we should live in a community, what are our obligations to other people simply as they are (not as brothers, sisters, wives, husbands, friends, professional colleagues, etc.). The focus is on community affairs, the basic principles of living in a community of other people. What are the basic guidelines for community order and organization? In what ways can a community of human beings be a good one?

Quite apparently, community life is of advantage to us. We benefit in crucial respects from living among others. Even if community life is unavoidable, clearly we can see how and where it adds to a life of possible solitude. For example, people can learn from one another. We have the ability to plan for the future, so we, unlike other animals, can use knowledge acquired in the past so as to change the future as we want it, for better or for worse. A particular bird of a certain kind simply carries out the actions that other members of its species have carried out, with only inessential changes, most of which people produce anyway. We can build on the successful (or unsuccessful) lives of our ancestors, and we can do so well or badly. But when we do it well, we can enjoy immense benefits in many areas of human life.

Thus, being a member of a community is a potentially beneficial thing, but it can also be of considerable harm. A resident of the Soviet Union or Nazi Germany would be in far better shape living on some desert island, unless he or she belonged to the ruling elite (where it is still doubtful that a person is well off, at least psychologically). In a repressive society, with total control over people's lives, a person talented in architecture or music would be in very bad shape. For such a person, also, community life could be worse than living on a desert island. For a young person following a career in architecture who is forced by members of his community to fight in some war, living in a community could be disastrous.

However community life came about, it seems clear that not all communities are equally good or bad. Regardless of what we identify as being good or bad in human life, some communities will enhance the good life, while others will be obstacles to it. This is where the question of political philosophy arises: What are the basic principles of a good human community? Or, what is *politically right?*

There are as many different answers to these kinds of questions as there are people who have tried to give them. The character of the good human community as such is just what political philosophy aims to identify. It may also be that there is no final answer to the question, in which case that becomes part of what the political philosopher has to consider and investigate.

As already pointed out, most philosophers today, and an even greater segment of the public with an opinion of these sorts of matters, deny that one could ever identify *correct* answers to these questions.

Nonetheless, the questions arise, even in an atmosphere of hopelessness and despondency. There are people in all ages who forge answers. We will be looking at the answers that have been offered by the major philosophers. I will not usually name them but merely outline various positions that are now fairly identifiable: socialism, communism, libertarianism, and the similar doctrines of democracy, monarchy, and so forth. These discussions will help the reader determine whether there is some hope for correct answers, even where anticipation of their widescale acceptance and implementation is not warranted.

POLITICS AND LAW

As mentioned earlier, political philosophy can produce a theory of political organization. If such a theory is widely accepted and implemented, a political system will emerge in the society which will reflect, with reasonable approximation, the tenets of the theory.

The tenets, or basic features, of a political theory have their influence on the legal system of a society. A legal or political system tends to reflect a political theory. Since this last is (usually) the product of a philosophical inquiry into political matters, it is fair to say that political philosophy aims at generating a legal system for purposes of solving the political problems of human beings. Not all systems exhibit some precise theory put into effect. Many systems are mixtures, involving elements of different political theories that may even be inconsistent. But even in such mixed systems traces of the different doctrines can be found. And those supporting the various elements usually cite some theories in their efforts to sustain them.

As an example we can consider the legal system of the United States. Its basic features are in the Constitution and its legal code. Most of us know enough of the Constitution to be able to check on its theoretical content. Moreover, the various documents surrounding the American Revolution, such as the Federalist Papers, Cato's letters, and the many prerevolutionary pamphlets, clearly discuss political issues from various philosophical perspectives. The Declaration of Independence makes clear reference to ideas advanced by one of the most important political philosophers, John Locke. Our current idea of human rights can be traced to Locke's theory of natural rights, a theory that reflects not just one man's political philosophy but the results of several centuries of political thought.

In the American system the theory of natural rights has its effects upon various legal provisions relating to property ownership, the right of free press, civil rights legislation, and the *due process* provision of the entire legal code.   By now the American legal system includes many other elements, of course.   These, too, can be traced to political ideas and ideals developed within a number of different or related political theories.   But we can clearly discern the traces of the political theory of natural rights.   These are the rights all individuals are supposed to possess.   Thus, when we say the system is .individualism, we are referring to its political theory.

POLITICAL THEORIES

The practical consequences of political theories are evident in many political systems.   Of course, some would dispute this, but on a commonsense level it is easily demonstrable.

Democracy

Democracy is the system of politics in which the politically active members of the citizenry decide, by various means, what principles should govern society.   This is one system with which most of us are familiar.   Even though most of us have an idea of what democracy is, it is still a rather complicated system.   It is also evident that it will be difficult to discuss democracy without touching on issues of political organization, the details and intricacies of contemporary politics.   But political philosophy does not deal with these matters directly.   Instead, once democracy is being implemented, many others, mostly social scientists, study its various features in practice. Today, democracy is discussed mostly by political scientists, sociologists, and even economists.

When political philosophers consider democracy, they are not generally concerned with the details (except as examples to illustrate their points, problems, or criticisms).   Instead, the political philosopher focuses on the central, crucial, or essential features of democracy. Without a clear idea of these essentials, of what democracy *must be* in the first place, those who study its details would not have a clear guide to what can be included in and excluded from their studies. Political philosophers are also concerned with comparing democracy to other political systems, to see how, in general, a democratic system would determine and achieve the proper goals of a human community. By learning what the essential aspects of a democratic political community are, political philosophers are better able to explain what will happen in a democratic community.

Those political philosophers who conclude in favor of democracy hold that among the various alternative ways of organizing human communities or societies, the democratic way is possible and is the most successful we could embark upon. They would advocate it on those grounds.

Democracy is possible, so the theory holds, because there are various ways of reaching decisions; the process of consulting the people involved and identifying the policies that most accurately reflect the majority's choice is one of these. Democracy, then, is seen as a possible way of organizing a human community, even if some of its variations may not be pure enough to be called democratic. (For example, the modification "representative" may have to be added in order to accommodate large communities.)

Consulting the citizenry and then putting into effect what the majority of the people consider best is regarded as the superior method of political organization for various reasons. This is where the issue of what is politically good comes in. Political theorists argue that their alternative for organizing a human community is the best. This is often called the *ideal* system, that is, one that is best for the purpose at hand. Sometimes "ideal" is used to point to something unreachable and yet worthy of pursuit. This distinction may be important at some level of discussion, but for now let us simply concentrate on the issue of why democracy is thought to be the ideal or best possible (more or less precisely implementable) political system.

Among the many theoretical justifications of democracy, we will focus on one. It is often presented in connection with the American system, but it is much older than that. The argument runs as follows. When all people are regarded as capable of contributing to their community's organizing principles and policies, they have a stake in learning about political issues. Although not everyone will be equally careful about studying what is good for the community at large, it is more likely that those who have a stake in the laws of a community will do more to understand what is best for it than those who have no stake in such a system. Thus, if we are interested in answering the questions facing all the people in a community, consulting all the people will very likely produce the best possible answers, or at least the best compromise. The good of the community, or the best for all the members, is better identified when all who reside in it attend to the problems than when only some select group or one person participates in seeking answers.

In short, the argument for democracy is an argument about how best to identify and implement the correct answers to our political questions. The underlying idea is simply that people seek to make the best of their communities and, when this is possible to them, they are likely to succeed (whereas such success would not be likely by other means). As with many other theories, democracy must be evaluated comparatively. Many answers to the question about how to organize a political community exist and democracy is one of them. Its answer is that the people as a whole will more likely produce the right answers to questions of political conduct and policy, provided they can all participate in this production. It is generally held by supporters of democracy that everyone is equally capable of giving correct answers to political questions, so that if the opportunity exists, all individuals will register what they consider the best way to live in a community. In essence, the right answer to the question of what is politically best is something that is determined by all of the people, or so proponents of democracy would argue. Underlying their view we could find numerous theories bearing on other areas of philosophy and the various sciences relating to human affairs. But concerning the specifically political views advanced by supporters of democracy, they hold that what is politically right must be decided by (consulting) everyone in a community.

The United States of America is often called a democracy, but it is clearly not purely democratic. Some laws are not enacted by simple majority rule but require approval by two-thirds of those involved in voting on various measures. Other laws and statutes are immune to virtually all decisions opposing or critical of them (e.g., the structure of the Constitution itself, *due process* measures, and lately many federal, state, county, and municipal regulations or ordinances that are established by small, temporary or permanent agencies such as the Food and Drug Administration or the local architectural boards). Nevertheless, the above basic features of democracy provide the first insight into the underlying principles of the democratic elements of American political life.

Challenging Democracy

The most important challenge facing the democratic theory of politics is the complicated issue of the very limited content of the position. When we recall that the only substantive point contained in the theory pertains to the best or appropriate *means* to be used to arrive at sound answers, we can appreciate how limited this content really is. Nothing other than relying on full participation by the people is said to be politically right. By proposing this answer, however, the theorists have gone beyond the answer's own provisions. Those who argue for democracy have allowed an answer to at least one political question without majority consultation. This answer is democracy itself. But if this answer is possible to arrive at without consulting the entire political membership of a community, why could we not provide some others, also? If some people—namely, proponents of democracy—can offer one answer— namely, the theory of democracy—as a correct political answer without going through the democratic process, then there is reason to doubt that the democratic process is needed for arriving at sound answers. In one instance, at least, it does not seem to be needed.

The foregoing problem is inherent in the democratic theory. Another inherent problem is that the majority of members of a human community could arrive at the conclusion that relying on democracy is wrong. If the best way to arrive at answers about political matters is the democratic way, then democracy contains the possibility of its own destruction. Indeed, some people argue that, among others, Hitler's rise to power came about by a semidemocratic process. And even if the real possibility of this is demonstrable— never mind the historical issue of Hitler's rise to power—then democracy has internal, theoretical problems, barring it from successful implementation. The point is crucial, although perhaps a bit complicated. A critic would argue as follows: Any theory whose central feature can be abandoned through its own implementation is not a successful theory.

There are other problems with democracy, but these are not internal problems. That is to say, one must already have alternative political ideals to criticize democracy in these ways; the internal criticism involved only the requirement that the theory be self-consistent.*

One external criticism of democracy might be that before we even come to political issues we have to find answers to questions of human conduct, specifically in ethics. If some kinds of actions and institutions are found immoral within a sound ethical framework, it could be wrong to allow majorities to pass and implement just any judgments about them within the political sphere. Thus we can imagine that a sound ethical theory concludes that éach person ought to make the best efforts to tell the truth unless some more important principles would be threatened by so doing. Suppose a majority of the political community chooses policies that violate this moral principle (without any demonstration that the violation is made necessary to protect higher-order values, e.g., human lives). But, given the soundness of the ethical conclusion, it could not be that this is right, even if the majority stands by the judgment. Thus, it may be a serious defect of the democratic theory that it can allow, as part of a legal system, political principles that violate moral principles that *all* people ought to abide by. In short, there is a serious threat that the democratic approach to politics will violate a sound moral position, whatever that would be. To make it possible to compel people to do what is morally wrong is a serious flaw of a political position.

Democrat's Answer. To these objections the proponent of democracy would offer several answers. Before looking at them I want to emphasize that some of these answers may not really work, just as some of the objections may not. We simply cannot trace out the implications and problems of these points at our present level of analysis. Hopefully, however, by touching on them to some extent, we will provide a basis for further inquiry.

---

* The reader may recall that logic is a basic tool for learning whether an answer is adequate. If an answer to the central political question includes elements that contradict each other, then it is flawed. In effect, one need either find some way to explain away the apparent contradiction or dismiss the theory as unworkable.

The pure democrat will probably reply to our first internal challenge by claiming that we are wrong to think that his is a political principle on the order of other, more substantive ones. A political theorist must provide the best possible answers to political questions that arise in a community. This is a methodological issue. It is not itself an answer to the *same type* of questions to be dealt with by using the method itself. In other words, the democrat will probably tell us that we are confused to put his answer and those provided by means of following the democratic method into the same category.

If we want to press further, the democrat may abandon his purism and allow that a few other substantive answers must be provided before democracy can be implemented. Some of these answers will come up as we look at other political theories. Many political theorists admit that the democratic method would indeed be helpful for certain purposes in a political community. They do so without advocating that this methodological principle is the *only* one that should be accepted as fundamental to the political framework of a human community. Besides, many nonpolitical organizations use the democratic method for reaching decisions. Civic and social clubs may use democratic methods for electing officials, scheduling social affairs, or formulating policies. But what interests us here is how well pure democracy fares under scrutiny.

To the second objection dealing with internal problems the democrat may reply by pointing out that no political system can *guarantee* against its rejection by those who operate by it. A dictatorship may be under the rule of someone who decides, all by himself, to abandon dictatorial powers. A socialist society may come to a state where the government commands the restoration of the principle of private ownership. There is then nothing odd about democracy's inability to guarantee against its own rejection.

Finally, the democrat may say that it is a myth that the answer to ethical questions has a bearing on political affairs. Certainly, in the main that is desirable. But political society has numerous unique problems. Sometimes the answers to questions in politics must conflict with the answers given in ethics. Spying, for instance, involves cheating, lying, fraud, and even killing. And war, even a defensive war, cannot abide by certain moral principles. Taxation itself involves a form of theft. It is not possible to ask of a political theory and system that it accommodate the dictates of even the soundest ethical position. The hope that the political and the ethical are consistent is naive. Any careful observer of actual political affairs will note that even the greatest statesmen lie. And while CIA or FBI activities may be morally objectionable, they could be politically proper.

In a sense, the democrat would continue, this is necessitated by ethics itself. The dictates of democracy override the dictates of any sound ethical position as it would apply to nonpolitical life. The common good is more important than the private ethical life of individuals. So, indeed, we seem to be faced with the occasional need to conflict with ordinary ethics. But this is only apparent: in political conduct more is at stake than is covered by personal ethics. If the state requires that we follow laws that are in conflict with our personal ethics, we must follow the state because it deals with higher values—the preservation and protection of the *entire* community.

These are some of the possible responses of the pure democrat. The theory of political affairs known as democracy is an important one, especially in modern Western societies. Furthermore, many societies, including those we call communist and socialist, maintain that their systems include democracy as a crucial element. The one-party political systems of many Eastern European countries call themselves democratic. Just how much the idea of a democracy may be stretched to allow for the inclusion of those systems is questionable. Perhaps a problem of democracy is just that such systems can justifiably consider themselves democratic. But it is also argued by its defenders that a well-developed democratic political system would never tolerate the provisions of those countries that exclude many people from participating in political affairs. On the other hand, many people are critical of American politics for its alleged pretentions to being a democratic system. Can the ordinary person, an artist, plumber, high school football coach, or the author of a philosophy textbook really influence politics? Here, too, the democrat may say that America is really far from being a democracy and that is partly responsible for the dissatisfaction with it.

Monarchy

The form of government called **monarchy** may not be of great interest to readers of this book. Most Americans are only vaguely familiar with monarchies, mostly through history and comparative government courses.

Monarchy is a form of government in which the principles by which the community is ruled are (ultimately) established by one person. From *archy*, meaning simply "rule" or "law," plus the term *mon* (or *mono*), we have the idea of single or one-person rule within a human community. As in *mono*poly, *mono*gamy, and *mono*phonic, the unit one is the central idea. A monarchy, then, involves a single ruler who determines the proper laws for a human community.

Often monarchies practice rule by inheritance, so that the single ruler must be a descendant of the prior ruler, and so forth. And in certain theories of monarchy this is considered an essential element, based mainly on the idea of a paternalist view of human social organization. Paternalism is the position that the ruler(s) of a community stands in the relationship of father or elder to the members (subjects or dependents). While this is crucial to some theories of monarchy, reference to family lineage is not essential to having a community be governed by one ruler. Where the argument for monarchy is mainly paternalistic, this reference to lineage could become crucial.

What argument may be offered in support of the political system of monarchy? We have noted already that the theory is not widely supported. Even in those countries where a version of monarchy exists (e.g., England and Spain), the existing political institutions impose severe limitations on the actual monarch. Nevertheless, simply because it is not one of the frequently entertained alternatives these days, the theory of monarchy should not be neglected. Some critics of the various forms of government familiar to us believe that current problems could be remedied, and might even have been avoided, with the institution of a monarchy. For example, although most people believe the political system of mainland China is a variety of socialism or communism, in the strictest sense it has been a monarchy of sorts for a long period of time. To the extent that some social commentators consider mainland China a good human community, they must be prepared to support the theory of monarchy, even if in a less than pure (and clearly nontraditional) format.

In its purest form the theory of monarchy starts with a belief in the natural inequality of human beings. Just consider that we all tend to rank people. Sometimes we do it by reference to social class, and other times by reference to economic success or power. It is generally believed that the distribution of intelligence and capacity for abstract thought in a community can be represented by a bell-shaped curve, so again inequalities are accepted as virtually inherent in human nature. Most of us certainly make qualitative distinctions among individuals. At times these have to do with our own preferences, likes, special interests, or aesthetic conceptions. (The very idea of someone's being an attractive person, among the "beautiful people," members of the enlightened or consciousness-raised class, and so forth testifies to the prevalence of this differentiation.) Instead of picking those whom we prefer or like we sometimes claim that some people are great, outstanding, excellent human beings, while the rest mediocre or even evil, putting it often in terms of "great guy," "bore," and "rotten bastard" (to use some familiar terminology). So we see that people accept both minor and serious differences of status.

The theory of monarchy assumes that there is a valid moral distinction we can always make with respect to all people, and that we can generally identify the best human being within some particular human community. Since the best person would be one who is both extremely wise or knowledgeable and most virtuous, this person's ability to judge matters of great importance must surpass anyone else's. The affairs of the human community are, of course, those we can easily construe to be the most important. This is because although your affairs and mine have great importance to you and me, respectively, the affairs of the entire community are of importance to us all. Anything that is of importance to everyone in a human community must be of the greatest importance. The opposite would be nonsense. And if the wisest and best person is one who would have the ability to judge matters of great importance, such a person ought to judge the affairs of the community at large. This person, then, should pass judgment and then implement the policies to be followed within the community at large.

The main point of this argument is that the best person should establish the laws of the society. This idea has been expressed not infrequently even in the United States. When people ask for a great leader to help us through some crisis or even to take the reins of government from the inept bureaucrats who simply serve special interests; or when they hope for a powerful but benevolent individual to control other, subsidiary governing elements (e.g., Congress); or again when they approve of the institution of absolute one-person rule in some emerging nation in Africa or Latin America—on these occasions it is the theory of monarchy that is being defended by them, even if not explicitly. My point here is that to understand the alternatives that are proposed among those commenting on political affairs, the theory of monarchy certainly must be considered as a serious contender. In short, could it not turn out, after all, that a human community would be best organized by obtaining the absolute authority of a benevolent king or queen (or emperor or dictator or whatever title is used)?

Before we raise some critical objections to this defense of the political system of monarchy, it will be useful to consider another way of arriving at a similar conclusion. The argument itself is different, but the conclusion is effectively the same: a monarchical arrangement is best for a human community.

In this argument we begin by noting that people are generally motivated to act by their fear of harm or death. The plausibility of this idea is easily confirmed when we pick cases such as everyone's concern with safety, with a healthy diet, with medical care, or with the host of activities in personal life and the array of governmental decisions that aim at safeguarding life.

The next point this argument takes into consideration is that people will do whatever they can get away with in order to help themselves unless some law exists that threatens punishment for certain kinds of conduct. To avoid the disaster of the "dog eat dog" human community, it is necessary that a very powerful agent assume the authority to impose strong prohibitions against the kinds of conduct that will produce a constantly warring community. Law and order must be upheld. Unless some agent possesses the full power and legal authority to devise and implement the best means for preserving peace in a human community, the motive for self-preservation would rage uncontrollably and indeed destroy rather than preserve human lives. The rational solution to the problem of imminent internal war within a human community is the selection of a powerful, unlimited authority whose full-time job is to oversee the affairs of state and secure peace within the community at large.

The main point of this defense of monarchy is that certain realities of human motivation and the threat of death establish that only with a firm, complete, and sovereign authority fully devoted to his or her task can a community maintain peace.

I have tried in both these cases to offer arguments that are at least plausible, that is, able to stand their ground without appeal to extrarational considerations. The theory of monarchy has, of course, been defended by reference to religious or supernatural considerations. In many specific cases kings and queens (or their apologists) defended their authority and power by reference to divine decree—"God selected me to rule!" This approach to justifying one-person rule, called the doctrine of the divine right of royalty, will not be considered here. We are attempting to offer the natural, rational arguments for various political systems. Of course, anyone who believes that the existence of God is a natural feature of reality, not requiring reference to supernatural, extrarational, and extrascientific considerations, would object to the implications of the approach I am taking. Nevertheless, the tradition of theism is mainly nonnaturalistic. To include considerations of God in an effort to provide alternative attempts at rational defense of various political systems is, therefore, incompatible with the well-known versions of theism. However much monarchy may have been defended along theistic lines, the defense that does have a claim upon our attention as human beings is one that *aims* at complete rationality. In the final analysis, the philosophical approach to various topics does require appeal to human reason rather than to some other element in us.

The First Argument Criticized.   Let us now turn to some critical considerations of each of the arguments for monarchy. One difficulty with the idea that the best and most knowledgeable person should rule is that selecting such a person is almost impossible, even ·if we admit to the existence of the greatest, morally most worthy person in the community. It will not do to deny that someone might indeed be the greatest human being in a community. It is possible. But it is difficult to specify some means of assuring his or her success as a political leader. The problem may not arise in a human community where *everyone* is as great as he or she could be—in a community of morally perfect people. These people would then be able and willing to identify with full honesty who is the greatest among them. The most brilliant and virtuous person would be the right choice, but it isn't clear why such people would need a ruler.

But would that individual be recognized as such by others who are far less virtuous than they could be? In other words, suppose that most of us are not excellent, outstanding people, even within our limited powers. It is unlikely that we would admit this outright. We would mistakenly regard ourselves good. So if a community contains many like us, will we identify the truly great person as indeed truly great? It is not likely. Instead, we will claim that those who are doing what *we believe* is right are the good people and the best of them is the best individual. There would be incredible discord among us about who is the greatest human being.*

There are two more important questions: (1) Assuming that we could identify the community's greatest citizen, would that person continue to be great *as a leader?* (2) Having achieved the position of greatness, would such a person choose his or her new situation or consider it best to remain as before, the best in the community but not a leader?

We must first ask what constitutes greatness, what makes someone morally outstanding. Presumably, given the nature of moral excellence, the great person has freely chosen to live by moral principles, to cultivate virtues, and to become a great human being. Would such a person of great virtue or character consider absolute reign over a community suited to the good human life? Does "I want to rule others for the common good!" indicate the best characteristics or virtues in human life? To express this in somewhat more traditional terms: Would a great human being choose to rule others?

Before we can learn whether being a monarch is even compatible with the character of a great human being, we need to know what such a person would be like. It seems quite probable that a great person, knowing what it is to become one, would never act in a way that could prevent others from reaching greatness. Would being an absolute ruler not involve doing at least some things that deprive others of their power to secure their own achievements, accomplishments, and greatness in life? If so, as is reasonable to suppose, then the individual best suited to be the monarch would refuse the position of rulership, at least in ordinary circumstances. (In emergency situations it is difficult to foretell what anyone, great or inadequate,

---

* Here it might be noted that some monarchists would claim that it is unimportant what anyone else believes, so long as the greatest person, aided by those who recognize his or her as such, knows who is great and proceeds to wrest power in order to produce the best human community possible. Yet the difficulty of recognizing greatness does not vanish. It is merely confined to a smaller circle of individuals.

should do, even regarding the common good.)   The objection here is that any truly outstanding, morally excellent individual would be the first to realize that virtue requires liberty, so such a person would be the last to seek absolute power over others.

Finally, absolute one-person rule by a great human being could turn out to be an impossibility because one's knowledge of others' affairs must be extremely limited.   Therefore, what is good for the community at large, which depends a great deal on knowledge of what is good for the members of the community individually, will not be attainable by depending on the wisdom and virtue of one person, however great.   Greatness will not automatically ensure a person's capacity to learn all of what is needed to evaluate the ways of an entire community of human beings.   It is not that one cannot know what is right for other people—although some critics object to monarchy on such skeptical grounds.   One individual, however, cannot find out what is right for everyone, including for all members together.   It is difficult even for a large group of rulers to find out what is best for the community and its membership.   For one person alone this would be impossible, especially if the ruler's own moral excellence must also be preserved.

Other objections could be raised to the great person theory of monarchy.   We might note in passing that being a great person for a while does not guarantee staying one forever, so the risks of assigning absolute rule to a great person are considerable.   Nor would other people remain static; they could achieve moral greatness beyond that of the monarch, in which case the community would no longer be led by the greatest person within it.   But the other objections are sufficient to challenge monarchy for now.   Let us see what responses could be made to the above points.   Then we can go on to scrutinize the other argument for monarchy.

Monarchy Defended.   The response to the first objection is not elaborate.   Suffice it to note that however difficult it may be to select the great person to rule the community, unless there are other problems with the argument for monarchy, we can insist that people should try harder.   If a decent, successful political community is our aim, we must find the greatest person to lead it, however difficult this may appear at first.

The next objection is more difficult to meet.   Would a great person consider absolute rulership a morally proper role?   To answer this the monarchist will need to add a few items to his theory. He may observe that the bulk of the people are in need of moral guidance and cannot be left to achieve moral excellence on their own. The bulk of humanity are like children. Most people are not free spirits such as the greatest person of the community. They are blind and morally stunted, and they require the leadership of someone who is indeed a moral giant. In effect, the monarchist's argument has turned into an explicit argument for paternalism, which should not, however, be related to monarchy exclusively.

Most people agree with the implementation of some paternalistic legal measures. The argument that in our complex society the government *must* regulate broadcasting, commerce, medicine, air travel, education, etc., is generally based on the view that people *cannot* cope with these matters on their own. So the monarchist simply believes that the individual leader would be more effective in dealing with the need for protecting people against themselves (and the shrewder among them) than would, for example, a federal bureaucracy in a quasi-democracy. The main point of the monarchist here is that people are far too weak to assume full responsibility for their own lives. Therefore, the leader would not tread on their moral responsibility by lending a helping hand. The monarch would be more like a gentle parent than a brutal master. Then the monarchist could argue that the greatest person, in this parental role, is duty-bound to provide guidance to the community's members. He could claim that when a great human being can contribute to the moral welfare of the masses, it would be cruel (immoral!) not to do so. Perhaps it would be like refusing to help an injured man on grounds that standing the pain and recovering on his own would strengthen his character. The monarchist would not accept that a great human being would refrain from benevolent human engineering.

The objection that a great leader could not acquire the knowledge needed to direct the community could be answered as follows: If certain facts could be discovered about human beings in general and could guide the monarch's judgment, the monarch would not require much detail in the effort of governance. There may be no need for knowing everything about each citizen. All that is necessary is that general principles of good conduct be implemented. The monarch would make sure that all obey these principles, which would be the law of the land. And the monarch would not have to respond to every deviation at each step; these general guidelines would serve as permanent guidelines in foreign policy, enforcement, punishment, etc.

In a way, the objection underestimates the capacity of a truly great leader. A brilliant ruler could well know a great deal about human affairs. Furthermore, being morally good, such a person would use his or her knowledge to the advantage of all, whether they know it or not.

Besides, the objection assumes that the good of the community consists of the good of each member. Perhaps the crucial and relevant moral goal is independent of individual welfare, desire, or want. A monarchist would probably insist that the great leader's function is to direct the entire community to the achievement of a common goal—or what in our day has been called the national purpose, or the public interest. There is an illusion in the objection that the good of the community coincides with the good of the individual members. What may have to be considered is that the good of the individuals must be made subservient to the good of the community. This may not appeal to the individualistic tendencies remaining in the American culture. But even in America there is now widespread belief in the irrelevance of the selfish aims of individuals. As the famous psychologist B. F. Skinner has argued in his book *Beyond Freedom and Dignity* (Knopf, 1971), it is the survival of the culture that ought to be the concern of all the members. And, the monarchist will maintain, this goal is best achieved when power is centralized in one great knowledgeable and virtuous person.

A Second Argument Criticized.   Having considered the responses to objections raised against the first argument for the political system of monarchy, let us now turn to the second argument and see what problems it raises. The main point of this argument was that the motive for self-preservation would, when rationally assessed, require a monarchy so as to avoid constant warring within a human community. What objections can be raised against this view?

First, we may object that human action is not solely motivated by fear of death. Most generally put, the importance of the quality of human life is omitted from consideration in this argument. Thousands of people have faced the danger (or even imminence or high probability) of death in order to secure a chance for a life of honor, liberty, and excellence. While some people may not care much for anything beyond living, even when the life possible to them is that of serfdom and dishonor, many others have made determined, even valiant, efforts to strive for much more.

Thus it seems unlikely that the rational way to organize a human community consists of relegating control of one's own life to an absolute ruler whose only role is to keep the community peaceful. Peace without liberty is no better than peace in a concentration camp. Although peace would appear to be the highest good when other values seem secure enough, one can easily understand that most people, even the best among human beings, would reject peace if it meant subservience. Since it is unlikely that the assumption (about the governing motive for human action) in this theory is correct, a defense of monarchy based on it fails by virtue of omitting other factors from consideration, ones that may count against monarchy.

Next we can object to the claim that without fear of punishment everyone would do anything that seems to enhance the narrow pursuit of self-preservation. This idea assumes again that all human beings are motivated by desires for immediate well-being: for the avoidance of pain and the procurement of pleasure. If it is false that the essential human motive is fear of death, then we might have to search for some other motives that could underlie human actions in a community. Perhaps some people strive for creative achievements—artistic, scientific, technological, and the rest possible to them. Perhaps people can pursue goals that give avoidance of pain and danger less prominence than the theory assumes. There is evidence to support this as we consider what human beings have done and are doing every day. If these objections hold against the theory, it may not be necessary to rule human communities by absolute power held by an agent exclusively responsible for peace. The kind of political system required for a human community would have to take into consideration the many different motives that may govern people. Only a system that encourages the best of them to flourish, while preventing the worst from reigning unchecked, could claim superiority. Since the theory being considered here limits all of us to a very narrow set of motives, it cannot be considered successful.

Monarchy Defended Again.   The most readily available response to the foregoing objections is based on certain scientific theories. Many psychologists hold that however complex and noble we may think human motives are, human conduct is nevertheless governed by the instinct or motive for self-preservation. Human beings, like other animals, instinctively strive for self-preservation, even when their actions seem far removed from such goals. Kittens seem to play with no overt regard for their self-preservation; birds whistle fancy tunes with no apparent connection to their self-sustenance; and fish swim about apparently aimlessly. Human beings, too, engage in all sorts of complex activities that appear to have no bearing on self-preservation. Nevertheless, this apparent lack of concern for simple survival is refuted by the general laws of animal biology and psychology. We act because our needs have to be fulfilled, and our basic need is to keep on living. Even those who commit suicide do so only because they misperceive their situation and believe that life cannot be lived by them. Those who risk life and limb for such noble myths as liberty and honor are, in the end, simply unaware of the correct means to achieve their self-preservation. It is the business of a wise and forceful leader, however widely resisted by mistaken beliefs and "ideals," to channel human action toward the harmonious continuance of community life.

The idea that without threat of legal punishment human beings would still, quite often, refrain from harmful interaction is also a myth. The prescientific notions of religion and morality must be abandoned so that we can come to grips with the facts scientists have uncovered through their careful research. Ever since human beings have populated the earth, every community has observed taboos to keep the human animal in check. Without these measures humanity would have destroyed itself. If the idea of a modern monarchy is not· invoked soon, human beings will surely suffer the consequences of the myth of liberty, rights, and the unchecked, unregulated pursuit of happiness—total annihilation. The rational way to organize a society, then, is to leave its governance to a wise person who fully understands these facts and will be totally devoted to the task of keeping peace within the human community.

These responses are not all structured in a clear argument. To determine their force, their truthfulness as proposals for solving our political problems, scholarly work is indispensable. To that end, the political philosopher must often get involved in what others regard as dry and dull reflections and research. Yet, as with the surgeon who embarks meticulously on the crucial task of saving a life with the calmest of hands and the clearest awareness of the situation, so the political theorist must attend to these gravest of human problems with what someone has called a passionate devotion to passionless truth.

Socialism

Our next task will be to examine a rather new political theory, **socialism.** As with other such labels, the term *socialism* is applied to many different ways of coming to similar conclusions.   Some versions of socialism are defended by appeal to religious viewpoints. The general idea of fraternity, of the brotherhood or intimate unity of humanity, collectively embarking on achieving the highest hopes defined within Christianity, for example, is part of many socialist positions.   But the most forceful of the socialist positions has been developed by Karl Marx.   Marx was, of course, a proponent of communism also, but he held that socialism must be achieved first. Since he believed that socialism is in fact a scientific approach to community problems, we will consider his view on socialism and leave the others aside.   It should not be forgotten, however, that others have defended this theory also.

Scientific Socialism.   Thus far the political theories I have outlined included moral elements in their arguments.   In other words, democracy and monarchy are theories that include statements about how a human community *ought to* be organized, or what a *good* or *just* community is.   Some features of the second argument for monarchy came close to involving predictions of what sorts of political developments *must* occur, based on what the theorist considered to be scientific ideas and analyses.   But even there the conclusion amounted to a statement that a certain way of organizing society is rational, which is another way of saying that it is the *best* or the *right* way.

Now we come to a political theory that is often defended on scientific rather than on moral grounds.   When someone defends a position on what are called "scientific" grounds, it is often taken that only descriptions of what has happened, is happening, and will happen could be involved.   That is, science is held to involve no more than descriptions of what occurs in the world.   When such descriptions are followed by statements of what people ought to do, which are not descriptive statements, one is no longer involved in the kind of scientific enterprise initially claimed for the theory, unless, of course, the goals to be achieved are somehow set out beforehand. One of the crucial features of much of modern philosophy is the prohibition against using science to defend the *goals* human beings may or, especially, *should* aim for. This is why, when some political philosophers offer judgments about what human beings should do, once the evidence of science has been obtained, they in fact go beyond what they themselves take to be science—description, prediction, explanation, analysis, etc.

When students of philosophy and political theory encounter the claim that some system is scientifically defensible, it is important that they make sure what the theorist has in mind. Although we cannot examine this issue here in full, it is worth pointing out that the common term *scientific* is not really that simple to understand (especially when it is used by practically anyone who aims at respectability in the modern world).

The above remarks are important because socialism, as offered to us by Marx, is advanced as a scientific viewpoint. But Marx did use the term *science* in a reasonably familiar way. He had a view of nature that involves a kind of basic, metaphysical principle. Marx held that this principle is proved scientifically, made evident by a careful observation of nature, including its physical and chemical processes. At any rate, when Marx held that the socialism he was talking about is a scientific analysis of social affairs, he was using the term *scientific* in a relatively familiar but not uncontroversial way. In the subsequent discussion we will see just how this enters into his doctrine and where the idea poses some difficulties.

The socialism we are considering is the result of what its proponents regard the laws of reality, especially the laws of human history and progress. The theory holds, basically, that everything in reality undergoes change in a revolutionary fashion, in accordance with the dialectics of nature. From the start, whatever exists will generate its opposite (or negation). When this clashes with its opposite, a brand new item emerges which then produces its own opposite. The process continues throughout nature until a point of total harmony is reached.

In the social sphere, for example, when industrial capitalism emerged, it consisted of the propertied or land-owning class of people, which then produced a class generally referred to as the proletariat, the workers, or wage laborers. According to Marx, these two social or economic classes cannot coexist for long and must eventually clash in revolution. From that clash will emerge the dictatorship of the proletariat. The accompanying economic and political arrangement is socialism.

Many elements contribute to the development of a socialist society, but these are not crucial for now. Suffice it to note that the initial opposition involves alienation of the workers from their livelihood (work) as well as the fierce competition of members of the propertied class for monopolistic or oligopolistic status in the market place and the political structure.*

Whatever the details of the process that leads to socialism, the process itself is regarded by Marx as inevitable, and in general those who hold to this theory as a scientific analysis of society believe the same. This is one unique feature of this system of community life. For many socialists it means that what we should or should not do is irrelevant, since the future will turn out the socialist way by virtue of historical necessity.

Mentioning the name of Karl Marx is very risky in a brief outline. Volumes have been written in efforts to clarify what thinkers such as Marx have said and meant. However, since Marxist socialism is not only a prominent scholarly topic but also a major ideological movement in our times, we need to outline the crucial features of the theory.†

Economic Features. Socialism is that political / economic arrangement in which the control of production and the distribution of the goods and services of a society rest ultimately in the hands of those

---

* A monopoly is a *single* firm that succeeds in keeping the production of some desired goods or services to itself. An oligopoly is a small *group* of such firms.
† The reader may have noticed that some of the political systems discussed here are conceived mainly in terms of their economic implications. In modern times many political systems (e.g., socialism, capitalism, communism, national socialism, and their varieties) are characterized by reference to their economic features. In short, the focus seems to be on the arrangement of material relations in society. Production, exchange, and consumption of goods and services are crucial for modern political theorists. Indeed, the term *political economy* is prominent within the intellectual community. As a distinctive field of inquiry, widely pursued in universities, this area of study explicitly presumes intimate ties between political or legal and economic or commercial affairs. One reason for this is that a very prominent view of human nature emerged some centuries ago in which people were conceived of as primarily material entities subject in all their activities to the same laws of behavior characteristic of physical nature.

who provide the labor to produce such goods and services—"the workers." By "rest" I mean that socialist communities aim at letting economic affairs be controlled by representatives of the workers. Such control is comprehensive. Once a group of workers has been selected to organize the economic affairs of society, that group is in total control of the major economic elements of society.

It may be simpler to understand this when we consider that in a socialist society no major firm producing vital goods and services is operated by individuals or their associations (corporations, partnerships). Most people have heard of the idea of **nationalization.** This means that an industry is taken over by the government. It is a bit misleading, however, to call socialist factories nationalized, since socialism need not have any national boundaries. Thus, the firms are owned by workers, in time throughout the world, and they administer them through representatives, that is, a socialist government. Private property, competition, profit, and other elements typical of free enterprise are not part of the socialist arrangement. Instead, the government of the people—workers—runs the firms for the purpose of eliminating the scarcity of badly needed goods and services. By the tenets of this theory, the people work for themselves by working for the government.

The crucial point here is that in socialist systems the entire society is organized to serve the interest of the working class. Opposition to this goal is discouraged if not completely prohibited. But, according to Marx, in a socialist society people gradually are changed so that their inclinations toward self-gratification and their desire for private gain eventually cease to exist. According to this theory, human beings as a group are in a process of growth throughout history, and human nature will be fully realized only in the post-socialist era. (Many people who discuss socialism are unaware of this feature of the Marxist versions of socialism and communism. Within Marxism the human race is conceived somewhat on the model of a single individual who goes through the various stages of development from childhood to adolescence and to full maturity.) The full realization of human nature will occur only in communism. But even by the time socialism emerges, that part of the developing human species that expresses itself in greed, self-centeredness, and personal ambition (including the desire for more and more wealth) will be transcended. Socialist human beings are beyond the stage where the species's "adolescent" characteristics are dominant— namely, capitalism.

But in Marx's theory capitalism must precede socialism. In the capitalist era the machinery and wealth needed to sustain the socialist order are created *via* the fierce competition among various capitalists who are seeking monopolistic status. In socialism, with control of production in the hands of the workers, and with the discontinuation of profiteering, all the needs of the members of society are met. And with the satisfaction of their basic needs, people will be able to develop their creative potential, not for profit but for the sheer joy and value of it, as well as the flourishing of the entire community. (Socialism emphasizes a concern with the society as such, not so much with the individuals of the community who may have false ideals or corrupt desires and conceptions of what is historically necessary.)

The specifics of the organization of such a political system differ, and Marx did not spell out the details. But the basic idea is to develop channels of communication between leaders and workers so that needs can be met efficiently. Since socialism, as conceived by Marx, is a preliminary stage to the ultimate development of a human community—that is, to one suited to the fully matured human species as opposed to one that serves fragmented, incomplete classes of adolescent varieties of "prehumans"—its aim is to eventually eliminate the need for a coercive state. At the stage of socialism, however, coercive powers are still needed to enable the community to cleanse itself of counterrevolutionary elements. Those who would linger in the past and revert to profiteering, acquisitiveness, selfishness, and other leftovers of capitalism must be dealt with sternly. Until the stage of the "new man" is reached, which ushers in communism—the stateless and fully harmonious human (or posthuman) society—coercive measures are needed. Therefore, although class division and warfare are no longer present in a socialist community, the state still exists to provide efficient guidelines to production, exchange, and consumption.

Humanistic Socialists. Not all socialists are Marxists. Some non-Marxist or revisionist Marxist socialists envision the best human community as a socialist one, with no need or possibility of reaching beyond this stage. These socialist theorists do not believe that humanity will develop into a more perfect version of itself. They believe the state is needed to keep up the efficient and just production and distribution of goods and services. Some do not accept the idea that socialism will come about by way of the forces of a

process in history.   The dialectics of nature, described at the beginning of the sketch of the Marxist system, cannot be counted on,
according to these theorists.   It will require the choices of human
beings, in accordance with moral ideals, to bring about a socialist
society.   The moral ideal to serve as the guiding principle for the
development of the non-Marxist type of socialist may be the Christian
view of the brotherhood of all persons—"You are your brother's
keeper"—or the secular idea that justice consists in the equal well-
being of all people on earth.   As such, socialists tend to be inter-
nationalist, except for national socialists.*

It is well to realize that socialism is best interpreted as a worldwide program, not aiming for the development of independent,
sovereign human communities.   Both Marxist and non-Marxist socialists would admit to this, although Marx would consider the
development of worldwide socialism as historically inevitable.   Non-
Marxists would consider it a proper goal of conduct, however likely
or unlikely its realization.

Marxism Untenable?   A crucial problem with the Marxist system
appears to be its basic premise that history moves in a virtually
preordained direction.   The dialectical principle, whereby everything develops its opposite and then, through their clash, resolves
into a new kind of thing, is difficult to confirm.   The process simply
does not appear to occur with sufficient regularity to qualify as a scientifically supportable law of nature and human social development.

Another problem is that if the theory is correct, then we are
all caught up in it, and our perception and understanding of reality
are actually forced upon us by our situation. within the dialectical
process.   As a result, it does not seem likely that anyone could ever
know of the existence of the process itself; reality could only be
known as determined by one's circumstances.   Marx seemed to want
to have it both ways: all people are moved by the forces of history—
mainly economic forces, which also govern their thinking and pre-

* Many people do not realize that Nazi Germany started out as a program for **national
socialism.**   Since racism or ethnic chauvinism is not part of socialism, national socialism
was distinguished from most other socialist systems.   But the claim that Nazi Germany
exemplified capitalism, namely, the system of private property and free enterprise, is
false.   The fact that business magnates supported some of Hitler's programs is often
the ground for this belief, but there is no justification for identifying the free market
economy with one where wealthy people, by use of political power and legal privilege,
stay closely tied to the policies of a dictatorial government.

vent the resolution of class conflicts by peaceful means—but Marx himself could break out of these forces and see the entire process from start to end. But if Marx, a human being, could break out, why could not others? And if others could, there is no way to guarantee the outcome; they could adjust to history or choose a different direction, leading away from socialism instead of leading toward it.

Finally, and this is perhaps the most important point, it appears that socialism is really irrelevant to those who are concerned with improving their communities in the lifetimes of human beings. Marxist socialism suits beings who are not really human but who are at a stage between human (our kind) and posthuman (those of a communist society). When one considers that Marxism often serves as a critical frame of reference by which to assess contemporary political affairs, a puzzle emerges. How could a frame of reference appropriate to a kind of being in the future be used to judge the lot of present human beings? Would that not be like judging the conditions of the life of a pig by the standards suited to a horse?

Rebuttal. The first objection may perhaps be met by pointing out that some laws do not operate like others, with precise temporal sequence. The seasons of the year do not come all that regularly, and the maturation of individuals varies considerably. Could nature not admit of more comprehensive principles that are not exact with respect to time sequence? Marx himself never offered a precise timetable for the revolution between workers and capitalists in the various industrial societies. He even allowed, late in his life, that some countries would move toward socialism without open revolution.

The problem of being caught up within the historical process and therefore trapped in a relative and limited perspective on reality is serious. However, it can be answered by noting that when Marx discovered the science of socialism, whereby he escaped the narrow perspective of class consciousness even though others were limited in their understanding, the possibility of revolutionary consciousness came about. It is just this development that makes it possible to eventually escape all such limitations and move toward a harmonious resolution of the dialectical process of social growth. Moreover, not even Marx claimed to have ultimate knowledge of reality. He held that by employing the science of socialism and by using the dialectical principles not just as an explanation of the past but as a tool for analysis of current events, he could offer probabilistic predictions.

Finally, concern for our present political situation without reflection on the future is utterly futile. It is only with the limited, narrow, and selfish attitude of mankind today that anyone would raise this objection. The present is unimportant by itself. It is the ultimate realization of communism that is crucial, and all present events must be judged by how they contribute to it. It is not that the objection does not fit within Marx's analysis of the limited perspective of contemporary, premature, or prehuman beings. It is quite predictable. But a true revolutionary consciousness will liberate a person from such tunnel vision. It is the fact of (or, as recent Marxists have said, the faith in) the full development of humanity's essential nature into a future community of unflawed beings that is important. The objection, then, has significance, but it is simply that whoever offers it shows a lack of full perspective.

Problems of Socialism Galore.   Concerning non-Marxist, nontheistic socialism, the objections center on the underlying moral ideal. To claim that lack of full equality in human beings is an injustice is to ascribe to nature a will, or a conscious design. Nature is not unjust or just. The ideal of justice applies only to character, conduct, and institutions governed by choice. Someone is unjust if he treats another cruelly, but not if he is thrown against another by a hurricane. If a beautiful child has some advantages over a homely one, it is not the child's fault. To produce forced equalization is to penalize the beautiful child for something the child has not done. Since there is reason to think that true excellence arises from choice and brings with it its own rewards, focusing on natural inequalities may indeed undermine human dignity.

There is also the assumption that some people are in a position to make others good in crucial ways. Who are these people to be— the best among us, those who know what is good? But would it not be unjust for these people to take advantage of their natural assets and use them to govern the lives of others? This system appears to deny the principle of essential equality and utilizes its opposite, the fact of natural inequality. The socialist, who wishes to implement an ideal of full equality among persons, appears to negate it in the process of selecting some people as privileged to make decisions about other people, which rejects any measure of equality in the final analysis.

Finally, the very idea of equalizing all people appears to be a negation of the necessary fact of nature that individual things are individual precisely because they are not in all respects like other things. At least time and space separate people, and these elements can be responsible for certain advantages. Must the process of equalization go on forever? If the socialist replies that only essential aspects are to be equalized, we need to discover what these are. It seems that the one quality we all share is our capacity for choice, for exercising our unique human capacities to become what we choose to be. But the socialist would violate just this equality among us by becoming an equalizer instead of leaving all free to exercise their only true, essential equality.

Rebuttal to Critics of Ideal Socialism. The non-Marxist socialist will probably respond to the first objection by reminding us of our ability to conquer nature. We divert the path of natural streams and rivers to form dams. We bring together disorderly sources of natural energy to develop nuclear energy. We build instruments and develop chemicals and nutrients to eliminate natural threats, diseases, and dietary deficiencies. Is it not sensible, also, to make efforts to repair nature's shortcomings when it produces human beings with serious natural disadvantages? If we do know how to do all these constructive things, is it not sensible and even obligatory for us to use human reason and work to bring about human equality? If we know what would bring about the betterment of all, is it permissible to abstain from acting on that knowledge? The objection, so the socialist says, caters to an old notion of human excellence, one that favors personal achievement without active regard for those faced with conditions that prevent them from aspiring to these goals. Perhaps at one time, when we did not know how to conquer nature, letting nature have such a significant influence on human welfare could be tolerated. There was no better way. But now that we have learned to correct problems caused by "nature's neutrality," there could be a way, and we are duty-bound to seek it out.

The second objection may be answered by reminding us that through proper self-discipline and adequate protection against abuse, it is safe enough to let those who know better do what they can for the rest. We do choose leaders in many fields of human endeavor— chiefs of hospitals, heads of college departments, foremen of work-crews, captains of football teams, and so forth. These need not be abusive about the position of leadership. Their duty is to serve the goal involved in the activity of the group they lead. Because they are knowledgeable and decent people, they should guide us, at least until we can all stand on our own feet. The belief that a select group, which aims at bringing about the equality of members of society (by a rational organization and management of production and distribution of wealth), will take advantage of its position is unduly pessimistic about human nature. While there is risk in this in some cases, the effort must still be made to strive to perfect the human race. Therefore, the socialist goal of equal well-being for all in a human community—even in the world at large—is worthy of pursuit, regardless of obstacles.

Finally, there may *appear* to be necessary inequalities in nature but this is not decisive. Many living things exhibit virtually total equality among members of the species. True, some animal groups exhibit what is sometimes called social ranking. But not all do. For example, fish do not seem to exhibit this, at least not uniformly. Many insects do not live by such inequality. But even if the bulk of the animal kingdom and nature exhibited inequality, does this make it necessary for human beings to live with what nature produced initially? Our special capacity for changing nature might be extended to changing our own nature. There is then reason to suggest that we should strive for change.

As for the one thing with respect to which we are equal, namely, our capacity for choice, it is just this capacity that makes the sensible, progressive transformation of human nature a realistic alternative as well as a duty. It is only the arrogance of narrow individualism that has promoted the fatalist thesis that human nature cannot be changed. Of course, those who are well off by nature will attempt to combat the sensible way of humanity. But we need to overcome this narrow perspective.

Final Points

We have outlined the disputes that surround the socialist theory, Marxist or non-Marxist. Anyone even meagerly aware of the intellectual climate, for example, as it occurs in the national media (which is not the most reliable source, however), can encounter elements of these disputes. One point about my own rendition of the socialist political system must be clarified. In the main, socialism concentrates on the economic aspects of human life, people's material needs and wants. At the same time, socialism holds that by improving the material conditions of human beings, their "spiritual" welfare is also enhanced. By "spiritual," most socialists who are close to Marxism do not mean something religious or mystical. Instead, they are referring to something in the area of psychological well-being. Still, the primary emphasis is put on material well-being and progress. This is evident from the widespread concern every socialist voices for the poor, the underprivileged, the economically underdeveloped regions of the world, and other aspects of human life pertaining to people's physical well-being.

Yet socialism is not alone in viewing human life primarily with reference to material factors. Many theorists who advocate capitalism do so because they believe that capitalism will foster great wealth, productivity, and prosperity for all segments of society. Adam Smith and other proponents of the essentials of a free enterprise and private property economy conceived of individuals as motivated largely by the desire for material well-being. Contemporary advocates of capitalism often make the very same point.

Yet, just like socialists, advocates of capitalism claim that the spiritual aspects of human life are best fostered in their type of system. Socialism is not alone in focusing on people's material or physical welfare, making room for spiritual matters only as a secondary feature of its tenets. Of course, not all socialists are materialists, as shown by the fact that numerous religious doctrines promote what are most properly conceived of as forms of socialism. Nor are all capitalists materialists. Here, too, numerous advocates of the capitalist system support it from an idealist and even a religious framework.

These points are raised here only to call attention once again to the deeply rooted and multifaceted philosophical underpinnings of the various political theories discussed in this chapter. We can detect this fact in connection with our next political system also.

Welfare Statism

The name of this political system, **welfare statism,** makes clear its central goal. The idea is that the government of such a system should strive to secure the welfare of the people. The legal system is geared toward that aim. This is the system's prime goal. Since there can be different types of welfare states, it is not possible to characterize such a system with one simple statement that will imply all of its features. The welfare state could be democratic or totalitarian; it could adhere to direct or representative democratic procedures; and there could be limitations on the government's power, especially in such areas of civil liberties as freedom of religion, assembly, expression, and political advocacy. All these could be ways in which a welfare state is designed to function for the purpose of securing the welfare of the people.

The welfare in question is usually material welfare, mixed now and then with the goals of equal education, and fostering the arts, science, etc. While the term *welfare* could be used to mean spiritual, artistic, moral, or other types of well-being, historically it has been used to refer to physical and economic well-being, with only some attention to these other areas. The method by which the welfare state proposes to achieve the purposes thought proper to a legal system is by regulation of the economic affairs that ensue in a society.

Those who propose welfare statism as the proper political system rest their argument on the acceptance of two central values: liberty and well-being. Supporters of the welfare state argue that the equal liberty of every citizen is a central political goal, based on the moral dignity of the individual. They also argue that the well-being of each individual is a crucial value that should be pursued by political means. Indeed, welfare statists hold that the equal liberty of individuals (e.g., to participate in determining political leadership, to pursue self-realization, to enjoy life, to speak openly) could not be achieved without first achieving the equal well-being of everyone. Those with more favorable economic conditions would otherwise enjoy greater liberty, even to the point of using their advantage against those without equal power to implement their goals.

These two values, however, tend to conflict, so that the welfare state strives for a balance between them. For instance, freedom of expression may have to be curtailed in order to prevent some people from advertising services and goods that (the government believes) could be harmful (e.g., pornographic movies, cigarettes, gambling facilities, and experimental drugs). On the other hand, equal well-being may have to be obstructed to protect the liberty of individuals, as in the case of those who are amassing considerable wealth via free expression in movies, song writing, publishing, and so forth.

The welfare state is a system in which a compromise is sought between two equally crucial but often mutually exclusive values, liberty and well-being. However, those who choose either of these political values as primary criticize the welfare state severely. Thus, socialists deemphasize liberty of human interaction in trade, communication, and other areas wherever the danger exists that such freedom of activity will lead to substantial inequality of well-being. Libertarians decry the sacrifice of liberty for what they consider to be mainly a private issue, namely, the responsibility of each person to achieve his or her own well-being.

Those who advocate the welfare state usually insist, however, that only by *balancing* the values of freedom and welfare can a community remain stable and prosperous. They emphasize that human life is a very complex affair and cannot be adjusted to a simple, consistent system of values. They admit that liberty is necessary for human creativity, thus seeing the need for its political protection. But to insist of the political priority of liberty is to ask for a kind of consistency from a government of which human beings and, therefore, human institutions are incapable. Insisting on the superior and thus exclusive political value of liberty is irresponsible to those who are less able to carry on for themselves if left completely free to do so. On the other hand, the view that government should manage human life completely is equally unacceptable, since that would stifle the energies that can be used to help eliminate human misery. It is the obligation of good people in power who represent us all to harness the creative energies of the productive elements of a community for the benefit of the less fortunate and less productive. It is the government's responsibility, also, to secure some measure of liberty, thus doing justice to human dignity and to humanity's general requirement of moral autonomy.

The welfare state is perhaps the least systematic political theory we will consider. Its proponents tend to be pragmatists—people who consider insistence on basic principles of politics an idle dream of utopians that is both unrealistic and ultimately destructive. It is wiser, they argue, to have flexible policies. Let us confront problems as they arise, without preconceived ideals in terms of which they *must* be solved. They claim that only this flexible, cautious, undogmatic approach will enable a community to face the challenges of an uncertain future.

We can easily learn the characteristics of the welfare state by simply looking at our own human community. To advocate the welfare state is, in the main, to advocate what essentially has been the *status quo* in America for more than half a century. To criticize it requires only to advocate some value as politically prior to any others, to reject compromise. All other systems discussed here do just that.

Communism (Collectivism)

This is one of the most widely discussed and least well understood political systems. **Communism** as a political theory should not be confused with communism as the vague notion employed to discuss the political regimes within the sphere of influence of Soviet Russia and Communist China. It is true that the latter often claim to *aim for* a communist community, and are often identified as such by outsiders. None of them claims to *be* a communist community, however. Whether the conditions that prevail in these actual societies are related to their political leaders' announced goal of building a communist world is not our question. What is important is that the nature of the communist human community cannot be learned from simply observing so-called communist countries.

The term *communism* is used to mean the sort of community in which human affairs are carried out in a society-wide, communal fashion. In other words, human affairs are considered to be affairs of the entire community, to be approached with all the tools the community can employ, on a cooperative, noncompetitive, harmonious basis. The most well-developed idea of the communist political system arises out of Marx's theory of social development. In that system communism refers to the culmination or completion of "prehuman" history.

According to the Marxist thesis described previously, after capitalism experienced its self-destructive revolution and gave rise to socialism, progress pointed toward the ultimate elimination of all coercive human institutions. Government is the main coercive institution in most societies and has ruled for the benefit of the few throughout most of history. Gradually government came to rule for the benefit of more and more, and in socialism government is to rule for the benefit of all. By that time, however, society is internally harmonious enough so that government is no longer at odds with the great majority of the people.   Once this stage is completed, the purpose of government—to use force against enemies of the ruling group—ceases.   This is when communism can emerge and the state or government with coercive status can wither away.   When people no longer divide into classes and the power of production has been harnessed to provide for the needs and wants of all, government is no longer needed.   Human beings will have changed into a mature new species and nature will contain all that members of this new species require for a peaceful, cooperative, flourishing life.

In effect, humanity will have reached perfection.   No longer flawed due to material scarcity and the accompanying lust for profit, the community can enjoy the communal life on a worldwide basis. We are now different and flawed, but all members of the communist society will be "brothers" and perfect.   They will have reached in their personal lives the essence of humanity, and they will have fulfilled the promise of human nature in all respects.   As a child embodies the potential for becoming an adult, we embody the potential for the development of a mature human species.   This will amount to each person's exhibiting only the actions that are fully consonant or in accord with man's essence: conscious, rational, useful productivity.   A community of such members does not need government; it is an anarchical society, a society without rules to be imposed on its members, and thus without rulers.

The fundamental value underlying communism seems to be the equality of all people and the resultant harmony in the community.   Perhaps to speak of this as a value is misleading. .We have been using the idea *value* in this and previous chapters to mean goals that (according to some theory) people *should* strive for and try to achieve or implement.   But in Marxist communism people will have reached their goal as a matter of natural historical evolution, irrespective of personal choices, and fully moved by forces outside them.   There are some Marxists who deny that communism is the inevitable result of history's development (according to dialectical force).   Still, it is Marx's own thesis and the most consistent way of understanding Marxism.   (To research the matter further one needs to study the communist idea in greater detail, of course.)

Still, it is fair to take social harmony and equality among all persons as the guiding *value* of communist political theory—just as class conflict and antagonism are the *evils* or deficiencies of the precommunist stages of prehuman society.   So for Marx the values to be achieved had both a moral and a scientific status; he held that it was both *good and necessary* to achieve communism. Although it may sound odd to claim both that something *should* be achieved and that it *must* and *will* be achieved, in the complete Marxist philosophy the oddity fits without much difficulty. So it is best to leave this matter undisturbed for now. Instead let us raise some objections to communism.

Anti-communism. A fundamental feature of communism concerns the character of social evolution. According to communist theory, social life proceeds along an upward-moving continuum. From what we could regard a stage of infancy, the entire human race is supposed to be moving toward a golden age where people will no longer experience any problems. The principle of dialectical development is supposed to explain this historical phenomenon. This principle is not confined to the processes of social development but to developments throughout nature. It is as if reality itself, including the human race, resembled an actual person. Each person begins as an infant, incapable of coping with reality successfully, gradually becoming more and more capable, and eventually growing to maturity, at which stage the person is capable of fully independent existence. This final stage for society is communism, in which humanity itself is no longer dependent on such earlier natural forces as economic necessity—the need to grab what one can from limited supplies of goods and services.

Yet the dialectical principle is not well established. Although Marx's partner, Friedrich Engels, wrote a book (*The Dialectics of Nature*) in which he tried to show that all areas of nature exhibit the operations of the dialectical principle, the book did not succeed in its task. This is understandable, since the principle was borrowed from another philosopher who never viewed it as a scientific law of nature. Hegel, from whom Marx borrowed the idea of the dialectic, viewed this principle as a fundamental feature of reality, established by *metaphysical* inquiry. But Marx rejected Hegel's metaphysics for a scientific analysis. And without the metaphysics it is difficult to see how the dialectical idea can be supported.

Without the dialectical principle—the idea that things produce their opposites and after a clash, between the positive and negative, a new thing emerges—the basis of the communist theory is substantially lost. That is one of the objections that many people raise against communist theory. If the objection is sound, communism amounts to nothing more than a fancy, an unsupportable dream, or a promise. It is no longer possible, then, to view communism as an ideal society. Instead, it becomes a cruel hoax, an image to which reality cannot conform; and when we try to make it so conform, disaster is bound to strike. Communist society becomes a utopian ideal that some people try desperately to force upon the world's peoples. It is this criticism that underlies the view that Stalinism, a recent era of the U.S.S.R. filled with massive brutality and complete tyranny, was the inevitable result of trying to make communism work. Indeed, some of Joseph Stalin's ideological supporters, guided by his own books on Marxism, tried to *create* "the new man." They tried, through genetic manipulation, to change human nature so that a communist being, drastically different from what we (human beings) are, would emerge in the Soviet Union.

The above criticism aims at the core of the communist theory. It does not address communist society itself but the grounds for believing that it could be instituted at all. It charges communist theory with having no rational, realistic foundation.

Others criticize communism by considering what kind of society it would be. These criticisms do not look at problems inherent in communist theory. They focus, instead, on what communism would amount to for the kind of people we are. The criticism presupposes that human *nature* is not changeable. People can change individually; they can grow into mature and responsible persons or fail to do so even though physically they age. But as a species the human race remains *essentially* the same throughout the ages. Of course, details change, because people can create and build on the creations of their ancestors, or they can destroy what others did for human life. However, the fact of each person's nature as a potentially creative as well as destructive being does not change.

From this position the criticism of communism amounts to the charge that communist society is unsuited to human life. Instead of being a general improvement on the human condition, communism is a distortion. For instance, the ideas that individuals should not own things privately, that children should be brought up by the community, and that cooperative production instead of competitive economic activity should be instituted are met with the charge that communism is based on a misunderstanding. As long as people are what they are, and as long as they can choose either to carry on with the business of living or to refrain from so doing, to collectivize property is to deprive those who think and work hard from what is theirs. It would also lead to the general reduction of production because the hardworking citizens will not produce for those who do not work for themselves. Communal ownership would only lead to general neglect of the land and its fruits because responsibility would be severed from reward. Children who are everyone's are not anyone's children, so they, too, would be neglected, in the main. Ultimately, there is no way to guarantee the perfection of society. Success in life depends on whether the individuals who make up a society do their best at living their lives— a virtue that cannot be inherited by their offspring.

Finally, communist theory is criticized for ambiguity. The actual structure of communist society was never discussed by Marx. Today Marxist theorists differ so much among themselves on just what Marx had in mind (and on what follows from his views) that it is hardly possible to consider the matter intelligently. Even more important is the explicit Marxist idea that only those who have reached Marx's own level of understanding of social affairs can perceive and implement the best ways of arranging society. Critics consider this responsible for the absolute power of the communist parties of the so-called communist countries. (However, there is debate among Marxists as to whether such parties have a legitimate role in communist society or even in its precursor, Marxist socialism.) The very existence of internal and widespread ambiguity raises reasonable doubts at least about the clarity of Marx's ideas. The critics can then claim that when a political theory is as confusing as Marxism, it cannot possibly provide guidelines for organizing a good human community.

There are other objections that could be raised against Marxism, if for no other reason than because there are so many critics of Marxism. I have said nothing of the relentless objections raised by those who view human affairs from a primarily theistic perspective. Marxism has no room for a deity. Instead of a God in another world, Marxism offers the promise of a better society in the future of humanity. But theistic criticisms cannot be of prime interest to us as we are attempting to deal with political affairs without referring to religious doctrines, ones that explicitly abandon the primary roles of reason and nature in human affairs.

Communist Replies. Contemporary Marxists deny that the dialectical principle has a determining role in Marxist political theory. At least the majority of Western Marxists deemphasize it. Even without the dialectic, the development of society toward communism would be the best thing for human beings—so the reply might go. Granted that without the dialectic communism is not inevitable. Yet it is still the best way of resolving the apparently constant and repeated problems of human society. Moreover, there is justified hope for the emergence of communism. How long it will take to achieve it cannot perhaps be predicted as some Marxists would have liked. But certain trends can be detected throughout society that would lead any reasonable observer to suggest the eventual creation of communism.

For example, does it not appear that gradually more and more people have experienced material improvement and have managed to escape subjugation by tyrants or monarchs? Starting from ancient Egypt where the masses had no power to determine their lives, all the way to modern democracies, is there not a trend toward less paternalism—rule by some who take it upon themselves to protect and rule others, with the eventual result of exploiting the "protected"? Marxism holds that this is an ongoing process that will culminate in a communist, classless, anarchical (i.e., governmentless) society. If we take the past seriously, is there not some ground for hope? Instead of a kingdom of heaven, in death, should we not have faith in an eventual peaceful and harmonious human life on earth? And this is not a blind faith either. Thus, however problematic the dialectical base of orthodox Marxism may be, the justification of the communist political system may be secure without such absolutist foundations. (The famous French philosopher-novelist Jean Paul Sartre now regards himself as a Marxist, even though he totally rejects an inevitable dialectical scheme, the historical determinism of Marx.)

The next objection against communism—that human nature is not changeable—simply reveals a fundamental pessimism. There has been evolution within various animal species. Other living things have come to adjust to the requirements of reality so as to achieve an optimal state. Perhaps the model of a child growing into a mature adult is in error, but evolutionary theory seems to support Marx. There is ample evidence of the self-destructive character of the kind of things human beings are today. Some even suggest that humans are freaks of nature and would "self-destruct" so as to give rise to the development of a more adapted species. Surely it is not idle speculation to suppose this. Human history is a relatively brief span of time, considering the infinite dimension of existence with regard to time.   So there is ample opportunity for improvement of the human race and even for being superseded by a well-balanced, unflawed kind of being.   It is, in the end, sheer defeatism to suggest that each generation of human beings must repeat the ups and downs of the previous one.   Communist theory rejects this vision in favor of the ultimate success of the species. That, in turn, will produce the kind of individuals who will take care of property they do not own privately, who will care for children they rear collectively, and who will produce goods to sustain the entire community.   This may not be possible for the kind of beings we are.   But it *will* be to the *new people!*

The objection that communist theory does not advance a detailed scheme for the organization of society may not be very difficult to meet.   Those who will comprise the membership of the new human community will be very different beings from us.   Even with hard work we can know only of the most crucial elements of their makeup.   Outside of this it would be futile speculation to spell out the details.   The ingenuity of a free and creative new human species cannot be matched by the likes of even Karl Marx.   When the proper time comes, the membership of the communist community will stand ready to institute the specific conditions that will make its flourishing possible.   We can know that much.   To demand more would be to demand to know ahead of time the results of creative geniuses.

Obviously some leadership is necessary to facilitate transition from one stage to the next.   The brutality of the so-called communist cadre under the Soviet system is not, however, a fair model of that leadership.   It is highly questionable whether the developments in the Soviet Union fit within the Marxist communist theory.   It would be more accurate, perhaps, to look to Communist China for a concrete test of how communism could be achieved.   The leadership offered there by Mao Tse Tung and those around him may sometimes become brutal.   But it is mainly educational.   It is by relying on the continuous education, the "permanent revolution" of the people's consciousness, that the answers to the questions of the communist society will emerge.   Such open-endedness is no shortcoming. It avoids relying on old ideas and makes creative socialization and communization possible.

Communism is today a very widely discussed theory of social organization.   This section has focused on its essential features. From the point of view of what is required for a political theory not much more needs to be discussed, except for making the points above with greater precision and detail and carrying out the investigation on the many theoretical fronts touched on by communist political theory. The rather narrow scope of the present investigation is due to our focus on political matters. Communist theory reaches far beyond the strictly political realm. Marx was a *political economist*. To a large extent he considered political issues secondary to economic ones.

For Marx, the political institutions of a society followed from its economic situation, not the other way around. Other, especially classical political theorists tend to disagree because they are interested, first of all, in the character of a political system and generally believe that the economic situation of a society is determined by its political structure. This, in turn, is concluded on grounds that the moral and political concerns of human beings are essential to human life as such; that is, human nature involves the need for identifying general principles of personal and social conduct in terms of which all other human concerns should be governed. But Marx believed that the mind of man did not and could not operate free from the influences of his economic conditions. It is these conditions that determine or cause what human beings will think concerning moral and political issues. As with socialism, in Marxist communism the basic concern is with man's material situation. This differs from monarchy and what are generally regarded as the more "right wing" forms of statism. These are usually concerned with the moral and intellectual improvement of humanity.

It is important to note at this point that political theory is very closely related to the general philosophy that is assumed or advocated by the theorist in question. More often than not, people who view human beings as primarily spiritual beings build their political system so as to govern the intellectual and moral life of the people. (Thus, conservatives in the United States tend to advocate laws that would prohibit immorality, e.g., obscenity and gambling. They generally think that what is important in human life, the spiritual part of man, requires close control by the state.) On the other hand, the people who view human beings as mainly material creatures, governed by the laws of matter—ruled by physical drives and instincts or by the physical and economic environment—advocate political systems that are geared to control people's economic activities. In short, generally speaking—but not exclusively—the Left focuses on each of us as primarily a *material* being, whereas the

Right focuses on each person as predominantly a *spiritual* being. So it seems that the metaphysical positions underlying the political systems we have been discussing are very influential, however much some of the political theorists might wish to disavow concern with metaphysics.

In the next section we will consider a political theory with sometimes explicit metaphysical underpinnings.

Libertarianism

The term **libertarianism** is a recent one for designating varieties of individualist political systems. The theory of libertarianism emphasizes the value of individual liberty in human community affairs. Within this position, the freedom of the individual is considered the supreme political value, even if now and then other important goals might be achievable by sacrificing the liberty of certain individuals. For example, although it might be possible to foster the spread of classical music appreciation by limiting the liberty of some people to spend their income as they would want, libertarianism advocates that their liberty is more valuable than promoting this admittedly valuable endeavor. Education about the harmful effects of pornography is perhaps a valuable prospect. But every individual's liberty to attend to other matters is to be protected against those who would force this value upon him. In short, individual freedom, or liberty, is the prime political value within the libertarian system of law and politics.

The American or Anglo-American tradition of politics displays strong libertarian tendencies. The rights referred to in the Declaration of Independence indicate this clearly. They aim to specify the individual's sphere of authority and the function of governments as agencies to protect and preserve that sphere.

However, as with other political theories, there are variations in the support offered in behalf of libertarianism. The conclusions advanced by different supporters are virtually the same: liberty is the prime political value, the basic condition of a good human community. But the arguments vary.

Then, even where this conclusion is accepted differences exist about the means by which individual liberty should be secured. Thus, the system of community organization is not identical in all versions of libertarianism. For example, some of its theorists advocate the establishment of a government that is authorized to act only so as to protect and preserve the liberty of the members of the community it serves. They support the institution of a proper government, one based on a constitution that defines the government's function in terms of its purpose of protecting and preserving liberty. Other theorists hold that governments as such cannot refrain from abridging the liberty of the citizens. These anarcho-libertarians make provisions for private protection of human rights but reject government as a means to such an end. They see any government as a necessary means toward the limitation of human liberty.

Many libertarians throughout history, especially those individualists well known in the Anglo-American political tradition, advocate a certain form of government as the means by which liberty, and thereby political or legal justice, must be secured. But there are other individualists, especially in America's intellectual and political history, who reject this idea. John Locke and Tom Paine accepted the positive role of government in securing liberty. Benjamin Tucker and Josiah Warren rejected it.

Among nonanarchist (or archist) libertarians, two arguments for the supreme political value of liberty are prominent. Those two arguments will receive our attention here, leaving aside for now the issue of whether anarchism is indeed the proper consequence of the libertarian argument for freedom. These arguments can be tied to some familiar figures in our intellectual tradition and in the present day. Among proponents of the value of liberty on grounds that it is the morally justified condition of human beings in a community are such philosophers as John Locke, Herbert Spencer, and, more recently, Ayn Rand, Murray Rothbard, and Robert Nozick. Among those who argue for liberty on grounds that it is the only sensible social condition in view of our complete or widespread ignorance of any moral values are such thinkers as David Hume, John Stuart Mill, and, in our time, Milton Friedman and F. A. Hayek.

The above characterization can be contested, since I have not specified the finer distinctions that are evident between the various people mentioned. Mill, for example, might not properly be considered a moral skeptic, although this is doubtless the case with Friedman. In the main, however, the arguments on the two sides can be characterized as above without too much distortion.   Instead of dwelling over the nuances, it will be valuable to summarize the arguments.

Skeptical Libertarians.   Libertarianism has been defended on grounds of moral skepticism or toleration.   The idea here is that human beings can do well or ill as they act and create in order to flourish in life, but it is never possible to be certain whether they do the right or wrong things.   To avoid ever making a mistake in imposing judgments on people concerning what is or is not right, it is best to allow everyone maximum individual liberty.   Of course, actions that limit others' maximum liberty are not allowed.   If we can never really know what is right or wrong in human affairs, it is always wrong or counterproductive to force others to do what one believes they should do.   Perhaps such beliefs are right on occasions, but it is always possible that one is wrong.   Therefore, to impose the course of conduct one believes to be right (or prevent that which one believes to be wrong) can never have sound justification.   Thus, the argument concludes, no one's liberty may ever be abridged (except, perhaps, to ward off someone who has initiated some abridgment).

The political system of a community works best when it protects people against those who would impose their judgments on others.   In general, the government of a community is most workable when it enforces the principle that no one is permitted to act aggressively against another.   The only law-making function of governments should be to explicate or expand the existing main principle or law of the community, so that new circumstances in which aggression could occur may be dealt with effectively.

The proper government does not act to achieve justice but to prevent interference with people's pursuit of what they think is good—even if what they think could be bad and one would wish that it not be implemented.   Laws would simply clarify this basic goal as new situations develop in which it is to be pursued.

It is also held by these libertarians that with such a narrow domain of governmental concern, people will tend to take on responsibility for their own lives and secure for themselves what they need and want with greater care than if they were to rely on the force of others, namely a government, in order to carry out the job of achieving human welfare.   Since the government, like any other kind of thing, is best at performing its specific function, in this case peacekeeping, the government is best kept away from the voluntarily undertaken projects of individuals and groups.   The argument puts heavy emphasis, also, on the government officials' inability to tell what is right and wrong for people to do—whether making lots of money is right or wrong, whether advertising cosmetics is good or bad, etc.   This follows from the general skepticism about identifying what is morally good.   In the light of that skepticism, there would be enormous danger in interfering with the lives of people, however much this appears to be desired by some on certain occasions.

This general skepticism is sometimes supplemented with the view that human beings are easily corrupted, so the less power they have, the less likely they are to do dangerous things to one another. Since government has the power of the gun—it is the only institution in society legally empowered to use weapons against people premeditatedly—it is very dangerous to let it do more than the minimum that is needed, which is to prevent violence.

Moral Libertarianism.   The second argument for libertarianism emphasizes that human beings are free agents, capable of moral choice and responsible for living by moral principles.   The basic moral principle that should be implemented in human life is that each individual should pursue his or her happiness.   Such happiness consists of success in life *qua* human being—success in terms of what it is to be a human being, to have the capacity to live rationally.   To achieve happiness or success as a person, we must choose to activate this capacity within our own individual circumstances.

But to be able to embark on this kind of life, for better or for worse, we require that others recognize our moral status and abstain from imposing upon us what they have decided should be done. Such imposition would deprive people of their capacity for moral choice, that is, of their dignity.   Thus, governments should be established to provide needed protection and preservation of the liberty each person is due by nature, as a moral agent.   Thus, this view of political life is based on a doctrine of natural human rights, derived from each person's nature as a moral agent.   Once correctly identified, the rights serve to define the proper authority of each person, including that of a government hired to protect everyone's proper sphere of authority.

In this argument it is not considered impossible to tell whether people are doing right or wrong. The position holds, however, that there is no justification for concluding, from the fact that someone is doing wrong, that another should stop him. Only when the wrong involves obstructing others own moral responsibilities could there be grounds for prohibiting and defending against it.

Basic Political Features.   Despite a serious difference between the two prominent arguments for the libertarian political system, the conclusion is the same: liberty is the prime social value all of us (by means of establishing governments) should act to protect and preserve. Politics in the libertarian theory is confined to a specific area of human life—securing the best possible protection and preservation of human rights, the result of which would be the best possible administration of justice available to people in a community. Libertarians argue, then, that their theory of politics would *depoliticize* society, leaving the bulk of human life to voluntary interaction instead of coercive regimentation by those in possession of the legal authority to use force. The realm of voluntary interaction would include anything from sex, religion, or education to commerce, art, or science. Governments could enter with justification only where the principle of liberty is itself either being violated or in clear and present danger of violation.

It may be worth noting that ample room for democracy exists within libertarian political theory. The selection of administrators of justice, the appointments of the lawmakers who would work on the logical extension of the principles of a libertarian community— these matters could be, though need not be, carried out democratically. But democracy would not enter the area of what principles should govern the community; any principle (law) that would violate anyone's liberty could not be imposed by a majority.

Libertarianism is individualistic because it holds each individual as an end and regards his or her liberty fully required in a society of *human* beings, suited to *human* life. This system, then, stands opposed to socialism, communism, fascism, and other forms of government that are unique for putting most aspects of community life under governmental control.

It is fair to say that there are few supporters of libertarianism today, at least outside of Fourth-of-July speeches. But it is also fair to say that it is the main theoretical obstacle to the planned, politicized society.* Let us now consider some objections to this minority political theory.

Objections to Skeptical Politics. To the first argument in support of the political principle (that laws must aim to protect the individuals of a human community against those who would perhaps mistakenly force their way of life on them), the central objection goes as follows: Although the theory is based on the impossibility of knowing what is right or wrong in human conduct, it ends by stating that it is counterproductive (i.e., wrong) to limit another person's liberty. But if it is possible to know this much, there is now no general support for not knowing more of what is right and wrong in human conduct. The libertarian—classical liberal—who argues that we should refrain from imposing our judgment (or, as some call it, preference) on others because we cannot learn what is right for them, runs into serious logical difficulties. A self-contradiction seems to be involved. It is asserted that human beings cannot know what is right (and wrong), and also that it is wrong to impose one's preferences on others. But saying the last appears clearly to be going against the first: it implies that the theorist knows that it is wrong to aggress against others! That, however, obviates the earlier skepticism about issues of right and wrong.

Aside from this internal objection (that shows different features of the theory to be in conflict), we appear to be quite capable of knowing what is right for people. Maybe we would rarely take the trouble to find out about such matters in any careful way, and often we make careless judgments, even substitute our wishes. This does not prove that we *cannot* know what is right and wrong. It is obvious to us that some of our neighbors, even close friends or relatives, live in ways that are right (or wrong). Some people we know pursue their professions vigorously, excel as parents or students, and take good care of their personal responsibilities. Others are negligent, sloppy, constantly tardy, and irresponsible. By care-

---

* It is no accident that Professor B. F. Skinner, who advocates a planned society governed by behavioral scientists, took as his main target in his book *Beyond Freedom and Dignity* the libertarian political and social tradition—"the literature of freedom and dignity."

fully considering the individual's circumstances we could tell whether the person is blameworthy—in courts this is done all the time, and we sometimes go to the trouble of carefully evaluating others' actions in our personal lives.   There are those who harm no one and still manage to carry on a despicable sort of existence, while others are positively admirable.

Does the libertarian wish to claim that just as soon as we learn that someone is doing something wrong we may interfere with that person's action?   This would imply that if we know that someone is doing something wrong, then we should prevent this.   But this is a bad argument.   From the (possible) fact that I know that Johnny is doing the wrong thing it follows by no means that I should stop Johnny.   Before that conclusion can be proved true, additional premises are needed, for example, "Whenever someone does the wrong thing, those who know about it should stop the person."   Unless this is correct, the libertarian view that each person's liberty should be protected and preserved (and others may only be interfered with in direct or indirect retaliation) could be preserved without moral skepticism.   There seems to be no rational grounds for governing others' lives simply because we know that they are doing things they should not.*

Objections to Moral Libertarianism.   The most prominent objection to moral libertarianism centers on efforts to define the concept *human being*.   This argument for political freedom conceives of people as essentially rational animals, requiring for their good life both mental and physical liberty.   The critics object, however, that such a definition—discussed fully in more detailed treatments—is indefensible.   Too many people are inept at rational thinking. Many lack any freedom to assume responsibilities on their own.   A community based on this notion of what people are (essentially) would be drastically wrongheaded.   And then there is the difficult issue of freedom of will, or human choice.   We face here a serious philosophical problem.   The theory seems to require that the problem be solved.   However, it is nowhere near a solution, and unless people do see eye to eye on this matter, unless the fact of our

---

* Criticism of the content of libertarianism will follow the discussion of the moral case for liberty.   For now only the different arguments are being scrutinized.

capacity to choose and be morally responsible is established, the argument cannot begin to get off the ground.

Finally, there is the dubious theory of classical ethical egoism, the moral position that people should strive for their own success and happiness, which underlies this political theory. Even assuming that we could know what human nature is and thus that people are by nature free and responsible moral agents, it is questionable that our moral responsibility consists of striving to be happy. Not only is "happiness" or "success" a terribly difficult idea to define, but by making happiness our moral goal and designing a society in terms of this goal, we may eliminate very many people as possible members of a human community. Libertarianism seems to neglect the less fortunate amongst us and to favor those with the ambition to become successful. Should a political community really serve the needs and wants of the more ambitious elements of society? By doing so it seems that such a system fails to prepare for the likelihood that success corrupts. Would not the successful combine to oppress not only the less successful but also those who are offspring of the less successful? Would the successful not try, eventually, to ensure their position by influencing the administrators of the legal system so that those trying to compete with them would not get a chance?

Objections to the System. In general, the political system of libertarianism appears to be either a very brutal idea for a human community, leading to widescale neglect of the less fortunate among the population, or, alternatively, a utopian idea, entrusting to free people the care of human problems that the government may not touch. Is it not a proved fact that capitalism, the economic corollary of libertarianism, allows for the rise of monopolies that can exclude potential competitors? Has capitalism not produced hordes of poor people whom the government had to rescue from the clutches of greedy businessmen? And has it not encouraged permissiveness in society? At any rate, would it not allow for widespread immorality —prosititution, gambling, drinking, drug addiction, pornography? In a libertarian society it is legally impossible for governments to protect people against their own ignorance and against the sly and shrewd elements of society who would lure the weak into irresistible traps. These and similar considerations appear to make libertarianism a hopelessly urealistic, inflexible, and ultimately cruel social and political community.

It is no wonder, the critic might argue, that American political reality has rejected the early naïveté that supported the libertarian elements of the American political tradition. Private property simply made it easy for the powerful to accumulate wealth and exploit the weak. Free trade benefitted only the rich, while the poor had to depend on the wealthy to hand out minimum payment for services rendered. Furthermore, the capitalist economy led to the neglect of precious natural resources. This form of government would not seem to suit human beings at all. It appears, instead, to suit only ambitious capitalists, those who strive for possession, for the rugged individualism that alienates people from one another and from their work.

Libertarianism Rescued? These charges are frequently and force-fully leveled against the libertarian political system and its economic corollary, capitalism. Let us now see how the libertarian might respond. First let us take the responses of the skeptical libertarian.

The objection on grounds of logical inconsistency might be answered by admitting that the freedom being advocated is indeed a preference. Those who defend freedom on grounds that we can-not know what is right and wrong do not deny that we have certain preferences as to what should be done and how society should be organized. Indeed, these are preferences for which one cannot offer logical arguments. A preference is not defensible by citing evidence and presenting a cogent argument.

It seems, however, that there are different types of preferences. Those who prefer to do certain private sorts of things do not auto-matically impose on others when they do what they prefer. Those who prefer to do more public kinds of things that involve others, whether or not these others accept it, do foster interference in others' lives, preventing others from pursuing their own preferences. The libertarian who argues along these lines will hold that the law should distinguish between assisting the first type of preferences and assisting the second type. By so doing, the law will leave it to the individuals to decide whether they will accept others' second-type preferences. Such a preference would be that other people do not see obscene movies or acquire great wealth. The law should serve everyone equally, and when it helps some people to bring about these second type of preferences, it automatically suppresses the first type of preferences of some people—in this case some people's preference, for example, to engage in the private activity of watching an obscene movie.

Perhaps there is a basic, unproved premise that these libertarians support, namely, that people should be treated as equals and no one should be prevented from satisfying his or her preferences so long as they pertain to private conduct. But the premise may not require any proof. The burden is on those who would deny it to prove that they should be allowed to impose their preferences on others. In other words, the libertarian may simply argue that he admits that he only has preferences to satisfy and does not know what people should do. But so long as others are in this same position, it follows that no one has grounds for *imposing* preferences on others. The situation that this implies for a political system is the maximum possible degree of liberty.

Those who object that we do in fact know that some people should do this or that are simply wrongheaded. The example of the negligent person is a case in point. Might it not be the case that such negligent conduct is in fact good for the person? More fundamentally, just what does it mean to say that a person should not neglect his life, health, security, education, and so forth? This kind of libertarian would classify that claim as an expression of an arbitrary preference. There seems to be no ground for rejecting the negligent person's preference in favor of another's to the effect that negligence should be avoided.

Furthermore, is lying, for example, really demonstrably wrong? How would such a demonstration go? Has it not been shown, by the failure of philosophers and theologians to conclusively prove any moral position, that even honesty is just a widespread preference— perhaps not widespread enough for those who prefer it, but still just a preference? We simply are left in the dark about what it would be to *know* that others *should* act in a certain way. All those who have claimed that they knew what was right for people to do seem to have managed to move on to the next step and impose what they "knew" on others. Perhaps there is no clear logical justification for this move. However, there appears to be ample psychological inclination behind it; otherwise, why would people often move against each other when they have convinced themselves that others are doing wrong or not doing right.

In the end, it is far better to admit to human ignorance, remain modest about our capacities, and protect ourselves against those who see things differently. That sort of social climate is more likely to breed progress; people will not be able to dismiss the activities of others and thereby stifle the chances for something new, something that may bring us all many benefits. There appears to be ample evidence for this last supposition. The "free world" may not have the artistic and spiritual traditions of other regions, but it seems to produce more of what people really need—so much so that the rest of the world depends on America's faltering free economy, still, to feed itself. This much is easy to show by reference to what economists have discovered. Therefore, let us leave aside the moralistic arguments and concentrate on manageable facts.

Turning now to objections to the second libertarian argument, let us note that the challenges are very sweeping. It becomes clear here that a political theory is closely tied to other branches of philosophy. The objection that it is impossible to define the concept *human being* would have to be answered by an epistemological argument that refutes this claim. Those libertarians who offer a comprehensive philosophical defense of their political theory of the sort under discussion have made serious efforts in this direction. Basically, they would claim that human beings, as part of nature, can be understood in the same way that other features of reality are, and that this understanding can lead to a clear definition of the idea *human being*, a statement of what human nature is. The fact that some people are crucially incapacitated and may not exhibit the essential features of humanness can be explained. Such "borderline" cases are still human, of course. As with mutations in nature, these cases require that we make the appropriate adjustments. In short, there is nothing fundamentally difficult about accommodating severely handicapped people in this definition of *human*. The definition of human beings as beings capable of choosing to reason is still the one that holds up against others, which is what is crucial.

As to the problem of free will, this may be omitted here. The libertarian will provide the best argument for free will and let the case rest there. The objection that many still debate the issue has no bearing on the soundness of their arguments (*if* they are sound). It may pose a social problem that others do not accept the proof being offered. But this is not a theoretical problem; others can be stubborn or blind. Many problems have been solved by those who attend to them while the rest of the world still believes myths about the subject.

The matter of classical ethical egoism has already been discussed and the libertarian who bases his or her arguments on this ethical position holds that it is the most successful moral theory that has been proposed. So, as with other fields of inquiry, the best that is available deserves support. Rational people will, then, support it. It is not theoretically but socially important that many people do not accept good arguments. Yet there is a point to the issue of defining happiness. This term is so frequently used to mean something like pleasure or fun that the egoist and libertarian may have trouble defending the view that all people should seek it as their primary goal. Unless the happiness people ought to seek can be pursued by everyone without abridging others' efforts to do so, it may be difficult to defend the doctrine that each person should seek happiness. Here one might say that the happiness in question can be achieved to the maximum only by rational thought and action, and rational thought and action would avoid the kinds of conflict that mere pursuit of pleasure and fun cannot.

Perhaps more important for political theory specifically is the objection that libertarianism seems to favor those with the ambition to become successful. Indeed this charge is true. Only the libertarian would see nothing wrong in it. If his moral theory is correct, then it cannot be wrong to want to succeed in life, whether as a scientist, teacher, musician, plumber, or banker. Ambition is wrong only when it violates the rights of others. Of course, then it is not ambition but the violation of others' rights that is wrong. The libertarian defends the value of each person's pursuit of success in life and admits that a legal system geared to make this possible—to forbid letting the less successful oppress those who make the effort— is for that very reason a good and just system.

The libertarian will deny that libertarian law *prevents* helping the less fortunate. Indeed, it is only in a free human community that help to others can be truly commendable, a case of *bona fide* generosity. This is because in this system the government does not exist for the purpose of forcing some to help others (via taxing and redistribution). Forced help is not help but extortion, so the (moral) libertarian will argue. It is the violation of each person's right to do with his or her own what he or she will, so long as it is done in peace. In general, libertarians leave personal moral matters, including whether to try to help people protect themselves from others (who might try to trick them) or even from themselves (their own negligence), outside the scope of political affairs. By arguing that politicians should focus their minds and energies on truly political problems, they would claim that their case helps to make a free people more self-reliant and able to handle personal and voluntary social and ethical matters competently and justly.

The libertarian would admit that political agents, like other people, may be influenced and even corrupted by the successful who want to secure their own position. Corruption would be less likely with a legal system that prohibits government from helping special interest groups, since any official doing so would be in violation of the law. Nevertheless, there is simply no guarantee against the possibility of human error and immorality! Any system that promises this is a fraud. Human life and its quality depend on how well people attend to it. No *system* alone can prevent people from becoming bad. However, a free political order would not permit that to be a burden on those who do lead a productive and successful life. So when such a political system is in force, those who would undermine it (by first refusing to make their own way in life and later by trying to force others to serve them) would meet with considerable obstacles.

As such, libertarianism is not utopian. Neither is it brutal; it simply disallows the use of force to secure help even for good causes, not to mention questionable ones. It has confidence, not faith, in the capacity of free human beings and entrusts to them the responsibility to lead a good human life. Researchers of the issue have argued that the conditions of poor people during the early days of capitalism would have been far worse without the free market. They have studied those historical periods and have come up with conclusions that contradict common ideas on that topic.

A free society would also not *encourage* irresponsible permissiveness, although, of course, no law could be used to upgrade those who wish to spend their lives in prostitution, gambling, dope, or the like. But the existence of such activities does not seem to be avoided by coercive, paternalistic governments.

Finally, private property is a moral issue, not merely an economic one. And on the economic side, there are numerous studies which show that its accumulation has not led to monopolistic practices. In fact it is only by getting favors from government that some

firms have grown so large.   Capitalism or private (property) accumulation did not lead to the neglect of natural resources and the
ecosystem.   Again, quite the contrary, it is more sensible to explain
these problems by reference to the existence of *public* or *collectively
owned* places such as lakes, forests, freeways, beaches, and parks.
Because "everybody owns" these, no one has a direct interest in
and responsibility for avoiding their pollution.   It is also part of the
libertarian answer to the objection that capitalism causes ecological
disaster, that population growth gets out of bounds only when people
can count on "free" goods and services, that is, government or
communally supplied education, health care, etc.   The libertarian
therefore considers the objections to capitalism unfounded, more a
creation of the critics of the free society than a historically defensible
position.   Generally speaking, the libertarian, though in a small
minority these days, credits periods of history when some human
communities came close to adopting his political theory with producing a better life for people than any other period. Resting
responsibility with individuals, not governments, has produced
abundance and relative peace.

Overview

With libertarianism we have reached the last political system that
will be discussed in this book.   There are, of course, other political
theories. History abounds with various forms of political and social
organization and most have had intellectual supporters who have
provided these systems with detailed arguments. But those we have
discussed are the best known—if not always by the name under
which they were discussed above.   For example, democracy could
have been called "majoritarianism," and monarchy might have been
labeled "authoritarianism."   The one system I have not discussed is
the republican form of government, mainly because republicanism
is a variety of democracy—indirect or representative democracy with
severe limits on what can be subjected to democratic rule. I have
not discussed fascism, although a system in which government regu-
lates human lives almost completely but does not actually own legal
title to people and their property comes close to many contemporary
social orders.   Again, libertarianism has often been called the theory
of the free society, the doctrine of laissez-faire or strict constitutional

democracy (where the constitution contains the principles advanced by libertarians). The systems discussed in this chapter represent a fair and rich sample of humanity's efforts to answer the central question of politics: How should a human community be organized?

There is one answer to this question that I have not mentioned thus far—mainly because it is not an answer but a rejection of the question. This is the theory of anarchism.

Anarchism

The central thesis of **anarchism**—meaning, literally, "no rule"—is that establishing any organized institution with the authority to use force is evil (or, less moralistically, inefficient). There are several arguments for anarchism and the one worth discussing is the most up to date. The case is put as follows: Since each person is a free, rational, morally responsible agent, it is immoral for anyone to order anyone else to do anything. Submitting to authority is itself wrong. To do so is to try to renounce what cannot be renounced, namely, one's moral autonomy. It is to choose to be what one is not, that is, a subservient, dependent creature. To delegate (to a government) the responsibility for defending oneself against aggressors is impossible. One cannot make another person one's moral agent.

According to the anarchist, all governments exist by unjustified force. We can explain why government is often corrupt, why wars are initiated by governments, why the legal system of every country reeks of bad laws: the very existence of a government is immoral, so obviously what is essentially related to government must be immoral.

For the anarchist, saying this much is often sufficient. Anarchists do not have an answer to people's questions about how to live life; it is their responsibility solely to answer that question. The anarchists see no role for law and order, such façades rob people of their essential moral nature and are used to exploit the bulk of the community. So, by getting rid of this inherently corrupt institution and its fancy façade, the legal system, people could make their own way in life just as they should.

Other anarchists do offer alternative solutions to general problems of community life. Sometimes they advocate communal forms of society—small versions of communism. Others offer the idea that little communities of individualistic property owners should combine on an *ad hoc* basis to defend themselves against possible aggression. Individualist as well as communalist anarchists stress, however, that the likelihood of war and crime is decreased substantially when no governments exist. The concentrated power to wage war is missing. The attractiveness of conquering entire bodies of land and massive groups of people is lost when anarchism is in effect.

Moreover, the problems that have plagued human communities throughout human history are explainable, so the anarchist holds, by reference to numerous artificial social and "legal" institutions. Behind this explanation there lies, in the theories of some anarchists, a conception of human nature as basically good. With the rise of social and political institutions this basically good human nature became corrupted. The social and political environment, not the individuals themselves, is responsible for most of the problems faced in modern societies. By now this environment consists of not only laws and enforcers but also widely propagated ideas—moralities, customs, manners, etc.—that have become parts of the consciousness of human beings who were certainly born without such notions. Only by the drastic reformation of human beings, by the sustained rejection of modern institutions, including the sort of phony conscious life these have created for people, can we recapture the peaceful and harmonious existence that a natural, free life promises for us.

Anarchist ideas may seem strange, but it will help to remember that the other theories presented, those in support of various governmental systems, also appear unusual in their outline form. The theories of democracy, monarchy, the welfare state, socialism, communism, and libertarianism all provide outlines of social systems that rarely exist in pure form. Anarchism, too, is a distant goal its proponents believe we *should* pursue. However difficult it may be to achieve it, if the case for anarchism is sound, if that kind of community life is indeed *the right kind*, then all should attempt to secure it.

It seems evident that we will all make political choices now and then, and at the fundamental level we should begin by selecting from these alternatives one that is most rational, most defensible, and most suited for human beings. Time and place may require slight or even drastic differences in details. Nevertheless, human beings should strive for the good human community, however remote it may be. It must, of course, be possible for us to strive for it and also to achieve the common good implementing it. Once we have discovered which type of human community will meet these requirements, we prove our concern for justice or some other political virtue by working for that kind of a society without compromise.

The anarchist view may not seem plausible. But there are features of it that do emerge from many views today. Those who want to go back to nature; those who have concluded that government in all its varieties leads to corruption and tyranny; those who see modern man alienated and frustrated, hardly able to give a sign of genuine, natural life—all these and many others give voice to essentially anarchist ideas.

I will not present objections to anarchism here because each of the political systems discussed earlier aim to do this in one way or another. They are arguments to the effect that social organization, political systems, laws, and their administration are proper for us. They thus reject anarchism as wrongheaded. So to evaluate the anarchist thesis in detail one needs to judge the political theories we have presented.

POLITICAL VALUES

Our next task is to consider and clarify some of the usual political ideas and ideals. These are goals that many political theorists identify as worthy of everyone's pursuit. I will not debate these ideas but merely make an initial attempt to explain them.

Stability

A crucial idea in many political theories is that the stability of a society is good and necessary for human life in a social or community context. The concept *stable* is familiar enough—we can distinguish stable chairs from wobbly ones, for instance. The point of calling some social or political system stable is not very different. A stable system is considered to be capable of continuation, whereas an unstable system has weaknesses. There is supposed to be a vulnerability about a political system that has no stability. Such instability is usually characterized by frequent changes in policy, variations in the effectiveness of the laws to achieve the goals of the society, danger of foreign intervention in domestic affairs, absence of uniform loyalty to the goals of the community, and similar problems. Stability in the processes of community life is one of the goals that political systems often aim for. When it does not require the sacrifice of other values, stability enhances the normal, prudent, somewhat routine but very necessary processes of community life. It also gives the impression, rightly or not, that the members of the community, the citizens, are relatively satisfied with how the community is governed. Of course, stability alone might be achieved by the inducement of fear, but it is possible to argue that the apparent stability of a totalitarian, police state is just that—apparent. In fact, the potential for disorder—revolution, rebellion, violent turnovers brought about from the inside or the outside—is always present if it is only by brute force that a system can remain stable.

Related to stability, if not interchangeable with it, is the idea of order. One difference between a stable political system and an orderly one is that there can always be a question about order regarding the standard by which orderliness is to be judged. When people insist that law and order must be secured and preserved in society, one can usually ask whether the *order* in question is a just or an unjust order. If it is the latter, then the order achieved is at the expense of political values that would have to be part of an orderly but good human community. Only the type of order that incorporates justice, that is in tune with the requirements of a good human community, can be given full philosophical support. It could even be argued that on those occasions when order is imposed by engendering injustice for some members in a society (e.g., when martial law is imposed), the only goal achieved is that the will of some people in society is given prior significance, without regard to whether it has merit. The extreme emphasis on stability and order, which is usually associated with extreme emphasis on national unity and perpetuity, has often resulted in an almost blind imposition of order by brute force.

However difficult it is to define justice and to make sure that it has a firm place in the affairs of a human community, there appear good reasons for the view that without justice, order is of very dubious value. It can also be argued that justice itself requires, under certain circumstances, the destruction of stability and order, as when it is right to upset the order that exists in a concentration camp to achieve the liberty of the inhabitants.   Nevertheless, the concern for order is not arbitrary.   It pertains to the human need for long-range planning and peace.

Justice

From the beginning of political philosophy the idea of justice has been of primary concern.   There have been those, also, who concluded that justice is a hopelessly confused notion, an impossible dream best forgotten, or in fact of negative value.   The latter is especially true when the notion of justice is tied closely to vengeance and the practice of violent punishment, but some philosophers have dismissed all ideas of justice as useless for purposes of making sense of political affairs.

Most people have some idea of the nature of justice. They usually associate justice with an accurate assessment of the worth of others and of others' actions.   Doing justice to someone, recognizing the true worth of another person, is understood widely enough not to pose grave difficulties in day-to-day living.

Being unjust to someone is also well known to most of us. Falsely accusing someone is a case in point.   Rejecting a person because of a prejudice—a judgment made prior to knowing the relevant facts—is also understood to qualify as injustice in some circumstances.   We justly admire those who achieved worthy goals by individual effort, but we unjustly gloat over shallow fame and fortune, which we might come by without any merit.

The idea *justice* is used when we think of our judgment of, regard for, and relations to others.   Do we act toward them in accordance with objective standards or act arbitrarily?   Justice may be an ideal we aspire to but rarely reach in our dealings with others. It can also be a goal we aim for in the way we regard ourselves.   It is generally thought, although not often discussed outside philosophy, that an ethical life requires justice, that acting unjustly is wrong and blameworthy, even punishable.   (Consider the term *obstruction of justice*, which was heard so often during the Watergate hearings.)

What Is Justice?   Philosophers have made many attempts to define justice.   They have tried to identify the crucial aspects of just actions and just institutions.   As with most topics in philosophy, they have seldom reached agreement, although often their views have converged on certain common ideas.

One well-known philosophical treatment of justice reaches the conclusion that justice consists primarily of being fair. A just person is a fair person, and just actions are actions carried out with fairness. By this view a just person is one who is unbiased in applying standards of human worth and the worthiness of actions, so that if one person is considered worthy because she helps the poor, then another who helps the poor must also be so considered. It would also be unjust to praise one person for something and disregard a similar fact about another. These and similar cases indicate why some philosophers would regard fairness as a crucial ingredient of justice.

Other philosophers consider fairness to be limited to a narrow set of cases where justice applies. They believe that being fair sometimes has nothing to do with justice, as when we treat animals fairly as we feed them, or as we are fair to our friends in distributing Christmas gifts to them even though there may be nothing *due to them* at all, so that no justice is involved in the situation.

In the political domain, the idea that justice equals fairness supports programs usually associated with the welfare state. If one of the central goals of a political and legal system is to foster justice, and if it is held that justice equals fairness, then the government of a human community is likely to be concerned with fairness, especially with the idea of the equal distribution of money, protection, education, health care, and whatever else governments distribute to people. The fairness involved in justice cannot usually be understood apart from what is due to people. Thus, in political affairs the fairness a government owes to people will have a great deal to do with what the government ought to provide. If its function is mainly to protect and preserve the rights of the citizens, this protection and preservation of rights must be carried out with fairness: the rich must not be favored, men must not receive better protection than women, blacks and whites must be equally well protected, and so forth. If the function of government is thought to be the achievement of people's economic well-being, or providing everyone with education and health care, then the doctrine that justice is fairness requires that all citizens receive these goods and services in equal proportions.

The justice-is-fairness idea is just one of those currently being debated among political theorists. Another view holds that justice involves treating everyone as a moral agent, so that governments must not sacrifice the liberty of citizens to achieve for them some other desirable goal, such as education or health care. The justice-as-due-process theory, or what I will call such for the present, sees the nature of justice, especially in the political sphere, as requiring that every individual be regarded morally capable, as possessing dignity, and as deserving treatment that is due anyone with the capacity for good and evil. Depending on what it is that such a capacity would entitle a person to in an organized human community, justice requires it. And since the central requirement for moral agents from their fellow citizens is that no one should voluntarily interfere with their moral capacity, justice demands the strictest protection and preservation of human liberty in a human community.

Upholding justice, usually taken to be the goal of a sound legal system, depends on how it is conceived. If every person is owed a thorough education, then justice will require that such education is administered throughout the society. If each person is due protection against bad influences (e.g., dirty movies, violence, and sex on television), then justice will be thought of as requiring that such protection be delivered. Clearly, then, what we believe justice is and what we believe people are due from us have a great deal to do with the kind of political system we will have.

A political system that does not aim for justice, at least in the social realm, is to that extent seen by most as defective. A just society, whether just in all respects or in relation to the kind of laws that are accepted and enforced, is the central goal of many a political thinker's labors and many a political activist's complicated, even violent, strategies. There may be fervent debate about what justice is. However, the opinion of most who have thought the matter over carefully is that justice is crucial to the successful processes of a human community.

Justice and Legality.   Finally, while justice is often a property of one or another law or political institution—so that the law is said to be a just law—legality alone does not guarantee that a policy or practice is just. There is dispute, of course, as to whether a system that does not even aim at justice could be a *legal* system or a valid political system. Thus Hitler's Germany claimed legal validity, but because it ignored justice to the extent most rational observers agree that it did, the Third Reich could be considered a tyranny and not a political or lawful system. The same can be said about Soviet Russia, especially under Stalin. This view regards many societies as lacking the institution of law and only carrying on the façade of legality. Others reject this and claim that law and justice are independent of one another. Justice is a matter of morality and it would, of course, be good to have the legal system conform to it. Yet, even when the system does not seek justice, it is still a lawful system so long as those who live by it accept its authority without much resistance.

Regardless of doubts about the nature and existence of justice, and despite the occasional attempts (by cynics, nihilists and political "scientists" of a certain orientation) to deny the very meaningfulness of the idea, the crucial importance of justice is undeniable. Justice is essentially related to how closely we abide by sound moral notions in our dealings with others, and political theory concerns itself with the basic principles of a good human *community*; so justice is the most crucial and challenging idea with which political theorists must come to grips.

Sovereignty

Whoever has sovereignty concerning an issue possesses the supreme, exclusive, final, and independent authority of leadership on how the issue must be decided. The sovereignty claimed either by individuals or by governments signifies the belief these have in their supreme position regarding the authority to decide. In a monarchy, for example, the king or queen would be the court of last resort, the final authority on matters related to the entire community. In a quasi-democracy the issue of sovereignty is confused, but usually the individual citizen is understood to have limited sovereignty within the entire social domain—for example, it is everyone's proper authority to contribute to a decision on many issues by way of casting a vote. On the other hand, the U.S. Supreme Court has final authority to settle disputes. However, the Court is not itself sovereign; it represents the people as specified in the Constitution. So again, it is in some sense the citizens who are sovereign, at least in principle, in a system such as that of the United States of America.

Who is sovereign in a given community is, of course, a matter of which theory of the good political order is correct. If, for instance, communism is right, the sovereign must be the *entire* community, the commune, as it were, to which the powers and will of any individual should be made subservient.   If one holds all of humanity or one's entire community to be of greater significance than the individuals who compose that community, the final authority in various matters will be that of the community or collective.   Quite apart from any derisiveness in the term, *collectivism* indicates that in a community the collective is sovereign.   On the other hand, in a pure democracy the majority is sovereign, while in libertarianism the individual has sovereignty within a definite domain (so that each individual has sovereignty in some areas but none has sovereignty in all).   In socialism and welfare statism it is usually the government that possesses sovereignty, although there can be qualifications concerning the extent of this sovereignty and the means by which it can be acquired.   In democratic socialism the government is sovereign in its accurate reflection of majority will, and in a welfare state the individual with limited liberty shares sovereignty with the government with its emphasis on limited paternalism.

General Welfare

Because of the preamble of the United States Constitution, the idea of general welfare is closely related to the American political system. To promote the general welfare, then, is viewed as a proper goal of our political system.

The idea seems closely linked with such older notions as the common good or common purpose.   It is often invoked to explain the need for certain policies.   The idea is familiar, but what exactly is the general welfare?   How could and should it be promoted?   The first question is answered most frequently by two different political theories.   One holds that the general welfare is the well-being of all people in the community, and the function of the law is to bring the welfare of everyone to full realization.   This answer is given by those who defend what I have earlier discussed as the welfare state.

The other answer, which is given quite often, although less frequently these days, is that the general welfare is the well-being of each citizen, but the way to bring it about or promote it is to protect each person's liberty to pursue it as he or she sees fit. When taken in the context of the Declaration of Independence and the Bill of Rights, this second answer appears to be more defensible for the American system. Yet, by concentrating on the point that the Constitution has as one of its goals to *promote* the general walfare, it is possible to defend the view that all means chosen by a democratic process may be employed to achieve this goal.

Another issue is not with the meaning of "welfare," but with the meaning of "general." The latter term can be interpreted in this context as follows: whatever is of general benefit should be promoted by the Constitution. And very few things may be of truly general benefit. People differ in many respects because although they are all people, they are also individuals who have talents, characteristics, goals, capacities, and personalities shared with very few or no others. Therefore, some political theorists have argued that only when their common, shared traits are in question can the political system promote their welfare. Just what these characteristics are is not at issue here. Some have called these the general need for security, the general goal of success in material well-being, the general requirement for moral virtue, the general capacity to make independent judgments about how to live, and so forth.

Others reject this interpretation because they deny that anything generally good for all people can be identified. So they defend the view that the system should abandon this goal or concern itself with everyone in just the respects that everyone or anyone may be better off. And the debate goes on. Here, again, whatever one can rationally take to be the general welfare and however one can defend the political system's method of promoting it, the idea is politically significant.

Equality

Today, equality is perhaps the most widely defended political goal. From prominent political philosophers, intellectuals in general, economists, and sociologists to artists, entertainers, and, of course, politicians, the majority of politically concerned citizens in the United States, as well as in the world community, defend the view that political systems should aim for establishing human equality.

In the American political tradition the ideal of equality relates most prominently to how the laws of the society should be administered. Equality under the law is the kind of equality that has been a prime concern within this tradition. Depending upon the proper purpose of the law and the government, the crucial concern with equality relates to applying the law equally throughout the citizenry. If law requires the prevention of pollution, then everyone's polluting activities (including the government's) must be stopped. Only where severe mitigating circumstances arise can someone justify escaping the force of the equal protection (and application) provision of law within this tradition.

Here it will help to reflect briefly on the belief that equality and freedom are in necessary conflict. If the government, through law, has as its essential goal to secure the liberty of each citizen (whether by protecting free speech, free trade, free religious exercise, free artistic or scientific activity), then equality enters in its responsibility to secure *everyone's* liberty, not just some favorite person's or group's.

Another sense of equality is prominent, especially of late. Equality here involves the idea that all human beings deserve to enjoy an equally good life. If this is so, the emphasis on liberty diminishes, since equalizing living standards will involve governments in making the services and creations of some people available to others whether the former choose this or not. But if fredom is not a crucial political value, this loss is of little importance.

Equality under the law is an ideal that involves the processes of legal administration and enforcement. It requires that no citizen receive less than he or she is due from government. But what a citizen is due from government is not itself specified in the call of equality. As long as the law applies equally to all, the equality spoken of in this tradition is achieved. On the other hand, the equal conditions of life of the citizenry, at least with respect to economic well-being, can involve the government in unequal administration of laws, the administration of laws toward some people but not others, and the enactment of different laws for different groups of people. All these may be required in order to produce the results of equal living standards for all people in society.

In evaluating which idea of equality is defensible as a goal for a society, we must consider several issues. Is it possible to achieve either kind of equality (or some other not discussed here)? If the achievement of equality is possible, can its value be demonstrated? Is there some sound argument to show that equality is good and worth striving for, so that the actions taken to ensure it (which are sometimes quite costly and even violent) could be seen to be warranted? Are political means of achieving equality, for example, in educational opportunity, in dealing with members of different racial, sexual, or age groups, the best means, or do they violate some other values that are more important to protect and preserve by political means?

In evaluating the place of equality within the area of community life and organized politics, these and similar questions deserve careful consideration. Even if today the community may exhibit thorough confusion on the issues involved, the citizens of such a community owe it to themselves to make some headway in reaching an understanding of the problems. Unless citizens make the effort to understand (and then to communicate through available channels), both the present community and the communities of future generations could be seriously damaged. It is clear that these issues of political philosophy are no mere academic amusements.

Liberty

Liberty is the most prominent political ideal associated with the American tradition, although it has had significance throughout human history. The term *liberty* has been defined in several different ways, as have other crucial terms in political philosophy and theory. In our own society two prominent senses can be identified.

First, liberty (or political freedom) means living and acting without unjust interference from others. The freedom of the press, freedom of assembly, freedom of trade, and freedom of artistic creativity are instances of such liberty. Its essence is that it would be unjust for anyone to prevent our acting by our own decisions, making our own ways in life, and our liberty is intact when no one does so. The details are many, and those who would agree with the above concept of liberty still disagree about the specifics.

For example, many would think it unjust to interfere with people's artistic creativity but find it perfectly proper to regulate people's commercial activities, so they would mean by liberty something different from those who see it the other way around or consider interference in both instances unjust.

This conception of liberty is often called negative because it emphasizes not interfering in others' lives. But that is not an entirely justified characterization. Positively, we are *doing what we choose to do* instead of what others might make us do. Nevertheless, the idea is that others should not interfere in what we do (appropriately detailed), so the negative element is evident.

Second, liberty (or freedom) is viewed as the power to do something. Thus, a paralyzed person lacks freedom because of the limitations of his or her power of movement. More relevant to social and political circumstances, those who are not free to move from one place to another because they are very poor are understood to lack liberty in this sense. When we speak of freedom from fear, hunger, ignorance, guilt, economic scarcity, and hardship, we are referring to liberty in this second sense. To secure liberty for all could mean under this interpretation that in various ways we should remove all obstacles that prevent people from reaching their highest potential in life.

Those who think that political systems should promote liberty in its first sense believe that political action, either private or governmental, should aim toward the protection and preservation of individual rights. No unjust interference in people's lives should be tolerated. Most of those who conceive of liberty along these lines see individuals as agents of their actions and responsible, in voluntary cooperation with others, for removing natural obstacles to their success in life. The political problem is to make sure that other people stay peaceful and not impose themselves as obstacles; the rest of nature is then reasonably manageable.

Those who think law should promote liberty in its second sense hold governments responsible for ensuring security, safety, health care, education, consumer guidance, and other forms of protection, as well as for making sure that people obtain these goods and services.

These two ideas of liberty are in opposition. If the first type of liberty is fully protected, then it is impossible to achieve the liberation of people from hunger, ignorance, etc., via governmental means. If a government must protect citizens against those who would take their work, property, even life without their permission, then that government could not obtain food, education, or health care for people who are unable to obtain these by themselves or with the voluntary assistance of others. That is, if the government must protect citizens from ignorance, hunger, and ill health, it must obtain the resources to do so from those who produce them, and thus engage in abridging the very liberty that under the first tradition it is supposed to preserve.

Because of these mutually exclusive senses of the term *liberty* or *freedom,* many theorists argue that one or the other kind of liberty should be relabeled. Some even believe that those who perpetuate these mutually exclusive senses of the term are perpetrating fraud.

Yet both ways of conceiving of liberty appear to be common and even commonsensical. Therefore, a solution to the problem of their conflict might be to distinguish between liberty that can be secured (or should be sought) by political means and liberty that politics could not achieve. Protecting people's liberty from other people could be the goal of political organization; it could be the one *common* good to be achieved by way of law. Achieving the freedom from other obstacles that nature poses, such dangers as flood, illness, scarce resources, and lack of knowledge, could be the task assumed by individuals as they live in a community free from others' forcible interference.

Many theorists have objected to this distinction between the liberty that is to be advanced by political means and the liberty that is to be left for private accomplishment. We cannot take up the issue here in full. Suffice it for now to have observed some elements of the common human concern with liberty. It should be evident also that concern with liberty is not clearly separated from the concerns with the other suggested political values, such as justice, discussed above.

POLITICS AND PRINCIPLES—
CONCLUDING REMARKS

It is not by accident that this has been the longest chapter of the book. The political systems and ideals described briefly here have a ·prominent place within our intellectual history.

The problems faced by people in relation to political affairs are constant. No one escapes them, and no age or place wherein community life exists could be without them. The view that politics is of no concern to a person would have to be false if it means that some person living among others has no relation to the politics of some community. Maybe a person does not *care!* It may even be that caring will accomplish little in some communities, especially those controlled by some powerful group or person. In fact, however, politics has a direct bearing on all our lives. Everyone in the community should have some idea of the alternatives open to us in the matter of how communities should be constituted, or how we could best govern ourselves. From the very denial of any need for systematic law and government to the advocacy of totalitarianism, the alternatives address our natural concern with human community life and how to live it best.

In our day more and more aspects of life seem to be under political supervision, although, with few exceptions, in most periods of history people's lives were fully governed by monarchs, emperors, pharaohs, polit-bureaus, assemblies, legislatures, and the like. Yet previously in the United States there has not been so much state involvement in human affairs as in recent times. Of course, some individuals, such as blacks, women, or members of the Indian tribes, have for long received less than full recognition of their individual rights (and responsibilities). But in the main those were exceptions to the system's general direction. Today the various governments have entered human affairs from banking to architecture, dentistry to barbering, drug manufacture to publishing books on how to watch football games; few aspects of contemporary life are totally exempt from government regulation. And this is more so in other regions of the world. Science, religion, art, sports, education, business, medicine—all the affairs, aspirations, miseries, and concerns of people are supervised by their political institutions.

It is hardly controversial to conclude, therefore, that all of us should pay some heed to politics. To do so comprehensively, with the hope of reaching some basic and clear understanding, it is necessary to become familiar with political philosophy and the various political theories that philosophical attention to politics and law has produced.

To appreciate the importance of such familiarity, consider how much power lies within the hands of those who claim to have political and legal authority. The police officer orders you to stop, and is authorized to shoot you if you do not. Why? And what defines whether his command is justified? The Internal Revenue Service agent seizes your bank savings and if you try to resist, you can be put in jail. Why? How does the IRS agent acquire such authority where you have none like it toward your neighbor? A person in a black robe delivers a judgment that can mean fifty years in prison. Why? What distinguishes judges and the sentence they hand down from you and some order you may issue? What about the authorities in some countries who put artists, newspaper reporters, and scientists in "mental hospitals"? Is the claim in behalf of such authority valid? Is the argument in support of it sound? When Soviet secret police drag a farmer to Siberia because he sold goods he produced without state permission, is the action of the police justified, their authority just? When South African police officers prevent a black citizen from entering a public building, are they acting with proper authority? Is the existence of a government document sufficient for political suppression—in any system, including the Third Reich?

These and many other problems arise for consideration within the area of political philosophy and theory. Also related to this area is the philosophy of law, in which the details of the legal system of the various political theories are ironed out and debated. Here such issues as the difference between intentional abridgment of another's liberty and accidental intrusion on another are considered. What is the difference between manslaughter and premeditated murder? What are the proper rules of evidence in a criminal case? What is the difference between criminal and civil law? Why should the burden of proof lie on the prosecution (yet why, in the case of the IRS, this should not be so)?

It is plainly important for us all to give political matters some of our attention. The Russian physicist and human rights advocate

Andrei Sakharov was asked once why he engages in political inquiry and advocacy when there is so little hope that his ideas will have impact on the Soviet government. His answer explains better than I could why politics must be of concern to us:

> ... You always need to make ideals clear to yourself. . . . You always have to be aware of them, even if there is no direct path to their realization. Were there no ideals, there would be no hope whatsoever. Then everything would be hopelessness, darkness—a blind alley.

QUESTIONS FOR DISCUSSION

1. Based on what has been discussed in the first part of this chapter, why would one have to be concerned with political philosophy?
2. What is the relationship of ethics to political theory?
3. In terms of the political system that exists in your community, what connections are evident between law and political theory?
4. Describe two types of democracy and explain how they differ from each other.
5. Outline and criticize one of the arguments for monarchy.
6. Which of the arguments for monarchy has no relationship to ethics? Why?
7. What are the crucial features of Marxist socialism and what arguments can be advanced to support this system?
8. What is the relationship between Marxist socialism and Marxist communism?
9. How do socialism and communism differ? What do they have in common?
10. Why is libertarianism an individualist political theory?
11. Explain the crucial differences between the two arguments for libertarianism. Evaluate these comparatively to see which is the better argument.
12. Defend anarchism.
13. Discuss any two of the political values covered in the chapter and defend with argument the more important one.
14. Explain what aspects of your own political society have been discussed in this chapter.
15. Which of the positions discussed would you advocate?
16. Relate the political systems discussed to the ethical positions considered in the previous chapter.

Epilogue:
Truth and Philosophy

7

At this point several issues could be discussed, depending on what an author considers to be the most important issue in philosophy or in some other area. As far as the purpose of the present book is concerned, we have covered numerous important topics in philosophy and further elaboration could not achieve progress within our present scope. What may be of some value is to address a question that has surely been on the minds of most readers. I am thinking of the question: What is to be concluded from all these disputes before us?

In short, the issue I think worth exploring in this final chapter is whether there are any truths in philosophy. The question of the nature of truth itself is at the crux of most philosophical systems and methods. However, when a reader first encounters philosophy, usually many philosophical positions will be presented. This is unlike introductory courses in other fields. Thus, the question of the possible truth of these various positions on numerous topics arises quite naturally. Is there freedom of the will or can none of us help what happens to us? Is nature composed of matter alone, or, if not, is it entirely spiritual? Is pragmatism or subjectivism or empiricism the correct epistemology? What about ethics—is altruism or egoism right? Should we take pleasure as our highest goal or should we serve the will of God? Is communism, socialism, monarchy, or libertarianism the proper political solution for us?

Encountering so many different, often contradictory ways of thinking about the world can be discouraging, even disturbing. It should awaken most of us to the realization that we do not know where we stand. The resulting perplexity might lead one to the view that philosophy is useless and possibly even destructive, so why not cast it aside and attend to more manageable matters?

This view is itself a position within philosophy, so we are back to the same puzzle again: what is right or true in philosophy?

It is pointless to wait for the "united association of philosophers" to come out of hiding and settle the issues. In other fields of inquiry we seem to find it acceptable enough to come up with answers that are both perfectly sound and quite open to revision, modification, and updating. It is best not to expect from philosophy something that is not promised in any other area, namely, a final settlement of the problems. Instead, one would probably do well to take up the task as a personal one and ask in earnest whether there are any right or nearly right answers to the questions raised in philosophy. Reading this book will not be enough for that task, admittedly. Reading all the other books in philosophy will not do the job, either. Yet, even after this brief survey one might attend to the task just a little while. To assist in this endeavor, I will suggest where I have ended up thus far in my own investigations concerning the matter of truth in philosophy.

THE SUBJECT MATTER OF PHILOSOPHY

In the first chapter I indicated what philosophy studies. The proper, valid subject matter of philosophy is the basic features of reality and our essential relationship to them—not, however, the various special domains studied in other fields of inquiry. Metaphysics studies basic facts; epistemology asks what knowledge is; ethics considers how human beings should live; and politics addresses the problem of how human communities should be set up. These, briefly, are the central issues treated within the branches of philosophy discussed in this book. Among the many branches and subbranches of human inquiry it is philosophy that considers these issues; however, they pertain to us all.

To make some headway toward coping with the issue of whether there can be truth in philosophy, it will help to consider that the purpose of philosophy is not itself a philosophical issue, although many philosophers discuss it. The knowledge of what philosophy studies is not philosophical knowledge—to be more precise. In any area of study the field must be well enough known; it must be distinguished from other fields and assimilated into the broader categories, such as sciences, arts, and humanities, before work can begin in it. This is a gradual process in human evolution, but when we think the matter through for ourselves, it is noticeable enough that whatever philosophy amounts to, this is not itself the consequence of philosophical inquiry. That would amount to having things upside down.

People can have a good deal of understanding of philosophy without having obtained philosophical understanding. Moreover, it is quite likely that this knowledge about philosophy is hidden; that is, people are not aware that they have it. Once we have some knowledge about philosophy, we can begin to develop a more rigorous, systematic approach to reaching some answers in the field.

The realm of existence studied in philosophy is crucial in determining the character of good judgments in the field. What is being studied requires that it be studied in certain distinctive ways. In a pluralistic world one can get seriously sidetracked by studying one subject matter in the fashion proper to another. Sometimes this can pay off, but more often the transplantation of methodology produces serious omissions. Methods used in chemistry are not all appropriate to the study of psychology, even though certain features may be common to both fields. Standards of good judgments emerge in the light of what we are investigating. Thus, physics develops its own tests for checking whether judgments in the field are good guesses, reliable estimates, firmly supported beliefs, or knowledge. The same is true in philosophy. Here, as in other fields, the methods to be employed have developed alongside the greater and greater curiosity and work being devoted to the subject matter.

One might think that there is a chicken-or-egg problem here: which came first, the subject matter or the method? Yet this is like asking what came first, reality or our knowledge of it? It is safe to suggest here that in the case of every individual the two come hand in hand—but reality has been around (at least) prior to any of us. Whatever the result of philosophical inquiry shows here, for our purposes the only crucial point is that because of philosophy's very broad scope of inquiry, and its concern with such basic issues, its primary tool of investigation is logic—the most general method of inquiry discovered by human beings.

All criticism invokes at least logic. Even where nothing else is presupposed, where one looks only at some theory's internal features, it is usual to criticize on grounds that some view is inconsistent, leads to contradictions, or reduces to incoherence. Examples may clarify issues in philosophical exposition, but they never can be decisive. This is because philosophy itself studies the issue of what counts as an example. How do we tell whether something does exemplify a particular principle, definition, or theory? The criterion of logical propriety is virtually universal; even those who reject its universal applicability argue for their views by means of its extensive use.

This is as it should be. Logic is a methodology that accommodates the character of reality itself. The subject matter, which is reality, or the very essence of being, gives rise to the method of inquiry. The field that studies this subject matter must make use of logic first and foremost.

THE GROUND OF PHILOSOPHICAL KNOWLEDGE

In philosophical inquiries, the arguments, theories, and even most esoteric issues can be traced to the basic problems in the field; these give each nuance its philosophical significance. All major and minor philosophical issues are traceable to the first or main question of philosophy: what is it to be something? This issue is dealt with in metaphysics. If the questions of that field can be given correct answers, then some guidelines may be available for purposes of proceeding, with promise of success, to other areas and problems in the field. In reference to the question raised earlier about the perplexing problem of whether there are truths in philosophy, we can now see how there might be. Exploring this question itself leads back to the central question of metaphysics. To have identified a basic fact of reality, a metaphysical fact, is to have provided oneself with some point of departure. That is, after all, the point of calling such facts basic. But we must now recall what it would be to be such a fact. What would characterize a metaphysical fact?

To this question I direct the reader back to chapter 2, and provide only a reminder here that if what one believes to be basic facts of existence really are such facts, then one will find them to be fully capable of integration with the rest of what one knows. To put this briefly, basic facts must be very generally, broadly, or *universally* applicable—facts found everywhere and at any time—with no exceptions. The test of whether one has identified a metaphysical fact is whether it squares with everything to which it is meant to apply—to *all of reality!* It must, therefore, square with any meaningful statement and with any realistic possibility (as specified in other branches of knowledge). Only after a good sampling of these has shown that in each and every case, without exception, some principle or fact has been exemplified do we have firm grounds for claiming that a basic fact of reality has been identified.

It is not enough, of course, to find any kind of statement or judgment to which everything can be fitted. Thus, a claim such as "If everything is a unicorn, then that thing is horned" is without any contradiction from nature. But these sorts of claims are hypothetical. A metaphysical fact, being a fact, can only be related by way of a categorical or existential claim—to the effect that something *is* the case, not that *if it is,* then something else follows.

If such facts exist and can be identified, then it is possible, however difficult that could turn out, to obtain answers to other philosophical questions. Keeping very much in focus the metaphysical facts of reality, it is possible to proceed by the use of logic, careful perception, and sometimes extensive analysis, and draw conclusions, in various areas of philosophy, that are as true as true can be. This is all that can be expected. To require that a person obtain a completely finished philosophy or theory is to ask for nonsense. (Here it may help to recheck the discussion of contextualism!)

The brevity of these comments should not lead the reader to conclude that it is easy to come up with solutions. It is an enormous task to make sure that one has come up with correct ones. Many great minds have tried and failed in several areas, even by their own admission. Also, in human history many people have accepted beliefs for which no support existed, or for which they

offered incredibly weak or even phony support. Many philosophers have come to think of themselves as morally responsible
never to encourage confidence in one's conclusions, theories, or
values. Some philosophers believe it to be their exclusive professional obligation to raise the most outlandish, fantastic objections
to some proposed idea, just to make sure that conclusions are not
accepted hastily. This, in turn, has led to philosophical meekness,
which may account for why people have, now and then, turned
away from philosophy to such occult fields as astrology and the less
analytic areas such as religion to obtain solutions to problems within
the philosopher's domain.

The answer here lies in striking a balance—a suggestion well
worth taking in numerous areas of life. An extremely, fruitlessly
demanding standard of truth is as unjustified in philosophy as anywhere else, but careless conclusion-chasing can be even more harmful. The reader has every reason to conclude for now that much
more work is needed to obtain philosophical knowledge. My purpose here is to indicate that such knowledge is not impossible.
Nothing has been done to entitle anyone to think that here it has
been reached!

KNOWLEDGE AND PHILOSOPHY

It is, of course, extremely difficult to suspend whatever philosophical orientation we have in life. We all grow up with ideas on
human freedom, the soul, values, God, knowledge, and politics.
We use these ideas to make sense of things we come upon in our
lives.

No matter how attached we are to such views, we will gain
considerable independence by taking a fresh view every now and
then. Even once independent investigations have led to some well-
thought-out conclusions, it is wise to renew the policy of rechecking
our premises. I am not suggesting pathological self-doubt, only
intelligent caution. I am not suggesting some phony attitude of
neutrality, only the effort to be objective in the broad sense specified in chapter 1 of this book. The recognition that we may make
mistakes should be coupled with the knowledge that we can be
right, as well.

The fact that in philosophy, specifically, it is somewhat difficult to provide controlled tests makes it crucial that we commit everything to careful scrutiny by way of logical analysis. The seriously advanced and carefully elaborated theories of other philosophers deserve attention—not primarily because we owe their authors respect, but because we should never neglect valuable help in our search for understanding. These other perspectives should, when possible, be considered at their best. For example, we should ignore those who distort the views of Marx in their fear that without distortion they might have to admit there is something of value in that outlook. We should reject the quick and shallow caricatures of communism, capitalism, and fascism.

Most important, it is advisable to confront ideas not just with their own internal shortcomings but with the competing ideas that are available to use in comparison. Even after numerous difficulties have been identified with various positions, we may still find that without a fully developed better idea, one of the flawed theories has to suffice. In the natural search for solutions that so many people undertake, the absence of a correct theory can easily prompt us to return to make reparations on ones found lacking.

At times people reject the prospect of solving some problem on grounds that previous philosophical efforts have failed. Here, too, care should be taken not to demand too much of the short history of humanity. The time could not be spent, even with the best of efforts, just on settling philosophical problems. Nor is it necessarily true that simply because according to current opinion these problems were left unsolved, this is in fact the case. Perhaps it is wrong to view others' solutions as bad. In general, some patience is certainly advisable in one's attempt to solve any problem, including philosophical ones. Even if a person does not wish to embark on the solution, it need not be concluded that no solution is possible.

We should remember that seeking philosophical understanding is not very different from seeking any other kind. In more specialized fields we try to "get it together" before we are satisfied with the result. On each occasion when new generations set out on the journey, the aim might well be to get it together once again. Gradually, if one wants to find answers in philosophy, one can begin to investigate and try to discover which answer makes more sense, which squares with one's own experiences, seen in a cool, calm light (not with a lot of wishful thinking injected!). With even more work, with the major philosophies in contention thoroughly studied, a person could well come to have philosophical knowledge. Very good ideas of what is right at least in certain narrow areas will be possible. One might wish to study the free will / determinism issue; or the existence of God; or skepticism; or the nature of perception. In each case one could keep an eye on other important work being done and eventually make the careful advance to a solid conclusion.

The problem is often that people are very impatient about obtaining philosophical knowledge. Most of us take it for granted that learning about the psychology of monkeys or the orbits of a subatomic particle would be very difficult. Biology, physics, computer science, horticulture—all these require hard work. Then, maybe, some knowledge has been obtained. Something like this happens in philosophy, too. Since all of us deal with philosophy, unlike chemistry or farming, in virtually all our waking moments— judging what exists, seeing if we have knowledge, making decisions about what to do, etc.—it appears at first that not much work is needed here to find out what is true and what isn't. But that is wrong. To understand and come to grips with philosophy, and then perhaps find some answers in the field—all these are very difficult tasks.

Many people, as we have noted, deny that knowledge is possible, not to mention philosophical knowledge. This last would be knowledge of some philosophical fact, some claim one could support as true within the area of philosophy. But in a sense, of course, they are claiming to knowing something when they offer this view. So when we consider their views together with all the others, we find that there is a lot to choose from. The question is raised again, Are there philosophical truths, is there philosophical knowledge? To put it differently: Is there a correct philosophical position, or could there be one?

ON THE CORRECT PHILOSOPHICAL POSITION

The possibility of formulating a correct philosophical position has nothing to do with whether there *will* be agreement about it. Not everyone is interested in finding a correct philosophical system or answer. Some people are bogged down with other problems and have no time for philosophizing. Even among those involved in philosophizing, many reject the very idea of a correct philosophy from the start, so their disagreement is assured. Then even if the bulk of philosophers and people were to see eye to eye on some philosophy, it is doubtful that they would all express their position in similar words. Finally, there are philosophers who do not want to *solve* philosophical problems, just as there are other professionals who are counterproductive.

Assuming, however, that a philosophical position is identified and found to be right—assuming someone's philosophy does indeed answer all philosophical questions correctly, solves all philosophical problems, it still would not close off the business of philosopy. Perhaps because many believe this is *not* so people have rejected the very idea of such a correct philosophical position. In a way it seems that philosophical positions get reintroduced over and over again, just as people are born over and over again. Because philosophical concerns are so basic to human life, in some sense each generation must ask and answer the questions anew, so that the many ways of approaching life get introduced and tested again and again.

In the various philosophies of the world some ideas are probably better, some worse. Sometimes a philosopher's way of bringing together good ideas, those that do best at solving problems and answering questions, is more successful than another's. And it is possible that occasionally a philosopher produces a correct philosophical system.

Clearly this system would not have to be one which produces final answers to all philosophical questions—if it is also discovered that no such final answers are possible, at least not about everything that philosophy investigates. As in the sciences, a correct philosophical position would have to be *the system of best answers* within the field. Such answers would rest on a clearly identified metaphysical foundation, on some (or one) metaphysical principle or fact, and have all areas of inquiry and answers fully integrated.

Some feature of such a system would have to have a claim to finality: in metaphysics only those answers can be right which are right pertaining to all of reality, *including the future.* But not all of philosophy deals with metaphysics, so final answers need not be required of such a system in all branches of philosophy.

What I am suggesting would appear to reflect most people's lives. Some values or life plans remain reasonably firm for each of us, but we must make decisions in most areas time and time again. Problems facing us now may be given the best, a mediocre, or worst answer, within the available batch of suggestions. Tomorrow we might find a better solution, but if we cannot wait, today's best is indeed *the* best. In considering the task of identifying the best philosophy, we can view the matter somewhat analogously. We can expect to find clear and firm answers in some areas, ones that will hold forever, and others that we have very good reason to consider correct,. barring only minor modifications as we learn more and more about reality. Some areas may really require much better familiarization before answers to the questions which we face there can be obtained.

This approach to the issue of the prospects of truth in philosophy, whether even some entire system of philosophical thought might be correct, appears to make sense. Our knowledge tends to develop in all areas, both in our individual lives and in human history, although it is also possible that in some epochs we lose sight of what others have discovered earlier. Reality itself undergoes changes, sometimes crucial ones. We are reasonably sure that this situation obtains in science. There, however, only some people become very upset with the results and disputes, whereas in some branches of philosophy everyone could get excited.

At any rate, even while we admit that further work is warranted in all areas of inquiry, we might also have very good reasons for drawing firm conclusions. If our research has been thorough, it is sensible to admit also that our conclusions merit support and even some partisanship. In areas such as morality and politics this can lead to the institution of policies and cultivation of practices and habits, as well as to serious conflicts and wars. To stick to one's conclusions stubbornly is hazardous in any domain but especially so in these last. One should be ready to consider honestly motivated and carefully advanced persuasion, and even yield to sound arguments and criticism, so as to avoid dogmatism, the attitude that makes learning impossible. On the other hand, wishy-washiness can lead to the neglect of crucial values in life; therefore, indiscriminate open-mindedness (often advocated by the unprincipled as "civilized ·tolerance") should be rejected as a viable alternative. However obvious and even pedestrian these considerations may be, it is probably most appropriate for anyone to approach philosophical positions, especially those concerned with values, accordingly.

PERSONAL ANSWERS

I have suggested a possible conception of what could be the correct philosophical position. Answering some questions by this approach in areas of philosophy could not lead to shutting the doors on the field. Times change; people grow up to ask the questions again; growth can continue—just as decay could set in.

The teacher's role in the search for answers by students and readers cannot include *giving* the answers. In some other fields this is not the case. In philosophy, because it deals with life in such a direct, intimate way, people must dig up the answers alone, perhaps with a little help from friends. This help would involve giving directions as to what has been thought about the issues by other serious investigators and how they have gone about trying to answer the recurring questions. Once this help has been provided, each person is quite alone. However much anyone has been influenced, pressured, cajoled, or even beaten into accepting various ideas from others, each person does appear to have to face some issues without others' assistance, at least at certain stages or moments of life. By examining the thoughts of some of the greatest thinkers in human history, by coming across some of the prominent systems of thought —or the rejection of the very idea of systems of thought—we are able to face the moments with a bit more strength and even with independence.

By now the reader can tell that philosophy is not an idle game for the clever. It need not be dull, of course, nor morbid. However, it is essentially serious. If what I have attempted to make clear in these last paragraphs is even partly true, then it seems that all cultures and the lives of all people have been under the influence of philosophical activities. For better or for worse, people live with or produce philosophical answers. That itself would be reason enough for someone who cares about life to give philosophy some attention. With these preliminary investigations the task should no longer seem so strange and confusing. It may even turn out to be a welcome adventure.

Glossary

The following terms are important within the field of philosophy. Some occur within the text and others are very likely to be used in philosophical articles and books, both classical and modern.

Absolutism. The general view that true statements must be unchangeable, final, and complete. Also used to characterize any view of reality regarded as final and incontrovertibly correct.

Abstract. Any term used to mean a group united by common features, several of a kind, nonspecific; opposed to concrete (individual or particular). Ideas are abstract because they apply to more than one of a kind, but names are concrete because they designate an individual or a particular being.

Aesthetics. The branch of philosophy concerned with the study of the nature of art and the standards to be used in evaluating artistic creations.

Agnosticism. The view that it is impossible to prove and know either that God exists or that Goes does not exist.

Altruism. The moral or ethical position according to which each person's proper goal in life is to further the interest(s) or happiness of other people.

Ambiguous. Applied to a term or an idea that can be used to mean two or more significantly different kinds of things, etc.

Amoralism. The position about the nature of human conduct according to which there is no moral difference between various kinds of actions, institutions, and the like. Science is often held to be amoral (or value-free).

Analogy. A type of reasoning such that if two or more items (things, actions, etc.) resemble each other in some respects, it is likely that they will resemble each other in other respects, also.

Analytic statement. The kind of statement that, according to certain philosophical positions, is true because the ideas contained in it mean what they do, and for no other reason.

Anarchism. The doctrine that holds that government is either unnecessary or actually inescapably immoral; the rejection of political communities. Anarchists may advocate certain types of human associations but not a legal or political system.

Antecedent. The first portion of a conditional or hypothetical statement; e.g., "If man is rational, then he has free will" has "man is rational" as the antecedent.

A posteriori. In characterizing statements: those whose truth could be known only after having experienced the facts that make them true. When used about facts: those that could be known only after being experienced.

A priori. In characterizing statements: those whose truth could be known without reliance on information gained from experience. When used about facts: those that could be known without reliance on experience.

Argument. A systematic development of support in behalf of some statement, claim, or theory.

Aristocracy. An organized human community governed by a group of individuals considered to be the morally outstanding members. Sometimes used to mean a community ruled by the refined and well-bred members.

Atheism. Disbelief or denial of ground for belief in a supreme being or God; denial that anything of the sort God is supposed to be exists.

Authoritarianism. The political system in which the laws (which, unlike the laws in totalitarianism, may have limited scope) gain their binding character because a person or group of people declared them binding. The view that a statement is true because a certain person asserts it.

Autonomy. The condition of having sole authority to make decisions pertaining to one's life, especially one's morally relevant conduct.

Axiom. A statement whose truth cannot be denied (within some domain of knowledge) without undermining the entire domain. A self-evident or obvious truth.

Behaviorism. The view, especially in psychology and theories of human action, that only those features of human affairs are real that involve the behavior of the organism, the overt movements of our bodies. Also the view that nonobservable aspects of human life may exist but are irrelevant to a scientific study of human beings.

Category. A group or class for which a clear place exists within the system of ideas or language we use to think and communicate; classifications into which a system of ideas is divided. A place in a system (of language, science, organization) clearly specified on the basis of the appropriate rules of division. "To fit into a category" is to have a precise place within an organization or system of diverse membership.

Categorical imperative. A moral law or supreme duty that is supposed to hold without qualification; the central moral law in the ethical theory of the philosopher Immanuel Kant. A type of moral judgment distinguished from those we state in terms of an "If . . . then. . . ." proposition or hypothesis.

Categorical statement. An unqualified statement; the simple type of assertion that is used in syllogistic arguments.

Circular argument. An argument in which the conclusion is supported with premises that contain the conclusion itself. A case of begging the question.

Circular definition. An attempted definition in which the statement that is supposed to define an idea or a term contains the idea or term being defined (explicitly or hidden).

Class. Either a naturally or an objectively justifiable grouping of items, or an artificially arranged group suited for some special purpose (which may or may not itself be justified). Consider also the idea of classification or categorization. In Marxism: economic group.

Cognition. The act of awareness, of obtaining knowledge, or of knowing. All mental aspects of the knowing process are involved in cognition.

Coherence theory. The position that holds that the truth of any statement is to be established by reference to whether the statement fits within the whole network of our judgments without inconsistency. As in "This is a coherent position."

Collectivism. The general term for those political systems which focus on the concerns and welfare of groups, the duties we have to them, and the authority and responsibility the group has over the individual.

Communism. A collectivist social system without government.

Concept. An idea or abstraction produced by thought, by the mental activity of integration (bringing items together) and differentiation (distinguishing items from one another), based on observation or thinking. Concepts are what we use to think abstractly, about things or items of a kind, whereas percepts are what we obtain by observing individual or particular items. As in "Our concept of government" or "The updated concept of the atom."

Confirm. To produce evidence that serves to give (usually conclusive) support for a theory or supposition. As in "My suspicions—that is, theory or hypothesis—were confirmed when we examined the evidence."

Consequent. The second portion of a conditional or hypothetical statement; e.g., "If man is rational, then he has free will" has "he has free will" as its consequent.

Conservatism. The approach to social and political affairs in terms of which what has lasted for some time as a feature of a human community is worth preserving. An emphasis on what the community's traditions contain. Conservatism does not itself propose any principles of political organization but concentrates on the method for identifying the principles worthy of preservation.

Contextualism. The epistemological view that to know that something is the case one must possess the best possible support for the belief in question, with "best possible support" specified in terms of the highest level of development of human understanding regarding the area of the subject matter and other relevant factors.

Continuum. A gradually changing range of different items (alternatives) between some point of beginning and a very different end.

Contradiction. Logical incongruity; when two statements are held to be true concerning some item and the first asserts what the second denies or vice versa. As in "Dogs bark and dogs do not bark" or "It is a sunny day and it is not a sunny day." (Since a contradiction is rarely uttered in the same breath, the examples here seem unrealistic.)

Contrary. The relationship that exists between two statements when the truth of one implies the falsity of the other while the falsity of either does not guarantee either the truth or falsity of the other. As in "The dog barks, so it is not silent; but the dog is not silent, so we don't know whether it barks, howls, or whines."

Correspondence theory. The position that holds that the truth of any statement is to be established by reference to whether the statement correctly identifies a fact of reality, that is, whether it fits (corresponds to) the facts.

Cosmology. A branch of metaphysics concerned with the origin, character, and development of the universe.

Counterexample. A fact supposedly explained by a theory that serves to show that the theory is inadequate because it does not manage to explain the fact in point.

Criterion. A basis or ground that serves as the standard by which the applicability or value of something is to be judged. As in "The Playmate of the year is his criterion for femininity" or "His criticism was based on an inappropriate criterion of excellence."

Cynicism. A doubtful, even belittling outlook on the supposition that values could be achieved or could even be important to strive for. Demeaning toward ideals.

Deduction. A form of reasoning by means of valid argumentation. Sometimes held to be the only kind of completely valid reasoning, as opposed to induction, which is said to yield only probable conclusions based on the evidence used to support them.

Definition. A statement of the essential features (or attributes, characteristics, properties, aspects) of the items referred to or correctly meant by the idea or term being defined. A statement of the nature of something. The statement of the necessary and sufficient requirements for something being what it is. (There are different theories of what definitions are.)

Deism. The view that God is the cause of the world but outside of that he takes no part in it. The God of deism is indifferent and incapable of having any effect on or relationship to the world now.

Determinism. The view that everything that occurs in the universe must be the effect of some cause, must be produced, is dependent on and conditioned by what brought it into existence. Some determinists specify the character of the causes to be events. Others leave open the issue of what kinds and types of things could be the causes of the events that must have a cause. Quite often determinism is thought to contradict the view that human beings are free or can choose their own actions. But self-determinism is not contradicted by determinism. It is contradicted by predeterminism and fatalism.

Dialectic. Reasoning so as to establish truth by questioning and testing answers by sustained scrutiny through counterexamples. In the writings of Hegel and Marx, the dialectic principle characterizes the process by which reality, including social affairs, develops toward perfection (e.g., the communist society).

Dichotomy. A relationship that characterizes two classes of items (statements, entities, events) that are mutually exclusive. As in the (alleged) dichotomy between values and facts.

Differentiation. Mental classification of items by reference to observed or otherwise established qualities they do not share. Establishing the existence of a difference. Upholding a difference.

Dilemma. A situation in which one must choose between alternatives, with equally forceful reasons for both choices. As in moral dilemmas, where mutually exclusive courses of conduct are equally obligatory.

Disjunctive statement. A proposition that, when true, has segments which cannot all be false. Thus, if the disjunctive statement "He is either rich or poor" is true, it could not be the case that he was of moderate but adequate means—he has to be *either* rich *or* poor.

Distributed.   When terms in a statement are used to refer to all items they could mean; when the terms are fully extended over their referent class. As in "All students are people," where "students" is distributed since *all* are referred to.

Dogmatism.   An approach to theories, viewpoints, doctrines, and the like that rejects the need to subject them to examination, scrutiny, tests, confirmation, or criticism but rests satisfied by simply asserting that they (or at least their basic features) are true beyond question.

Dual aspect theory.   The view of the relationship between body and mind in terms of which the mind is an aspect or objective (or real) characteristic of the human organism (specifically the brain).

Dualism.   The view that reality consists of two separable and fundamentally different irreducible realms of being or type of stuff or substance. Sometimes used to refer to any view that permits the possibility that both body and mind (or matter and spirit) exist in the universe, however they are related to each other as long as they are not the same thing.

Egoism.   In ethics, the view that each person should act so as to achieve his or her happiness; the doctrine that rational self-interest is the proper goal of human conduct. Sometimes taken to be the view that everyone should (or even necessarily must) follow his or her desires of satisfaction, pleasure, enjoyment, etc.

Emotivism.   The position about the nature of ethical judgments in terms of which these are either expressions of one's emotions and/or efforts to create certain emotions (pro or con) toward something in those who are being addressed with the judgment. Denies that ethical judgments could be either true or false.

Empiricism.   The position in epistemology that knowledge must always be of sensory experience, that only when one can derive all of what one claims to know from such experience could it be true that one does in fact know. Less strictly, empiricism emphasizes the role of sensory observation in efforts to obtain knowledge.

Epistemology.   The branch of philosophy that studies the nature of knowledge.

Equivocation.   The mixing up of two different senses of a word so that a point is established that may otherwise be unsupportable.

Essence.   The aspects or features of something without which it would not be what it is. As in "The essence of love is admiration coupled with intense loyalty and intimacy." If the statement is false, then love could exist, but not as characterized by the above features; if true, all love must exhibit them.

Ethics.   The branch of philosophy in which the nature of the good life for human beings is studied.

Existential statement. A statement that asserts the existence of some thing or some fact. A claim asserting the objective reality of something.

Existentialism. A philosophical position that stresses the importance of attending to a person's concrete existence instead of attending to abstract systems concerning man and reality. It denies the existence of human nature and emphasizes each person's freedom to choose what he will be. It also proclaims that while we cannot know what we should do, we are nevertheless responsible for what we choose as if we had spoken for all of mankind by our choice. Much of existentialism is communicated through literature instead of systematic philosophical discussion.

Faith. Belief in something that is neither self-evident nor demonstrable, i.e., not provable.

Fallacy. Reasoning that does not accord with the appropriate rules or that violates them.

Fatalism. The position that what will occur, is now happening, or has happened has at the outset or beginning of existence been fixed (programmed?). Destined.

Form. The structure, character, or essence of something as contrasted with or distinct from its matter or stuff. In Plato's philosophy forms are the immaterial, nonspatiotemporal, fixed ideas (definitions, natures, essences) that exist in the truly real realm of intelligible things. In Aristotle's philosophy that which makes something what it is—its essence, nature, or definition; the form of something is distinguishable but inseparable from the thing (activity, event, object, entity) itself. (We can *distinguish* the shape of a chair from its materials but we cannot *separate* the two.)

Formal. Pertaining to structure or character. In logic the formal features of arguments involve the logical principles exhibited, independent of the content of the argument.

Free will. Human freedom of choice. The ability human beings have to cause (will) some of their actions on their own.

Freedom. Either the capacity to choose or the condition to implement one's choice without interference from others (political liberty). Sometimes used in "I am free of trouble" and thus meant to indicate the absence of obstruction or impediments from within (ignorance, psychological blocks, or physical disease) or without (limits set by human beings or other natural forces).

Function. The role or place something has in a system that could be either designed (purposive) or determined independent of human choice. As in "The function of the police is to keep the peace" or "The function of the heart is to pump blood."

Generalization.   A statement based on information about some members of a class of items but applied to all or most members of the class.   As in "Hungarians are medium-height people" based on information about an adequate sample of Hungarians who fit the characterization.

Genus.   A class of items further divided into distinct groups (species). In "Human beings are rational animals" "animal" is the genus and "rational (animals)" the species.

Hard determinism.   The view that from the outset in existence everything was set into motion in a precise, strictly governed fashion (either by God or by necessary laws of reality).

Hasty generalization.   A statement about all or most members of a class based on limited or inadequate information obtained by encountering a few members.

Hedonism.   In ethics, the position that each person's moral responsibility is to seek to obtain as much pleasure and as little pain as possible.

Humanism.   The view in terms of which the ideals to pursue are identified by reference to human potential—either individual or collective.   In Marxism, humanism signifies the progress of mankind toward the full realization of human essence (in communism).

Hypothesis.   A statement suggested as possibly true based either on some evidence or on imagination alone.   In science many hypotheses are considered in order to test and discover what in fact is the case, what explanation is correct, or what theory is true.

Hypothetical syllogism.   A type of argument, though not strictly syllogistic, with conditional premises.   For example, "If horses are speedy runners, and if speedy runners are dangerous, then horses are dangerous."

Idealism.   The position in terms of which reality consists of mental elements alone—ideas, images, mind, spirit, soul, etc.

Identify.   To learn or establish (by various appropriate means) what something is.

Identity.   The condition of being something specific, determinate (not necessarily determin*ed*!); to have a specific nature is to have some identity.   Identity is a very basic attribute of anything so that it is not easily defined without an entire system.   The Law of Identity is the principle of existence or reality in terms of which whatever exists must be a specific something, a thing of some kind.   The law is also fundamental in the science of logic.

Idol.   Something intensely admired, usually without merit for it.   False god.

Immanent.   Immersed in something; inherent; dwelling within.   If God, for example, is immanent, he would be in everything all at once.

Implication.   In logic the relationship that holds between the premises and the conclusion of valid arguments; thus "A is B," and "B is C" *imply* that "A is C."

Indeterminism.   The view that there are some events that are not caused and are random.

Induction.   A method of reasoning from premises to conclusions in which the conclusions may turn out to be false even though the premises support them, and where the premises usually consist of statements about particular facts, whereas the conclusions tend to go beyond the knowledge of these particular facts to broad generalizations.   The bulk of scientific research, detective work, and the like involves inductive reasoning, although both of these fields involve a good deal of deductive reasoning as well.

Inference.   The mental act of affirming that some belief, conclusion, theory, or statement is warranted or justified by reference to available information.   As in "From the evidence he discovered, the detective inferred that the butler did it."   Or "From 'As are Bs' and 'Bs are Cs,' I inferred 'As are Cs.' "

Innate ideas.   Judgments supposedly true and known as such by a rigorous inspection of our own minds, without reliance on evidence from the sense organs.

Introspection.   The mental act of awareness of one's own emotional states or mental processes.   As in "By introspection I became aware of my feelings for him."

Intuition.   In some philosophical theories, a special type of awareness or knowledge.   Also used to mean being aware of something without knowing how the awareness came about or how to justify or prove the content of one's awareness.   Intuitive awareness is often regarded as coming about very rapidly.   Also, knowing from habit or practical, unexamined familiarity.

Judgment.   The mental act of forming a belief, conclusion, or opinion.

Justification.   The act of providing (good) reasons for one's conduct, including what one has concluded about something.   As "He was perfectly justified in breaking off the relationship" or "He had an excellent justification for what he said (believed) about Harry."

Laissez faire.   The term that in French means "let do" or "let act," usually applied to the economic system of a society where trade, commerce, production, etc., are conducted free of governmental interference.   Free enterprise capitalism, based on private ownership of goods and services.

Liberalism.   In "classical liberalism," the social / political theory in terms of which human beings are understood to be capable of free choice and most reliable about matters of self-improvement and the improvement of their community.   In "modern liberalism," the social / political theory in terms of which human beings ought to utilize the central authority of their community's laws so as to improve on the general well-being of the members of the society.

Libertarianism.   The social / political theory in terms of which each person should enjoy freedom from the forcible imposition of others either because no one can know what others should do, or because forcing others to do what is right makes them incapable of moral responsibility of their own.   The central principle is that no one ought to force his or her ways on another person or another's property.   Libertarianism either rejects all government or considers government an agency established so as to provide the sole service of protecting and preserving the liberty of every member of the community.

Libertarianism (metaphysical).   The view that there exist uncaused events in nature.   Sometimes used to characterize all views that uphold the freedom of human beings to choose their own conduct.

Linguistic analysis.   The philosophical school or approach in which the method of solving philosophical problems is detailed and careful investigation of the meanings and / or implications of the terms used in language.   Some varieties of this approach require the translation of all common terms into artificial (symbolically expressed) languages.   Some require the study of language as it is used in ordinary discussions.   While often claimed to be philosophically neutral, the approach can be traced to various philosophical theories.

Logic.   The system of principles of correct thinking to be used in obtaining and testing knowledge.   Often used for purposes other than learning, as in the construction of logical games, artificial (formal) systems, etc.

Logical atomism.   The philosophical view that in reality there exist only tiny, individual, isolated items that are constructed into systems by the employment of the rules of logic.   These systems are *the world* for us.

Logical empiricism.   The view that the crucial task of philosophy is to discover the proper way to fix the meaning of terms in the language.   There are only two possible ways that terms can be meaningful, according to this school: by being open to verification via sensory experience (observation) and by occupying a place in a system of meanings (determined by logical analysis).

Machiavellian.   An adjective used to characterize conduct that is shrewdly and carefully scheming; based, very loosely, on the doctrine of Niccolo Machiavelli (1469–1527), a political thinker from Florence, who argued that political leaders (monarchs, especially) ought to abandon Christian morality when in office and use power as harshly as needed but always subtly, because that is the only way to keep a country independent, free, and stable.

Materialism. The metaphysical position that all of what exists consists of matter (physical stuff) or that all events are explainable in terms of (caused by) matter in motion, material factors.

Metaethics. The branch of epistemology concerned with the nature of ethical judgments and the meaning of ethical terms. In contemporary philosophy discussions of ethics and metaethics are usually combined.

Metaphysics. The branch of philosophy concerned with identifying and investigating the nature of reality, that is, the most fundamental aspects of existence. The term *metaphysics* means "beyond physics" but this does not accurately explain the field itself even though sometimes that is used to help explain it. "First philosophy" is the most accurate rendition of the meaning Aristotle, one of the most detailed metaphysicians of ancient times, would have wanted to convey by the term *metaphysics,* which was the title given to his studies in the field. Sometimes, very misleadingly, considered to mean occult, supernatural, or mystical fields of concern.

Mind. The aspect or feature of a thinking being (one that is conscious or aware by use of ideas, concepts) which carries out the functions required for intellectual or conceptual awareness of reality. Human reason; reason; the faculty of rational thought and awareness.

Miracle. An event for which no rational, natural explanation is possible; something that is fundamentally mysterious but has an effect on nature in defiance of known and possible natural laws. An event to be explained by reference to supernatural or divine intervention.

Monarchy. A political system of single and complete authority and sovereignty. A system of government in which one person establishes laws. Sometimes a system of government in which a single person stands as a figurehead but does not actually possess decisive authority.

Monism. The metaphysical position that there exists one, unified reality of which the particular things and groups or kinds of things are continuous, integrated features, parts, aspects, etc.

Monotheism. The doctrine that there exists one single God.

Moral code. A system of principles concerning what every and any individual should use as general guidelines so as to live a good human life.

Morality. The sphere of human concern where moral codes are considered of great importance. The field of philosophy where various answers to "How ought human beings live in view of the fact that they are human?" are examined and evaluated. The branch of philosophy called *ethics*.

Mores. Well-established social rules usually upheld by custom and public pressure.

Mysticism. The approach to or view of life in terms of which reality—or true reality, highest being—is known or experienced by way of nonrational or nonscientific means. Sometimes mysticism is held to be unexpressible, incapable of being spoken about, ineffable—at least the mystical aspects of reality and life are held to be so. Sometimes mysticism involves the view that no individual minds (or even bodies) exist but everyone is one being (at least in the state of full realization). Often associated primarily with Eastern philosophy and religion but part of virtually any culture's religious heritage.

National Socialism. The political system in terms of which socialism should be confined to the sphere of a given nation. The general designation of the political system in which the Nazis held power. Fascism (which is less directly socialist) is frequently substituted for national socialism as the more accurate description of social and political affairs in historically Nazi regimes.

Nationalism. The political attitude (more than viewpoint) that the obligation of every citizen is to be fully loyal to his country above all else.

Nationalization. An act of government to expropriate the belongings of private individuals and put these under governmental management. Usually applied to the expropriation of large firms.

Natural law. Either the body of laws (principles) that govern the actions of things incapable of choice or the laws that should govern human conduct. Laws of nature and moral laws that exist independently of the desires, wishes, or decisions of human beings.

Natural right. In classical moral philosophy, any *moral* principle to be identified by reference to the nature of man and his community. In modern *political* philosophy, any principle of social conduct or relations allegedly universally applicable because of the nature of human beings. Thus, the right to life, liberty, or the pursuit of happiness was held by John Locke to be a natural right; judging by human nature it is right that each person in society be protected against intervention into or abridgment of living, acting, or pursuing well-being. More recently referred to as human rights. Also recently expanded to include rights not directly justified by reference to the nature of human beings. (Contrast the three rights referred to in the Declaration of Independence with the many rights listed in the United Nations Charter "Universal Declaration of the Rights of Man.")

Naturalism. In metaphysics, the position that whatever exists is part of one, knowable, scientifically accessible existence. In metaethics, the view that it is possible to acquire knowledge of answers to ethical questions by means used in other fields of study. Sometimes held to be the view that everything that exists can be known by way of sensory experience alone. In ethics, the view that holds that the answers to questions about proper human conduct must be obtained by a study of human nature; or that "good" is definable by reference to sensible facts. (Also the term used to designate a belief in the superiority of wildlife as opposed to civil society, technology, etc.)

Neo-Platonism. Any more or less faithful later variety of the philosophy Plato developed; theories with an essentially Platonist emphasis.

Nihilism. The doctrine that there are no values or that the alleged values are sham and should be abolished. Often considered a prerequisite of a better culture to come out of the ruins of a culture with (false) moralities that are artificial, stultifying, and limiting.

Nominalism. The theory that words are names for more or less arbitrarily but habitually grouped items. Nominally: in name (as distinguished from: by necessity); by assignment of the name.

Normative. The characteristic of judgments that are made to express what is considered right or wrong, good or bad.

Noumenon. In the philosophy of Kant, the being of something as it exists within itself, independently of what it is *for us,* what it *appears* to be. Thought by Kant to be inaccessible to human knowledge since the process of knowing something prevents us from being in contact with it as it really is.

Objective. The characteristic of judgments or statements in terms of which they must be capable of proof or support based on what is actual, real, and independent of our wishes, decisions, or desires.

Objectivism. The philosophical position that what exists does not constitute part of human invention, creation, or wishing but is independent of these. In epistemology: the view that knowledge must be based on evidence or reasoning involving facts and principles not invented but discovered. In ethics: the view that moral judgments must be founded on objective facts. Sometimes used to refer to any view that considers as meaningful only those judgments and theories that can be confirmed by sensory evidence. (Also the philosophical system developed by Ayn Rand.)

Ontological argument. A case for the existence of God based on the type of entity God is supposed to be, namely, supremely perfect.

Ontology. The branch of metaphysics that studies the types of being there are or could be. Also the study of the basic kinds of items in reality.

Onus of proof. The burden of having to provide the proof for some claim.

Opinion. A serious, but admittedly weakly or slightly supported, judgment about something.

Ostensive definition. The establishing of the essential meaning of a term by way of offering directly observable examples of what it means. Definition by direct indication or pointing.

Pacifism. An ethical (and political) doctrine in terms of which forcible action, or violence, is never justified. Pacific: peaceful.

Pantheism. The theistic view that God is an essential part of everything. The position that God and nature are one and the same.

Paradox. A case in which two positions on some topic exclude each other but appear equally plausible or well justified. Any position that gives rise to paradoxes has to be revised so as to eliminate them; otherwise, it ends in inconsistency.

Parsimony, principle of. Using the fewest and least complicated assumptions possible to explain anything.

Paternalism. A conception of government that ascribes to it caretaker responsibilities. Any political system in terms of which the law and its administrators must act as moral and / or economic supervisors of the citizenry. View of the state as father.

Perception. The mental act of becoming aware of some particular event or object.

Phenomenon. Anything as it appears to consciousness as opposed to what it might be in itself. Thought by Kant to be the only aspect of reality capable of being known by us.

Platonism. The philosophy associated with Plato. It emphasizes the superior status of the intellectual (ideal, spiritual) realm of reality.

Polytheism. The view that there exist more gods than one.

Positivism. In epistemology the view that we can only know what is observable by sense organs. The view in terms of which metaphysics is impossible. In ethics and politics the position that judgments concerning right and wrong cannot be shown to be true or false. In the philosophy of law the view that there exists no other source of binding law than what is contained in documents produced by governments. A view opposed to natural law. Sometimes used to indicate that a theory, idea, or viewpoint is imposed upon the raw data of sense, or posited—constructed rather than discovered to exist independently of the mind. Sometimes used to indicate the crucial role of empirical evidence within a field (e.g., positive economics).

Post hoc, ergo propter hoc. Literally translated: "after something; therefore, because of it." A fallacious inference because it assumes that succession in time is identical to causal interaction.

Postulate. A hypothesis or suggestion. We often postulate that something is so and so to see whether we could thereby make sense of or explain something we know to be the case.

Pragmatism. The philosophy in terms of which there are no objective (ultimate) principles of existence, knowledge, or value but only practical consequences in terms of which these make sense. Truth, then, is determined by what works out in practice. Fundamental principles in both metaphysics and ethics are always relative to some concern or inquiry, never permanent and independent of the inquirer.

Predestination. The view that whatever occurs has been so determined or willed by God.

Predicate. The term in a proposition used to state something about the subject. In "Politicians are powerful" the predicate is "powerful."

Prejudgment (prejudice). A judgment offered prior to obtaining the evidence that would justify it. Sometimes used to indicate judgments based on irrelevant information (as in condemning a person for having black skin, when in fact this is not something wrong, nor anything one can determine) .

Premise. A statement offered in support of a conclusion. The first two statements in a syllogistic argument.

Probability. Chance; likelihood. The degree of support for some belief or statement. As in "The probability is 50–50 that the road is washed out by now." Sometimes it is suggested that reality itself contains probabilistic states, that some facts are intrinsically probabilistic. Also, a field of mathematics that studies degrees of chance or possibility.

Process metaphysics. The metaphysical view that the basic material of reality is process, event, or occasion. The position developed most fully by the philosopher Alfred North Whitehead.

Proof. A valid argument in support of some statement, belief, or theory. Usually held to be possible only in connection with deductive arguments but views vary about whether valid inductive arguments are possible.

Property. In metaphysics, an attribute, quality, feature, or aspect of something. In political theory and economics, the items that can be owned by people.

Proposition. A statement, claim, or assertion. There are simple and complex and many other kinds of propositions that can be categorized within a system of propositions (e.g., formal, propositional calculus).

Quality. In logic, the negative or affirmative feature of a proposition. In metaphysics, used to refer to features of items such as shapes, color, size, etc. Also used to speak of the magnitude of the value of something.

Quantifier.   The "all," "no," and "some" terms that precede statements in arguments.   In "All men are mortal" the "all" is the quantifier. In mathematical logic: "(x)" and "$(\exists\, x)$."

Rationalism.   The epistemological position that the source of knowledge must ultimately be precisely thought-out ideas. The view that we can obtain knowledge by unaided reason.   Also the conception of knowledge as comparable to mathematical truth or formal logical reasoning.   Usually based on the metaphysical view that material things are inferior, even less than real, too changeable to qualify as objects of knowledge.   In political theory, the view that the state should be constructed in terms of progressive principles that aim to upgrade the society.   In ethics, see *Objectivism*.

Rationality.   The feature of human consciousness in terms of which people are capable of awareness of reality by the use of ideas, concepts, theories, systems, etc.   The view that human beings have this capacity is independent of the special doctrine of rationalism.   It is often thought that rationality must be in conflict with human emotions.   This view is a consequence of certain philosophical theories and not necessarily implied by the rationality of human beings.

Rationalization.   The act of feigning or pretending to have reasons for what one has done or is doing (where in fact one does not know or acted from impulse).   Often confused with reasoning, especially because some psychologists argue that there is no difference—as if we always simply invented reasons for our beliefs and actions.

Realism.   The metaphysical position that reality exists independently of human consciousness (of it).   In epistemology, the view that what we perceive and know exists just as we see and know it and is not *conditioned* by our way of perceiving and knowing it.

Reason.   The human faculty of awareness by way of concepts, ideas, etc., as abstracted from perceptions by way of differentiation and integration (noticing differences and similarities).

Reductio ad absurdum.   Showing a position absurd by proving that if it were true, something absurd would follow.   A way of arguing that is very frequent in philosophy, logic, mathematics, and law.

Reductionism.   A position which holds that by analysis we can show that there is just one kind of thing, event, or item in existence even though it appears in a variety of ways.   By reducing the appearances through analysis of the elements, we can reach the reality that underlies them all.   This reality could be pure matter, pure mind, God, souls, mathematical principles, etc.   Reductionism does not presuppose what the ultimate and only kind of existence is. One could advocate reductive materialism, reductive idealism, etc.

Reductive materialism. The metaphysical view that reality is composed only of bits of matter in motion and everything that does not appear to be material can, in time, be fully understood as varieties of such matters.

Referent. The item being referred to by a word, symbol, sign, etc.

Refutation. The act of demonstrating that some claim, statement, or theory has not been proved true. A refutation need not involve showing the falsity of some view, although this could be part of it.

Relativism. The epistemological view that our knowledge is always what it is in terms of some conditions; that our judgments are true or false as related to some framework that governs them (our economic condition, culture, religion, race, age, sex, epoch, climate, etc.). In ethics, the view that what is morally right and wrong is always related to some conditions, etc. The idea that there is nothing firm, fixed, objective, or certain.

Revelation. A means of obtaining knowledge whereby God designates someone for special communication or witness of certain events. It is crucial about such knowledge that human beings cannot obtain it for themselves, with just their own efforts.

Right. A condition justified either by law or by moral argument. As in "I have a right to vote because the Constitution states so" or "I have a right to know because you promised to tell (and promises ought to be fulfilled)." More generally, right means correct, true, or proper in its various contexts. See also *Natural right*.

Rightist. A rather vague term used to designate those whose political views tend toward the authoritarian and are often based on religious doctrine. Favoring spiritual, moral, and legal discipline and strict order. Sometimes used to designate conservatives. In the United States, often used to designate those who favor traditional (American) political principles. In general, the term does not specify political persuasions, so that there could be rightist democrats, communists, socialists, etc.

Scientific method. Generally held to be the strict observance of rules of evidence and reasoning in an effort to identify facts about a certain realm of reality. The rules are often thought to involve careful sensory observation, experimentation, use of statistical theory, etc. However, some sciences may employ the scientific method without making use of the same rules as other sciences. Broadly: precise, careful, systematic study of a special area of reality.

Scientism. The viewpoint that knowledge can be obtained only through the scientific method. Usually this view accepts a somewhat restricted conception of the scientific method, namely, that only information based on sensory observation may be used to develop scientific theories and conclusions. The view tends also to reject the idea that philosophy can produce knowledge. Metaphysics, ethics, and political theory are also rejected by scientism (unless they are interpreted as dealing only with describable facts) .

Self-determinism. The version of determinism applied to human action in terms of which (some of) what human beings do is or can be caused by them. The idea that some of the things people do are up to them. When the nature of the self, what each individual uniquely is as a person, is specified, the view traces the cause of human conduct to people's essential characteristic(s).

Self-evident. A characteristic of statements whose truth is determinable or provable simply by understanding them. A characteristic of facts whose existence need not be demonstrated or proved. A characteristic of statements whose truth can be denied only at the cost of immediate absurdity. In Descartes's philosophy, "It is false that I think" would be the denial of "I think" and would thus be immediately absurd, since "I think" is a self-evidently true statement whenever uttered. Sometimes said of any obvious truth.

Selfishness. Often used to characterize a concern only for one's shallow gain, immediate benefit, and satisfaction of desires. Strictly speaking, selfishness is a concern for what is (in fact) one's best, ultimate interest or benefit, what is good for oneself. The attitude encouraged by ethical egoism (when taken in the second, broad sense).

Self-realization. In ethics, the view that the moral good of every person consists in achieving his or her greatest potential. In some ethical theories the nature of the self (human nature) is specified and principles can therefore be identified so as to guide one toward self-realization. In some recent (existentialist-oriented) psychological theories a person achieves full mental health by striving for self-realization.

Semantics. The study of meanings, their alterations, the linguistic aspects of thought and communication. Often used to indicate a concern for words as signs or symbols. As in "It is a matter of semantics" or "The peculiarities of English semantics."

Sensationalism. The epistemological view that whatever is known consists of sensory impressions, sensations, sensory experiences, the data of the senses, etc. Sometimes used to designate the view whereby true statements refer to or name (composites of) sensory impressions, and meaningful statements are those that could be true statements of this kind (so that we can specify what it would take for them to be true by reference to the possibility of such sense impressions). An extreme version of empiricism.

Sense datum. A bit of sensation of which sense experience consists. Sense impression: a bit of experience impressed upon the senses.

Skepticism. The view that knowledge is not possible (pure skepticism). Mitigated skepticism denies that certain knowledge is possible. Other varieties of skepticism argue that no one ever knows anything. Sometimes used to designate religious doubting.

Socialism. The economic and political system with full or partial central regulation and ownership of the productive factors within a geographic area. In Marxist socialism the regulators and owners would have to be members and representatives of the working class. Generally, the existing government's regulation and nationalization of all major industries exemplifies a socialist system. In Marxism, the science of society as well as a stage in revolutionary social development preceding communist society.

Soft determinism. The view that human action is determined by human will and choice, and that human will and choice are themselves shaped by factors outside human control.

Solipsism. The metaphysical view that only I (as stated by any solipsist) exist and that all else is dependent for its being on and reducible to my being. Sometimes used to characterize a radically egocentric, introspective, antisocial conception of life.

Sophist. One who advances intricate, clever, and sometimes purposefully deceptive arguments that are actually unsound but tend to persuade initially.

Sophistry. A turn of reasoning characteristic of sophists. Sometimes sophistry is playful, sometimes vicious, and sometimes desperate; disguised fallaciousness as a characteristic.

Sorites. A chain of syllogistic argument with the conclusion stated but some premises left unstated.

Species. One group of members within a larger or additional class (kind). As chairs are a species of furniture.

Statism. Political theories according to which the individual member of a community is a part of the most important being of concern— the complete, whole, living, and subordinating community.

Stipulation. The act of assigning a meaning to some word or thing, usually provisionally and without implying that there is justification for doing so. As in "Let's call this a horse" even though it isn't one and may even be a sofa. Sometimes definitions are stipulated, as in "Let's accept that a horse is a long-legged jumping bear," although there is no justification for this and it may have to be withdrawn. Some views hold that all meanings and definitions are stipulated.

Stoicism. The ethical position that virtue is achieved through inner calm and contentment and worldly items ought not to be pursued for purposes of attainment of the good life. Thus, stoics are those, in ordinary discourse, who are able and willing to stand pain and misery and who do not become excited about pleasure and good fortune.

Subject. That about which something is claimed in a statement. In "Politicians are powerful" the subject term is "politicians." A person. Self.

Subjectivism. In epistemology, the view that what is known is conditioned by the individual who knows it. Generally, the view that things exist in relationship to minds (or, in subjective idealism, to one mind). In ethics, the view that what is right or wrong is determined by the will of one who is making the evaluation. Often certain philosophical trends are called subjectivist—e.g., existentialism and Eastern mysticism—because their focus is more or exclusively on the personal, introspective experiences of human beings rather than on systematic worldviews, all of reality, the external world.

Syllogism. A form of reasoning whereby some judgment is shown to be the logical, rational consequence of bringing two others together in mind. Thus, if one considers that all men are mortal and that some politicians are men, then it follows that some politicians are mortal.

Synthetic statement or judgment. One in which what is said could be proved true only by using sensory evidence. Often used in philosophy and other fields where systematic inquiry is carried out as if it were quite obvious that these sorts of statements are easily distinguished from analytic ones. Yet it is a controversial distinction that requires elaborate theoretical justification.

Tautology. Ordinarily a redundant statement, such as "All circles are round." Strictly true by virtue of logical form; technically a truth function that, when it is put on a truth table, is shown to have the value "true" regardless of the possible truth values taken by the propositions of its argument.

Teleology. The framework for explaining all or some events in the universe by reference to purposes, goals, design, or intention. Sometimes it is held that while human action must be explained teleologically—i.e., with reference to purposes and intentions—other events cannot be so explained. The view that there is room for purposive explanation and action in nature.

Theism. Any view in which the existence of one or more deities is defended and made central. Christianity is a form of theism.

Theology. The study of the nature of God. Approaches to philosophy in which the existence and nature of God are fundamental.

Theorem. A statement in a formal system that is implicit in the basic principles of the system.

Theory. A network of systematically related ideas and statements that explains and renders understandable some realm or area of reality.

Totalitarianism. The form of human community in which all (or nearly all) activities of the members are directly governed (regulated or controlled) by those designated as administrators and executors of the legal system.

Transcendent. What is beyond, overarching everything else. God, if not inherent in everything, is often said to be transcendent or above everything.

Tyranny. A regime in which a corrupt person rules solely by force.

Utilitarianism. The ethical position that holds the greatest satisfaction of the greatest number of people as the primary moral goal for each individual.

Utility calculus. The system whereby the rules of utilitarianism are worked out according to the measurement of the satisfaction produced by various (kinds of) actions. A system of measuring utility. Often suggested as the method by which to achieve the goals of the welfare state.

Utopia. Literally: No place. The perfect human community as conceived in terms of certain political theories. Sometimes a model to be used as a standard for conduct, sometimes a goal to be achieved.

Validity. A property of correct reasoning such that in a valid argument if the premises are true, the conclusion would have to be true.

Verification. Establishing the truth of some claim by making sure of it, i.e., obtaining the information firsthand that will show it to be true. Usually associated with showing something true by observation or testing.

Vicious circle. A fallacious method of arguing whereby one relies on premises to prove a conclusion that is already required for proving some of the premises used to prove it.

Virtues. Qualities of a person required so as to lead the morally good life. Morally good character traits.

Voluntarism. Any social system where nonaggressive human actions may never be prohibited and obstructed. Also a metaphysical position in terms of which the existence of reality and values depend upon the will of someone.

Bibliography

PHILOSOPHY AND ITS PURPOSE

ALSTON, WILLIAM P., and BRANDT, RICHARD B. (eds.). *The Problems of Philosophy*, ed. 2 (Allyn and Bacon, 1974). A good collection of essays in both classical and contemporary philosophy.

ARISTOTLE. *Metaphysics*. A classic that is very difficult to read. Still, some sections, especially in the first few books, are extremely helpful for purposes of understanding the nature of philosophy. The reader is advised to first pick up Wheelwright's edition of selections, called *Aristotle, Selections* (Odyssey Press, 1951).

EDWARDS, PAUL (ed.). *Encyclopedia of Philosophy* (4 volumes, found in all sizable libraries). This massive publication by Macmillan (1973) provides a somewhat contemporary version of comment and history pertaining to all problems in philosophy. While being critical is essential in reading these representations of philosophy, the effort needed to go through some discussions will pay off.

HARRE, ROM. *An Introduction to the Logic of the Sciences* (Macmillan, 1967). A modern-day Aristotelian analysis of science.

HARRE, ROM, and SECORD, PAUL. *The Explanation of Social Behaviour* (Littlefield, Adams, 1972). The most recent and impressive effort to show that the sciences are all naturalistic even when the methods used in the social sciences must accommodate the nature of human beings. Social science philosophy at its best.

Kuhn, Thomas S.   *The Structure of Scientific Revolutions* (University of Chicago Press, 1970).   Kuhn says scientific knowledge changes and truth is relative to theories or basic paradigms that gain acceptance from those in some field of science.   The issue of the link between change and reality is left unanswered, but the work has been very influential.

Matson, Wallace I.   *The Existence of God* (Cornell University Press, 1965).   Detailed consideration of the problem of God's existence.

Ortega y Gasset, J.   *What Is Philosophy?* (Norton, 1964) .   A clear book by a continental philosopher and profound observer of recent culture, discussing the place of philosophy in human societies.

Ross, James.   *Philosophical Theology* (Bobbs-Merrill, 1969).   A difficult work supporting the rationality of religion and theism.

Rudner, Richard.   *Philosophy of Social Science* (Prentice-Hall, 1966).   A clear exposition of the view that human behavior should be studied by methods used in the physical sciences, lest we fail to be scientific in our work.   A well-updated positivist approach to social science, clearly argued and informative about how many people today conceive of science.

Selsam, Howard.   *What Is Philosophy?* (International Publications, 1939).   An orthodox Marxist but not very detailed presentation of what philosophy is.   It is useful at least for purposes of seeing how Marxism addresses philosophy.

Smith, H. George.   *Atheism: The Case Against God* (Nash, 1974).   A readable, sustained criticism of arguments for God and religion in general.

Toulmin, Stephen.   *The Uses of Argument* (Cambridge University Press, 1964).   This book argues that both differences and similarities are identifiable within the various fields of science, and we must take this fact into account as we consider the relationships among the sciences and between science and the humanities.

Wheatley, Jon.   *Prolegomena to Philosophy* (Wadsworth, 1970).   A clear introduction to what many contemporary philosophers take to be philosophy at its best.   Breezy but not easy.

METAPHYSICS

Anderson, Alan Ross (ed.).   *Minds and Machines* (Prentice-Hall, 1964).   Several stimulating papers on whether machines can or could think.

BURTT, E. A. *The Metaphysical Foundations of Modern Science* (Anchor, 1954). A classic work showing the developments in modern science and their relationship to metaphysical issues.

FISK, MILTON. *Nature and Necessity* (Indiana University Press, 1973). A recent and clearly written defense of objective necessity and naturalism.

HICK, JOHN (ed.). *The Existence of God* (Macmillan, 1964). Essays on the problem of the existence of God.

MATSON, WALLACE I. *Sentience* (University of California Press, 1976). A development of the case for a materialist but nonreductionist theory of mind/body identity (very well written and short).

SEIDEL, GEORGE J. *A Contemporary Approach to Classical Metaphysics* (Appleton-Century-Crofts, 1969). A brief and clear discussion of major issues in metaphysics with a focus on ancient problems.

SMITH, H. GEORGE. *Atheism: The Case Against God* (Nash, 1974). A recent criticism of theism and defense of not believing in God's existence.

STRAWSON, P. F. *Individuals* (Anchor, 1965). A recent attempt at constructing a metaphysical system; concerned with the basic features of our way of thinking about reality.

TAYLOR, RICHARD. *Metaphysics* (Prentice-Hall, 1974). A clear, comprehensive, up-to-date discussion of major metaphysical problems.

EPISTEMOLOGY

ARNER, DOUGLAS G. (ed.). *Perception, Reason, and Knowledge* (Scott, Foresman, 1972). A good collection of excerpts from Hume, Locke, Berkeley, Descartes, Kant, and others.

AUSTIN, J. L. "Other Minds," in his *Philosophical Papers* (Oxford University Press, 1961). Defense of the performative theory of knowledge. Difficult but worth the trouble.

BRIDGMAN, P. W. *The Logic of Modern Physics* (Macmillan, 1961). Parts of this work contain the best statement of operationalism.

DEWEY, JOHN. *The Quest for Certainty* (Putnam, 1960). A clear statement of the pragmatism of John Dewey. See also William James's "Pragmatism's Conception of Truth," in *Essays in Pragmatism* (Hafner).

HAMLYN, D. W. *The Theory of Knowledge* (Anchor, 1970). One of the best treatments of the subject, clear and comprehensive.

LENIN, V. I. *Materialism and Empirico-criticism* (International Publishers, 1927). A Marxist-Leninist epistemology.

POPPER, KARL.   *The Poverty of Historicism* (Harper & Row, 1964).   A famous criticism of historicism and some doctrines and programs based on it.

RAND, AYN.   *Introduction to Objectivist Epistemology* (The Objectivist, Inc., 1970).   A theory of concepts and definitions advancing contextualist ideas.

STOUGH, CHARLOTTE.   *Greek Skepticism* (University of California Press, 1969).   An excellent survey and discussion of the ancient versions of skepticism.   It illustrates the ongoing character of philosophy.

UNGER, PETER.   *Ignorance* (Oxford University Press, 1975).   Defends the view that no one knows anything.

YOLTON, JOHN W.   *Thinking and Perceiving*   (Open Court, 1962).   A clear discussion of central problems in epistemology.   Informative, critical, and constructive.

LOGIC

ARISTOTLE.   *Works,* Volume 1 (Oxford University Press).   A very clear statement of the fundamentals of syllogistic logic.   Still better than most texts.

BANKS, P.   "On the Philosophical Interpretation of Logic: An Aristotelian Dialogue," in Albert Menne (ed.), *Logico-Philosophical Studies* (D. Reidel, 1962).   Excellent discussion.

CAPALDI, NICHOLAS.   *The Art of Deception* (Prometheus Books, 1974).   An elementary but very clear introduction to careful thinking; a clever, lively book.

PARKER, F. H., and VEATCH, H. B.   *Logic as a Human Instrument* (Harper & Row, 1965).   A comprehensive introduction to Aristotelian logic.   It also covers the essentials of modern propositional logic.

SCHAGRIN, MORTON L.   *The Language of Logic* (Random House, 1968).   A good introduction to the symbolism of modern logic.   Very useful to those interested in understanding contemporary philosophical discussions that use logical symbolism.

ETHICS

BAIER, KURT.   *The Moral Point of View* (Cornell University Press, 1966).   A very recent and often complicated statement of what is the minimum requirement for a position to count as an ethics initially. Baier's claims are often in conflict with those offered in this book.

EKMAN, R. (ed.). *Readings in the Problems of Ethics* (Charles Scribner's Sons, 1965). A good collection of recent treatments of issues surrounding the question of how moral judgments might be justified and understood.

HOSPERS, JOHN. *Human Conduct* (Harcourt, Brace & World, 1972). A very clear and detailed introduction to ethics. Virtually all ethical positions are discussed and debated in Hosper's clear but comprehensive treatment. The best single-author book on the subject.

LADD, JOHN (ed.). *Ethical Relativism* (Wadsworth, 1973). A good collection of articles about relativism.

MATTER, JOSEPH A. *Love, Altruism and World Crises* (Nelson-Hall, 1975). Examination of a recent theory of altruism in a relatively straightforward fashion.

MILO, RONALD D. (ed.). *Egoism and Altruism* (Wadsworth, 1973). A collection of articles on each of these ethical positions; not comprehensive.

RAND, AYN. *The Virtue of Selfishness* (New American Library, 1964). A collection of Rand's essays in vigorous defense of egoism. The most consistent and uncompromising version of egoism is advanced by Rand in these essays.

RAND, BENJAMIN. *The Classical Moralists* (Houghton Mifflin, 1909). The most comprehensive collection of excerpts from all of the major writers on ethics. If not in print, still worth picking up in the library.

SMART, J. J. C. *An Outline of a System of Utilitarian Ethics* (Melbourne University Press). A clear but difficult statement of utilitarianism.

STEVENSON, C. L. *Ethics and Language* (Yale University Press, 1944). The major statement of the school of ethical theory that rejects the objective foundation of moral judgment and analyzes ethical statements along mitigated subjectivist lines.

THOMAS, G. *Christian Ethics and Moral Philosophy* (Charles Scribner's Sons, 1955). A presentation of the issues dealt with in moral philosophy in terms of theism.

POLITICAL PHILOSOPHY

ACTON, H. B. *The Morals of Markets* (Longman, 1971). A clear defense of the classical liberal (capitalist) society against egalitarian and collectivist critics.

CRANSTON, M. (ed.). *Western Political Philosophers* (Capricorn, 1967). A selection of concise essays on political philosophers from Plato to Mill.

GUNNELL, JOHN G. *Philosophy, Science & Political Inquiry* (General Learning Press, 1975). Detailed discussion of political analysis.

HELLER, AGNES. "A Marxist Theory of Value," *Kinesis* (Fall 1972). A recent, nondeterminist, nonrationalist defense of Marx's conception of man's future.

LAKOFF, SANFORD A. *Equality in Political Philosophy* (Beacon Press, 1964). A serious and detailed discussion of various ideals of equality.

MACHAN, T. R. (ed.). *The Libertarian Alternative* (Nelson-Hall, 1974). A comprehensive collection of essays contributing to the defense and analysis of several varieties of libertarianism.

MARX, KARL. *Communist Manifesto* (Regnery, 1963). A clear and vehement statement of the program of communism.

PERELMAN, CHAIM. *Justice* (Random House, 1967). An analysis of justice by the methods of contemporary conceptual inquiry.

SCHWARTZ, THOMAS (ed.). *Freedom and Authority* (Dickenson, 1973). A very good collection of crucial excerpts from classical and modern theorists.

STRAUSS, LEO, and CROPSY, JOSEPH. *History of Political Philosophy* (Rand McNally, 1963). A collection of excellent but difficult essays on the major political thinkers of human intellectual history.

Index